Taste of Home
COOKING SCHOOL
50TH ANNIVERSARY COOKBOOK

You've Just Struck Gold—
50 Years of Great Recipes

*I*f you've attended a Taste of Home Cooking School, you know we cook up lots of fun, excitement *and* great food. What you might not know is that we've been doing it for 50 years.

In honor of our golden anniversary, we've collected the 627 *best* recipes—those that have been shared on stages across America and have stood the test of time—into one big book. Yes, we're *proud* to present the *Taste of Home Cooking School 50th Anniversary Cookbook.*

It all began in 1948 with a business venture called Homemaker Schools. One busy home economist loaded up her station wagon and drove across the Midwest, stopping at small-town appliance dealerships to conduct cooking classes for dozens of "homemakers". In the 1990s, the Cooking School was acquired by *Taste of Home*, the most popular cooking magazine in the country.

Learning from the Pros

These days, a dozen friendly, hard-working cooking experts put on 260 cooking demonstrations per year from the East Coast to the West, and from North to South. Auditoriums are jam-packed with women, some men and even a few children eager to have a good time, learn preparation techniques and take home a cookbook filled with family-pleasing recipes.

We're still partial to small- and medium-size towns. We're always impressed how communities of 2,000 can easily fill an auditorium with 900 folks eager to experience a Cooking School session. Tickets typically sell out within hours—even at venues that seat 2,400.

The home economist who plans and hosts the show becomes a local celebrity for the day—complete with a photo and feature story in the newspa-

per and guest appearances on the radio.

Each Cooking School show is part instruction and part entertainment. We figured out long ago that learning and laughter go well together. A typical session includes 11 to 14 demonstration recipes, a question-and-answer session with the host home economist, a few jokes and dozens of door prizes for the audience.

Names You Can Trust

The recipes in this book are from well-known, trusted companies that have co-sponsored the Cooking School over the years. Nestlé, Campbell's, Tyson, Del Monte and Pillsbury are just a few examples. (The recipe sponsors are listed at the opening of each chapter.)

The *Taste of Home Cooking School 50th Anniversary Cookbook* isn't like traditional cookbooks. Mixed in with the recipes are historical food facts and short stories about how classic dishes like "Green Bean Bake" came to be. Each of the last five decades has its own "flashback" section to help you recall those bygone days.

The book is thoroughly indexed beginning on page 273. The General Index identifies recipes by ingredient or cooking method. The Alphabetical Index of recipe titles starts on page 284. And a third index on page 288 highlights special features, such as the history pages.

By using and enjoying this book, you'll help us celebrate our 50-year anniversary, plus you just might create some "golden" memories of your own. Happy cooking!

> **Cooking School home economist Tamara Becwar shows off the 11 recipes she made onstage in 1989.**

NOW AND THEN.
Full-color photos accompany many of the recipes in this book.
Some classic recipes, such as Green Bean Bake (above), include
stories explaining how they came to be. Each decade—from the
'50s to the '90s—has its own memory page (right).

Taste of Home
COOKING SCHOOL
50TH ANNIVERSARY COOKBOOK

Editors:
Patricia Wade, Heidi Reuter Lloyd

Art Director:
Bonnie Ziolecki

Assistant Editors:
Jean Steiner, Julie Schnittka, Faithann Stoner

Cooking School Director:
Sandy Bloom

Editorial Assistant:
Kari Staus

Food Photography:
Rob Hagen, Dan Roberts

Food Photography Artists:
Stephanie Marchese, Vicky Marie Moseley

Photo Studio Manager:
Anne Schimmel

Production:
Ellen Lloyd, Catherine Fletcher

Art Associate:
Jami Zewen

Publisher:
Roy Reiman

Taste of Home Books
©2002 Reiman Media Group, Inc.
5400 S. 60th St., Greendale WI 53129
International Standard Book Number: 0-89821-349-5
Library of Congress Control Number: 2002107540
All rights reserved.
Printed in U.S.A.

PICTURED ABOVE: Home economist Sophie Petros demonstrated recipes to attentive audiences throughout the Midwest during the 1960s.

PICTURED ON FRONT COVER: Herbed Parmesan Loaf (p. 71), Perfectly-Chocolate Chocolate Cake (p. 230) and Golden Chicken and Autumn Vegetables (page 112).

TO ORDER additional copies of this book or for information about other Reiman Publications books, write *Taste of Home* Books, P.O. Box 908, Greendale, WI 53129. To order with a credit card, call toll-free 1-800-344-2560 or visit our Web site at **www.reimanpub.com**.

Page 54   *Page 124*   *Page 268*

TABLE *of* CONTENTS

Chapter 1
SNACKS & BEVERAGES

Turn to these selections when you're looking for a special beverage or appetizer to start a meal...or when the midday munchies or late-night hunger strikes.

Recipes in this chapter provided courtesy of these past sponsors...

Bertolli	Miracle Whip
Blue Bonnet	Moody Dunbar
Campbell's	Nabisco
Chicken of the Sea	Nestea
Del Monte	Nestlé
Equal	Oster
Farmland	Pillsbury
Grey Poupon	Reynolds
Hellmann's	Sargento
Hidden Valley	Schilling
Hormel	Spice Islands
Karo	Stouffer's
Knox	Sunbeam
Lawry's	Taster's Choice
Lipton	Tyson
McCormick	Velveeta

SEA-IT-DISAPPEAR SHRIMP DIP

(Pictured at left)

Tempt your troops with this versatile dip served in an attractive bread bowl. A touch of dill is the perfect complement to the delicate flavor of shrimp. This recipe was a favorite in our fall 2001 cooking schools.

> 1 can (10-3/4 ounces) condensed cream of mushroom soup, undiluted
> 1 package (8 ounces) cream cheese, softened
> 2 cans (6 ounces *each*) small shrimp, rinsed and drained
> 1/2 cup *each* finely chopped celery, green onions and water chestnuts
> 1/4 cup mayonnaise
> 1/2 teaspoon dill weed
> 1 unsliced loaf (1 pound) round Italian bread
> Assorted vegetables *and/or* crackers

In a large saucepan, bring soup to a boil, stirring frequently. Reduce heat to medium-low; add cream cheese and stir until smooth. Stir in shrimp, celery, green onions, water chestnuts, mayonnaise and dill; heat through. Cut the top fourth off loaf of bread; carefully hollow out bottom, leaving a 1-in. shell. Cube removed bread; set aside. Spoon dip into bread shell. Serve with bread cubes, vegetables or crackers. **Yield:** 10-12 servings.

EL POLLO NACHO PLATTER

The popularity of Mexican food exploded in the 1980s as many folks took their first taste of nachos, fajitas and enchiladas—dishes that are now commonplace in many households. This fast-to-fix platter is guaranteed to disappear in a hurry.

> 12 ounces Mexican process cheese, cubed
> 1 cup chopped cooked chicken
> 1/2 cup chopped onion
> 1/2 cup chopped green pepper
> 1/4 cup milk
> Tortilla chips
> 2 cups shredded lettuce
> 1 cup chopped tomato

In a saucepan, combine cheese, chicken, onion, green pepper and milk. Cook and stir over low heat until cheese is melted. Arrange tortilla chips on serving platter. Top with chicken mixture, lettuce and tomato. **Yield:** 6-8 servings.

TOLL HOUSE PARTY MIX

Most folks find it impossible to stop eating this unique twist on traditional party mix. Hundreds of party mix recipes have been created since Rice Chex cereal was introduced in 1950. This chocolaty version blending sweet and salty is one of our favorites.

> 2 cups toasted cereal squares
> 2 cups small pretzel twists
> 1 cup dry-roasted peanuts
> 1 cup (about 20) caramels, coarsely chopped
> 1 package (11 to 12 ounces) semisweet chocolate, milk chocolate, butterscotch *or* white morsels

In a large bowl, combine cereal, pretzels, peanuts and caramels. In a medium microwave-safe bowl, microwave morsels on medium-high power for 1 minute; stir. Microwave at additional 10- to 20-second intervals, stirring until smooth. Pour over cereal mixture; stir to coat evenly. Spread mixture in a greased 13-in. x 9-in. x 2-in. baking pan; cool for 30-45 minutes or until firm. Break into bite-size pieces. **Yield:** 8 servings.

ORIGINAL RANCH OYSTER CRACKERS

(Pictured below)

In the late 1950s and early 1960s, Steve and Gayle Henson's 120-acre Hidden Valley Ranch near Santa

Barbara, California was favored by weekend visitors. Guests loved the creamy salad dressing Steve created and soon began taking it home in glass jars. Eventually he packaged prepared dressing and a mix, both of which are still popular.

> 8 cups oyster *or* soup crackers
> 1/4 cup vegetable oil
> 1 envelope ranch salad dressing mix

Place crackers in a large resealable plastic bag. Pour oil over crackers and toss to coat. Add dressing mix; toss to coat. Spread in a jelly roll pan. Bake at 250° for 15-20 minutes; cool. Store in an airtight container. **Yield:** 8 cups.

CAJUN-STYLE CHICKEN NUGGETS

Microwave ovens became common in American kitchens during the 1980s, and soon there was an abundance of snack food recipes that could be cooked in a jiffy. Barbecue sauce and blue cheese dressing are delicious alternate dipping sauces for these tender seasoned nuggets.

> 1 envelope onion *or* onion-mushroom soup mix
> 1/2 cup dry bread crumbs
> 1-1/2 teaspoons chili powder
> 1 teaspoon ground cumin
> 1 teaspoon dried thyme
> 1/4 teaspoon cayenne pepper
> 2 pounds boneless skinless chicken breasts, cut into 1-inch cubes
> 3 tablespoons butter *or* margarine, melted
> Prepared mustard, optional

In a large bowl, mix soup mix, bread crumbs and seasonings. Dip chicken in bread crumb mixture, coating well. Arrange chicken in a 13-in. x 9-in. x 2-in. baking dish; drizzle with butter. Microwave, uncovered, on high for 6-8 minutes or until chicken is no longer pink, turning chicken once; drain on paper towels. Serve warm with mustard if desired. **Yield:** 5 dozen.

SCARLET PUNCH

This sweet punch has instant tea as its base, but its pretty pink blush comes from the addition of cranberry juice. Cranberries were named by the Pilgrims, possibly for the cranes that fed on the small scarlet berries along what is now the Massachusetts coast.

> 3/4 cup limeade concentrate

2 cups cranberry juice cocktail
5 tablespoons unsweetened instant tea
1-1/2 quarts cold water
3/4 cup light corn syrup
1 lime, sliced
Fresh mint leaves, optional

In a large pitcher, combine limeade concentrate, juice and tea. Add water and corn syrup. Stir well. Pour over ice in individual glasses or over block of ice in punch bowl. Garnish with lime or mint leaves if desired. **Yield:** 16 servings.

SMOKY SALMON SPREAD

Once an inexpensive mainstay of middle-class menus, canned salmon is frequently used today in spreads, dips and savory loaves.

2 packages (8 ounces *each*) cream cheese, softened
3 tablespoons lemon juice
3 tablespoons milk
1-1/2 teaspoons dill weed
2 cans (6 ounces *each*) skinless boneless salmon, drained
1/4 cup thinly sliced green onions
3 to 4 drops liquid smoke, optional
Sliced French bread *or* crackers

In a small mixing bowl, beat cream cheese, lemon juice, milk and dill weed. Stir in salmon and green onions. Season with liquid smoke if desired. Cover and refrigerate for several hours to blend flavors. Serve with bread or crackers. **Yield:** 3-1/2 cups.

FRUIT TEA SPARKLER

Cool and refreshing, this bubbly beverage combines the bold citrus flavors of orange and lemon.

4 cups cold water
1 can (12 ounces) frozen orange juice concentrate, thawed
1 can (12 ounces) frozen lemonade concentrate, partially thawed
1/2 cup sugar
3 tablespoons unsweetened instant tea
2 liters club soda

In a medium pitcher, combine water, concentrates, sugar and tea; stir until sugar and tea are dissolved. Fill glasses with ice. Add two parts tea mixture and one part club soda; stir. Serve immediately. **Yield:** 12-15 servings.

CREAM CHEESE & HAM TORTILLA ROLLS

(Pictured above)

In the 1990s, a bevy of roll-up recipes became popular, as they're the perfect fuss-free food for entertaining. Roll-ups are fast to fix, plus you can make them ahead and keep them wrapped in the refrigerator until you're ready to serve.

1 carton (4 ounces) spreadable chive and onion cream cheese
1 jar (4-1/2 ounces) marinated artichoke hearts, drained and finely chopped
1 jar (4 ounces) diced pimientos, drained
2 flour tortillas (10 inches)
6 ounces thinly sliced fully cooked ham
4 ounces thinly sliced provolone cheese

In a bowl, combine cream cheese, artichokes and pimientos; mix well. Spread on one side of tortillas. Layer each tortilla with ham and cheese. Roll up tightly; wrap in plastic wrap. Refrigerate for at least 2 hours. Slice into 1-in. pieces. **Yield:** 1-1/2 dozen.

CHICKEN PECAN TARTS

(Pictured at left)

Pecans have a starring role in these scrumptious treats. Southern orchards produce 250 million pounds of pecans each year, primarily for cooking and baking.

> 2 tablespoons butter *or* margarine
> 1 cup finely chopped pecans
> 1 cup finely chopped cooked chicken
> 1/2 cup chopped celery
> 1/4 cup mayonnaise *or* salad dressing
> 1 tablespoon Dijon mustard
> 1 package (3 ounces) cream cheese, softened
> 1/4 teaspoon salt
> 1/2 teaspoon ground nutmeg
> 1 tube (7-1/2 ounces) refrigerated buttermilk biscuits

In a large skillet, melt butter; add pecans and saute until lightly browned. In a bowl, combine chicken, celery, mayonnaise, mustard, cream cheese, salt and nutmeg. Add pecans; mix well. Separate biscuits; roll each into a 4-in. circle. Press into 10 foil bake cups, letting dough cover bottom and sides. Place bake cups in muffin pans. Spoon chicken mixture into bake cups. Bake at 425° for 12 minutes or until crust is golden brown. **Yield:** 10 servings.

MEXICAN BLACK BEAN DIP

Folks love the burst of flavor in every bite of this delicious dip. Black bean soup thrived during the 1990s, and this luscious legume increased in popularity. At your supermarket, labels may read Frijoles Negros, the Spanish term for black beans.

> 1 can (16 ounces) refried black beans
> 1/2 cup plus 2 tablespoons salsa, *divided*
> 1-1/2 cups (6 ounces) Mexican-style shredded cheese, *divided*
> 1 cup prepared guacamole
> 1 cup diced tomatoes
> 1/2 cup thinly sliced green onions
> 1/2 cup sour cream
> 1/4 cup chopped fresh cilantro *or* parsley

Tortilla chips

Combine beans, 2 tablespoons salsa and 1/2 cup cheese; mix well. Spread on 12-in. round serving plate. Drop small spoonfuls of guacamole over beans; top with tomatoes and green onions. Drop small spoonfuls of sour cream and remaining salsa over tomatoes and green onions. Top with remaining cheese; sprinkle with cilantro. Serve with chips. **Yield:** 12 servings.

CONFETTI BITES

These bite-size bits provide a delicious way to enjoy fresh vegetables—broccoli, carrots, bell pepper, tomatoes. McCormick's Salad Supreme Seasoning, which can be found in the spice aisle of most grocery stores, is the flavor secret.

> **2 cans (8 ounces *each*) refrigerated crescent rolls**
> **2 packages (8 ounces *each*) cream cheese, softened**
> **3 tablespoons mayonnaise *or* salad dressing**
> **1/2 teaspoon dried basil**
> **1/4 teaspoon garlic powder**
Finely chopped fresh vegetables
Salad Supreme Seasoning

Press dough into 15-in. x 10-in. x 1-in. jelly roll pan to form crust. Bake at 350° for 12-15 minutes; cool. Combine cream cheese, mayonnaise, basil and garlic powder; spread thinly over crust. Top with vegetables. Sprinkle generously with seasoning. Cut into squares. **Yield:** 2 dozen.

PINEAPPLE TEA

The addition of pineapple juice offers a simple change of pace for traditional iced tea. Flavored teas took prominence in the 1970s, and herbal teas gained popularity.

2-1/2 cups pineapple juice
> **1 cup water**
> **1/4 cup unsweetened instant tea**
> **1 tablespoon sugar**
Cinnamon sticks

In a large saucepan, combine pineapple juice, water, tea and sugar. Cover and allow to simmer for 5 minutes. Serve hot with cinnamon sticks. **Yield:** 4 (6-ounce) servings.

HOLIDAY CHEESE BALL

A cheese ball is easy to prepare and provides a showcase for fine American cheeses. Wisconsin, New York, Vermont and Oregon are some of the states recognized for producing extraordinary domestic cheese.

1/4 cup milk
3/4 cup crumbled blue cheese
1/4 cup cubed cheddar cheese
> **1 small wedge of onion**
> **1 teaspoon Worcestershire sauce**
> **1 package (3 ounces) cream cheese, cubed**
1/4 cup butter *or* margarine

1/2 cup pecan halves
> **6 sprigs fresh parsley**
Assorted crackers

In a food processor, combine milk and blue cheese. Cover and process until smooth. While processing, add cheddar cheese. Add onion, Worcestershire sauce, cream cheese and butter. Process until smooth. Place cheese mixture on plastic wrap; shape into ball. Chill at least 1 hour. In a food processor, process pecans and parsley until finely chopped. Roll ball in mixture of nuts and parsley. Serve with crackers. **Yield:** 1 cheese ball.

LAYERED ARTICHOKE TORTA

(*Pictured below*)

The eye-catching appearance and satisfying flavor of this savory spread make it a surefire party-pleaser.

> **2 packages (8 ounces *each*) cream cheese, softened**
> **1 envelope ranch salad dressing mix**
> **1 jar (6 ounces) marinated artichoke hearts, drained and chopped**
> **1/3 cup roasted red peppers, drained and chopped**
> **3 tablespoons minced fresh parsley**
Assorted crackers

In a small mixing bowl, blend cream cheese and dressing mix. In a separate bowl, stir together artichokes, peppers and parsley. In a 3-cup bowl lined with plastic wrap, alternate layers of cheese and vegetable mixtures, beginning and ending with a cheese layer. Refrigerate 4 hours or overnight. Invert on plate; remove plastic wrap. Serve with crackers. **Yield:** 10-12 servings.

BERRY AND APRICOT FRAPPE

(Pictured above)

Whether you call them frappes, shakes or smoothies, blended fruit beverages have remained all the rage throughout the past few decades.

> 2 cups orange juice
> 1 cup ice cubes
> 1/2 cup frozen strawberries *or* raspberries
> 1/2 cup peeled apricot pieces *or* canned apricots in juice, drained
> 1/2 cup fat-free plain *or* flavored yogurt
> 2 tablespoons wheat germ
> 4 to 5 packets sugar substitute

In a blender or food processor, combine all of the ingredients. Cover and process until smooth. Serve immediately. **Yield:** 2 servings.

CHEDDAR CHICKEN SPREAD

When late-night munchies strike, turn to this recipe for an easy way to satisfy your cravings.

> 2 cans (5 ounces *each*) chunk breast of chicken, drained, flaked
> 3/4 cup shredded cheddar cheese
> 1/2 cup mayonnaise *or* salad dressing
> 1/4 cup sweet pickle relish
> 2 tablespoons dried minced onion
Lettuce leaves *or* crackers

In a bowl, combine chicken, cheese, mayonnaise, relish and onion. Cover; refrigerate until ready to serve. Serve on lettuce leaves or crackers. **Yield:** 2 cups.

BACON-CHEESE APPETIZER PIE

This cheesecake is great for an open house or neighborhood get-together. It's easy to make and tastes delicious.

Pastry for a single-crust pie
> 3 packages (8 ounces *each*) cream cheese, softened
> 4 eggs, lightly beaten
> 1/4 cup milk
> 1 cup (4 ounces) shredded Swiss cheese
> 1/2 cup sliced green onions
> 6 bacon strips, cooked and crumbled
> 1/2 teaspoon salt
> 1/8 teaspoon pepper
> 1/8 teaspoon cayenne pepper

Roll the pastry into a 13-1/2-in. circle. Fit into the bottom and up the sides of an ungreased 9-in. springform pan. Lightly prick the bottom. Bake at 450° for 8-10 minutes or until lightly browned. Cool slightly. In a mixing bowl, beat cream cheese until fluffy. Add eggs and milk; beat until smooth. Add the Swiss cheese, onions, bacon, salt, pepper and cayenne; mix well. Pour into the crust. Bake at 350° for 40-45 minutes or until a knife inserted near the center comes out clean. Cool for 20 minutes. Remove sides of pan. Cut into thin slices; serve warm. **Yield:** 16-20 servings.

ROSY NECTAR PUNCH

Fruity nectar adds a special richness to this pretty thirst-quencher.

> 2 cups hot water
> 1 cup light corn syrup
> 6 tablespoons unsweetened instant tea
> 1 teaspoon ground nutmeg

4 cups apricot nectar
3 cups cold water
1/2 cup lemon juice
4 cups raspberry, cherry *or* strawberry
　　soda, chilled

In a 3-qt. container, combine water, corn syrup, tea and nutmeg; stir. Add apricot nectar, cold water and lemon juice; chill in refrigerator until ready to serve. Pour into punch bowl; gradually stir in soda. **Yield:** about 28 (1/2-cup) servings.

EASY CHICKEN NACHOS SUPREME

(Pictured below)

This fun finger food is great for a party or whenever you want a zesty treat. Lower-fat ground chicken provides a nice alternative to traditional ground beef.

1 pound fresh ground chicken
1/4 cup chopped onion
2 garlic cloves, minced
1 tablespoon chili powder
1-1/2 teaspoons ground cumin
4 ounces tortilla chips, *divided*
2 cups (8 ounces) shredded Colby-Jack
　　cheese, *divided*
1/4 cup sliced ripe olives, *divided*
3 tablespoons diced green chilies, *divided*
Chopped tomato, sour cream, salsa and
　　guacamole, optional

In a nonstick skillet, combine chicken, onion, garlic, chili powder and cumin. Cook over medium-high

heat for 6-8 minutes or until chicken is no longer pink, stirring frequently. Spray pizza pan or baking sheet with nonstick cooking spray. Layer half of chips, 1/2 cup cheese and half each of chicken mixture, olives and green chilies. Repeat. Top with rest of cheese. Bake at 350° for 15-20 minutes or until hot. Top with chopped tomato and serve with sour cream, salsa and guacamole if desired. **Yield:** 6 servings.

FOUR-CHEESE PIMIENTO SPREAD

Christopher Columbus discovered a mysterious little cousin of the bell pepper on one of his voyages to the New World. Today, folks are discovering that pimientos add vibrant color and fun flavor to almost any savory dish.

3 cups (12 ounces) shredded white
　　cheddar cheese
2 cups (8 ounces) shredded orange
　　cheddar cheese
1 cup (4 ounces) shredded Parmesan cheese
1 package (4 ounces) crumbled feta *or* blue
　　cheese
1 jar (4 ounces) diced pimientos, drained
2 teaspoons sweet pickle juice
3 tablespoons prepared mustard
1 cup mayonnaise

In a large bowl, combine all ingredients; mix well. Chill if desired. Serve with burgers, open-faced sandwiches or assorted crackers. **Yield:** 6 cups.

CHILI CON QUESO DIP

It's hard to believe such a simple recipe—only two ingredients—can produce such a yummy dip. The recipe was introduced in the '70s and soon became a favorite across the country.

> **1 pound process cheese, cubed**
> **1 can (15 ounces) chili with beans**
> **Tortilla chips *or* assorted crackers**

In a 1-1/2-qt. microwave-safe dish, stir together cheese and chili. Cover. Microwave at 50% power for 8-10 minutes, stirring occasionally, until cheese is melted and dip is smooth when stirred. Serve with chips. **Yield:** 3-1/2 cups.

BLACK BEAN SOUTHWEST SALSA

(Pictured below)

Vine-ripened tomatoes, spicy jalapenos and savory onions are just a few of the garden-fresh ingredients that jazz up plain black beans to create this Southwest taste explosion.

> **3 cans (15 ounces *each*) black beans, rinsed**
> **and drained**
> **1-1/2 cups vinaigrette *or* Italian salad dressing**
> **1 jar (7 ounces) diced pimientos, drained**

> **cup thinly sliced green onions**
> **1 medium tomato, chopped**
> **1 medium green pepper, chopped**
> **1/2 cup chopped fresh parsley**
> **3 jalapeno peppers, seeded and finely**
> **chopped**
> **1 tablespoon hot pepper sauce**
> **1 tablespoon Worcestershire sauce**
> **1 teaspoon pepper**
> **1 teaspoon dried oregano**
> **3 garlic cloves, minced**
> **Tortilla chips**

In a large bowl, combine all ingredients except chips. Mix well. Cover and refrigerate at least 4 hours to blend flavors. Serve with tortilla chips. **Yield:** 9 cups.

MOCHA COCOA

For generations, children have loved to snack on cookies and mugs of hot cocoa. This version has a sweet mocha flavor with a hint of cinnamon.

> **1/3 cup water**
> **1/4 cup baking cocoa**
> **1/4 cup packed brown sugar**
> **2 tablespoons instant coffee granules**
> **1/8 teaspoon salt**
> **3-1/2 cups milk**
> **Whipped cream**
> **4 cinnamon sticks**

In a saucepan, combine first five ingredients. Bring to a boil and simmer 2 minutes. Gradually stir in milk and continue cooking until hot. Pour into mugs; top with whipped cream. Garnish with cinnamon sticks. **Yield:** 4 servings.

FRUIT JUICE KNOX BLOX

Jiggly gelatin snacks are a favorite of the preschool set. This simple recipe allows you to use your favorite flavor juice for added nutrition.

> **4 envelopes unflavored gelatin**
> **4 cups cold fruit juice, *divided***

In a microwave-safe bowl, sprinkle gelatin over 1 cup juice; let stand 3 minutes. Microwave on high for 1 minute 20 seconds; stir thoroughly. Let stand 2 minutes or until gelatin is completely dissolved; stir in remaining 3 cups juice. Pour into an 8- or 9-in.

square pan; chill until firm, about 3 hours. Cut into 1-in. squares. **Yield:** about 6 dozen.

BANANA-YOGURT STRAWBERRY SHAKE

This thick, wholesome drink combines the refreshing flavors of berries, yogurt, banana and honey. Once you start sipping it, you won't be able to stop!

  1 cup frozen whole strawberries, partially
     thawed
  1 carton (8 ounces) plain yogurt
  1 ripe banana
  2 tablespoons honey
1/4 cup milk
1/2 teaspoon vanilla extract

In a blender, combine all ingredients. Cover and process until smooth and frothy. **Yield:** 2 servings.

PARTY PINWHEELS

(Pictured at right)

These special snacks are fast to assemble—you can make them in advance and refrigerate until serving time.

  2 packages (8 ounces *each*) cream cheese,
     softened
  2 green onions, finely chopped
  1 envelope ranch salad dressing mix
  4 flour tortillas (12 inches)
  1 jar (4 ounces) diced pimientos
     or 1/3 cup finely chopped red pepper
  1 can (4 ounces) diced green chilies
  1 can (2-1/4 ounces) sliced ripe olives
1/2 cup chopped celery
Salsa, optional

In a bowl, combine cream cheese, onions and dressing mix; mix well. Spread mixture on tortillas. Drain pimientos, chilies and olives; blot dry with paper towels. Sprinkle pimientos, chilies, olives and celery over cream cheese. Roll up tortillas tightly; wrap individually in plastic wrap. Refrigerate at least 2 hours. To serve, cut rolls into 1-in. pieces, discarding ends. Arrange on plate; serve with salsa if desired. **Yield:** 3 dozen.

TUNA DIP

A favorite for over 30 years, this creamy dip is delicious on crackers. Add a bit of chopped celery if you enjoy some added crunch.

  1 can (6 ounces) tuna, drained and flaked
  1 cup cottage cheese
1/2 cup mayonnaise
1/2 teaspoon onion salt
  2 tablespoons sweet pickle relish
Saltine crackers

In a medium bowl, combine all ingredients except crackers. Mix well. Serve with crackers. **Yield:** 2 cups.

VANILLA ALMOND COFFEE

In recent years, flavored coffees have become more available, but in the 1980s, hostesses often made their own using flavor extracts.

  1 pound regular *or* decaffeinated ground
     coffee
  1 bottle (1 ounce) vanilla extract
  1 bottle (1 ounce) almond extract

Place coffee in a large resealable plastic bag. Add vanilla and almond extracts to coffee. Shake to blend thoroughly. Best if stored in refrigerator. Prepare coffee according to package directions. **Yield:** 1 pound flavored coffee.

BARBECUE BACON CHESTNUTS

(Pictured above left)

An appealing appetizer, this dish may remind you of Rumaki, a traditional recipe featuring chicken livers and water chestnuts wrapped in bacon. By skipping the chicken livers, you avoid the fuss.

> 1 can (8 ounces) whole water chestnuts, drained
> 1 pound sliced bacon
> 6 tablespoons chili sauce *or* ketchup
> 3 tablespoons brown sugar
> 1 tablespoon Dijon mustard
> 1 tablespoon bourbon, optional

Wrap each water chestnut with 1/2 slice bacon and secure with wooden pick. Arrange bacon-wrapped water chestnuts in a single layer in a shallow baking pan. Broil until crispy, about 5 minutes on each side. Drain well. Blend chili sauce, brown sugar, mustard and bourbon if desired. Pour over chestnuts. Bake at 350° for 20 minutes. **Yield:** 30 appetizers.

BACON DELIGHT DIP

(Pictured above right)

This delicious dip is great on a holiday buffet. Try serving it inside a loaf of bread.

> 1 pound sliced bacon
> 1 round loaf (1 pound) sourdough, rye *or* pumpernickel bread
> 1 package (8 ounces) cream cheese, softened
> 2 cups (16 ounces) sour cream
> 1 can (4 ounces) chopped green chilies, drained
> 6 green onions, chopped

Cook bacon until crisp. Drain; crumble and set aside. Cut top off bread to form a cover. Remove bread inside loaf, leaving a 1/2-in. shell of bread. Cut removed bread into 1-in. cubes and set aside. Combine cream cheese, sour cream, chilies and onions. Stir in bacon. Spoon mixture into bread and replace bread top. Wrap bread in heavy aluminum foil and bake at 350° for 1-1/4 hours. Serve bread bowl with bread cubes reserved for dipping. **Yield:** 10-15 servings.

FOUR-CHEESE BALL

A quick glance at this recipe from the 1970s, and you'll recognize a mainstay at many cocktail parties.

> 1 package (3 ounces) cream cheese, softened
> 1/4 cup mayonnaise *or* salad dressing
> 1 cup (4 ounces) shredded Swiss cheese, at room temperature
> 4 ounces process cheese, cut in small cubes

2 tablespoons chopped pimiento
1 teaspoon Worcestershire sauce
1/2 teaspoon onion powder
1/4 teaspoon hot pepper sauce
1/2 cup crushed saltines (about 15 crackers)
1-1/2 teaspoons grated Parmesan cheese
Assorted crackers

In a small mixing bowl, beat cream cheese and mayonnaise. Add Swiss and process cheese; mix well. Add pimiento, Worcestershire sauce, onion powder and hot pepper sauce. Chill at least 1 hour. Shape into a ball. Combine crushed saltines and Parmesan. Roll cheese ball in saltine mixture. Cover and chill. Remove from refrigerator 15 minutes before serving. Serve with crackers. **Yield:** 1 cheese ball (2 cups).

DEVILED SPREAD

You'll find it hard to stop munching this snack once you start! It's easy to make and special enough for a holiday party.

1 package (8 ounces) cream cheese, softened
1 can (4-1/2 ounces) deviled ham
1/4 cup mayonnaise *or* salad dressing
2 teaspoons prepared mustard
1/8 teaspoon salt
Dash pepper
2 tablespoons sweet pickle relish
Saltine crackers

In a small bowl, beat cream cheese, deviled ham, mayonnaise, mustard, salt, pepper and pickle relish. Chill several hours. Serve with saltines. **Yield:** 6-8 servings.

YOGURT BERRY SMOOTHIE

(Pictured at right in foreground)

These velvety smooth shakes make a special snack. The refreshing flavor of strawberries adds a special tang.

2 cups unsweetened frozen strawberries
   or raspberries
1 carton (8 ounces) vanilla yogurt
1/4 cup milk *or* water
3 tablespoons unsweetened instant tea
2 tablespoons sugar

In a blender, combine all ingredients. Cover and process until mixture is smooth. Pour into glasses. **Yield:** 2 servings.

CITRUS REFRESHER

(Pictured below in background)

For a special occasion, serve this tea in a punch bowl, using a pretty ice ring. To create one, fill a ring mold halfway with prepared tea. Freeze until solid. Top with lemon slices. Add tea to cover. Freeze until solid.

5 cups cold water
1 cup unsweetened pineapple juice
3/4 cup lemonade concentrate
1/2 cup orange juice
6 tablespoons unsweetened instant tea
1/4 cup sugar

In a large pitcher, combine water, pineapple juice, lemonade concentrate, orange juice, tea and sugar; stir until tea and sugar are dissolved. Serve over ice. **Yield:** 6-8 servings.

ITALIAN BEAN DIP

(*Pictured at right*)

If you enjoy hummus, a Middle Eastern dip traditionally made with chick peas, you'll certainly enjoy this updated variation. Consider spreading the dip as a base on pizza crust or in pita pockets to create exciting new combinations.

> 1 can (16 ounces) white kidney beans, rinsed and drained
> 3 tablespoons lemon juice
> 3 teaspoons extra virgin vegetable *or* olive oil, *divided*
> 1 teaspoon chopped garlic
> 1 teaspoon chopped fresh oregano *or* 1/4 teaspoon dried oregano, *divided*

Salt to taste
Assorted fresh vegetables

In a food processor, combine beans, lemon juice, 2 teaspoons olive oil, garlic, 1/2 teaspoon oregano and salt. Process until smooth. Spoon into a small shallow bowl and drizzle with remaining oil. Sprinkle with remaining oregano. Serve as a dip for vegetables. **Yield:** 12 servings.

HERB CHEESE BALL

This basic cheese ball is easy to make with help from a food processor. Mix chopped nuts with the parsley flakes or cracked pepper to add flavor and texture.

> 1 package (8 ounces) cream cheese, softened
> 1/2 cup butter *or* margarine, softened
> 1 tablespoon chopped chives
> 1 garlic clove, minced
> 1 teaspoon pepper

Dried parsley flakes *or* cracked black pepper
Assorted crackers

In a food processor, blend cream cheese, butter, chives, garlic and pepper. Chill until firm enough to handle. Using a piece of waxed paper, shape into a ball. Roll in parsley flakes or cracked pepper. Serve with crackers. **Yield:** 6 servings.

GOLDEN WEDDING PUNCH

In a simpler time, wedding receptions were effortless affairs, featuring a fruity punch served with a slice of homemade wedding cake.

> 2 cups water
> 2 tablespoons unsweetened instant tea

> 3 cups orange juice
> 1 cup lemon juice
> 1 cup pineapple juice
> 1/2 cup sugar
> 1/4 cup grenadine
> 1 bottle (28 ounces) ginger ale

Prepared ice ring
Pineapple tidbits, optional
Strawberry halves, optional

In a large pitcher, combine water, instant tea, juices, sugar and grenadine; stir briskly until tea and sugar are completely dissolved. Chill. Place ice ring in a punch bowl. Pour tea mixture and ginger ale over ice. Garnish with pineapple and strawberries if desired. **Yield:** 22 (1/2-cup) servings.

DILLY SHRIMP DIP

The flavor of seafood is subtle in this thick, creamy dip. It's terrific on crackers or vegetables such as carrot and celery sticks.

> 1 package (8 ounces) cream cheese, softened
> 1/3 cup butter *or* margarine
> 1 can (4-1/4 ounces) tiny shrimp, rinsed and drained
> 1 tablespoon grated onion
> 1/4 teaspoon dill weed

Milk
Assorted crackers

In a mixing bowl, combine the cream cheese and butter. Beat until well blended. Stir in the shrimp, onion and dill weed. Chill until ready to serve. If necessary add milk by teaspoonful until reaching the desired consistency. Serve with crackers. **Yield:** 1-2/3 cups.

SPICY BEAN SALSA

(Pictured below)

Variations on traditional chunky salsas became all the rage in the 1990s. Black-eyed peas and whole kernel corn add interest to this zesty favorite featured onstage in fall 1997.

    1 can (15-1/2 ounces) black-eyed peas, rinsed and drained
    1 can (15 ounces) black beans, rinsed and drained
    1 can (15 ounces) whole kernel corn, drained
1/2 cup chopped onion
1/2 cup chopped green pepper
1/2 cup finely chopped jalapeno peppers
    1 can (14-1/2 ounces) diced tomatoes, undrained
1/2 teaspoon garlic salt
    1 bottle (8 ounces) Italian salad dressing
Tortilla chips

In large glass bowl, combine all ingredients except tortilla chips; mix well. Cover and refrigerate several hours or overnight to blend flavors. Serve with tortilla chips as an appetizer. May also serve as a side dish. **Yield:** 12 servings.

DIJON AND HONEY MEATBALLS

Miniature meatballs are always a favorite at cocktail parties. Yogurt makes the unique sauce extra creamy.

    1 pound bulk pork sausage
1/2 cup dry bread crumbs
    1 egg
    1 cup honey Dijon barbecue sauce
1/2 cup plain yogurt

In a bowl, combine sausage, crumbs and egg; shape into 1-in. balls. Brown meatballs in a 10-in. skillet until no longer pink; drain. Pour sauce over meatballs; stir and heat through. Remove from heat; blend in yogurt. **Yield:** 3 dozen.

Festive Fondues

Cold and Snowy Swiss Winter Sparks a Warming Trend

Surrounded by snow in the Swiss Alps, some hungry person came up with a brilliant idea: how to turn hardened cheese and stale bread into delicious dining.

Fondue, from the French word meaning "to melt", began out of economic necessity. Cheese made by local townspeople during the summer became dry and unpalatable by winter. Roads were impassable, and fresh food was scarce.

Peasants discovered that warmed with wine in a big earthenware pot, cheese turned tasty and creamy—a feast fit for a crowd.

Cherry brandy and garlic added flavor while the alcohol kept the cheese from curdling. Old bread, even crusts, became delicious and soft when dipped and twirled in gooey cheese sauce. Eventually, long-handled forks with two tines were made especially for fondue meals.

Cheese fondues surged in popularity in the 1950s and desserts soared in the 1970s. Both were hot again in the '90s.

CLASSIC SWISS FONDUE

A bit of cornstarch or all-purpose flour helps keep cheese in suspension, so it doesn't separate while heating. Keep the temperature low to avoid scorching.

> **2 cups dry white wine**
> **1 pound Swiss cheese, cubed**
> **3 tablespoons cherry brandy *or* dry white wine**
> **3 tablespoons all-purpose flour**
> **1 garlic clove**
> **Dash *each* of white pepper, paprika and ground nutmeg**
> **1/8 teaspoon baking soda**
> **1 loaf French bread, cut into 1-inch cubes**

Bring wine to a boil. Place cheese, brandy, flour, garlic and seasonings in blender or food processor. Add wine. Cover and process until smooth. Transfer to a fondue pot. Cook over medium heat, stirring constantly until mixture is hot and bubbly. Add baking soda; mix well. Keep fondue at a gentle simmer over low heat. Serve with bread. **Yield:** 8-12 servings.

WISCONSIN CHEESE FONDUE

When stirring cheese into a simmering liquid such as beer or wine, stir in a zigzag pattern, not a circle. This will help break up the cheese. A good fondue pot is heavy, wide and shallow.

> 4 cups (1 pound) shredded cheddar cheese
> 2 tablespoons cornstarch
> 1/2 teaspoon ground mustard
> 1 cup beer
> 1 teaspoon Worcestershire sauce
> Pumpernickel *or* rye bread, cubed

In a large bowl, toss cheese, cornstarch and mustard to coat cheese. In a 2-qt. saucepan over low heat, heat beer and Worcestershire until hot, but not boiling. With a fork or wire whisk, gradually stir in cheese. Cook over low heat until cheese is melted and mixture is smooth and bubbling, stirring constantly. Pour into fondue pot for serving. Keep warm over low heat on fondue stand. To serve: Let each person spear chunks of bread on long-handled fondue fork and dip into fondue. **Yield:** 2-3/4 cups.

SPICED CHOCOLATE FONDUE

It was only a matter of time before two Swiss passions—fondue and chocolate—were married. Classic combinations include chocolate with cinnamon, caramel, coconut or marshmallow.

> 1 package (12 ounces) semisweet chocolate morsels
> 1/2 cup light corn syrup
> 1/4 cup milk
> 2 tablespoons coffee-flavored liqueur
> 1/8 teaspoon ground cinnamon
> Strawberries, pineapple *or* banana chunks, apple slices, cubed angel food *or* pound cake

In a microwave-safe bowl, combine chocolate morsels and corn syrup. Microwave, uncovered, at 50% power for 1-1/2 to 2 minutes; stir. Microwave at additional 10- to 20-second intervals, stirring until smooth. Stir in milk, liqueur and cinnamon. Microwave, uncovered, at 50% power for 2-3 minutes or until warm, stirring frequently. Transfer to a fondue pot and keep warm. Serve with fruit and/or cake. **Yield:** 2-1/2 cups.

BRAZILIAN COFFEE

Served hot or over ice, this delightful beverage will bring your meal to a magnificent conclusion.

> 2 cups water
> 1/4 cup instant coffee granules
> 1 square (1 ounce) unsweetened chocolate
> 1/4 cup sugar
> 1/8 teaspoon salt
> 2 cups milk

In a saucepan, combine water, coffee granules and chocolate. Cook over low heat, stirring constantly, until chocolate is melted. Add sugar and salt; bring to a boil. Reduce heat and simmer 4 minutes, stirring constantly. Gradually stir in milk and heat until hot. Whisk until light and frothy. Serve hot or pour over cracked ice. **Yield:** 4 (1-cup) servings.

PEANUT-SUNFLOWER SPREAD

Peanut butter lovers will want to try this rich spread. A touch of maple syrup enhances the nutty flavor.

> 1/4 cup salted sunflower kernels
> 1 cup cocktail peanuts
> 2 tablespoons cold butter *or* margarine, cut into chunks
> 1 tablespoon maple syrup
> Celery stalks and apple wedges

In a food processor, process sunflower kernels until coarsely chopped; remove and set aside. Process peanuts until paste forms. Add butter and syrup; process until smooth. Add sunflower seeds; pulse until blended. Serve with celery and apple. Store in refrigerator. **Yield:** 4 servings.

TANGY GRAPE REFRESHER

Quench your thirst with this tangy, unexpected combination of grape juice and tea.

> 3 cups grape juice, chilled
> 1/2 cup orange juice
> 1/2 cup cold water
> 1/2 cup unsweetened instant tea
> 1/4 cup sugar
> 1 orange, sliced
> 1 lemon, sliced
> 1 can (12 ounces) lemon-lime soda

In a 2-qt. pitcher, combine grape juice, orange juice, water, instant tea and sugar; mix well. Stir in fruit. Refrigerate at least 2 hours or until ready to serve. Just before serving, add lemon-lime soda. **Yield:** 6 servings.

ORANGE SPICE COFFEE

You won't have to remind yourself to stop and smell the coffee—or drink it either—when you whip up this comforting beverage.

> **1 tablespoon sugar**
> **6 whole cloves**
> **1 cinnamon stick (3 inches)**
> **Peel of 1 small orange**
> **2 cups hot water,** *divided*
> **2 teaspoons instant coffee granules**

In a small saucepan, combine sugar, cloves, cinnamon and peel with 1/2 cup hot water; heat for 5 minutes. Strain mixture into a pitcher, discarding spices and orange peel. Stir remaining hot water into spice liquid; add coffee granules. Let stand about 1 minute. Pour into cups. **Yield:** 2 cups.

SPINACH AND SAUSAGE STUFFED MUSHROOMS

(Pictured below)

Restaurants featured a wide variety of stuffed-mushroom recipes during the 1970s and '80s. Fillings ran the gamut—sausage, crabmeat, herb stuffing, cheese combinations and more.

> **1 package (12 ounces) frozen spinach souffle**
> **3 tablespoons chopped onion**
> **2 tablespoons butter** *or* **margarine**
> **3/4 cup water**
> **2-1/3 cups herb-seasoned stuffing mix crumbs**
> **8 ounces bulk Italian sausage, cooked, crumbled and drained**
> **1/4 cup grated Parmesan cheese**

2-1/2 to 3 pounds whole large mushrooms
Additional grated Parmesan cheese, optional

Defrost spinach souffle in microwave on 50% power for 6-7 minutes. In a medium saucepan, cook onion in butter until tender. Add water; bring to a boil. Remove pan from heat. Add stuffing mix; stir until moistened. Stir in spinach souffle, sausage and cheese. Remove mushroom stems. Arrange mushrooms in a 15-in. x 10-in. x 1-in. baking pan; fill with spinach mixture, mounding slightly. Sprinkle with additional cheese if desired. Bake at 400° for 10-15 minutes or until cheese and mushrooms are lightly browned. **Yield:** 8-10 servings.

DRIED BEEF BALL

Dried meat has been made in America since the Indians made jerky by drying buffalo or venison. Colonists followed their example by drying beef using a good deal of salt.

> **2 packages (about 2 ounces** *each***) sliced dried beef,** *divided*
> **1 package (8 ounces) cream cheese, softened**
> **1/4 cup grated Parmesan cheese**
> **2 tablespoons milk**
> **1-1/2 teaspoons prepared horseradish**
> **Assorted crackers**

In a food processor, shred 1 package dried beef. Remove and set aside. In processor, place remaining dried beef, cream cheese, Parmesan cheese, milk and horseradish. Process until well blended, scraping sides as needed. Place mixture on a sheet of plastic wrap; form into a ball. Roll in reserved dried beef; chill. Serve with crackers. **Yield:** 6 servings.

VEGGIE BLOX

These good-for-you snacks taste great, too. Use a colorful combination of your favorite vegetables. Waist watchers are sure to appreciate this healthful selection.

> **3 cups finely chopped fresh vegetables (carrots, celery, peppers, etc.)**
> **5 envelopes unflavored gelatin**
> **3/4 cup cold water**
> **2 cups tomato juice**
> **1 tablespoon lemon juice**
> **2 tablespoons sugar**
> **1 teaspoon Italian seasoning**
> **3 drops hot pepper sauce, optional**
> **Additional cucumbers** *or* **zucchini, thinly sliced**

Sprinkle gelatin over cold water; let stand 1 minute.

In a small saucepan, bring tomato juice to a boil. Add to gelatin; stir until gelatin is completely dissolved. Stir in vegetables, lemon juice, sugar, seasoning and hot pepper sauce. Pour into a 13-in. x 9-in. x 2-in. baking dish and chill until firm. Cut into 1-in. squares. To serve, place a square on a slice of cucumber or zucchini. **Yield:** 10 dozen.

LUNCHBOX SNACK MIX

As parents know, children enjoy munching on dry breakfast cereal. With the addition of peanuts and raisins, this crispy combo appeals to youngsters and adults alike.

> 2 cups fruity sweetened corn puffs cereal
> 1-1/2 cups lightly sweetened crisp rice and corn squares cereal
> 1 cup dry roasted peanuts
> 1 cup chocolate-covered raisins *or* raisins

In a large bowl, combine cereal, peanuts and raisins. Store in airtight containers. **Yield:** 8 servings.

FRESH VEGETABLE SPREAD

The first food processors were introduced to America in the 1970s, providing a speedy alternative to many cumbersome kitchen tasks. Flavorful spreads like this one could be swirled together in a matter of seconds, saving home cooks time and effort.

> 1 carrot, cut into 2-inch pieces
> 1 celery rib, cut into 2-inch pieces
> 1/2 medium green pepper, cut into chunks
> 1 small onion
> 2 bacon strips, cooked
> 1 package (8 ounces) cream cheese, cubed
> 1/4 cup milk
> 2 cups (8 ounces) shredded sharp cheddar cheese
> Fresh vegetable dippers

In a food processor, finely chop carrot, celery, green pepper, onion and bacon. Add cream cheese, milk and shredded cheese; process until well blended. Refrigerate before serving. Serve with fresh vegetables. **Yield:** 8 servings.

1-2-3 FRUIT PUNCH

Dazzling drinks add color and flavor to snacktime. This simple punch refreshes on a summer day and is perfect for brunches and showers.

> 1 can (46 ounces) red fruit punch, chilled
> 3 teaspoons unsweetened instant tea
> 3 cups cold water
> 3/4 cup lemonade concentrate

In a large pitcher or small punch bowl, combine all ingredients; stir. Add ice. **Yield:** 10-12 servings.

OLD-FASHIONED CORN DOGS

(Pictured above)

The all-American hot dog actually is an import named after the German city of Frankfurt. After serving the sausages on buns, creative cooks found a way to encase them in a crunchy cornmeal batter.

> Vegetable oil *or* shortening for deep frying
> 1 cup self-rising flour
> 3/4 cup self-rising cornmeal mix
> 3/4 cup milk
> 1 egg, lightly beaten
> 2 tablespoons vegetable oil
> 1 package (1 pound) hot dogs, at room temperature
> Mustard and ketchup, optional

In a large saucepan or electric deep fryer, heat 2-3 in. of oil over medium-high heat to 375°. Stir together flour and cornmeal in a mixing bowl. Add milk, egg and oil; stir until smooth. Set batter aside for 10 minutes. Insert skewers into hot dogs. Dip hot dogs into batter. Carefully drop corn dogs into hot oil. Fry until golden brown and floating on top. Drain on paper towels. Serve hot with mustard and ketchup if desired. **Yield:** 8-10 corn dogs.

1 envelope ranch salad dressing mix
1 package (8 ounces) cream cheese, softened
1 cup roasted red peppers, drained
Sliced bread and vegetable dippers

In a food processor, combine first three ingredients. Cover and process until smooth. Transfer to a serving bowl and refrigerate until ready to serve. Serve with bread and vegetable dippers. **Yield:** 2 cups.

SPICED TEA

Pretty and refreshing with citrus undertones, this flavored tea is an ideal summertime thirst-quencher.

2-1/2 cups boiling water
  3/4 cup sugar
    2 tablespoons unsweetened instant tea
  1/4 teaspoon ground nutmeg
  1/4 teaspoon ground cinnamon
  1/4 teaspoon ground allspice
1-1/2 cups water
  1/2 cup orange juice
  1/3 cup lemon juice

In a saucepan, combine first six ingredients; mix well. Let stand until cool. Stir in remaining ingredients. Chill thoroughly. Serve over ice cubes in tall glasses. **Yield:** 4-6 servings.

CHICKEN DRUMMETTES

(Pictured above right)

Decades ago, chicken wings cost only pennies per pound. Clever restaurant managers found a way to cash in by serving savory wing appetizers.

  1 envelope ranch salad dressing mix
1/4 cup vegetable oil
 24 chicken drummettes (about 2 pounds)
Prepared ranch salad dressing

In a large bowl, combine dressing mix and oil. Add drummettes; toss well to coat. Arrange on rack in a foil-lined baking pan. Bake at 425° for 25 minutes. Turn drummettes; bake an additional 20 minutes. To serve, dip in salad dressing. **Yield:** 2 dozen.

ROASTED RED PEPPER SPREAD

(Pictured above left)

At your next dinner party, tempt your guests with this quick-to-fix spread. By serving an inexpensive appetizer, you can offset the cost of a more expensive entree.

BIG COUNTRY BISCUIT WRAPS

A special surprise awaits folks inside these fast, flavor-packed snacks. The selection of fillings provides something for everyone.

  1 tube (12 ounces) refrigerated buttermilk
    biscuits
3/4 cup chopped cooked ham
3/4 cup shredded cheddar cheese

Separate dough into 10 biscuits. Press each biscuit into a 5-in. round. In a small bowl, combine chopped ham and cheddar cheese; mix well. Spoon about 2 tablespoons mixture onto center of each biscuit. Fold dough in half over filling; press edges with fork to seal. Place on ungreased baking sheet. Bake at 400° for 10-13 minutes or until golden brown. **Yield:** 10 wraps.

FILLING VARIATIONS:

HONEY-MUSTARD HAM FILLING:
  1 cup chopped cooked ham
  2 tablespoons honey mustard
  1 tablespoon finely chopped red onion

TURKEY SWISS FILLING:
  3/4 cup chopped cooked turkey
  1/2 cup shredded Swiss cheese
  1/4 cup chopped tomato

COUNTRY SAUSAGE FILLING:
  6 ounces bulk pork sausage, cooked and crumbled
  1/2 cup shredded cheddar cheese
  1/2 cup chopped apple

WESTERN BARBEQUE FILLING:
  1/2 cup prepared sloppy joe meat mixture
  1/2 cup baked beans
  2 tablespoons barbecue sauce
  1 teaspoon dried minced onion

PIZZA POCKET FILLING:
  1 cup sliced cooked Italian sausage
  1/3 cup shredded mozzarella cheese
  1/3 cup chopped green pepper
  1/3 cup pizza sauce

CHICKEN TACO FILLING:
  1 cup chopped cooked chicken
  1/3 cup Mexicorn
  1/3 cup shredded Monterey Jack cheese
  1/4 cup chunky salsa

CHICKEN BROCCOLI FILLING:
  1 cup chopped cooked chicken
  1/3 cup chopped cooked broccoli
  1/3 cup shredded cheddar cheese
  2 tablespoons mayonnaise
  1 tablespoon finely chopped onion

PHILLY CHEESESTEAK FILLING:
  1 cup chopped cooked roast beef
  1/3 cup shredded mozzarella cheese
  1/4 cup chopped green *or* red pepper

ITALIAN BISTRO TART

(Pictured at right)

People will rave over this rich-tasting onion tart. Frozen puff pastry allows you to prepare the flaky crust in a jiffy with little fuss.

  1/2 package (17-1/4 ounces) frozen puff pastry (1 sheet), thawed
  5 yellow onions, thinly sliced
  2 tablespoons butter *or* margarine
  1/2 pound sliced bacon, cooked and crumbled
  1 egg
  3/4 cup whipping cream

  1 teaspoon garlic salt
  1/2 cup shredded Swiss cheese

Roll pastry to fit an ungreased 10-in. tart pan or pie plate; flute edges. Pierce crust with fork. Bake at 350° for 15 minutes. Remove from oven and let cool. In a covered skillet, cook onions in butter over low heat until soft and tender. Do not allow to brown. Spread cooked bacon and onions in crust. In a bowl, beat egg, cream and garlic salt. Pour over onion mixture. Sprinkle with cheese. Bake at 350° for 25 minutes or until egg mixture is set. Let stand 5 minutes before cutting. **Yield:** 6 servings.

MOROCCAN COFFEE MAGIC

We have all heard about England's taxation on teas, which led to revolt during the Boston Tea Party. Later, the War of 1812 interfered with shipping in the tea trade but not with South American coffee imports. Both events helped make coffee America's most popular hot beverage.

  3 cups boiling water
  1/4 cup instant coffee granules
  1/4 cup sugar
  1 tablespoon ground cinnamon
  1/4 teaspoon ground cloves
  1/4 teaspoon ground allspice

In a large pitcher, combine water and coffee granules; stir until coffee is dissolved. Add sugar, cinnamon, cloves and allspice; stir well. Cover and let cool about 1 hour. Serve over ice in glasses. **Yield:** 4 (6-ounce) servings.

Chapter 2

SALADS & DRESSINGS

Whether cool and crunchy or warm and wonderful, salads can be served as a meal starter, side dish or main course. The tangy flavor of homemade dressings will dazzle your taste buds.

Recipes in this chapter provided courtesy of these past sponsors...

GRILLED STEAK SALAD WITH PINEAPPLE SALSA

(Pictured at left)

Tender strips of grilled steak are served on a bed of salad greens, then topped with a medley of fruits, tomatoes and peppers.

> 1 pound boneless beef sirloin steak (1 inch thick)
> 2 teaspoons Mexican seasoning
> 1 can (15 ounces) mandarin oranges, drained
> 1 can (14-1/2 ounces) diced tomatoes with mild green chilies *or* jalapeno peppers, undrained
> 1 can (8 ounces) pineapple tidbits, undrained
> 1/2 cup chopped green *or* sweet red pepper
> 6 cups torn salad greens *or* 1 package (10 ounces) assorted salad greens

Trim fat from steak. Rub both sides with seasoning. Grill, uncovered, directly over medium heat for 12-15 minutes or until steak reaches desired doneness. Meanwhile, for salsa, combine oranges, tomatoes, pineapple and pepper. Thinly slice steak across the grain. Serve steak and salsa over salad greens. **Yield:** 4 servings.

ORIGINAL HOT CHICKEN SALAD

Throughout the 1970s, this down-home favorite was served at many potlucks and showers. Crunchy almonds and colorful pimientos make this satisfying dish something special.

> 2 cups cubed cooked chicken
> 2 cups chopped celery
> 1/2 cup chopped almonds
> 1 jar (2 ounces) diced pimientos
> 1/2 teaspoon salt
> 1/4 teaspoon pepper
> 2 tablespoons lemon juice
> 1/2 cup mayonnaise
> 1 cup sour cream
> 1 cup crushed saltines
> 1 cup (4 ounces) shredded Swiss cheese

In a large bowl, combine the first six ingredients. Blend lemon juice, mayonnaise and sour cream. Stir into chicken mixture. Spread in a greased 9-in. square baking dish. Mix saltines and cheese. Sprinkle on top of casserole. Bake at 350° for 25 minutes or until heated through. **Yield:** 4 servings.

STRAWBERRY MARSHMALLOW MOLD

During the 1960s, no buffet was complete without a tempting gelatin salad. Luscious strawberries add vivid color and sweetness to this cool treat, which draws raves from kids and adults alike.

    1 package (3 ounces) strawberry gelatin
    1 cup boiling water
    1 package (10 ounces) frozen sweetened
      sliced strawberries
1-1/2 cups miniature marshmallows

In a large bowl, dissolve gelatin in boiling water. Add strawberries; stir until fruit separates and mixture thickens. Fold in marshmallows. Pour into a 1-qt. mold coated with nonstick cooking spray; refrigerate until firm. Just before serving, unmold onto a serving platter. **Yield:** 4-6 servings.

FESTIVE LAYERED SALAD

(Pictured below)

While layered salads enjoyed immense popularity in the 1970s, new combinations are being created even today. With lots of vegetables and delightful fresh flavor, this salad makes a wonderful summer lunch.

    1 can (16 ounces) julienned pickled beets,
      well drained
    2 cups shredded carrots
    4 cups torn fresh spinach
    2 cups (8 ounces) shredded cheddar *and/or*
      Monterey Jack cheeses, *divided*
    2 cups halved cherry tomatoes
    1 package (10 ounces) frozen peas, thawed
1-1/3 cups ranch salad dressing
    1/2 teaspoon pepper
Herb *or* garlic croutons, optional

In a large glass serving bowl, layer beets, carrots, spinach, 1 cup cheese, cherry tomatoes and peas. Combine salad dressing and pepper; spoon evenly over top. Sprinkle remaining cheese over dressing. Cover with plastic wrap; refrigerate for 2-12 hours before serving. Sprinkle with croutons if desired. **Yield:** 8 servings.

EGGPLANT PASTA SALAD

The Spaniards introduced eggplant to the Americas around 1600. By 1800, purple and white varieties were grown in the United States for ornamental use. It wasn't until the 1950s that folks began to serve eggplant dishes. Even today, eggplant is most associated with Middle Eastern and Mediterranean cooking.

    2 cups uncooked large shell pasta
    2 cups peeled and cubed eggplant
    2 small zucchini, cubed
    2 garlic cloves, minced
    1 tablespoon olive *or* vegetable oil
    1 can (14-1/2 ounces) diced tomatoes with
      basil, garlic and oregano, undrained
    1/3 cup crumbled feta cheese
Chopped fresh basil leaves, optional

Cook the pasta according to package directions; rinse and drain. In a skillet, cook the eggplant, zucchini and garlic in oil over medium-high heat for 3 minutes, stirring frequently. Add the tomatoes. Cover and cook over medium-low heat for 5 minutes. Cook, uncovered, for 3 minutes or until thickened. Cool; stir in the pasta and feta cheese. Serve at room temperature or chilled. Garnish with basil if desired. **Yield:** 4-6 servings.

VEGETABLE SALAD STACK-UP

Offering a unique twist on traditional layered salad, this version features corn, peppers, zucchini and tomatoes draped in a tangy dressing.

4 cups shredded lettuce
1 cup chopped green pepper
1 can (12 ounces) whole kernel corn with
  sweet peppers, drained
1 cup sliced zucchini
2 cups chopped tomato
1 cup chopped celery
1 cup mayonnaise *or* salad dressing
1 cup French salad dressing
2 cups (8 ounces) shredded cheddar cheese
6 bacon strips, cooked and crumbled

In a 2-1/2-qt. serving bowl, layer lettuce, pepper, corn, zucchini, tomatoes and celery. In a small bowl, combine the mayonnaise and French dressing. Pour over the vegetables, coating the entire top layer. Cover and chill several hours or overnight. Sprinkle with cheese and bacon just before serving. **Yield:** 6 servings.

COOL 'N' CREAMY HAM SALAD

A sweet and creamy dressing lends old-fashioned goodness to this ham and pasta salad.

2 cups uncooked spiral pasta
3 medium apples, diced
2 cups cubed fully cooked ham
1 medium green pepper, cut into strips
1 can (14 ounces) sweetened condensed
  milk
3/4 cup lime juice
1/4 cup vegetable oil
1/4 cup prepared mustard
2 teaspoons onion salt
1 tablespoon celery seed

Cook pasta according to package directions; drain. In a large bowl, combine pasta, apples, ham and green pepper. In a small bowl, combine condensed milk, lime juice, oil, mustard, salt and celery seed. Pour over ham mixture and toss to coat. Cover and refrigerate at least 3 hours. **Yield:** 8-10 servings.

CLASSIC CHICKEN CAESAR SALAD

(Pictured above right)

During warm-weather months, this cool salad offers a refreshing change from the heavier meals served other times of the year. The chicken stays moist and tender, while the zesty dressing wakes up the taste buds.

1/4 cup olive *or* vegetable oil
2 tablespoons lemon juice

1 garlic clove, minced
3/4 teaspoon salt
1/2 teaspoon pepper
4 boneless skinless chicken breast halves
2 tablespoons mayonnaise
6 cups torn romaine *or* mixed salad greens
1 cup (4 ounces) Parmesan, mozzarella
  and/or Romano cheeses, *divided*
1/2 cup garlic croutons

In a large bowl, whisk oil, lemon juice, garlic, salt and pepper. Remove 2 tablespoons oil mixture from bowl. Brush onto chicken. Grill or broil chicken 5 inches from heat for about 5-6 minutes per side or until chicken juices run clear. Add mayonnaise to remaining oil mixture. Add lettuce, 3/4 cup cheese and croutons; toss to coat. Arrange salad on four serving plates. Cut chicken crosswise into 1/2-in. slices; arrange on top of salads. Sprinkle with remaining cheese. **Yield:** 4 servings.

"CRABBY" GAZPACHO SALAD

(Pictured above)

In Japanese, surimi means minced fish. Pronounced "Sir-Ree-Mee", this is the generic term for all of the imitation crabmeat products that were introduced to consumers in the 1980s.

> 1 cup uncooked small shell pasta
> 1 tablespoon olive *or* vegetable oil
> 1 package (8 ounces) imitation crabmeat, coarsely chopped
> 3/4 cup seeded and chopped cucumber
> 3/4 cup chopped celery
> 3/4 cup medium chunky salsa
> 1/4 cup *each* diced red onion, sweet red pepper and green pepper
> 1/4 cup Italian salad dressing
> 1 tablespoon lemon juice
> Salt and pepper to taste

Cook pasta according to package directions; drain. In a large bowl, combine pasta and oil. Add remaining ingredients and toss. Cover and refrigerate for at least 1 hour before serving. **Yield:** 8 servings.

CREAMY POTATO SALAD

If you're always looking for good traditional recipes, this tasty potato salad is a classic. It can be served on greens, with a sandwich or as an accompaniment to baked ham.

> 2 pounds red potatoes
> 2 green onions, chopped
> 1/2 cup mayonnaise
> 1/2 cup sour cream
> 1 jar (2 ounces) diced pimientos, drained
> 1-1/2 tablespoons prepared mustard
> 1 tablespoon sugar
> 1 tablespoon white wine vinegar *or* cider vinegar
> 1/2 teaspoon salt
> 1/2 teaspoon celery seeds
> 1/4 teaspoon pepper
> 1/8 teaspoon garlic powder

In a medium saucepan, cook potatoes in boiling water for 25 minutes or until tender; drain and cool. Peel and cube potatoes. In a large bowl, combine remaining ingredients. Add potatoes; toss to coat. Serve immediately or cover and chill overnight. **Yield:** 6-8 servings.

CHICKEN WALDORF SALAD

Waldorf salad was created by maitre d' Oscar Tschirky for the Waldorf Astoria Hotel's grand opening in 1893. Over the years, dozens of versions have been created using an apple, mayonnaise and celery base.

> 3 cups cubed cooked chicken
> 3 medium tart apples, cored and diced
> 1/2 cup chopped celery
> 1/2 cup mayonnaise
> 1/2 cup sour cream
> 2 tablespoons honey
> 1 tablespoon lemon juice
> 1/2 teaspoon ground nutmeg
> 1/2 head iceberg lettuce, torn

In a large bowl, combine chicken, apples and celery. In a small bowl, combine mayonnaise, sour cream, honey, lemon juice and nutmeg. Pour over chicken mixture. Toss gently to mix well. Serve over lettuce. **Yield:** 4 servings.

RED, WHITE AND BLUEBERRY MOLD

Add patriotic pizzazz to your next get-together by serving this layered gelatin salad.

1 package (3 ounces) raspberry gelatin
3 cups boiling water, *divided*
1 cup strawberry pie filling
1 package (3 ounces) lemon gelatin
1 package (8 ounces) cream cheese,
   softened
1 package (3 ounces) grape gelatin
1 cup blueberry pie filling
Frozen whipped topping, thawed, optional

Spray a 9-in. square baking dish or 10-cup glass bowl with nonstick cooking spray. In a medium bowl, dissolve raspberry gelatin in 1 cup boiling water; stir until completely dissolved. Stir in strawberry filling. Pour into prepared baking dish. Refrigerate 30 minutes or until set but not firm. In a small bowl, dissolve lemon gelatin in 1 cup boiling water; stir until completely dissolved. Place cream cheese in a medium bowl. Gradually add lemon gelatin, beating with wire whisk until well blended. Spoon over raspberry layer in baking dish. Refrigerate 30 minutes or until set but not firm. In a medium bowl, dissolve grape gelatin in 1 cup boiling water; stir until completely dissolved. Stir in blueberry filling. Spoon over lemon layer in baking dish. Refrigerate until firm, about 4 hours. Garnish with whipped topping if desired. **Yield:** 10 servings.

ZIPPY PASTA SALAD

In recent years, homemakers have become more aware of the health benefits of cooking with olive oil. Back in 1986, when this salad was featured in our onstage demonstrations, we simply knew that it tasted delicious.

2-1/2 cups uncooked spinach noodles
2-1/2 cups uncooked egg noodles
   3 cups broccoli florets
1/2 cup plus 1 tablespoon olive *or* vegetable oil,
   divided
1/2 cup chopped red onion
   1 package (5 ounces) sliced pepperoni
   1 jar (4 ounces) diced pimientos
   1 can (6 ounces) ripe pitted olives, drained
   and sliced
   1 tablespoon Dijon mustard
1/4 cup red wine vinegar *or* cider vinegar
   1 teaspoon sugar
1/2 teaspoon salt
Dash pepper
   1 garlic clove
   2 tablespoons minced fresh parsley
1/2 cup grated Parmesan cheese

Cook noodles according to package directions, adding broccoli for 1 minute at end of cooking time;

drain. Place noodle mixture in a large bowl. Add 1 tablespoon oil, onion, pepperoni, pimientos and olives and toss to coat; refrigerate. In a food processor, combine mustard, vinegar, sugar, salt, pepper, garlic and parsley. While processing, gradually add remaining oil in a steady stream. Add dressing and Parmesan cheese to pasta mixture; mix well. Cover and refrigerate until serving time. **Yield:** 8-10 servings.

ZESTY ORANGE CHICKEN PASTA SALAD

(Pictured below)

Always a hit at summer celebrations, this delightful salad looks beautiful on a buffet and is very refreshing on a hot day.

   1 cup mayonnaise *or* salad dressing
1/2 cup orange juice
   2 teaspoons dried basil
1/4 teaspoon ground ginger
   4 boneless skinless chicken breast halves
   (about 1-1/4 pounds), cooked and cubed
   2 cups spiral pasta, cooked and drained
   1 can (11 ounces) mandarin oranges, drained
1/2 cup chopped pecans

In a large bowl, mix mayonnaise, orange juice, basil and ginger. Add remaining ingredients; toss lightly. Cover and refrigerate at least 2 hours to blend the flavors. **Yield:** 6 servings.

Watergate Salad

What does this sassy salad have in common with the political scandal that rocked America in the 1970s? Not a lot, as it turns out.

IT'S BEEN 30 years since what appeared to be a small-time burglary at a Washington, D.C. hotel sparked an investigation that resulted in indictments against 40 government officials and the resignation of the president.

And the scandal even gave a new name to an old salad.

Cause and effect? Hardly.

As a scandal, Watergate (named after the Watergate Hotel) mixed political spying, sabotage and bribery. As a salad, Watergate blends pistachio pudding, crushed pineapple and walnuts for a taste that's, well…intriguing.

Pistachio Pineapple Delight was renamed Watergate Salad by a Chicago food editor who wanted to promote interest in the recipe in her news column around the time of the scandal. It worked, and the name stuck.

Now, the only question that pops up more often than "Where'd that salad get its name?" is "Can I have the recipe?" And the answer is yes. See below.

WATERGATE SALAD

(Pictured above)

You don't need to break in to our recipe vault to learn the secrets of this salad's success. And it's no crime to enjoy the taste and texture of this crunchy tangy concoction.

- **1 package (3.4 ounces) instant pistachio pudding mix**
- **1 can (20 ounces) crushed pineapple in juice, undrained**
- **1/2 cup chopped walnuts**
- **3-1/4 cups miniature marshmallows,** *divided*
- **2 cartons (8 ounces** *each***) frozen whipped topping, thawed,** *divided*
- **Maraschino cherries**

In a large bowl, combine pudding mix, pineapple with juice, nuts and 1 cup marshmallows; stir until blended. Fold in one carton of whipped topping. In a separate bowl, combine 2 cups marshmallows and remaining whipped topping. Spoon one half of pudding mixture into a large serving bowl; top with one half of marshmallow mixture. Repeat layers. Garnish with cherries and remaining marshmallows. Cover and refrigerate until serving. **Yield:** 16 servings.

GERMAN POTATO SALAD

Germans dress hot cooked potatoes with a mixture of bacon, vinegar and sugar. The proportions of sugar and vinegar may change depending on the cook's personal taste.

6 medium potatoes
6 bacon strips, cut into 1/2-inch pieces
1 medium onion, chopped
1 celery rib, chopped
1 tablespoon all-purpose flour
1/2 cup water
1/3 cup white vinegar
2 tablespoons sugar
1 tablespoon chopped fresh parsley
1 teaspoon salt
1/8 teaspoon pepper

Place potatoes in a 4-qt. saucepan; add water to cover. Over high heat, bring to a boil. Reduce heat to medium-low. Cover; simmer 20-30 minutes or until fork-tender; drain. Cool potatoes slightly. With sharp knife, peel potatoes; discard peels. Cut potatoes into 1/4-in. slices. In a 10-in. skillet over medium heat, cook bacon until crisp. Remove bacon to paper towels to drain; set aside. Discard all but 2 tablespoons drippings. In bacon drippings, cook onion and celery until tender. Add flour; stir until blended. Gradually stir in water, vinegar, sugar, parsley, salt and pepper; bring to a boil, stirring constantly. Add potatoes; toss gently to mix well. Heat through. Garnish with bacon; serve immediately. **Yield:** 5 cups.

SAUERKRAUT SALAD

Cabbage salads have been made in America for more than 300 years. You'll find this unique recipe, with its sweet-and-sour flavor, a perfect complement for pork entrees. Diced pimientos and red and green peppers provide visual interest as well as a spark of flavor.

1 can (27 ounces) sauerkraut, drained
3 celery ribs, sliced
1 medium onion, diced
1/2 medium green *or* sweet red pepper, diced
1/2 cup diced pimientos
1/3 cup vegetable oil
1/4 cup white wine vinegar *or* cider vinegar
18 packets artificial sweetener
Salt and pepper to taste

In a medium bowl, combine the first five ingredients. In a small bowl, whisk together oil, vinegar and sweetener. Pour over salad and mix thoroughly. Season with salt and pepper. Cover and chill overnight

or place in freezer for 40 minutes, stirring after 20 minutes. **Yield:** 10 servings.

MEXICAN CHOPPED SALAD

(Pictured below)

Sure to be an instant favorite with family and friends, this garden-fresh Mexican-style salad is terrific after a fun day in the sun.

6 cups sliced romaine lettuce
1-1/2 cups (6 ounces) cheddar *and/or* Pepper Jack cheese
1 cup diced peeled jicama
1 medium avocado, peeled and diced
1 cup chopped tomato
1 cup canned black beans, rinsed and drained
1/2 cup frozen whole kernel corn, thawed
1/4 cup thinly sliced green onions
1/4 cup vegetable oil
2 tablespoons white wine vinegar *or* cider vinegar
1 jalapeno pepper, minced
1/2 teaspoon salt

In a large bowl, combine lettuce, cheese, jicama, avocado, tomato, beans, corn and green onions. In a small bowl, combine remaining ingredients; mix well. Add to salad mixture; toss to coat. **Yield:** 4 servings.

NUTTY BROCCOLI-BACON SALAD

The name broccoli comes from the Italian word for "cabbage sprout" and, indeed, broccoli is a member of the cabbage family. An excellent source of vitamins and minerals, broccoli tastes good and is good for you.

    1 container (8 ounces) plain yogurt
    1 tablespoon cider vinegar
    2 tablespoons sugar
    4 cups broccoli florets
    1/4 cup crumbled cooked bacon
    1/2 cup pecan pieces

In a bowl, combine yogurt, vinegar and sugar. Add broccoli; toss to coat. Just before serving, stir in bacon and nuts. **Yield:** 8 servings.

CURRIED HAM AND RICE SALAD

(Pictured below)

Widely used in Indian cooking, curry powder is actually a blend of up to 20 spices, herbs and seeds. Among those most commonly used in commercial blends are cardamom, chilies, cinnamon, cloves, cumin, nutmeg and turmeric. Turmeric is what gives curried dishes their characteristic yellow color.

    1 can (14-1/2 ounces) diced tomatoes with
      garlic and onion, undrained

    1 cup uncooked long grain rice
    1/2 cup mayonnaise
    2 tablespoons lemon juice
    1 tablespoon curry powder
    1-1/2 cups diced fully cooked ham
    1/2 cup sliced green onions
    1/2 cup raisins
  Chopped parsley, optional
  Toasted sliced almonds, optional

Drain tomatoes, reserving liquid; set tomatoes aside. Pour reserved liquid into a measuring cup; add water to measure 2 cups. Pour into saucepan; bring to a boil. Add rice; reduce heat. Cover and simmer for 20 minutes or until done. In a large bowl, combine tomatoes, mayonnaise, lemon juice and curry. Stir in ham, onions, raisins and rice; chill. Garnish with parsley and almonds if desired. **Yield:** 6 servings.

BLUE CHEESE CHICKEN SALAD

Blue cheese tends to be strong in flavor and aroma, so it may take time to develop an appreciation for its characteristic taste.

    1 can (14-1/2 ounces) diced tomatoes,
      undrained
    1/2 pound boneless skinless chicken breast
      halves, cut into strips
    1/2 teaspoon dried tarragon
    6 cups torn salad greens
    1/2 red onion, thinly sliced
    1/2 cucumber, thinly sliced
    1/3 cup crumbled blue cheese
    1/4 cup Italian salad dressing

Drain tomatoes, reserving liquid; set tomatoes aside. In a large skillet, cook reserved liquid until thickened, about 5 minutes, stirring occasionally. Add chicken and tarragon; cook until chicken juices run clear, stirring frequently. Cool. In a large bowl, toss chicken, tomatoes and remaining ingredients. Serve immediately. **Yield:** 4 servings.

GRAPEFRUIT AND ORANGE ASPIC

Aspic is a savory jelly made with gelatin. It's traditionally served as a relish alongside cold meat or fish. Though tomato aspic is probably more common, this fruity medley is delicious as well.

    2 envelopes unflavored gelatin
    1 cup cold water
    2 cups unsweetened pink grapefruit juice
    2 tablespoons lemon juice

1/4 cup sugar
2 drops red food coloring, optional
2 large pink grapefruit, peeled and sectioned
1 orange, peeled and sectioned

In a medium saucepan, sprinkle gelatin over cold water; let stand 1 minute. Stir over low heat until gelatin is completely dissolved. Stir in grapefruit juice, lemon juice, sugar and food coloring if desired. Chill, stirring occasionally, until mixture is consistency of unbeaten egg whites. Fold in grapefruit and orange sections. Turn into a 5-cup mold or bowl; chill until firm. Just before serving, unmold onto a serving platter. **Yield:** 6-8 servings.

GOLD COAST SALAD

Carrots were brought to America by European colonists. They grew so well that wild carrots quickly spread across the country in the form of a weed known as Queen Anne's lace. This salad combines carrots and fruits.

2/3 cup vegetable oil
1/3 cup red wine vinegar *or* cider vinegar
3 tablespoons honey
1 teaspoon poppy seeds
1/2 teaspoon salt
6 cups torn salad greens
2 cups orange segments
1-1/2 cups shredded carrots
1/2 cup raisins

In a jar with a tight-fitting lid, combine oil, vinegar, honey, poppy seeds and salt; shake well. Refrigerate to blend flavors. Combine salad greens, orange segments, carrots and raisins in a large bowl. Just before serving, pour dressing over salad; toss lightly. **Yield:** 6-8 servings.

CHICKEN SALAD CANTON

(*Pictured above right*)

Soy sauce is an extremely important ingredient in Asian cooking. The salty dark sauce is made by fermenting boiled soybeans and roasted wheat or barley. Soy sauce is used to flavor a wide array of sauces, marinades and dressings.

1 cup fresh snow peas *or* 1 package
  (6 ounces) frozen snow peas, thawed
1 can (14-1/2 ounces) diced tomatoes with
  garlic and onion, undrained
3 tablespoons vegetable oil
3 tablespoons cider vinegar
1 tablespoon soy sauce

4 cups shredded cabbage *or* iceberg lettuce
1 cup cubed cooked chicken
1/3 cup chopped fresh cilantro *or* sliced green
  onions
Pepper to taste
Toasted sesame seeds

If using fresh snow peas, dip in boiling water for 30 seconds; cool. Drain tomatoes, reserving 1/4 cup liquid; set tomatoes aside. Combine reserved liquid with oil, vinegar and soy sauce. In a large bowl, combine snow peas, tomatoes, cabbage, chicken, cilantro and pepper. Pour dressing over salad; toss lightly. Sprinkle with sesame seeds. **Yield:** 2 servings.

SEVEN-LAYER SALAD

This multi-layered salad makes a beautiful presentation and can be made a day in advance, which is a great help to a busy hostess.

1 head iceberg lettuce, shredded
1/2 cup chopped celery
1/2 cup chopped green pepper
1/2 cup chopped onion
1 package (10 ounces) frozen peas, thawed
1-1/2 cups mayonnaise
2 tablespoons sugar
1-1/2 cups (6 ounces) shredded cheddar cheese
8 bacon strips, cooked and crumbled

Place lettuce in the bottom of a 4-qt. glass salad bowl. Layer with celery, pepper, onion and peas. Spread mayonnaise over top of salad. Sprinkle with sugar. Layer with cheese and bacon Cover and chill several hours or overnight. **Yield:** 8-10 servings.

and dressing; pour over the pasta mixture. Toss to coat well. Cover and refrigerate for at least 1 hour before serving. **Yield:** 8 servings.

FRUIT GEM SALAD

Featured onstage in 1969, this salad highlights a colorful variety of fruits draped in a sugary sauce.

> 1 egg
> 1 cup sugar
> 2 tablespoons all-purpose flour
> 1 can (20 ounces) crushed pineapple, undrained
> 1 jar (10 ounces) maraschino cherries, undrained
> 2 medium oranges, peeled, chopped and seeded
> 2 medium apples, diced
> 3 firm bananas, sliced
Flaked coconut *or* chopped walnuts

In a saucepan, combine egg, sugar and flour. Drain pineapple and cherries, reserving juices; add juices to saucepan. Cook over medium heat, stirring constantly, until mixture has thickened, about 3-4 minutes. Cool. In a serving bowl, combine oranges, apples, bananas, pineapple and cherries. Stir sauce into fruit mixture. Sprinkle with coconut just before serving. **Yield:** 8-12 servings.

HONEY-POPPY SEED DRESSING

Delicious on salad greens or prepared fruit, this luscious dressing really shines through.

> 1/4 cup honey
> 1/3 cup vegetable oil
> 2 tablespoons cider vinegar
> 2 teaspoons poppy seeds
> 1/2 teaspoon salt

Thoroughly blend all ingredients. Serve with fruit salad or salad greens. Refrigerate leftovers. **Yield:** 3/4 cup.

ITALIAN ROTINI SALAD

(Pictured above)

With a wonderful combination of colors and flavors, this hearty, one-of-a-kind Italian pasta salad is a satisfying meal in itself.

> 1 package (12 ounces) tricolor spiral pasta, cooked and drained
> 2 cups cubed cooked roast beef
> 2 cups broccoli florets, blanched
> 1 cup cubed Provolone cheese
> 1/3 cup roasted red peppers, coarsely chopped
> 3/4 cup steak sauce
> 1/2 cup Italian salad dressing

In a large bowl, combine pasta, beef, broccoli, cheese and peppers. In a small bowl, combine steak sauce

TENNESSEE CORN BREAD SALAD

Leftover corn bread will never go to waste once you try this wonderful dish. Folks will happily dish up this satisfying salad.

> 1 package (8-1/2 ounces) corn bread/ muffin mix

3 large tomatoes, chopped
1 large green pepper, chopped
1 large onion, chopped
1/2 cup chopped sweet pickles
12 bacon strips, cooked and crumbled
1 cup mayonnaise
1/4 cup dill pickle juice

Prepare corn bread according to package directions; cool. Crumble half of the corn bread into bottom of a large serving bowl. In another bowl, combine tomatoes, green pepper, onion, pickles and bacon; blend well. Spoon half of vegetable mixture over corn bread. In a small bowl, combine mayonnaise and pickle juice; spread half of dressing over vegetables. Repeat layers with remaining corn bread, vegetables and dressing. Cover; chill 2-3 hours before serving. **Yield:** 6-8 servings.

MACARONI SALAD

In the early 1960s, typical macaroni salad included cheese, green pepper and onion in a creamy dressing. The following recipe got our audiences talking because of its unique combination of ingredients.

1 package (7 ounces) uncooked elbow macaroni
2 cups diced cooked shrimp, chicken *or* ham
1/3 cup French salad dressing
1 cup diced celery
2 tablespoons chopped pimientos
1/2 cup finely chopped green onions
3 hard-cooked eggs, sliced
1/4 cup sweet pickle relish
1 cup mayonnaise *or* salad dressing
1/2 cup sour cream
1/2 teaspoon salt
Lettuce leaves

Cook macaroni according to package directions; drain. In a large bowl, combine macaroni, shrimp, French dressing, celery, pimientos, onions, eggs and relish. Combine mayonnaise, sour cream and salt. Pour over salad; toss to coat. Serve on lettuce leaves. **Yield:** 6 servings.

NEW-WAVE POTATO SALAD

(Pictured at right)

Potato salad has never been easier, thanks to the convenience of frozen hash browns and the microwave oven. Chopped radishes and dill pickle add texture and flavor to this simple salad that we featured in 1999.

4 cups frozen cubed hash brown potatoes
2 tablespoons water
1/4 cup mayonnaise
1/4 cup sour cream
1 tablespoon dill pickle juice
1/2 tablespoon prepared mustard
1 teaspoon salt
1/8 teaspoon pepper
1/4 cup chopped celery
1/4 cup chopped radishes
3 tablespoons chopped dill pickles
2 tablespoons chopped onion
2 hard-cooked eggs, coarsely chopped
6 to 8 large tomatoes, optional
Snipped fresh dill, optional

Place hash browns and water in a shallow microwave-safe dish. Cover and microwave on high for 8-10 minutes or until hash browns are tender, stirring once during cooking. In a large bowl, combine mayonnaise, sour cream, pickle juice, mustard, salt and pepper; stir until smooth. Add celery, radishes, pickles, onion, eggs and warm hash browns; toss to coat. If desired, slice 1/2 in. off the top of each tomato and hollow out the inside. Spoon potato salad into the tomatoes. Garnish with dill if desired. **Yield:** 6-8 servings.

MEDITERRANEAN PASTA SALAD

The edible thistle, known as the artichoke, was prized by ancient Romans as food of the nobility. You'll often find artichokes and olives paired in Mediterranean dishes.

  1 package (10 ounces) spiral *or* large shell pasta
  1 can (14-1/2 ounces) diced tomatoes with basil, garlic and oregano, undrained
  1 jar (6-1/2 ounces) marinated artichoke hearts, undrained
  1 can (2-1/4 ounces) sliced ripe olives, drained
  1 small red onion, thinly sliced
Salt and pepper to taste
Minced fresh parsley

Cook pasta according to package directions; drain. In a large bowl, combine tomatoes, artichoke hearts, olives and onion; let stand 10 minutes to blend flavors. Toss tomato mixture with pasta. Season with salt and pepper. Garnish with parsley. **Yield:** 6 servings.

SWEET POTATO CHICKEN SALAD

(Pictured below)

A change of pace from traditional potato salad, this recipe receives great flavor and texture from two types of potatoes. The irresistible dill-flavored dressing adds a special spark.

  3 cups cubed cooked chicken
  1 pound small red potatoes, cooked and cubed
  1 pound sweet potatoes, cooked, peeled and cubed

  1 package (16 ounces) cut green beans, cooked and drained
  1/2 cup mayonnaise
  1/2 cup plain yogurt
  2 tablespoons milk
  2 teaspoons dill weed
  1/2 teaspoon salt
  1/8 teaspoon pepper
Toasted pecans, optional*

In a large bowl, combine chicken, potatoes and green beans. In a small bowl, combine mayonnaise, yogurt, milk, dill weed, salt and pepper. Pour mayonnaise mixture over chicken mixture; stir gently to coat evenly. Cover and refrigerate at least 30 minutes. Sprinkle with pecans before serving if desired. **Yield:** 4 servings. *Editor's Note:** Toast pecans in an ungreased skillet over medium heat, stirring frequently until golden brown. Or bake at 350° for 10-15 minutes, stirring occasionally.

PANZANELLA

(Pictured above)

Panzanella is a traditional Italian bread salad featuring tomatoes, olive oil and vinegar. For best flavor, combine ingredients at least an hour before serving.

  4 slices Italian bread (1/2 inch thick), toasted and cut into 1/2-inch cubes
  1 pound tomatoes, cored and cut into 1/2-inch chunks
  1/4 cup finely chopped red onion
  1/4 cup finely chopped fresh basil
  1 garlic clove, minced
  5 teaspoons olive *or* vegetable oil
Salt and pepper to taste

In a large bowl, combine bread, tomatoes, onion, basil, garlic, olive oil, salt and pepper; toss to blend. Let stand 1 hour. Serve at room temperature. **Yield:** 8 servings.

LAYERED PARTY SLAW

(Pictured at right)

The word coleslaw comes from the Dutch words kool (cabbage) and sla (salad). You'll enjoy the sweet and sour flavor of this layered version.

1 small head cabbage, shredded
1/2 medium head cauliflower, chopped
8 bacon strips, cooked and crumbled, *divided*
2 cups frozen peas, thawed
2 cups sliced fresh mushrooms
1/2 cup sliced green onions
1/2 cup grated Parmesan cheese
1-1/4 cups coleslaw dressing
2 medium tomatoes, cut into wedges

In a large glass serving bowl, layer the cabbage, cauliflower, half of the bacon, peas, mushrooms and onions. Top with cheese, coleslaw dressing and remaining bacon. Cover and chill several hours or overnight. Garnish with tomatoes before serving. **Yield:** 12 servings.

BANANA MOLD

When sweetened fruit-flavored gelatin came onto the market in the 1930s, it revolutionized the way Americans looked at salads.

1 package (3 ounces) strawberry gelatin
1-1/2 cups boiling water
2 packages (3 ounces *each*) orange gelatin
2 cups ginger ale, heated to boiling
1-1/2 cups pineapple juice
2 apples, peeled and chopped
2 large firm bananas, sliced
1/2 cup chopped pecans
Whipped cream

Dissolve strawberry gelatin in boiling water. Pour mixture into an 8-in. square baking dish. Chill until firm. Cut gelatin into 1/2-in. cubes. Dissolve orange gelatin in hot ginger ale. Stir in pineapple juice. Chill until mixture becomes slightly thickened. Fold in apples, bananas and pecans. Gently fold in strawberry gelatin cubes. Pour mixture into a 2-qt. mold and chill until firm. Unmold onto a serving platter. Top with whipped cream. **Yield:** 8 servings.

CALCUTTA TURKEY SALAD

Poultry has been a part of American tradition since Ben Franklin proposed the wild turkey as the symbol of the new nation. Today, major holidays such as

Thanksgiving are celebrated with a roasted turkey dinner with all the trimmings. You'll want to keep this salad recipe handy to jazz up any leftover poultry.

2 cups diced cooked turkey
1 can (11 ounces) mandarin oranges, drained
1/2 cup diced green pepper
1/2 cup sliced celery
1/2 cup blue cheese salad dressing
1 teaspoon curry powder
Lettuce leaves
Flaked coconut, chopped walnuts, crumbled cooked bacon *or* chopped hard-cooked eggs, optional

In a bowl, combine turkey, oranges, pepper, celery, salad dressing and curry powder. Toss to coat. Cover and refrigerate until serving time. Serve in lettuce-lined salad bowl. Garnish with coconut, walnuts, bacon or hard-cooked eggs if desired. **Yield:** 4 servings.

BLACK BEAN CHICKEN SALAD

(Pictured at left)

Medium-sized oval beans with earthy sweet flavor, black beans achieved immense popularity in the 1980s. This zesty salad combines tender chicken strips, a variety of vegetables and nutritious beans to create a flavor-packed main dish.

DRESSING:
　　1/3 cup tomato vegetable juice
　　　2 tablespoons lime juice
　　　2 tablespoons olive *or* vegetable oil
　　1/2 teaspoon ground cumin
　　1/2 teaspoon salt
SALAD:
　　　4 boneless skinless chicken breast halves
　　　2 tablespoons olive *or* vegetable oil
　　　1 garlic clove, minced
　　1/2 to 1 jalapeno pepper, finely chopped
　　3/4 teaspoon salt
　　　1 cup peeled and seeded diced cucumber
　　　1 cup sweet red pepper strips
　　　1 cup chopped tomato
　　1/2 cup chopped red onion
　　4 to 6 cups torn romaine
　　　1 can (15 ounces) black beans, rinsed and
　　　　drained

In a small bowl, whisk together dressing ingredients; set aside. Cut chicken into 2-in. strips. In a large skillet, heat oil over medium-high heat. Add chicken and stir-fry about 8 minutes or until juices run clear. Add garlic, jalapeno pepper and salt; stir-fry 30 seconds. Remove chicken mixture from skillet and place in a large salad bowl. Add remaining salad ingredients to bowl. Pour dressing into skillet; cook and stir over medium heat until slightly warm. Pour warm dressing over salad ingredients; toss to coat. **Yield:** 4 servings.

BEAN AND BACON SLAW

For a twist on traditional slaw, try this combination, which will pleasantly surprise you. Saucy baked beans and crumbled cooked bacon help accentuate the mild flavor of the shredded cabbage.

　　　1 can (16 ounces) vegetarian baked beans,
　　　　drained
　2-1/2 cups coarsely shredded cabbage
　　1/2 cup chopped celery
　　　2 tablespoons chopped green pepper
　1-1/2 tablespoons minced onion
　1-1/2 tablespoons cider vinegar
　　1/3 cup mayonnaise *or* salad dressing
　　1/4 teaspoon salt

1/4 teaspoon pepper
8 bacon strips, cooked and crumbled

In a bowl, combine beans, cabbage, celery, pepper and onion. In a small bowl, blend vinegar and mayonnaise; stir in salt and pepper. Pour dressing over bean mixture; toss gently. Cover and chill. Stir in bacon before serving. **Yield:** 8 servings.

Vegetable and Wild Rice Salad

Known for its nutty flavor and chewy texture, wild rice isn't really a rice at all. It's a long-grain marsh grass native to the northern Great Lakes area. Using a convenient rice mix, you can prepare this recipe in a jiffy.

    1 package (6-1/4 ounces) quick-cooking
        long grain and wild rice mix
    1 package (16 ounces) frozen cauliflower,
        carrots and pea pod combination, cooked
        and drained
    1/3 cup honey Dijon salad dressing
    2 green onions, thinly sliced
    2 celery ribs, diced

Prepare rice mix according to package directions. In a large bowl, gently combine rice, vegetables, salad dressing, onions and celery. Serve warm or cover and refrigerate until serving. **Yield:** 4 servings.

Pecan Salad Dressing

Pecan trees prefer a temperate climate and are widely grown in Georgia, Texas and Oklahoma. This luscious Southern dressing is ideal over fruit salad.

    1/3 cup mayonnaise
    1/3 cup orange juice
    1 tablespoon lemon juice
    1 tablespoon sugar
    1/4 teaspoon salt
    1 package (3 ounces) cream cheese, softened
    1/3 cup finely chopped pecan pieces
Prepared fruit salad

Combine the first six ingredients; beat until well blended. Stir in pecans. Chill. Serve with fruit salad. **Yield:** 1-1/3 cups.

Pineapple Coleslaw

Dutch settlers made slaws as soon as their first cabbages came up. Since that time, American slaws have taken many forms. Some are peppy with vinegar and spices, others are creamy and mild. This fruity version is accented with pineapple chunks, red apple and miniature marshmallows.

    4 cups shredded cabbage
    1 cup diced unpeeled red apple
    1 cup pineapple chunks
    1 cup miniature marshmallows
    1/2 cup chopped celery
1-1/2 cups mayonnaise *or* salad dressing
Romaine lettuce, optional

In a large bowl, combine the first five ingredients. Stir in mayonnaise. Toss lightly to coat. Cover and refrigerate. Serve over lettuce leaves. **Yield:** 12 servings.

Sunshine Mallow Waldorf

Marshmallows are commonly used to top hot chocolate and dishes such as candied sweet potatoes. Their fluffy goodness can also add a special touch to a variety of salad recipes.

    1 cup mayonnaise *or* salad dressing
    1/2 cup cup chopped walnuts
    1/2 cup raisins
    3 cups chopped apples
    2 cups miniature marshmallows
    1 can (11 ounces) mandarin oranges,
        drained

In a large bowl, combine mayonnaise, walnuts and raisins. Fold in remaining ingredients. Cover and chill at least 2 hours before serving. **Yield:** 8 servings.

Peach Melba Salad

The classic dessert Peach Melba was created in the late 1800s by the famous French chef Escoffier. It's made with two peach halves that have been poached in syrup and cooled. Each peach half is topped with a scoop of vanilla ice cream and a tasty raspberry sauce.

    1 cup (8 ounces) small curd cottage cheese
    1 can (29 ounces) sliced peaches, drained
    1 carton (8 ounces) frozen whipped
        topping, thawed
    1 package (3 ounces) raspberry gelatin
    1/4 cup maraschino cherries

Using half of each, layer cottage cheese, peaches and whipped topping in a large serving bowl. Sprinkle with half of the dry gelatin. Repeat layers. Gently fold ingredients to blend. Garnish with cherries. Cover and chill before serving. **Yield:** 8 servings.

AUTUMN AMBROSIA

According to Greek mythology, ambrosia was the food of the gods on Mt. Olympus. Nowadays, the word designates a combination of chilled fruit and coconut.

> 1 can (15 ounces) **pineapple chunks, drained**
> 2 firm **bananas, sliced**
> 1 cup **chopped dates**
> 1-1/3 cups **flaked coconut**
> 2 cans (11 ounces *each*) **mandarin oranges, drained**
> 1 carton (8 ounces) **plain yogurt**
> 1 tablespoon **lemon juice**
> 1 teaspoon **poppy seeds**

Layer pineapple, bananas, dates, coconut and orange sections in a serving bowl. Combine yogurt and lemon juice; spoon over fruit. Sprinkle with poppy seeds; chill. Toss lightly before serving. **Yield:** 8-12 servings.

PERFECT PASTA SALAD TOSS

(Pictured above)

Some historians believe that explorer Marco Polo brought the idea of pasta back with him to Italy from China. In fact, this staple dates back to at least 1000 B.C., long before Polo's expeditions.

> 8 ounces **uncooked tube pasta**
> 4 ounces **sliced salami, cut into strips**
> 1 jar (7 ounces) **roasted sweet red peppers, drained, cut into thin strips**
> 1 jar (6-1/2 ounces) **marinated artichoke hearts, drained**
> 1/3 cup **pitted ripe *or* kalamata olives, cut in half lengthwise**
> 1/4 cup **loosely packed fresh basil leaves, chopped *or* 2 teaspoons dried basil**
> 1/2 cup **Italian *or* Caesar salad dressing**
> 1 cup (4 ounces) **shredded Parmesan, mozzarella *or* Romano cheese**
> **Romaine lettuce leaves, optional**

Cook pasta according to package directions; drain. Meanwhile, in a large bowl, combine salami, peppers, artichokes, olives and basil. Add pasta and salad dressing; toss to coat. Add the cheese; toss well. Cover and refrigerate at least 30 minutes or up to 6 hours. Serve on lettuce-lined plates if desired. **Yield:** 4 servings.

CINNAMON-APPLE RING MOLD

This refreshing gelatin salad is the perfect accompaniment for roasted pork.

> 1 package (3 ounces) **raspberry gelatin**
> 1/4 cup **red cinnamon candies**
> 2 cups **applesauce, heated**
> 1 tablespoon **lemon juice**
> 1/2 cup **chopped red apples**
> 1 cup **chopped celery**
> 1/2 cup **chopped walnuts**

In a bowl, combine gelatin, cinnamon candies and hot applesauce; stir until candies and gelatin are dissolved. Add lemon juice; chill until mixture begins to set. Add apples, celery and walnuts; mix well. Pour into six individual molds or a 1-qt. ring mold coated with nonstick cooking spray. Chill until firm. Unmold before serving. **Yield:** 6 servings.

MEXICAN EGG SALAD

European colonists brought chickens to the New World for their eggs, and they have been an important part of American food ever since.

> 4 **hard-cooked eggs, chopped**
> 1 cup (4 ounces) **shredded mild cheddar *or* Monterey Jack cheese**
> 1/4 cup **coleslaw dressing**
> 2 to 3 tablespoons **chopped green chilies**

2 tablespoons finely chopped green pepper
2 tablespoons finely chopped onion
Salt and pepper to taste
Tomato slices
Taco sauce and tortilla chips

In a medium bowl, combine eggs, cheese, dressing, chilies, green pepper, onion, salt and pepper. Mix well. Garnish with tomato slices. Serve with taco sauce and tortilla chips. **Yield:** 2 servings.

SPINACH SALAD WITH BACON DRESSING

Wilted salads are made by pouring a dressing made with hot bacon drippings, vinegar and sugar directly over the salad greens. For variety, you may want to add fresh sliced mushrooms or Oriental accents such as water chestnuts and bean sprouts.

4 bacon strips, diced
1/4 cup sliced green onions
2 tablespoons brown sugar
1-1/2 tablespoons red wine *or* cider vinegar
1/4 teaspoon salt
1/8 teaspoon ground mustard
Dash of paprika
1 package (10 ounces) fresh spinach, torn

In a small skillet, cook bacon for 3 minutes, stirring to separate into pieces. Add onions, brown sugar, vinegar, salt, mustard and paprika. Cook until onions are tender and bacon is done, stirring occasionally. Just before serving, pour hot dressing over spinach. Toss to coat. **Yield:** 4 servings.

TORTELLINI TUNA SALAD

(Pictured at right)

There are hundreds of different pasta shapes and sizes available today. Tortellini, or "little twists", are a small stuffed pasta.

1 package (19 ounces) frozen cheese tortellini
1 can (8-3/4 ounces) kidney beans, rinsed and drained
1 can (6 ounces) tuna, drained and flaked
2 celery ribs, thinly sliced
1/2 to 3/4 cup ranch salad dressing
2 green onions, sliced
1 tablespoon capers, optional
Salt and pepper to taste
Leaf lettuce
Chopped fresh parsley

Prepare frozen tortellini according to package directions; drain. Meanwhile, in a large bowl, combine beans, tuna, celery, salad dressing, green onions and capers if desired; mix well. Add tortellini to tuna mixture; toss gently. Season with salt and pepper. Cover and refrigerate until serving. To serve, line a platter or bowl with leaf lettuce. Spoon pasta mixture over greens. Garnish with parsley. **Yield:** 4-6 servings.

LIME CREAM SALAD

In 1970, no potluck was complete without a fruity gelatin. This pastel-colored molded salad goes well with baked ham.

1 cup hot water
1 package (3 ounces) lime gelatin
2 packages (3 ounces *each*) cream cheese
1/2 cup vegetable oil
1 jar (7 ounces) marshmallow creme
1 cup whipping cream, whipped
1 can (20 ounces) crushed pineapple, drained

Place water and gelatin in blender. Cover and process until gelatin is dissolved. Place container in refrigerator until mixture is cool. When mixture is cool, add cream cheese, oil and marshmallow creme. Cover and process until smooth. Fold whipped cream into gelatin mixture. Fold pineapple into mixture. Pour into a 6-cup mold coated with nonstick cooking spray. Refrigerate until set. Unmold onto serving platter. **Yield:** 12 servings.

CITRUS SALAD TOSS

(Pictured below)

Salads came into their own in the early 1900s, as restaurant chefs developed new salad combinations and dressings. By 1920, the first commercial salad dressings were available. This tempting recipe from the 1990s pairs salad greens and fruits.

    2 tablespoons lemon juice
    2 teaspoons sugar
1/4 cup hazelnut *or* vegetable oil
    4 cups torn salad greens
1-1/4 cups shredded mild cheddar cheese
1/2 cup shredded Parmesan cheese
1-1/2 cups orange sections
    1 cup grapefruit sections
    1 cup seedless green grapes
    1 can (8 ounces) sliced water chestnuts,
        well drained
1/3 cup chopped hazelnuts *or* almonds, toasted

In a small bowl, combine lemon juice and sugar. Slowly add oil, whisking until smooth and thickened; set aside. In a large bowl, combine salad greens, cheeses, orange and grapefruit sections, grapes and water chestnuts. Add dressing; toss gently. Sprinkle with hazelnuts. Serve immediately. **Yield:** 8 servings.

HOT CHICKEN SALAD

Twenty years after we first featured hot chicken salad onstage, we offered an updated recipe made with prepared coleslaw dressing in 1998.

    1 to 1-1/2 cups diced cooked chicken
    1 package (10 ounces) frozen chopped
        broccoli, thawed and drained
    1 cup (4 ounces) shredded cheddar cheese
1/2 cup coarsely chopped almonds *or* cashews
1/2 cup chopped celery
1/2 cup coleslaw dressing
1/4 cup chopped onion
    1 teaspoon chicken bouillon granules
1/2 cup crushed potato chips

In a medium bowl, combine all ingredients except chips. Mix well. Spoon into a 1-qt. casserole dish. Top with chips. Bake at 350° for 25-30 minutes or until hot and bubbly. Let stand 5 minutes before serving. **Yield:** 4 servings.

CALICO POTATO SALAD

Found on picnic tables and at informal parties throughout the country, no salad is more varied or thoroughly American than creamy potato salad. The potatoes may be sliced or cubed, and the dressing may include mayonnaise, whipped cream, sour cream or yogurt. Familiar additions often include celery, hard-cooked eggs, chopped pickle or olives.

    2 quarts water
    1 tablespoon salt
    1 package (24 ounces) frozen potatoes O'Brien
1/2 cup mayonnaise
    2 tablespoons sweet pickle juice
    1 tablespoon prepared mustard
1/4 teaspoon celery seed
1/4 teaspoon pepper
1/2 cup chopped sweet pickles
1/2 cup chopped celery
    3 hard-cooked eggs, coarsely chopped

In a large covered saucepan, bring water and salt to a boil. Add potatoes; cook until fork tender, about 5 minutes. Drain well. In a bowl, blend mayonnaise, pickle juice, mustard, celery seed and pepper. Add pickles, celery and eggs. Add warm potatoes; toss lightly. Cover and refrigerate several hours.

Yield: 6-8 servings. **Microwave Directions:** Place frozen potatoes and 2 tablespoons water in a shallow microwave-safe dish; cover tightly. Microwave on high for 8-10 minutes or until potatoes are tender, stirring once during cooking. Complete recipe as directed above, adding 1 teaspoon salt to dressing mixture.

ORANGE CUPS

Today, busy cooks may find this recipe a bit time-consuming, but in 1969, these individually prepared salads were the height of elegance, meant to impress your guests.

> 6 large oranges
> 1 package (3 ounces) orange gelatin
> 1/2 cup boiling water
> 1/2 cup chopped walnuts
> 1 cup seedless grapes, halved
> 2 firm bananas, sliced
> 1 cup sliced strawberries
> 1 cup miniature marshmallows

Making V-shaped cuts, cut out a circle from the top of each orange. With a melon baller, remove all pulp and juice to a bowl. Remove seeds from pulp. Set orange cups aside. Dissolve gelatin in boiling water. Stir in orange pulp and juice. Refrigerate until slightly thickened. Stir in walnuts, fruits and marshmallows. Spoon mixture into orange cups. Refrigerate oranges until gelatin is firm. **Yield:** 6 servings.

GARDEN-FRESH SHRIMP AND PASTA SALAD

(Pictured above right)

Seafood salads are often a regional dish, their flavors based on the local catch and customs. If you are in the heartland, use canned or frozen seafood to create these specialities.

> 8 ounces tube pasta, cooked and drained
> 1 medium cucumber, peeled, seeded and sliced
> 1 cup fresh *or* thawed frozen sugar snap peas, trimmed
> 1/4 cup sliced green onion
> 1 tablespoon snipped fresh dill *or* 1/2 teaspoon dill weed
> 1/2 cup ranch salad dressing
> 1/2 cup mayonnaise
> 1 can (6 ounces) shrimp, rinsed and drained
> Lettuce leaves

In a large bowl, combine pasta, cucumber, peas, green onion and dill. Add dressing and mayonnaise; toss to coat. Gently fold in shrimp. Chill before serving if desired. Serve on a bed of lettuce. **Yield:** 6 servings.

MARINATED VEGETABLE SALAD

Here's a welcome change from ordinary vegetables. The zesty marinade adds exceptional flavor to this colorful dish.

> 3/4 cup mild chunky salsa
> 1/4 cup lime juice
> 1/4 cup chopped fresh cilantro *or* parsley
> 2 tablespoons olive *or* vegetable oil
> 2 medium tomatoes, chopped
> 1 can (15 ounces) kidney beans, rinsed and drained
> 1 medium ripe avocado, peeled, seeded and chopped
> 1 cup chopped zucchini
> 1 can (4 ounces) diced green chilies
> Lettuce leaves, optional

In a large bowl, combine salsa, lime juice, cilantro and oil. Add tomatoes, kidney beans, avocado, zucchini and chilies; toss to coat. Cover and refrigerate for at least 2 hours. Serve over lettuce leaves if desired. **Yield:** 6-8 servings.

Chapter 3

BREADS, ROLLS & MUFFINS

Oven-fresh yeast breads, coffee cakes, muffins and rolls are an enticing way to invite family and friends to the table…morning, noon or night!

PEANUT BUTTER CHOCOLATE PULL-APART ROLLS

(Pictured at left)

Your family will be pleasantly surprised when they bite into these delicate rolls filled with creamy peanut butter and chocolate. They are ideal for brunch or an afternoon snack.

    4 to 4-1/2 cups all-purpose flour
    1/2 cup sugar
    2 packages (1/4 ounce *each*) rapid-rise yeast
    1 teaspoon salt
    1 cup milk
    1/2 cup water
    3/4 cup creamy peanut butter, *divided*
    1 cup semisweet chocolate chips
ICING:
    1 cup confectioners' sugar, sifted
    2 tablespoons baking cocoa *or* creamy
       peanut butter
    1 to 2 tablespoons milk

In a large bowl, combine 2 cups flour, sugar, yeast and salt. Heat milk and water until very warm (120°-130°); stir into dry ingredients. Stir in 1/2 cup peanut butter and enough remaining flour to form a soft dough. Knead on a lightly floured surface until smooth and elastic, about 6-8 minutes. Cover; let rest on floured surface 10 minutes. To prepare filling, combine 1/4 cup peanut butter and chocolate chips in a small bowl. Stir to blend; set aside. Divide dough in half; roll each to 15-in. circle. Cut each circle into six pie-shaped wedges. Place 1 tablespoon filling at wide end of each wedge; roll up tightly from wide end and curve to form crescent. Arrange six crescents (with points down) on greased baking sheet, spoke fashion, with one end of each crescent meeting at the center. Pinch ends at center to seal. Repeat with remaining crescents on separate baking sheet. Cover; let rise in warm place until doubled in size, about 30-45 minutes. Bake at 375° for 15-20 minutes or until done, switching positions of baking sheets halfway through baking for even browning. Remove from baking sheets; cool on wire racks. For icing, combine sugar, cocoa or peanut butter and milk in a small bowl. Stir until smooth. Drizzle over rolls. **Yield:** 2 dozen.

PUMPERNICKEL BREAD

Delicious with a meal or to make a sandwich, this hearty dark bread has a distinct savory flavor. Best of all, your bread machine does all the work.

> 1 cup water (70° to 80°)
> 2 tablespoons dark molasses
> 1 tablespoon vegetable oil
> 4 teaspoons white vinegar
> 2 tablespoons brown sugar
> 2-1/4 teaspoons baking cocoa
> 2-1/4 teaspoons instant coffee granules
> 1-1/2 teaspoons whole caraway seeds
> 1-1/2 teaspoons minced onion
> 1 teaspoon salt
> 2 cups bread flour
> 1-1/2 cups rye flour
> 2 teaspoons bread machine yeast

In bread machine pan, place all ingredients in order suggested by manufacturer. Select the basic bread setting. Choose crust color and loaf size if available. Bake according to bread machine directions (check dough after 5 minutes of mixing; add 1 to 2 tablespoons of water or flour if needed). **Yield:** 1 loaf.

BUTTERSCOTCH STREUSEL MUFFIN TOPS

If you favor the crumb-topped caps crowning many muffins, you'll love this unique muffin-top recipe. For those with limited kitchen equipment, these are prepared on baking sheets rather than in muffin pans.

> 1-2/3 cups butterscotch chips, *divided*
> 2 tablespoons butter *or* margarine
> 3 cups all-purpose flour, *divided*
> 1 cup sugar
> 1-1/2 teaspoons baking powder
> 1/2 teaspoon baking soda
> 1/2 teaspoon ground cinnamon
> 1 cup pecan pieces
> 2/3 cup milk
> 1/4 cup vegetable oil
> 1 egg, lightly beaten

Microwave 2/3 cup chips and butter on high for 45-60 seconds or until chips are melted and mixture is smooth when stirred. Add 3/4 cup flour; blend until mixture forms crumbs. Set aside. Stir together sugar, baking powder, baking soda, cinnamon, nuts and remaining flour and chips. Combine milk, oil and egg; add all at once to flour mixture. Stir until just moistened (batter should be lumpy). Spoon batter in 2-tablespoon-size mounds, 2 inches apart, on

lightly greased baking sheet. Sprinkle reserved crumb mixture evenly over muffin tops. Bake at 350° for 10-12 minutes or until golden brown. Cool slightly; remove from baking sheet. Serve warm. **Yield:** 20 muffin tops.

CRUMB-TOPPED COCOA BANANA BREAD

This lovely loaf offers rich chocolate flavor married with fragrant spices and ripe bananas. Treat your family to a tempting slice today.

> 1-1/2 cups all-purpose flour
> 1-1/3 cups sugar
> 6 tablespoons baking cocoa
> 1 teaspoon baking soda
> 1/2 teaspoon salt
> 1/4 teaspoon baking powder
> 1/4 teaspoon ground cinnamon
> Dash of ground ginger
> Dash of ground mace
> 2 eggs
> 1/2 cup vegetable oil
> 1 cup mashed ripe bananas (2 medium)
> TOPPING:
> 3 tablespoons all-purpose flour
> 2 tablespoons sugar
> 1 tablespoon cold butter *or* margarine
> 1/8 teaspoon baking powder
> 1/8 teaspoon ground cinnamon

In a large bowl, stir together flour, sugar, cocoa, baking soda, salt, baking powder, cinnamon, ginger and mace. Add eggs, oil and bananas; stir until blended. Spoon batter into an 8-in. x 4-in. x 2-in. greased loaf pan. To make topping, combine flour, sugar, butter, baking powder and cinnamon in a small bowl; sprinkle evenly over batter. Bake at 350° for 55-60 minutes or until toothpick inserted near center comes out clean. Cool 10 minutes. Loosen sides of loaf from pan; remove to wire rack. Cool completely. (Loaf may be stored in refrigerator, well wrapped, for up to 1 week.) **Yield:** 1 loaf.

DATE AND NUT SCONES

Scones can be savory or sweet and are usually eaten for breakfast. This Scottish quick bread is said to have taken its name from the Stone of Destiny, or Scone, the place where Scottish kings were once crowned.

> 2 cups all-purpose flour
> 1/4 cup sugar

2 teaspoons baking powder
1/2 teaspoon salt
1/4 cup cold butter *or* margarine
2 eggs
1/3 cup whipping cream *or* whole milk
3/4 cup chopped dates
1/3 cup slivered almonds

In a large bowl, combine flour, sugar, baking powder and salt. With pastry blender or two knives, cut butter into flour mixture until crumbly. Make a well in center. Separate one egg; reserve egg white. Lightly beat egg yolk and one whole egg into cream; pour into well. Stir with fork until dough cleans sides of bowl. Stir in dates and almonds. Turn dough out onto lightly floured surface; knead about 10 times. Pat dough into 6-1/2-in.-diameter circle. Cut circle into 6 wedges. Place 1 in. apart on ungreased baking sheet. Lightly beat reserved egg white; brush on dough. Bake at 400° for 18-20 minutes or until lightly browned. Serve warm. **Yield:** 6 scones.

PRALINE COFFEE CAKE RING

(Pictured at right)

To many, a praline is a special patty-shaped candy from Louisiana made with brown sugar and pecans. This family-pleasing coffee cake highlights those two popular flavors.

3-1/4 to 3-3/4 cups all-purpose flour
1/4 cup sugar
1 package (1/4 ounce) rapid-rise yeast
1/2 teaspoon salt
1/2 cup butter *or* margarine, cut into pieces
1/4 cup milk
1/4 cup water
2 eggs
FILLING:
1/2 cup packed brown sugar
1/3 cup chopped pecans
1/3 cup flaked coconut, optional
1/4 cup butter *or* margarine, melted
1 teaspoon ground cinnamon
GLAZE:
1 cup confectioners' sugar, sifted
1 to 2 tablespoons milk
1/2 teaspoon vanilla extract

In a large bowl, combine 1 cup flour, sugar, yeast and salt. Heat butter, milk and water until very warm (120°-130°); butter does not need to melt. Gradually stir into dry ingredients; beat 2 minutes at medium speed, scraping bowl occasionally. Add eggs and additional 1/2 cup flour; beat 2 minutes at high speed. With spoon, stir in enough remaining flour to form a soft dough. Knead on lightly floured surface until smooth and elastic, about 4-6 minutes. Cover; let rest 10 minutes. Combine the filling ingredients in a medium bowl; mix well. Set aside. Roll dough to 24-in. x 9-in. rectangle. Spread filling to within 1/2 in. of edges. Beginning at long end, roll up as for jelly roll; pinch seam to seal. With a sharp knife, cut lengthwise through roll to separate into two long portions. Arrange both halves, side by side, so that cut sides are on top. Twist both portions together, keeping cut sides up to show layers. Bring ends together to form a ring; pinch ends to seal. Carefully transfer to greased baking sheet; reshape if necessary. Cover; let rise in warm place until doubled in size, about 45-60 minutes. Bake at 350° for 35-40 minutes, covering with aluminum foil after 20 minutes to prevent overbrowning. Remove from pan; cool on wire rack. In a small bowl, combine glaze ingredients; mix until smooth. Drizzle over coffee cake. **Yield:** 1 coffee cake.

OLD-FASHIONED BUTTERMILK BREAD

(Pictured above)

In times past, buttermilk was the liquid left after butter was churned. Today, it is made by adding a special bacteria to lowfat or nonfat milk, giving it a slightly thickened texture and tangy flavor.

5-1/2 to 6 cups all-purpose flour
   3 tablespoons sugar
   2 packages (1/4 ounce *each*) quick-rise yeast
   2 teaspoons salt
1/4 teaspoon baking soda
   1 cup buttermilk
   1 cup water
1/3 cup butter *or* margarine, cut into pieces

In a large bowl, combine 3 cups flour, sugar, yeast, salt and baking soda. Heat buttermilk, water and butter until very warm (120°-130°). Butter does not need to melt; mixture will appear curdled. Stir into dry ingredients. Stir in enough remaining flour to form a soft dough. Knead on lightly floured surface until smooth and elastic, about 6-8 minutes. Cover; let rest 10 minutes. Divide dough in half; roll each half to 12-in. x 7-in. rectangle. Beginning at short end, roll up tightly; pinch seam and ends to seal. Place each, seam side down, in a greased 8-in. x 4-in. x 2-in. loaf pan. Cover; let rise in warm place until doubled in size, about 30-45 minutes. Bake at 375° for 30-35 minutes or until done. Remove from pans; cool on wire rack. **Yield:** 2 loaves (12 slices each).

STICKY BUNS

In the late 1800s, Philadelphians could purchase these glazed sweet rolls from street vendors. The Pennsylvania Dutch originated the recipe and called them schnecken, or snails, because of their spiral shape.

   3 to 4 cups all-purpose flour
   2 tablespoons sugar
   1 package (1/4 ounce) active dry yeast
   1 teaspoon salt
   1 cup milk
1/4 cup butter *or* margarine
   1 egg
   5 tablespoons butter *or* margarine, melted, *divided*
1/2 cup packed brown sugar, *divided*
1/2 cup pecan halves
   2 teaspoons ground cinnamon
1/2 cup dark corn syrup

In a large mixing bowl, combine 1 cup flour, sugar, yeast and salt. Heat milk and 1/4 cup butter until very warm (120°-130°). Add to dry ingredients; beat 2 minutes, scraping bowl occasionally. Stir in egg and 1/2 cup flour; beat 2 minutes, scraping bowl occasionally. Stir in enough remaining flour to form a soft dough. Place in a greased bowl, turning once to grease top. Cover and let rise in a warm place until doubled, about 1-1/2 hours. Pour 3 tablespoons melted butter into a 13-in. x 9-in. x 2-in. baking pan. Sprinkle with 1/4 cup brown sugar and pecans. Punch dough down. Turn onto a lightly floured surface. Roll into a 15-in. x 9-in. rectangle. Brush with remaining melted butter. Combine cinnamon and remaining brown sugar; sprinkle over dough. Roll up, jelly-roll style, starting with a long side; pinch seams to seal. Cut into 15 buns. Place buns, cut side up, in prepared pan. Pour syrup over rolls. Cover and let rise in a warm place until doubled, about 40 minutes. Bake at 400° for 25 minutes or until golden brown. Cool in pan for 5 minutes before inverting onto a serving plate. **Yield:** 15 buns.

POTECA

A favorite for breakfast, Poteca is a rich Slovenian nut bread. It's customary to serve this traditional loaf at Christmas.

   3 to 4 cups all-purpose flour
1/4 cup sugar
   1 package (1/4 ounce) active dry yeast
   1 teaspoon salt
1/2 cup milk
1/2 cup water

1/4 cup butter *or* margarine
1 egg
WALNUT FILLING:
1/4 cup butter *or* margarine
1/2 cup packed brown sugar
1 egg
2 tablespoons milk
1 teaspoon orange extract
2 cups finely chopped walnuts
GLAZE:
1 cup confectioners' sugar
1 to 3 tablespoons milk

In a large mixing bowl, combine 1 cup flour, sugar, yeast and salt. Heat milk, water and butter until very warm (120°-130°). Gradually add to dry ingredients; beat 2 minutes, scraping bowl occasionally. Stir in egg and 1/2 cup flour; beat 2 minutes, scraping bowl occasionally. Stir in enough remaining flour to form a soft dough. Place in a greased bowl, turning once to grease top. Cover and let rise in a warm place until doubled, about 1-1/2 hours. To prepare filling, combine butter, brown sugar and egg in a small mixing bowl; blend in milk and extract. Stir in nuts. Turn dough onto a floured surface; roll into a 20-in. x 15-in. rectangle. Spread filling to within 1/2 in. of edges. Roll up, jelly-roll style, starting with a long side; pinch seams to seal. Gently pull roll to a 25-in. rope. Holding one end of rope, loosely wrap dough around, forming a coil on a greased baking sheet. Tuck end under; pinch to seal. Cover and let rise in a warm place until doubled, about 1 hour. Bake at 325° for 40 minutes or until golden brown. Remove from baking sheet and cool on wire rack. Combine glaze ingredients; drizzle over loaf. **Yield:** 1 loaf.

APPLE CINNAMON ROLLS

(Pictured at right)

Rediscover the satisfaction that comes from making and eating homemade baked goods by creating these mouth-watering rolls.

APPLE FILLING:
2 peeled and coarsely chopped apples
3/4 cup sugar
1/4 cup butter *or* margarine
2 tablespoons all-purpose flour
1 teaspoon ground cinnamon
1/2 teaspoon ground nutmeg
DOUGH:
5 to 5-1/2 cups all-purpose flour
1/2 cup sugar
2 packages (1/4 ounce *each*) quick-rise yeast
1 teaspoon salt

1/2 cup water
1/2 cup milk
1/4 cup butter *or* margarine
3 eggs
CINNAMON-SUGAR TOPPING:
3/4 cup sugar
1 teaspoon ground cinnamon
1/2 teaspoon ground nutmeg

In a medium saucepan, combine apples, sugar, butter and flour. Bring to a boil over medium-high heat. Cook 3 minutes. Reduce heat to medium-low. Cook 10 minutes, stirring constantly, until thick. Stir in cinnamon and nutmeg. Cool completely. To prepare dough, combine 1 cup flour, sugar, yeast and salt in a large mixing bowl. Heat water, milk and butter until very warm (120°-130°). Gradually add to dry ingredients. Beat 2 minutes at medium speed, scraping bowl occasionally. Add eggs and 1 cup flour. Beat 2 minutes at high speed, scraping bowl occasionally. Stir in enough remaining flour to form a soft dough. Turn onto a lightly floured surface. Knead until smooth and elastic, about 8-10 minutes. Cover; let rest 10 minutes. Divide dough into two equal portions. Roll each portion into a 12-in. x 8-in. rectangle. Spread filling evenly over dough. Beginning at long end of each, roll up tightly as for jelly roll. Pinch seams to seal. Cut each roll into 12 equal pieces. Place, cut sides up, in four greased 9-in. round pans. Cover; let rise in a warm place until doubled in size, about 45 minutes. To prepare topping, combine sugar, cinnamon and nutmeg. Stir until well blended. Sprinkle over rolls. Bake at 375° for 25-30 minutes or until golden brown. Remove from pans; serve warm. **Yield:** 2 dozen.

Oatmeal Bread

(Pictured below)

In cooler climates, oat crops withstood harsh growing conditions better than wheat, so sometimes wild oats took over wheat fields. Because oats grew so readily, they became a favorite for cooking.

2-1/2 to 3 cups bread flour
 1/2 cup quick-cooking oats
 2 tablespoons brown sugar
 1 package (1/4 ounce) rapid-rise yeast
 1 teaspoon salt
 1 teaspoon ground cinnamon
1-1/4 cups water
 2 tablespoons butter *or* margarine

In a large mixing bowl, combine 1 cup flour, oats, brown sugar, yeast, salt and cinnamon. Heat water and butter until very warm (120°-130°). Gradually add to dry ingredients. Stir in enough remaining flour to form a soft dough. Turn onto a lightly floured surface. Knead until smooth and elastic, about 6-8 minutes. Cover; let rest 10 minutes. Roll to a 12-in. x 7-in. rectangle. Beginning at short end, roll up tightly as for jelly roll. Pinch seam and ends to seal. Place, seam side down, in a greased 8-in. x 4-in. x 2-in. loaf pan. Cover; let rise in a warm place until doubled in size, about 1 hour. Bake at 375° for 30-35 minutes or until done. Remove from pan; cool on wire rack. **Yield:** 1 loaf.

Cinnamon Date Rolls

We guarantee that the aroma of these rolls baking is enough to get even the soundest sleeper out of bed. What a wonderful way to wake up!

 5 to 5-1/2 cups all-purpose flour
1-1/2 cups sugar, *divided*
 2 packages (1/4 ounce *each*) rapid-rise yeast
 1 teaspoon salt
 1/2 cup water
 1/2 cup milk
 3/4 cup butter *or* margarine, *divided*
 2 eggs
1-1/2 tablespoons ground cinnamon
 1 package (8 ounces) chopped dates
Glaze:
 1 cup confectioners' sugar
 1 to 3 tablespoons milk

In a large mixing bowl, combine 2 cups flour, 1/2 cup sugar, yeast and salt. Heat water, milk and 1/2 cup butter until very warm (120°-130°). Gradually add to dry ingredients; beat 2 minutes, scraping bowl occasionally. Stir in eggs and enough remaining flour to form a soft dough. Turn onto a floured surface; knead until smooth and elastic, about 6-8 minutes. Cover and let rest for 10 minutes. Turn onto a floured surface; roll into a 22-in. x 10-in. rectangle. Melt remaining butter; brush butter on dough. Sprinkle with cinnamon, dates and remaining sugar to within 1/2 in. of edges. Roll up, jelly-roll style, starting with a long side; pinch seams to seal. Cut into 15 rolls. Place rolls, cut side up, in a greased 13-in. x 9-in. x 2-in. baking pan. Cover and let rise in a warm place until doubled, about 45 minutes. Bake at 375° for 30 minutes or until golden brown. Cool in pan on wire rack. Combine glaze ingredients; drizzle over rolls. **Yield:** 15 rolls.

Daisy Coffee Cake

From the rhythmic, relaxing motion of kneading to the wonderful aromas that fill the kitchen, baking bread offers a simple pleasure. Slow down for a moment and try this flower-shaped loaf from the 1960s.

2-1/2 to 3 cups all-purpose flour
 3 tablespoons sugar
 1 package (1/4 ounce) active dry yeast

1 teaspoon salt
1/4 cup water
1/2 cup milk
3 tablespoons shortening
1 egg, beaten
1/4 cup apricot jam

GLAZE:
3/4 cup confectioners' sugar
1 tablespoon milk
1 tablespoon butter *or* margarine, melted
1/4 teaspoon vanilla extract

In a large mixing bowl, combine 1 cup flour, sugar, yeast and salt. Heat water, milk and shortening until very warm (120°-130°). Gradually add to dry ingredients; beat 2 minutes, scraping bowl occasionally. Stir in egg and enough remaining flour to form a soft dough. Turn onto a floured surface; knead until smooth and elastic, about 6-8 minutes. Place in a greased bowl, turning once to grease top. Cover and let rise in a warm place until doubled, about 1 hour. Turn onto a floured surface; roll to 1/2-in. thickness. Cut 12 circles with 2-1/2-in. doughnut cutter. Arrange 12 doughnut holes in center of greased baking sheet, overlapping edges. Stretch doughnut dough into 4-in. lengths. Twist each length once and arrange as petals around doughnut holes. Cover and let rise in a warm place until doubled, about 30 minutes. Bake at 350° for 15-20 minutes or until golden brown. Remove from baking sheet to wire rack to cool. Spoon jam into center of coffee cake. Combine glaze ingredients; drizzle over coffee cake. **Yield:** 1 coffee cake.

minutes or until a toothpick comes out clean. Cool in pan for 5 minutes before removing to a wire rack. Serve warm. **Yield:** 12 muffins.

COCONUT-ORANGE DATE MUFFINS

Fruit-flavored muffins are a popular choice for breakfast on the go. These palate-pleasers are also ideal for a wholesome snack.

1-1/4 cups all-purpose flour
1/4 cup packed brown sugar
1-1/2 teaspoons baking powder
1 teaspoon grated orange peel
1/2 teaspoon salt
1 egg
1/2 cup milk
2 tablespoons butter *or* margarine, melted
1/2 cup chopped dates
1/2 cup flaked coconut

In a bowl, combine flour, brown sugar, baking powder, orange peel and salt. In another bowl, beat egg, milk and butter. Stir into dry ingredients. Fold in dates and coconut. Fill greased or paper-lined muffin cups three-fourths full. Bake at 350° for 18-20

ONION SHORTCAKE

(*Pictured above*)

A contest-winning recipe from spring 1998, we featured this delightful accompaniment on the front cover of our fall 1998 Recipe Collection.

1 cup sliced onion
1/4 cup butter *or* margarine
1 package (8-1/2 ounces) corn bread/muffin mix
1 egg, lightly beaten
1/3 cup milk
1 can (8-1/2 ounces) cream-style corn
2 drops hot pepper sauce
1 cup (8 ounces) sour cream
1 cup (4 ounces) shredded sharp cheddar cheese, *divided*
1/4 teaspoon salt
1/4 teaspoon dill weed

In a large skillet over low heat, cook onion in butter until tender. Meanwhile, combine corn bread mix, egg, milk, corn and hot pepper sauce; stir until smooth. Spoon batter into a greased 9-in. square baking pan. Add sour cream, 1/2 cup cheese, salt and dill weed to onions in skillet. Spoon over batter in baking pan. Sprinkle with remaining cheese. Bake at 425° for 25-30 minutes or until golden brown. Serve warm. **Yield:** 9 servings.

    1 egg
    1 tablespoon water
Additional poppy seeds

In a large bowl, combine 1 cup flour, sugar, yeast and salt. Heat milk, water and butter until very warm (120°-130°); gradually stir into dry ingredients. Stir in egg and enough remaining flour to form a soft dough. Knead on a lightly floured surface until smooth and elastic, about 4-6 minutes. Cover; let rest 10 minutes. In a small bowl, combine filling ingredients; mix well. Set aside. Roll dough to 14-in. x 10-in. rectangle; cut lengthwise into two strips. Spoon half the filling down center of each. Bring up sides to enclose filling, pinching the seam and ends to seal. Arrange ropes, side by side, on greased baking sheet so that seam sides are on bottom. Twist both ropes together; pinch ends to join. Cover; let rise in warm place until doubled in size, about 20-30 minutes. In a small bowl, beat together egg and water; brush onto top of dough. Sprinkle with poppy seeds. Bake at 375° for 25-30 minutes or until golden brown. Remove from baking sheet; cool on wire rack. **Yield:** 1 loaf (12 slices).

SHEPHERD'S BREAD

Two crusty golden-brown loaves with terrific flavor and texture are what you'll get when you try this recipe. Your family will love it served with soup or stew on cold days. It also makes great toast for a super start to any morning.

    7 to 8 cups all-purpose flour
1/4 cup sugar
    2 packages (1/4 ounce *each*) active dry yeast
    1 tablespoon salt
1-1/2 cups water
    1 cup milk
1/4 cup butter *or* margarine

In a large mixing bowl, combine 2 cups flour, sugar, yeast and salt. Heat water, milk and butter until very warm (120°-130°). Gradually add to dry ingredients; beat 2 minutes, scraping bowl occasionally. Stir in 1 cup flour or enough to form a thick batter; beat 2 minutes, scraping bowl occasionally. Stir in enough remaining flour to form a soft dough. Turn onto a floured surface; knead until smooth and elastic, about 6-8 minutes. Place in a greased bowl, turning once to grease top. Cover and let rise in a warm place until doubled, about 30 minutes. Stir dough down; divide in half. Shape each half into a ball. Place each ball on a greased baking sheet. Cover and let rise in a warm place until doubled, about 30 minutes. Bake at 375°

ONION-POPPY SEED TWIST

(*Pictured above*)

While yeast breads may take some time to prepare, you'll agree that the effort is worth it after one bite of this fresh-from-the-oven savory loaf. Each slice is weaved with flavorful onions and poppy seeds.

2-1/2 to 3 cups all-purpose flour
    3 tablespoons sugar
    1 package (1/4 ounce) rapid-rise yeast
    1 teaspoon salt
1/2 cup milk
1/4 cup water
    3 tablespoons butter *or* margarine
    1 egg
FILLING:
    1 cup finely chopped yellow onion
    2 tablespoons butter *or* margarine, melted
    2 tablespoons poppy seeds
1/8 teaspoon salt

for 30 minutes or until golden brown. Remove from baking sheets; cool on wire racks. **Yield:** 2 loaves.

CINNAMON-RAISIN SWIRL BREAD

Cinnamon bread with raisins is a favorite breakfast treat. It is slightly sweet, is beautifully swirled and makes delicious toast.

    4 **cups all-purpose flour**
1/3 **cup nonfat dry milk powder**
    2 **tablespoons sugar**
    1 **teaspoon salt**
1/2 **cup chopped nuts**
1/2 **cup raisins**
    1 **package (1/4 ounce) rapid-rise yeast**
1-1/2 **cups water**
    2 **tablespoons butter or margarine**
1/4 **cup packed brown sugar**
    1 **teaspoon ground cinnamon**

In a large mixing bowl, combine 3 cups flour, milk powder, sugar, salt, nuts, raisins and yeast. Heat water and butter until very warm (120°-130°). Gradually add to dry ingredients; beat 2 minutes, scraping bowl occasionally. Stir in enough remaining flour to form a stiff dough. Turn onto a floured surface; knead until smooth and elastic, about 6-8 minutes. Place in a greased bowl, turning once to grease top. Cover and let rise in a warm place until doubled, about 45 minutes. In a small bowl, combine brown sugar and cinnamon. Stir dough down; divide in half. On a lightly floured surface, roll each half into a 12-in. x 8-in. rectangle. Sprinkle brown sugar mixture to within 1/2 in. of edges. Roll up, jelly-roll style, starting with a short side; pinch seams to seal and tuck ends under. Place in two greased 9-in. x 5-in. x 3-in. loaf pans. Cover and let rise in a warm place until doubled, about 30 minutes. Bake at 350° for 20-25 minutes or until bread sounds hollow when tapped. Remove from baking pans; cool on wire rack. **Yield:** 2 loaves.

FRESH APPLE POCKETS

(Pictured at right)

Johnny Appleseed established apple tree nurseries from Pennsylvania to Indiana in the early 1800s. Today, apple trees thrive in many parts of the country. The succulent apples in these pastries contribute to their flavor and moistness.

    2 **to 2-1/2 cups all-purpose flour**
    2 **teaspoons sugar**
    1 **package (1/4 ounce) rapid-rise yeast**

1/2 **teaspoon salt**
2/3 **cup water**
1/3 **cup butter or margarine, cut into pieces**
FILLING:
    2 **cups thinly sliced peeled apples (about 2 medium)**
1/3 **cup sugar**
    2 **tablespoons all-purpose flour**
1/2 **teaspoon ground cinnamon**
TOPPING:
    1 **egg**
    1 **tablespoon water**
Additional sugar

In a large bowl, combine 1 cup flour, sugar, yeast and salt. Heat water and butter until very warm (120°-130°). Butter does not need to melt. Stir into dry ingredients. Stir in enough remaining flour to form a soft dough. Knead on lightly floured surface until smooth and elastic, about 4-6 minutes. Cover; let rest 10 minutes. For filling, combine apples, sugar, flour and cinnamon in a medium bowl. Toss to coat evenly; set aside. Divide dough in half. Roll each piece into a 10-in. square; cut into 4 (5-in.) squares. Place about 1/4 cup filling onto center of each. Bring corners up over filling; pinch together to seal. Transfer to a greased baking sheet. Cover; let rise in warm place until doubled in size, about 20-40 minutes. In a small bowl, beat together egg and water; brush onto tops of dough. Sprinkle with sugar. Bake at 375° for 20-25 minutes or until golden brown. Remove from baking sheet; cool on wire rack. **Yield:** 8 servings.

APPLE CRUMB COFFEE CAKE

German settlers introduced an array of sweet breads and the coffee klatch—a time to enjoy coffee and cake while exchanging news. This practice fostered two American traditions, the coffee break and the coffee cake.

> 1 package (1/4 ounce) active dry yeast
> 1/4 cup warm water (105° to 115°)
> 1/2 cup butter *or* margarine
> 1/2 cup sugar
> 1/2 teaspoon salt
> 3 eggs
> 1/4 cup milk
> 2-1/3 cups all-purpose flour
> 3 large apples, peeled and sliced

TOPPING:
> 2/3 cup sugar
> 1/2 cup all-purpose flour
> 2 teaspoons ground cinnamon
> 6 tablespoons butter *or* margarine

In a small bowl, dissolve yeast in water; set aside. In a mixing bowl, cream butter, sugar and salt. Add yeast mixture, eggs and milk; mix well. Gradually add flour and beat until well blended. Spread batter into a greased 9-in. square baking pan. Arrange apples on top of batter. In a small bowl, combine the first three topping ingredients. Cut in butter until crumbly. Sprinkle over apples. Cover and let rise until doubled, about 1 hour. Bake at 375° for 35-45 minutes or until golden brown. Remove from pan; cool on wire rack. **Yield:** 9 servings.

HERB AND CHEESE BREAD

Bread machines enjoyed a heyday in the 1990s. The machines make bread from start to finish quickly and easily. Most recipes feature simple ingredients that don't require a lot of advance preparation.

> 1 cup plus 2 tablespoons water
> 1-1/4 teaspoons salt
> 3 cups bread flour
> 1/3 cup grated Parmesan cheese
> 2 tablespoons nonfat dry milk powder
> 2 tablespoons sugar
> 2 teaspoons Italian seasoning
> 2 teaspoons bread machine yeast

In bread machine pan, place all ingredients in order suggested by manufacturer. Select the basic bread setting. Choose crust color and loaf size if available. Bake according to bread machine directions (check dough after 5 minutes of mixing; add 1 to 2 tablespoons of water or flour if needed). **Yield:** 1 loaf.

CHOCOLATE-COCONUT BRAID

(Pictured at right)

Breakfasts and brunches get even better when this bread appears on the table. No one can resist the sweet chocolate-coconut filling peeking out of the tender flaky braid. Pecans in the filling and on top of the bread add crunch and flavor.

FILLING:
> 3/4 cup semisweet chocolate chips
> 1/3 cup evaporated milk
> 2 tablespoons sugar
> 1 cup flaked coconut
> 1/2 cup chopped pecans
> 1 teaspoon vanilla extract
> 1/4 teaspoon ground cinnamon

DOUGH:
> 2-1/2 to 2-3/4 cups all-purpose flour
> 2 tablespoons sugar
> 1 package (1/4 ounce) rapid-rise yeast
> 1/2 teaspoon salt
> 1/2 cup milk
> 1/4 cup water
> 1/2 cup butter *or* margarine
> 1 egg, at room temperature

Vegetable oil

GLAZE:
> 1 cup confectioners' sugar
> 1 tablespoon butter *or* margarine, softened
> 1/2 teaspoon vanilla extract
> 2 to 3 tablespoons milk

Additional chopped pecans

For filling, combine chocolate chips, milk and sugar in a small saucepan. Cook over low heat, stirring constantly, until chips are melted and mixture is smooth. Stir in coconut, pecans, vanilla and cinnamon; set aside to cool. For dough, combine 1-1/2 cups flour, sugar, yeast and salt in a large bowl. Heat milk, water and butter until very warm (120°-130°). Gradually add to dry ingredients; beat for 2 minutes on medium speed. Add egg and 1 cup flour; beat 2 minutes. Stir in enough remaining flour to form a stiff dough. Cover; let rest 10 minutes. Turn out dough onto well-floured surface; roll into a 10-in. x 18-in. rectangle. Transfer to a greased baking sheet. Spread filling lengthwise down center third of dough. Cut 1-in.-wide strips diagonally on both sides to within 3/4 in. of filling. Alternately fold opposite strips of dough at angles across filling. Shape into a ring; pinch ends to seal. Brush lightly with oil; let stand 20 minutes. Bake at 375° for 20-25 minutes or until lightly browned. Remove from baking sheet to wire rack. Cool completely. In a small bowl, beat confectioners' sugar, butter, vanilla and milk until smooth. Drizzle over braid. Sprinkle with pecans. **Yield:** 10-12 servings.

CINNAMON COCOA BREAKFAST BUNS

(*Pictured below*)

Early birds will snatch up these delightful breakfast buns. Tender and flaky, they're irresistible goodies that never last long!

DOUGH:
3-1/2 to 4 cups all-purpose flour
  1/2 cup sugar
    1 package (1/4 ounce) rapid-rise yeast
    1 teaspoon salt
  1/2 cup butter *or* margarine, cut into pieces
  1/2 cup prepared mashed potatoes
  1/4 cup milk
  1/4 cup water
    2 eggs
FILLING
    1 tablespoon butter *or* margarine, melted
  1/4 cup sugar
    1 tablespoon baking cocoa
  1/2 teaspoon ground cinnamon
TOPPING:
Confectioners' sugar
    1 teaspoon baking cocoa, optional

In a large bowl, combine 1 cup flour, sugar, yeast and salt. Heat butter, potatoes, milk and water until very warm (120°-130°); stir into dry ingredients. Stir in eggs and enough remaining flour to form a soft dough. Knead on a lightly floured surface until smooth and elastic, about 4-6 minutes. Cover; let rest 10 minutes. Roll dough to 15-in. x 9-in. rectangle; brush with melted butter. In a small bowl, combine sugar, cocoa and cinnamon; sprinkle evenly on dough to within 1/2 in. of edges. Beginning at long end, roll up tightly; pinch seam to seal. With sharp knife, cut roll into 12 equal pieces. Place, cut sides up, into greased muffin cups. Cover; let rise in warm place until doubled in size, about 45-60 minutes. Bake at 375° for 15-20 minutes or until done. Remove from cups; cool on wire racks. Lightly sift confectioners' sugar over tops. Sift cocoa over sugar if desired. **Yield:** 12 buns.

VIENNA BREAD

Nothing can beat the mouth-watering aroma of home-baked bread wafting from the kitchen. This wonderful recipe makes two loaves…one for you to serve to your family and one to share with a neighbor.

  7 to 8 cups all-purpose flour
  1 tablespoon sugar
  1 package (1/4 ounce) active dry yeast
  4 teaspoons salt, *divided*
  3 cups water, *divided*
  2 tablespoons butter *or* margarine
  1 teaspoon cornstarch
Poppy seeds

In a large mixing bowl, combine 2-1/2 cups flour, sugar, yeast and 3 teaspoons salt. Heat 2-1/2 cups water and butter until very warm (120°-130°). Add to dry ingredients; beat 2 minutes, scraping bowl occasionally. Stir in 1-1/2 cups flour or enough flour to form a thick batter; beat 2 minutes, scraping bowl occasionally. Stir in enough remaining flour to form a soft dough. Turn onto a floured surface; knead until smooth and elastic, about 6-8 minutes. Place in a greased bowl, turning once to grease top. Cover and let rise in a warm place until doubled, about 1 hour. Stir dough down; divide in half. Shape into 2 (12-in.) tapered loaves. Carefully transfer to greased baking sheets. Cover and let rise in a warm place until doubled, about 1 hour. Meanwhile, to prepare glaze, combine cornstarch and remaining water and salt in a small saucepan. Cook over medium heat until mixture thickens, stirring constantly. Remove from heat. Brush glaze on loaves. With a sharp knife, make four shallow slashes across top of loaves. Sprinkle with poppy seeds. Bake at 450° for 10 minutes. Reduce heat to 350° and bake 40-50 minutes longer or until golden brown. Remove from baking sheets; cool on wire racks. **Yield:** 2 loaves.

White Batter Bread

Batter breads can be prepared in a jiffy, because the yeast mixture doesn't require any kneading. For beginner bakers, this simple recipe will help you discover the appeal of working with yeast.

> 4 to 4-1/2 cups all-purpose flour
> 3 tablespoons sugar
> 2 packages (1/4 ounce *each*) active dry yeast
> 1 tablespoon salt
> 1 cup milk
> 1 cup water
> 2 tablespoons butter *or* margarine

In a large mixing bowl, combine 1-1/2 cups flour, sugar, yeast and salt. Heat milk, water and butter until very warm (120°-130°). Gradually add to dry ingredients; beat just until moistened. Stir in 1 cup flour or enough remaining flour to form a thick batter. Beat for 2 minutes, scraping bowl occasionally. Stir in enough remaining flour to form a stiff batter. Place in a greased bowl, turning once to grease top. Cover and let rise in a warm place until doubled, about 40 minutes. Stir batter down. Turn batter into a 9-in. x 5-in. x 3-in. loaf pan. Bake at 375° for 40-50 minutes or until golden brown. Remove from pan; cool on wire rack. **Yield:** 1 loaf. **Herb Batter Bread:** To the dry ingredients, add 1/4 teaspoon dried basil, 1/4 teaspoon dried oregano and 1/4 teaspoon dried thyme.

Streusel-Topped Peach Kuchen

(Pictured above right)

If you need to take a spectacular coffee cake to an early-morning gathering, this is the recipe to rely on. Folks are sure to ask for the recipe once they catch a whiff of the wonderful aroma and savor the fresh taste only homemade baked goods can provide.

> 2-1/2 cups all-purpose flour
> 1/3 cup sugar
> 1 package (1/4 ounce) rapid-rise yeast
> 1/2 teaspoon salt
> 1/2 cup butter *or* margarine
> 1/4 cup milk
> 1/4 cup water
> 2 eggs

> 2 cans (15 ounces *each*) sliced peaches in
>   heavy syrup, drained
> CINNAMON-NUT TOPPING:
>   1/4 cup cold butter *or* margarine
>   1/2 cup packed brown sugar
>   1/3 cup sugar
>   1/3 cup chopped pecans
>   1/4 cup all-purpose flour
>   1/2 teaspoon ground cinnamon

In a large mixing bowl, combine 1 cup flour, sugar, yeast and salt. Heat butter, milk and water until very warm (120°-130°). Gradually add to dry ingredients. Beat 2 minutes at medium speed, scraping bowl occasionally. Add eggs and 1/2 cup flour; beat 2 minutes at high speed, scraping bowl occasionally. Stir in remaining flour to form a stiff batter. Transfer to a greased 13-in. x 9-in. x 2-in. baking pan. Arrange peaches in rows on top of batter. To prepare topping, in a medium bowl, cut butter into brown sugar until crumbly. Add sugar, pecans, flour and cinnamon. Stir until well blended. Sprinkle evenly over peaches. Cover; let rise in a warm place until doubled in size, about 1 hour. Bake at 375° for 25-30 minutes or until done. Serve warm or cool. **Yield:** 1 coffee cake.

CHEESE BREAD

With specks of cheese peeking out of every slice, this tempting recipe is worth the effort. The result is two beautiful golden loaves.

> 7 to 8 cups all-purpose flour
> 1/3 cup sugar
> 2 packages (1/4 ounce *each*) active dry yeast
> 1 tablespoon salt
> 2 cups water
> 2/3 cup milk
> 3 cups (12 ounces) shredded cheddar cheese
> 1 tablespoon butter *or* margarine, melted

In a large mixing bowl, combine 2-1/2 cups flour, sugar, yeast and salt. Heat water and milk until very warm (120°-130°). Add to dry ingredients; beat 2 minutes, scraping bowl occasionally. Add cheese and 1/2 cup flour; beat 2 minutes, scraping bowl occasionally. Stir in enough remaining flour to form a stiff dough. Turn onto a floured surface; knead until smooth and elastic, about 6-8 minutes. Place in a greased bowl, turning once to grease top. Cover and let rise in a warm place until doubled, about 1 hour. Punch dough down. Turn onto a lightly floured surface; divide dough in half. Roll each half into a 14-in. x 9-in. rectangle. Roll up, jelly-roll style, starting with a short side; pinch seams to seal and tuck ends under. Place in two greased 9-in. x 5-in. x 3-in. loaf pans. Cover and let rise in a warm place until doubled, about 1 hour. Bake at 375° for 40 minutes or until golden brown. Remove from baking pans; cool on wire racks. Brush tops with butter. **Yield:** 2 loaves.

BANANA-PECAN WHOLE WHEAT LOAF

(Pictured at left)

The bread machine brought technology to tradition, renewing interest in bread baking. The machines are easy to use, and the result has universal appeal.

> 1/3 cup warm water (70° to 80°)
> 1/2 cup mashed ripe banana
> 3 tablespoons butter *or* margarine
> 2 eggs
> 3/4 teaspoon salt
> 1-3/4 cups bread flour
> 1-1/4 cups whole wheat flour
> 1/4 cup sugar
> 2 teaspoons bread machine yeast
> 1/2 cup toasted chopped pecans *or* raisins

In bread machine pan, place all ingredients, except pecans, in the order suggested by manufacturer, adding bananas with water. Select basic bread or fruit and nut cycle, adding pecans according to manufacturer's directions. Choose crust color and loaf size if available. Bake according to bread machine directions (check dough after 5 minutes of mixing; add 1 to 2 tablespoons of water or flour if needed). **Yield:** 1 loaf (1-1/2 pounds).

SESAME POCKET BREAD

Also called pita bread, this Middle Eastern flat bread splits horizontally to form a pocket. A wide variety of ingredients can be stuffed inside.

3-1/2 to 4 cups all-purpose flour
    1 package (1/4 ounce) active dry yeast
    2 teaspoons salt
1-1/4 cups warm water (120° to 130°)
    1 egg white, lightly beaten
    1 tablespoon cold water
    8 teaspoons sesame seeds

In a large mixing bowl, combine 1 cup flour, yeast and salt. Gradually add warm water to dry ingredients; beat 2 minutes, scraping bowl occasionally. Add 3/4 cup flour; beat 2 minutes, scraping bowl occasionally. Stir in enough remaining flour to form a stiff dough. Turn onto a floured surface; knead until smooth and elastic, about 6-8 minutes. Divide dough into 8 pieces. On a lightly floured surface, roll each into a 5-in. circle. Place circles on greased baking sheets. Cover and let rest 45 minutes. Turn dough circles over on baking sheets. Combine egg white and cold water; brush over circles. Sprinkle with sesame seeds. Bake at 500° for 10 minutes or until lightly browned. Remove from baking sheets; cool on wire racks. **Yield:** 8 individual loaves.

CINNAMON COFFEE BRAID

People will rave about this tender delicate bread spiced with a touch a cinnamon. The recipe makes two loaves...one for you to enjoy and one to share.

    4 to 4-1/2 cups all-purpose flour
3/4 cup sugar, *divided*
    2 packages (1/4 ounce *each*) active dry yeast
1-1/2 teaspoons salt
3/4 cup milk
1/2 cup water
    1 cup butter *or* margarine
    3 egg yolks
    2 teaspoons ground cinnamon
1/4 cup butter *or* margarine, melted

In a large mixing bowl, combine 1-1/2 cups flour, 1/4 cup sugar, yeast and salt. Heat milk, water and 1 cup butter until very warm (125°-130°). Gradually add to dry ingredients; beat 2 minutes, scraping bowl occasionally. Add egg yolks and 1/2 cup flour or enough to form a thick batter; beat 2 minutes, scraping bowl occasionally. Stir in enough remaining flour to form a stiff batter. Cover bowl with foil and refrigerate 4 hours. In a small bowl, combine cinnamon and remaining sugar. Turn dough onto a lightly floured surface; divide dough into 6 pieces. Roll each piece into an 18-in. rope. Place three ropes on a greased baking sheet and braid; pinch ends to seal and tuck under. Repeat with remaining ropes. Brush braids with melted butter and sprinkle with cinnamon-sugar mixture. Cover and let rise in a warm place until doubled, about 1 hour. Bake at 400° for 25 minutes or until golden brown. Remove from baking sheets; cool on wire racks. **Yield:** 2 loaves.

HAM 'N' SWISS LOAF

If brunch is your specialty, keep this hearty recipe handy. It's always a hit with family and friends. The braided appearance looks impressive, yet is easy to do.

3-1/2 to 4 cups all-purpose flour
    2 tablespoons sugar
    2 packages (1/4 ounce *each*) rapid-rise yeast
1/4 teaspoon salt
    1 cup warm water (120° to 130°)
1/4 cup prepared mustard
    2 tablespoons butter *or* margarine, softened
    3 cups chopped fully cooked ham
    1 cup (4 ounces) shredded Swiss cheese
    1 jar (4 ounces) diced pimientos, well drained
3/4 cup diced dill pickles
    1 egg, lightly beaten

In a large bowl, combine 1-1/2 cups flour, sugar, yeast and salt. Stir warm water, mustard and butter into dry ingredients. Stir in enough remaining flour to form a soft dough. Knead on lightly floured surface until smooth and elastic, about 4-6 minutes. Cover; let rest on floured surface 10 minutes. Roll dough to a 15-in. x 10-in. rectangle. Transfer to a greased baking sheet. Sprinkle ham, cheese, pimientos and pickles lengthwise over center-third of dough. With sharp knife, make cuts from filling to dough edges at 1-in. intervals along sides of filling. Alternating sides, fold strips at an angle across filling. Cover loaf; let rise in a warm place until almost doubled in size, about 20-40 minutes. Brush loaf with egg. Bake at 375° for 35 minutes or until golden brown. Remove from baking sheet to wire rack. Serve warm. **Yield:** 4-6 servings.

THREE-PEPPER CALZONES

(Pictured above)

Originating in Naples, Italy, calzones are half-moon-shaped stuffed pizzas. Use your imagination to create filling combinations of meats, vegetables and cheeses.

> 3/4 cup water (70° to 80°)
> > 1 tablespoon olive *or* vegetable oil
> 3/4 teaspoon salt
> 2-1/4 cups all-purpose flour
> > 1/4 cup cornmeal
> > 2 teaspoons bread machine yeast *or* rapid-rise yeast
> 1-1/2 cups sliced green *or* sweet red peppers
> > 1 medium onion, sliced
> > 2 ounces pepperoni, cut into thin strips
> > 2 garlic cloves, minced
> 1-1/2 cups grated mozzarella cheese
> > 1 cup grated provolone *or* fontina cheese
> Crushed red pepper, optional

In bread machine pan, combine water, oil, salt, flour, cornmeal and yeast in the order suggested by the manufacturer. Select dough setting (check dough after 5 minutes of mixing; add 1 to 2 tablespoons of water or flour if needed). In a large skillet over medium heat, cook peppers, onion, pepperoni and garlic until vegetables are tender, stirring frequently. Set aside to cool. When cycle is completed, turn dough onto a lightly floured surface. Divide into 4 equal pieces. Roll each into an 8-in. circle. Stir cheese into pepperoni mixture. Place 1 cup on one-half of each circle; moisten edges with water. Fold dough over filling and press with tines of fork to seal. Place on greased baking sheet. With sharp knife, make 3 (1-in.) slits across top of each calzone. If desired, brush tops with water

and sprinkle with crushed red pepper. Bake at 400° for 25 minutes or until golden brown. Serve warm. **Yield:** 4 servings.

RAPID-MIX BRIOCHE

This French creation is a light yeast bread rich with butter and eggs. Brioche dough is often used to enclose foods such as sausage or cheese.

> 3-1/2 to 4 cups all-purpose flour,
> > 1/3 cup plus 1 tablespoon sugar, *divided*
> > > 1 package (1/4 ounce) active dry yeast
> > > 1 teaspoon salt
> > 1/2 cup milk
> > 1/4 cup water
> > 1/2 cup butter *or* margarine
> > > 4 eggs

In a large mixing bowl, combine 1 cup flour, 1/3 cup sugar, yeast and salt. Heat milk, water and butter until very warm (120°-130°). Add to dry ingredients; beat 2 minutes, scraping bowl occasionally. Stir in 3 eggs plus 1 egg yolk (cover and refrigerate egg white); beat 3 minutes, scraping bowl occasionally. Stir in enough remaining flour to form a stiff batter. Cover and let rise in a warm place until doubled, about 2 hours. Stir dough down and beat for 2 minutes. Cover with foil and refrigerate overnight. Punch dough down. Turn onto a lightly floured surface. Cut one-fourth from the dough; set aside. Shape remaining dough into 24 balls and place in well-greased muffin cups. Divide reserved dough in 24 small balls. Make an indentation in the top of each large ball; place a small ball in each indentation. Cover and let rise in a warm place until doubled, about 50 minutes. Combine egg white and remaining sugar; brush over rolls. Bake at 375° for 15 minutes or until golden brown. Remove from baking pans; cool on wire racks. **Yield:** 2 dozen.

HERB PEEL-AWAY BREAD

This savory bread bakes up golden and delicious. Individual pieces of seasoned dough are coated with melted butter and mounded in a fluted tube pan. After baking, it's easy to peel away a portion of the baked loaf.

> 3-1/2 cups all-purpose flour
> > 1/3 cup sugar
> > > 2 packages (1/4 ounce *each*) rapid-rise yeast
> > > 1 teaspoon salt
> > > 2 tablespoons grated Parmesan cheese
> > > 1 tablespoon dried parsley flakes
> > > 1 teaspoon dried thyme

1/2 teaspoon dried basil
1/2 teaspoon dill weed
1/2 teaspoon dried rosemary, crushed
  1 cup water
  6 tablespoons butter *or* margarine, *divided*
  1 egg

In a large mixing bowl, combine 2-1/2 cups flour, sugar, yeast, salt, cheese and herbs. Heat water and 4 tablespoons butter until very warm (120°-130°). Gradually add to dry ingredients; beat 2 minutes, scraping bowl occasionally. Stir in egg and enough remaining flour to form a soft dough. Turn onto a floured surface; knead until smooth and elastic, about 6-8 minutes. Cover and let rest 10 minutes. On a floured surface, roll dough into a 12-in. square. Melt remaining butter; brush on dough. Cut dough into 25 squares. Arrange squares, butter side down, in a greased 10-in. fluted tube pan. Cover and let rise in a warm place until doubled, about 30 minutes. Bake at 375° for 20-25 minutes or until golden brown. Remove from pan; cool on wire rack. **Yield:** 1 loaf.

REUBEN LOAF

Arthur Reuben, owner of the now-closed Reuben's Delicatessen in New York, created this sandwich using corned beef, Swiss cheese and sauerkraut topped with Thousand Island dressing. This recipe melds those classic flavors into a tasty bread ideal for snacking.

3-1/4 cups all-purpose flour
  1 tablespoon sugar
  1 package (1/4 ounce) rapid-rise yeast
  1 teaspoon salt
  1 cup warm water (125° to 130°)
  1 tablespoon butter *or* margarine, softened
1/4 cup Thousand Island dressing
  6 ounces thinly sliced corned beef *or* 1 can
    (7 ounces) corned beef
1/4 pound sliced Swiss cheese
  1 can (8 ounces) sauerkraut, well drained
  1 egg white, beaten
Caraway seed, optional

In a large mixing bowl, combine 2-1/4 cups flour, sugar, yeast and salt. Add warm water and butter; beat just until moistened. Stir in enough remaining flour to form a soft dough. Turn onto a floured surface; knead until smooth and elastic, about 6-8 minutes. Roll dough to 14-in. x 10-in. rectangle; place on greased baking sheet. Spread dressing down center- third of length of dough. Top with layers of beef, cheese and sauerkraut. Cut 1-in.-wide strips along sides of filling out to dough edges. Alternating sides, fold strips at angle across filling. Cover and

let rest in a warm place 30 minutes. Brush with egg white; sprinkle with caraway seed if desired. Bake at 400° for 25 minutes or until golden brown. Cool slightly; serve warm. **Yield:** 8 servings.

ORANGE PECAN BREAD

(Pictured below)

You may want to make this bread a morning tradition at your home. Delicious pecans add crunchy texture to the orange-flavored loaf.

2-3/4 to 3-1/4 cups all-purpose flour
  1/3 cup sugar
    1 tablespoon grated orange peel
    1 package (1/4 ounce) quick-rise yeast
  3/4 teaspoon salt
  1/3 cup milk
  1/4 cup water
    3 tablespoons butter *or* margarine, cut
      into pieces
    3 eggs
  3/4 cup coarsely chopped pecans, toasted

In a large bowl, combine 1 cup flour, sugar, orange peel, yeast and salt. Heat milk, water and butter until very warm (120°-130°); stir into dry ingredients. Stir in 2 eggs, pecans and enough remaining flour to form a soft dough. Knead on a lightly floured surface until smooth and elastic, about 4-6 minutes. Cover; let rest 10 minutes. Divide dough in half; roll each to 12-in. rope. Arrange ropes, side by side; twist together. Pinch ends to join. Place in a greased 8-in. x 4-in. loaf pan. Cover; let rise in a warm place until doubled in size, about 45-60 minutes. Lightly beat remaining egg; brush on dough. Bake at 350° for 40-45 minutes or until done. Remove from pan; cool on wire rack. **Yield:** 1 loaf (12 slices).

GLAZED HUNGARIAN COFFEE CAKE

A multitude of wonderful baked goods have been introduced by the Hungarians. Their coffee cakes are generally nut-flavored yeast breads.

4 to 4-1/2 cups all-purpose flour
1-1/3 cups sugar, *divided*
2 packages (1/4 ounce *each*) active dry yeast
1 teaspoon salt
3/4 cup milk
1/2 cup water
1/2 cup butter *or* margarine
2 eggs
1 teaspoon ground cinnamon
1/3 cup butter *or* margarine, melted
1/2 cup chopped nuts, *divided*
1/3 cup light corn syrup

In a large mixing bowl, combine 1 cup flour, 1/3 cup sugar, yeast and salt. Heat milk, water and 1/2 cup butter until very warm (120°-130°). Gradually add to dry ingredients; beat 2 minutes, scraping bowl occasionally. Stir in eggs and 1/2 cup flour; beat 2 minutes, scraping bowl occasionally. Stir in enough remaining flour to form a stiff dough. Place in a greased bowl, turning once to grease top. Cover bowl with foil and refrigerate at least 2 hours or up to 2 days. In a small bowl, combine cinnamon and remaining sugar. Sprinkle one-third of cinnamon-sugar mixture into bottom of a well-greased 10-in. tube pan. Divide dough into thirds. Divide one-third into 12 pieces. Shape each into a ball. Dip each into melted butter. Arrange in an even layer in tube pan. Sprinkle with 1/4 cup nuts and one-half of the remaining cinnamon-sugar mixture. Shape remaining dough into 24 balls. Dip each into melted butter; arrange in an even layer in tube pan. Sprinkle with remaining nuts and cinnamon-sugar mixture. Cover and let rise in a warm place until doubled, about 45 minutes. Drizzle syrup over dough. Bake at 350° for 1 hour or until dark golden brown. Immediately invert onto serving plate. **Yield:** 1 coffee cake.

ITALIAN HERO LOAF

Skip the routine of everyday sandwiches by serving this delicious loaf stuffed with hearty fillings. Your family will rave over this lip-smacking combination of deli favorites.

3 to 3-1/2 cups all-purpose flour
1 tablespoon sugar
1 package (1/4 ounce) rapid-rise yeast
2 teaspoons Italian seasoning
1 teaspoon salt
1 cup water
1 tablespoon butter *or* margarine, softened
4 ounces thinly sliced fully cooked ham
4 ounces sliced provolone cheese
4 ounces thinly sliced salami
1 jar (2 ounces) diced pimientos, well drained
1/2 cup pitted ripe olives
1 egg white, beaten
Sesame seeds
Creamy Italian salad dressing, optional

In a large mixing bowl, combine 2-1/4 cups flour, sugar, yeast, Italian seasoning and salt. Heat water and butter until very warm (120°-130°). Gradually add to dry ingredients; beat 2 minutes, scraping bowl occasionally. Stir in enough remaining flour to form a soft dough. Turn onto a floured surface; knead until smooth and elastic, about 6-8 minutes. Place in a greased bowl, turning once to grease top. Cover and let rest for 10 minutes. On a greased baking sheet, roll dough in a 14-in. x 10-in. rectangle. Layer ham, cheese and salami down center of rectangle; top with pimientos and olives. On each long side, cut 1-in.-wide strips about 2-1/2 in. into center. Starting at one end, fold alternating strips at an angle across filling. Pinch ends to seal. Cover and let rise in a warm place, about 30 minutes. Brush with egg white; sprinkle with sesame seeds. Bake at 400° for 25 minutes or until golden brown. Remove from baking sheet to wire rack to cool slightly. Serve warm with salad dressing if desired. **Yield:** 1 loaf.

OLD VIRGINIA SPOON BREAD

This Southern dish may have evolved from suppawn, a Native American porridge. Perhaps its new name stuck because this comfort food is best eaten with a spoon. Thomas Jefferson ate spoon bread with every meal.

1 cup cornmeal
1-1/2 teaspoons baking powder
1/2 teaspoon salt
1-1/2 cups boiling water
3 eggs, *separated*
1 tablespoon butter *or* margarine, melted
1 cup buttermilk
1 teaspoon sugar

In a large mixing bowl, combine cornmeal, baking powder and salt. Pour boiling water over cornmeal mixture; stir until slightly cooled. Beat egg yolks in a separate bowl with mixer until lemon-colored. Stir egg yolks and butter into cornmeal; blend well. Stir in buttermilk and sugar. In a small mixing bowl, beat egg whites until soft peaks form. Gently fold egg whites into cornmeal mixture. Pour batter into a greased 2-qt. casserole. Bake at 375° for 45-50 minutes or until golden brown. **Yield:** 6-8 servings.

THREE-CHEESE TWIST

(Pictured above)

This simple bread is so eye-catching, people will think you fussed all day. It's literally bursting with savory cheese. Serve warm as a snack or with soup or salad.

DOUGH:
- 1/2 cup milk
- 1 egg
- 1/4 cup water
- 3 tablespoons olive *or* vegetable oil
- 1 teaspoon salt
- 3 cups bread flour
- 2 teaspoons bread machine yeast

FILLING:
- 1 cup (4 ounces) shredded sharp cheddar cheese
- 1/2 cup shredded Swiss cheese
- 1/4 cup grated Parmesan cheese

In bread machine pan, place the dough ingredients in order suggested by manufacturer. Select dough setting (check dough after 5 minutes of mixing; add 1 to 2 tablespoons of water or flour if needed). When cycle is completed, turn dough onto a lightly floured surface. Roll dough to 18-in. x 12-in. rectangle. Combine filling ingredients and sprinkle to within 1/2 in. of edges. Beginning at long end, roll up tightly; pinch seam to seal. Place, seam side down, on large greased baking sheet. With sharp knife, cut lengthwise down center of roll, about 1 in. deep, to within 1/2 in. of ends. Keeping cut side on top, form into "S" shape. Tuck both ends under center of "S" to form a "figure eight"; pinch dough to seal. Cover; let rise in warm place until doubled in size, about 30-45 minutes. Bake at 350° for 35-40 minutes, covering with aluminum foil after 25 minutes to prevent excess browning. Remove from pan; cool on wire rack. **Yield:** 1 loaf (12 servings).

OATMEAL MOLASSES BREAD

(Pictured below)

The aroma of this hearty bread is sure to bring hungry appetites to the table. The taste will keep them coming back for more.

1-1/2 cups boiling water
    1 tablespoon butter *or* margarine
    2 teaspoons salt
1/2 cup sugar
    1 cup rolled oats
    2 packages (1/4 ounce *each*) active dry yeast
3/4 cup warm water (110° to 115°)
1/4 cup molasses
1/4 cup packed brown sugar
    6 to 6-1/2 cups all-purpose flour

In a small mixing bowl, combine boiling water, butter, salt and sugar. Stir in oats; cool to lukewarm. In a large mixing bowl, dissolve yeast in warm water. Stir in molasses, brown sugar and 1 cup flour. Beat until smooth. Add oat mixture and enough remaining flour to form a stiff dough. Turn out onto a floured surface; knead until smooth and elastic, about 6-8 minutes. Shape into a ball. Place in a greased bowl, turning once to grease top. Cover and let rise until doubled, about 1-1/2 hours. Punch dough down; divide in half and shape into balls. Cover and let rest 10 minutes. Shape into loaves and place into two greased 9-in. x 5-in. x 3-in. loaf pans. Cover and let rise until nearly doubled, about 1 hour. Bake at 375° for 35 minutes. Cover loosely with foil the last 20 minutes if loaves are browning excessively. Remove from pans; cool on wire rack. **Yield:** 2 loaves.

BEAUTIFUL BASIC DOUGH

Most bakers possess a basic sweet dough recipe that can be used to create a variety of loaves. Use this one to prepare either of the tempting breads that follow.

1/2 cup milk
1/4 cup butter *or* margarine
    2 packages (1/4 ounce *each*) active dry yeast
1/2 cup warm water (110° to 115°)
1/2 cup sugar
    1 teaspoon salt
    3 eggs
4-1/2 cups all-purpose flour

Heat milk and butter to 110°. In a large mixing bowl, dissolve yeast in warm water. Add milk mixture, sugar, salt, eggs and 2 cups flour; beat until smooth. Add enough remaining flour to form a soft dough. Turn onto a floured surface; knead until smooth and elastic, about 8 minutes. Place in a greased bowl, turning once to grease top. Cover and let rise in a warm place until doubled, about 1 hour. Punch dough down. Use dough to prepare Coconut Crunch Loaf or Frosty Fruit-Nut Loaf. **Yield:** 1 recipe dough.

COCONUT CRUNCH LOAF

This delectable coffee cake is easy to prepare. Simply pat the dough into a baking pan, then crown with a flavorful coconut-walnut topping.

1/2 recipe Beautiful Basic Dough (recipe above)
3/4 cup flaked coconut
1/2 cup packed brown sugar
1/2 cup chopped walnuts
    3 tablespoons milk
    3 tablespoons butter *or* margarine, melted

Press dough onto bottom of a greased 13-in. x 9-in. x 2-in. baking pan. In a bowl, combine the remaining ingredients; sprinkle over dough. Cover; let rise in a warm place until doubled, about 1 hour. Bake at 375° for 25 minutes or until lightly browned. **Yield:** 1 coffee cake (15 servings).

FROSTY FRUIT-NUT LOAF

This yummy breakfast bread is studded with raisins and walnuts and offers a subtle orange flavor. Top it with prepared vanilla frosting for added sweetness.

1/2 cup raisins
1/4 cup chopped walnuts
  3 tablespoons grated orange peel
1/2 recipe Beautiful Basic Dough (recipe at left)
Prepared vanilla frosting, optional

Combine raisins, walnuts and orange peel. Knead into dough. Place in a greased 1-1/2-qt. casserole. Cover; let rise in a warm place until doubled, about 1 hour. Bake at 375° for 30 minutes or until golden brown. Cool. Frost with vanilla frosting if desired. **Yield:** 1 loaf (8-12 servings).

HEALTHY WALNUT BREAD

Throughout history, light-colored loaves of bread were admired because only the rich could afford the highly processed flours that produced them. Today, more folks seem to favor the unparalleled flavor and texture that darker loaves provide.

3-1/2 cups all-purpose flour, *divided*
2-1/2 cups whole wheat flour
1-1/2 cups chopped walnuts
  1/2 cup wheat germ
  1/3 cup sugar
    2 packages (1/4 ounce *each*) rapid-rise yeast
    2 teaspoons salt
1-1/2 cups water
  3/4 cup plain yogurt
  1/4 cup butter *or* margarine

In a large mixing bowl, combine 2-3/4 cups all-purpose flour, whole wheat flour, walnuts, wheat germ, sugar, yeast and salt. Heat water, yogurt and butter until very warm (120°-130°). Gradually add to dry ingredients; beat 2 minutes, scraping bowl occasionally. Stir in enough remaining all-purpose flour to form a stiff dough. Turn onto a floured surface; knead until smooth and elastic, about 6-8 minutes. Cover and let rest 10 minutes. Divide dough in half. On a lightly floured surface, roll each half into a 12-in. x 8-in. rectangle. Roll up, jelly-roll style, starting with a short side; pinch seams to seal and tuck ends under. Place in two greased 8-in. x 4-in. x 2-in. loaf pans. Cover and let rise in a warm place until doubled in size, about 1 hour. Bake at 400° for 25-30 minutes or until bread sounds hollow when tapped. Remove from baking pans; cool on wire racks. **Yield:** 2 loaves.

TEX-MEX CORN BREAD

(Pictured above)

Add south-of-the-border zest to your favorite soup or salad with this flavorful corn bread. Cream-style corn makes it extra moist and tasty.

    1 egg
    1 cup cornmeal
1-1/2 teaspoons baking powder
  1/2 teaspoon salt
    1 can (8-1/2 ounces) cream-style corn
  1/2 cup milk
    2 tablespoons vegetable oil
    1 teaspoon sugar
    1 cup (4 ounces) shredded sharp cheddar cheese
    2 tablespoons chopped jalapeno peppers *or* chopped green chilies

Beat egg in a large mixing bowl. Add remaining ingredients; blend well. Pour batter into a greased 8-in. square baking pan. Bake at 450° for 25-30 minutes or until golden brown. Cool in pan 10 minutes before serving. **Yield:** 6-9 servings.

CRISPY ONION CRESCENT ROLLS

(Pictured above)

A snap to prepare, these rolls bake up in a jiffy. The tasty results help round out most any meal without all the work traditional yeast breads require.

      1 tube (8 ounces) refrigerated crescent
          dinner rolls
1-1/3 cups french-fried onions, slightly crushed
      1 egg, beaten

Separate rolls into 8 triangles. Sprinkle each triangle with 1-1/2 tablespoons french-fried onions. Roll up triangles from short side. Place crescents on foil-lined baking sheet. Brush with beaten egg. Sprinkle any remaining onions on top. Bake at 375° for 15 minutes or until golden brown and crispy. Transfer to wire rack; cool slightly. **Yield:** 8 rolls.

BANANA NUT BREAD

Bananas were scarce in the United States until a railroad builder and an American sea captain founded the United Fruit Company in the mid-1800s. Since then, bananas have become a favorite year-round fruit.

1/3 cup shortening
2/3 cup sugar
  2 eggs
  1 cup mashed ripe bananas (3 medium)
  1 teaspoon grated orange peel
1/4 cup orange juice
1-3/4 cups all-purpose flour
  1 teaspoon baking powder
1/2 teaspoon baking soda
1/2 teaspoon salt
  1 cup chopped walnuts

In a large mixing bowl on medium speed, cream shortening and sugar. Add eggs, one at a time, beating well after each addition until light and fluffy. Beat in banana, orange peel and orange juice. Combine the flour, baking powder, baking soda and salt. Add to banana mixture; beat 1 minute. Stir in the nuts. Spread into a greased 9-in. x 5-in. x 3-in. loaf pan. Bake at 350° for 60 minutes or until a toothpick inserted near the center comes out clean. Cool in pan on wire rack for 10 minutes. Remove from pan; cool completely on wire rack. Wrap and store overnight. **Yield:** 1 loaf.

CHEESE BREAD KNOTS

Dinner rolls owe their popularity to quick baking and fabulous oven-fresh flavor. In this recipe, melted Swiss cheese is kneaded into the dough, so the distinct flavor appears in every bite.

      5 to 5-1/2 cups all-purpose flour
      2 packages (1/4 ounce *each*) active dry yeast
      2 cups milk
      6 ounces process Swiss cheese, cubed
1/2 cup sugar
1/4 cup butter *or* margarine
      1 tablespoon salt
      1 egg
Additional butter *or* margarine, melted

In a large mixing bowl, combine 2 cups flour and yeast. Heat milk, cheese, sugar, butter and salt until very warm (120°-130°). Add to dry ingredients; beat 2 minutes, scraping bowl occasionally. Stir in egg; beat 3 minutes, scraping bowl occasionally. Stir in enough remaining flour to form a soft dough. Turn onto a floured surface; knead until smooth and elastic, about 6-8 minutes. Place in a greased bowl, turning once to grease top. Cover and let rise in a warm place until doubled, about 1-1/2 hours. Turn onto a lightly floured surface; divide dough into 4 equal pieces. Shape each piece into 12 balls. To form knots, roll each ball into a 6-in. rope; tie into a knot. Tuck ends under. Place rolls 2 in. apart on greased baking sheets. Cover and let rise in a warm place until doubled, about 40 minutes. Bake at 375° for 10-12 minutes or until golden brown. Brush with melted butter. Remove from baking sheets; cool on wire racks. **Yield:** 4 dozen.

White Bread with Variations

The aroma of homemade white bread conjures memories of the American farm wife baking loaves to be spread with sweet homemade butter. Today, bread machines are making home bread-making almost magical, as the machine turns a few basic ingredients into luscious loaves. In addition to a basic white bread, here we offer several variations to the simple recipe.

LARGE:
(About 1-1/2 pounds)
1-1/8 cups water
1-1/4 teaspoons salt
1-1/2 tablespoons butter *or* margarine
    3 cups bread flour
    2 tablespoons nonfat dry milk powder
    2 tablespoons sugar
    2 teaspoons bread machine yeast

MEDIUM:
(About 1 pound)
    3/4 cup water
    3/4 teaspoon salt
    1 tablespoon butter *or* margarine
    2 cups bread flour
1-1/2 tablespoons nonfat dry milk powder
1-1/2 tablespoons sugar
1-1/2 teaspoons bread machine yeast

In bread machine pan, place all ingredients in order suggested by manufacturer. Select the basic bread setting. Choose crust color and loaf size if available. Bake according to bread machine directions (check dough after 5 minutes of mixing; add 1 to 2 tablespoons of water or flour if needed). **Yield:** 1 loaf.

VARIATIONS:

LIGHT WHEAT
(Use basic bread, delayed or rapid bake setting.)
LARGE: Replace 1 cup bread flour with 1 cup whole wheat flour.

MEDIUM: Replace 2/3 cup bread flour with 2/3 cup whole wheat flour.

CHEDDAR BREAD
(Use basic bread, delayed or rapid bake setting.)
LARGE: Omit butter and decrease water to 3/4 cup. Add 1-1/2 eggs with water. Add 1 cup shredded cheddar cheese with flour.

MEDIUM: Omit butter and decrease water to 1/2 cup. Add 1 egg with water. Add 2/3 cup shredded cheddar cheese with flour.

SALT-FREE WHITE BREAD
(Use basic bread, delayed or rapid bake setting.)
LARGE AND MEDIUM: Omit salt and use unsalted butter.

OAT DATE NUT BREAD
(Use basic bread, delayed or rapid bake setting.)
LARGE: Add 1/2 cup old-fashioned oats, 1/2 cup chopped dates, 1/3 cup chopped pecan pieces *or* walnut pieces and 1 teaspoon ground cinnamon with flour.

MEDIUM: Add 1/3 cup old-fashioned oats, 1/3 cup chopped dates, 1/4 cup chopped pecan pieces *or* walnut pieces and 3/4 teaspoon ground cinnamon with flour.

SWEET EGG BREAD
(Use basic bread, delayed or rapid bake setting.)
LARGE: Decrease water to 3/4 cup; add 1-1/2 eggs with water. Increase sugar to 1/4 cup.

MEDIUM: Decrease water to 1/2 cup; add 1 egg with water. Increase sugar to 3 tablespoons.

PIZZA DOUGH
(Use dough setting.)
Follow recipe for White or Light Wheat Bread (large or medium), except omit sugar and replace butter with olive oil. Process using dough setting. Remove dough. Grease appropriate pan or pans; sprinkle with cornmeal. Roll or pat dough to fit pan(s). Top as desired. Bake at 400° or until done.

LARGE: Recipe fits two 12-in. pizza pans or one 14-in. pizza pan.

MEDIUM: Recipe fits one 12-in. pizza pan, one 14-in. pizza pan or one 13-in. x 9-in. x 2-in. baking pan.

GREEN CHILI & CHEDDAR STUFFED BREAD

(Pictured below)

Here is a traditional French bread with a new twist—green chilie and cheddar cheese filling. This bread makes any soup or salad a memorable meal.

DOUGH:
   3/4 cup water (70° to 80°)
    1 tablespoon olive *or* vegetable oil
   3/4 teaspoon salt
2-1/3 cups bread flour
1-1/2 teaspoons bread machine yeast
FILLING:
1-1/2 cups (6 ounces) shredded sharp cheddar
       cheese
    1 can (4 ounces) diced green chilies, well
       drained
   1/4 cup chopped ripe olives
   1/4 cup chopped green onions
TOPPING:
    1 egg white, lightly beaten

In bread machine pan, place all dough ingredients in the order suggested by manufacturer. Process on dough/manual cycle. When cycle is complete, re- move dough to floured surface. If necessary, knead in additional flour to make dough easy to handle. Roll dough to a 14-in. x 10-in. rectangle. Mix to- gether filling ingredients; evenly sprinkle the filling to within 1/2 in. of the dough's edges. Pat down lightly. Beginning at long end, roll up tightly; pinch seam and ends to seal. Taper ends by gently rolling back and forth to make a 16-in.-long roll. Line large baking sheet with lightly greased aluminum foil. Place loaf, seam side down, on foil. Cover; let rise in a warm place until almost doubled in size, about 15-20 minutes. Brush loaf with egg white. With sharp knife, cut three 4-in. slits lengthwise down the center of loaf, cutting at a slight diagonal and cutting deep enough to expose filling. Bake at 400° for 25-30 minutes or until cheese is melted and

crust is golden brown. Cool 5 minutes before removing from pan. Serve warm. **Yield:** 6 servings.

ITALIAN EASTER BREAD

Both Italians and the Swiss prepare this festive Easter bread with colored eggs embedded in the dough. Not only do you get a beautifully baked bread, you get hard-cooked eggs that are ready to eat.

    3 to 3-1/2 cups all-purpose flour
    1/4 cup sugar
    1 package (1/4 ounce) active dry yeast
    1 teaspoon salt
    2/3 cup warm milk (120° to 130°)
    2 tablespoons butter *or* margarine,
        softened
    7 eggs
    1/2 cup chopped mixed candied fruit
    1/4 cup chopped blanched almonds
    1/2 teaspoon aniseed
Vegetable oil

In a mixing bowl, combine 1 cup flour, sugar, yeast and salt. Add milk and butter; beat 2 minutes on medium. Add 2 eggs and 1/2 cup flour; beat 2 minutes on high. Stir in fruit, nuts and aniseed; mix well. Stir in enough remaining flour to form a soft dough. Turn onto a lightly floured surface; knead until smooth and elastic, about 6-8 minutes. Place in a greased bowl, turning once to grease top. Cover and let rise in a warm place until doubled, about 1 hour. If desired, dye remaining eggs (leave them uncooked); lightly rub with oil. Punch dough down. Divide in half; roll each piece into a 24-in. rope. Loosely twist ropes together; place on a greased baking sheet and form into a ring. Pinch ends together. Gently split ropes and tuck eggs into openings. Cover and let rise until doubled, about 30 minutes. Bake at 350° for 30-35 minutes or until golden brown. Remove from pan; cool on a wire rack. **Yield:** 1 bread.

HERBED PARMESAN LOAF

(Pictured on cover)

Great with a spaghetti dinner, this soft loaf is easy to make and offers wonderful homemade flavor.

    3-1/2 cups all-purpose flour
    1/3 cup grated Parmesan cheese
    1 tablespoon sugar
    1 package (1/4 ounce) rapid-rise yeast
    2 teaspoons Italian seasoning
    1 teaspoon salt
    1 cup water

    2 tablespoons butter *or* margarine,
        softened
    2 eggs
    1 tablespoon cold water
Additional grated Parmesan cheese

In a large mixing bowl, combine 2-1/2 cups flour, cheese, sugar, yeast, seasoning and salt. Heat water and butter until very warm (120°-130°). Add to dry ingredients; beat just until moistened. Add 1 egg; beat until smooth. Stir in enough remaining flour to form a soft dough (dough will be sticky). Turn onto a floured surface; knead until smooth and elastic, about 6-8 minutes. Place in a greased bowl, turning once to grease top. Cover and let rest for 10 minutes. Stir dough down. Roll into a 15-in. x 8-in. rectangle. Roll up, jelly-roll style, starting with long side; pinch seams to seal and tuck ends under. Place, seam side down, on a greased baking sheet. Cover and let rise in a warm place until doubled, about 30 minutes. With a sharp knife, cut a lengthwise slash on top of loaf. Beat remaining egg and water; brush on loaf. Sprinkle with additional cheese. Bake at 400° for 20 minutes or until golden brown. Remove from pan; cool on a wire rack. **Yield:** 1 loaf.

60-MINUTE CLOVER ROLLS

A bountiful basket of delectable dinner rolls will add interest to any meal. They're especially scrumptious fresh from the oven.

    3-1/2 to 4-1/2 cups all-purpose flour
    3 tablespoons sugar
    2 packages (1/4 ounce *each*) active dry yeast
    1 teaspoon salt
    1 cup milk
    1/2 cup water
    1/4 cup butter *or* margarine

In a large mixing bowl, combine 1-1/2 cups flour, sugar, yeast and salt. Heat milk, water and butter until very warm (120°-130°). Add to dry ingredients; beat 2 minutes, scraping bowl occasionally. Add 1/2 cup flour; beat 2 minutes, scraping bowl occasionally. Stir in enough remaining flour to form a soft dough. Place in a greased bowl, turning once to grease top. Cover bowl; place bowl in a pan filled with 98° water. Let rise 15 minutes. Turn onto a floured surface. Shape dough into 24 balls and place in well-greased muffin cups. With kitchen shears, cut each ball in half, then into quarters, cutting through almost to the bottom of rolls. Cover and let rise 15 minutes. Bake at 425° for 12 minutes or until golden brown. Remove from baking pans; cool on wire rack. **Yield:** 2 dozen.

SOUR CREAM ROLLS

Your reputation as a baker will surely rise after you serve these rich dinner rolls. Serve them as part of your special-occasion meals.

2-1/4 cups all-purpose flour
  2 tablespoons sugar
  1 package (1/4 ounce) rapid-rise yeast
  1 teaspoon salt
  3/4 cup sour cream
  1/4 cup water
  2 tablespoons butter *or* margarine
  1 egg

In a large mixing bowl, combine 1 cup flour, sugar, yeast and salt. Heat sour cream, water and butter until very warm (120°-130°). Gradually add to dry ingredients. Beat 2 minutes at medium speed, scraping bowl occasionally. Add egg and remaining flour to form a soft batter. Spoon evenly into greased 2-1/2-in. muffin cups. Cover; let rise in a warm place until doubled in size, about 1 hour. Bake at 400° for 25-30 minutes or until golden brown. Remove from pans; cool on wire rack. **Yield:** 12 rolls.

FRUIT 'N' NUT SNACK BREAD

(Pictured below)

With a little effort, you can turn a few basic ingredients into a fresh fragrant snack bread. The chewy dried fruits and crunchy nuts will have folks coming back for more.

  3 to 3-1/2 cups all-purpose flour
1/4 cup sugar
  1 package (1/4 ounce) rapid-rise yeast
  1 teaspoon salt

1/2 cup milk
1/2 cup water
1/4 cup butter *or* margarine
1/2 cup chopped dates
1/2 cup snipped dried apricots, dried
    cherries *or* dried cranberries
1/2 cup chopped almonds *or* pecans, toasted
Confectioners' sugar, optional

In a large mixing bowl, combine 1-1/2 cups flour, sugar, yeast and salt. Heat milk, water and butter until very warm (120°-130°). Add to dry ingredients; beat 2 minutes, scraping bowl occasionally. Stir in dates, dried fruit, almonds and enough remaining flour to form a soft dough. Turn onto a floured surface; knead until smooth and elastic, about 6-8 minutes. Cover and let rest 10 minutes. Roll dough to a 12-in. circle or 15-in. x 10-in. rectangle. Place on a greased 12-in. pizza pan or large baking sheet. Cover and let rise in a warm place until doubled, about 30 minutes. Bake at 400° for 15-20 minutes or until golden brown. Remove from pan to wire rack to cool. Sprinkle with confectioners' sugar if desired. **Yield:** 1 loaf.

90-MINUTE DINNER ROLLS

The Egyptians first used wild yeast spores as a leavening agent more than 5,000 years ago. Today, scientists are able to identify the various types of yeast that are best for baking. These commercial yeasts help ensure successful results every time you bake.

  2 to 2-1/2 cups all-purpose flour
  2 tablespoons sugar
  1 package (1/4 ounce) active dry yeast
1/2 teaspoon salt
1/2 cup milk
1/4 cup water
  2 tablespoons butter *or* margarine

In a large mixing bowl, combine 3/4 cup flour, sugar, yeast and salt. Heat milk, water and butter until very warm (120°-130°). Add to dry ingredients; beat 2 minutes, scraping bowl occasionally. Add 1/4 cup flour; beat 2 minutes, scraping bowl occasionally. Stir in enough remaining flour to form a soft dough. Turn onto a floured surface; knead until smooth and elastic, about 6-8 minutes. Divide dough into 12 pieces. Shape into balls. Place in a greased 9-in. round cake pan. Fill a large baking pan with 1 in. boiling water. Place on bottom rack of cold oven. Cover rolls; set pan on rack above water. Close oven door; let rise 30 minutes. Remove rolls and pan of water from oven. Uncover rolls. Bake at 375° for 20-25 minutes or until golden brown. Remove from baking pan; cool on wire rack. **Yield:** 1 dozen.

Basic Sweet Dough

Experienced bakers possess a basic sweet dough recipe that can be used as a base for a wide array of coffee cake and pastry recipes. You may want to experiment with the basic dough on page 66 as well to see which texture and flavor you prefer.

4-1/2 cups all-purpose flour
   1/3 cup sugar
     2 packages (1/4 ounce *each*) active dry *or* rapid-rise yeast
     1 teaspoon salt
   3/4 cup milk
   1/2 cup water
   1/3 cup butter *or* margarine
     2 eggs

In a large bowl, combine 1-1/2 cups flour, sugar, yeast and salt. Heat milk, water and butter until warm (105°-115°). (Butter does not need to melt.) Gradually add to dry ingredients; beat 2 minutes at medium speed, scraping bowl occasionally. Add eggs and 1/2 cup flour; beat 2 minutes at high speed. With spoon, stir in remaining flour to form a stiff batter; grease top. Cover tightly with plastic wrap; refrigerate 2 hours or up to 3 days. Remove dough from the refrigerator. Punch dough down. Use dough to prepare one of the following variations.

Lemon-Nut Twists

1/2 cup sliced almonds, toasted
1/3 cup packed brown sugar
   1 tablespoon grated lemon peel
1/2 recipe Basic Sweet Dough
   2 tablespoons butter *or* margarine, melted, *divided*
   1 cup confectioner's sugar
   4 to 5 teaspoons lemon juice

Combine almonds, brown sugar and lemon peel. Roll dough to 21-in. x 8-in. rectangle. Brush middle third of dough with 1 tablespoon butter. Sprinkle buttered area with half of filling. Fold one of the remaining dough thirds over filling. Brush folded dough with remaining butter. Sprinkle with remaining filling. Fold remaining dough third over filling; pinch edges to seal. Cut into 8 (1-in. wide) strips. Holding each strip at both ends, twist in opposite directions 3 times. Place on greased baking sheet. Cover; let rise in a warm place until doubled in size, about 20-40 minutes. Bake at 375° for 15 minutes or until golden brown. Remove from sheet; cool on wire rack. Combine confectioner's sugar and lemon juice. Beat until smooth. Drizzle over twists. **Yield:** 8 twists.

Fresh Fruit Kuchen

1/2 recipe Basic Sweet Dough
   3 cups sliced fresh fruit (apples, pears, plums, peaches *or* nectarines)
1/2 cup all-purpose flour
   3 tablespoons sugar
3/4 teaspoon ground cinnamon
1/4 teaspoon ground nutmeg
   3 tablespoons butter *or* margarine, softened
   1 cup confectioners' sugar
   4 to 5 teaspoons milk
1/4 teaspoon almond extract

On a lightly floured surface, roll dough to 10-in. x 15-in. rectangle. Place on large greased baking sheet. Arrange fruit in lengthwise rows on dough. Combine flour, sugar, cinnamon and nutmeg. Cut in butter until mixture is crumbly. Sprinkle between rows of fruit. Cover; let rise in a warm place until doubled in size, about 20-40 minutes. Bake at 375° for 20 minutes or until golden brown. Remove from pan; cool on wire rack. Combine confectioners' sugar, milk and almond extract. Beat until smooth. Drizzle over fruit. **Yield:** 1 coffee cake (15 servings).

Bouquet Coffee Cake

1 recipe Basic Sweet Dough
1 egg
1 tablespoon water
5 tablespoons raspberry *or* strawberry jam

On a lightly floured surface, roll dough to a 14-in. x 7-in. rectangle. Cut into 14 (1-in.) strips. Twist 2 strips together. Form into coil and tuck end underneath. Repeat with remaining strips to make 7 coils. Place one coil in center of greased baking sheet. Arrange remaining coils around center coil in circle with sides lightly touching. Cover; let rise in a warm place until doubled in size, about 20-40 minutes. Lightly beat egg and water; brush on cake. With thumb, press deep indentations into centers of coils. Fill each with about 2 teaspoons jam. Bake at 375° for 20 minutes or until golden brown. Remove from baking sheet; cool on wire rack. **Yield:** 1 coffee cake (7 servings).

RYE FRENCH BREAD

Rye flour is milled from a hardy cereal grain. It contains less gluten than all-purpose flour. For that reason, it is usually blended with some higher-protein flour to produce a well-risen loaf. Rye flour is also heavier and darker in color than most other flours, which is why it produces dark dense loaves.

2-1/2 cups warm water (105° to 115°)
   2 packages (1/4 ounce *each*) active dry yeast
   1 tablespoon salt
   1 tablespoon caraway seed
   1 tablespoon butter *or* margarine, melted
   2 cups rye flour
4-1/2 cups all-purpose flour
Cornmeal
   1 egg white
   1 tablespoon cold water

Pour warm water into a large warm mixing bowl. Sprinkle yeast over water; stir until dissolved. Add salt, caraway seed, butter and rye flour. Beat until smooth. Add all-purpose flour and stir until well blended (dough will be slightly sticky). Place in a greased bowl, turning once to grease top. Cover and let rise in a warm place until doubled, about 30 minutes. Turn onto a lightly floured surface. Divide into 2 equal portions. Roll each into a 15-in. x 10-in. rectangle. Beginning at long end, roll up tightly toward you; seal edges by pinching together. Taper ends by rolling gently back and forth. Place loaves on greased baking sheets that have been sprinkled with cornmeal. Cover; let rise in a warm place until doubled, about 30 minutes. With sharp knife, make 4 diagonal cuts on top of each loaf. Bake at 450° for 25 minutes or until golden brown. Remove from oven and brush with egg white mixed with cold water. Bake 5 minutes longer. **Yield:** 2 loaves.

ORANGE ROLLS

The bold orange flavor of these sweet rolls satisfies at breakfast, dessert or snacktime. Moist and scrumptious, they come out perfect every time.

DOUGH:
2-3/4 to 3-1/4 cups all-purpose flour
   1/4 cup sugar
    1 package (1/4 ounce) quick-rise yeast
    1 teaspoon salt
    6 tablespoons butter *or* margarine

    1/4 cup water
    2 eggs
   1/2 cup sour cream
FILLING:
    1 cup flaked coconut
    2 tablespoons grated orange peel
   3/4 cup sugar
    2 tablespoons butter *or* margarine, melted
GLAZE:
   3/4 cup sugar
   1/2 cup sour cream
    2 tablespoons orange juice
   1/4 cup butter *or* margarine

To make dough, combine 1 cup flour, sugar, yeast and salt in a large bowl. Heat butter and water until very warm (120°-130°). Stir into dry ingredients. Add eggs and sour cream; mix well. Stir in enough remaining flour to form a stiff dough. Cover; let rest 10 minutes. To shape and fill, in a small bowl, combine coconut, orange peel and sugar; mix well. Divide dough in half. Roll each half to a 12-in. circle. Brush with butter. Sprinkle each with half of coconut mixture. Cut each circle into 8 wedges. Starting at outside edge, roll up each wedge to enclose filling. In a greased 13-in. x 9-in. x 2-in. baking pan, arrange rolls in two rows. Cover; let rise in a warm place until almost doubled in size, about 30-45 minutes. Bake at 375° for 25-30 minutes or until golden brown. In a small saucepan, combine glaze ingredients. Bring to a boil, stirring constantly. Boil 3 minutes. Pour hot glaze over hot rolls. Serve warm. **Yield:** 16 rolls.

PRUNE POCKET BUNS

Tucked inside these homemade buns is a delicious filling featuring prunes, nuts, raisins and a touch of cinnamon. Since the recipe requires no kneading, it's nice for bakers who want fresh buns without any fuss.

DOUGH:
    1 cup milk
    6 tablespoons butter *or* margarine
   1/2 cup sugar
   1/2 cup sour cream
    1 teaspoon salt
    1 package (1/4 ounce) active dry yeast
   1/4 cup warm water (105° to 115°)
    2 eggs
    4 cups all-purpose flour
FILLING:
1-1/2 cups chopped drained cooked prunes
   2/3 cup chopped walnuts
   2/3 cup sugar
   2/3 cup raisins

1-1/2 teaspoons ground cinnamon

Heat milk and butter to 130°. Stir in sugar, sour cream and salt. In a large mixing bowl, dissolve yeast in warm water. Stir in milk mixture, eggs and flour. Beat for 1 minute, scraping bowl frequently. Cover; let rise in a warm place until doubled, about 1 hour. Meanwhile, combine prunes, walnuts, sugar, raisins and cinnamon. Stir batter down. Spoon about 1 level tablespoon of batter into each well-greased and lightly floured muffin cup; top with about 1 level tablespoon of prepared prune mixture. Spoon another level tablespoon batter over prune mixture in each muffin cup. Let rise in a warm place until doubled, about 1 hour. Bake at 375° for 12-15 minutes or until golden brown. **Yield:** 2 dozen.

FRESH APPLE KUCHEN

Kuchens originated in Germany but are now enjoyed in many variations throughout the world. They are traditionally a fruit- or cheese-filled yeast coffee cake and are usually served for breakfast. Feel free to enjoy a slice of this apple version any time of day!

      2 to 2-1/2 cups all-purpose flour
      2 tablespoons sugar
      1 package (1/4 ounce) active dry yeast
   1/2 teaspoon salt
   1/2 cup milk
   1/4 cup water
      4 tablespoons butter *or* margarine
      1 egg

TOPPING:
      4 cups sliced peeled tart apples
   2/3 cup sugar
1-1/2 teaspoons ground cinnamon
      2 tablespoons butter *or* margarine

In a large mixing bowl, combine 3/4 cup flour, sugar, yeast and salt. Heat milk, water and butter until very warm (120°-130°). Add to dry ingredients; beat 2 minutes, scraping bowl occasionally. Add egg and 1/4 cup flour; beat 2 minutes, scraping bowl occasionally. Stir in enough remaining flour to form a stiff batter. Cover with foil and let rise in a warm place until doubled, about 1 hour. Stir batter down; divide in half. Spread batter to edges of two greased 12-in. pizza pans or 9-in. round cake pans Arrange apples evenly over batter. Combine sugar, cinnamon and butter; mix until crumbly. Sprinkle over apples. Cover and let rise in a warm place until doubled, about 1 hour. Bake at 375° for 25 minutes or until golden brown. Remove from baking pans. Serve warm. **Yield:** 2 coffee cakes.

ITALIAN CHEESE TWISTS

(Pictured above)

When there's no time to bake from scratch, turn to these tempting twists. Use of frozen bread dough provides a speedy shortcut to fresh-baked flavor.

      1 loaf (1 pound) frozen white bread dough, thawed
   1/4 cup butter *or* margarine, softened
   1/4 teaspoon garlic powder
   1/4 teaspoon *each* dried basil, oregano and marjoram
   3/4 cup shredded mozzarella cheese
      1 egg
      1 tablespoon water
      2 tablespoons sesame seeds *and/or* grated Parmesan cheese

On a lightly floured surface, roll dough into a 12-in. square. Combine butter and seasonings; spread over dough. Sprinkle with mozzarella cheese. Fold dough into thirds. Cut crosswise into 24 strips, 1/2 in. each. Twist each strip twice; pinch ends to seal. Place 2 in. apart on a greased baking sheet. Cover and let rise in a warm place until almost doubled, about 30 minutes. In a small bowl, beat egg and water; brush over the twists. Sprinkle with sesame seeds and/or Parmesan cheese. Bake at 375° for 10-12 minutes or until light golden brown. Serve warm. **Yield:** 2 dozen.

Flashback to the '50s

*T*wo of the most influential inventions of all time—television and rock 'n' roll—were introduced just about the time Homemaker Schools were gearing up across the U.S.

Coincidence? Well, sure. But what exciting, creative times those were! While Elvis Presley was playing to full houses with his soulful singing and controversial dance moves—the kind our mothers didn't want us to learn—home economist Mary Fenton was pulling in crowds of moms who did want to learn how to save time while feeding their families nutritious home-cooked meals.

The first Homemaker Schools were staged at appliance stores in 1948 and 1949, but they really got rolling—literally—in the 1950s. With her station wagon stuffed with pans and utensils, Mary Fenton drove across the Midwest, bringing the shows to tens of thousands of women while putting 50,000 miles per year on her car.

As the crowds grew, so did the venues. Soon, Mary and other home economists were filling auditoriums, sharing cooking techniques, recipes, prizes, camaraderie and fun—a clean-cut, informational afternoon out with the girls.

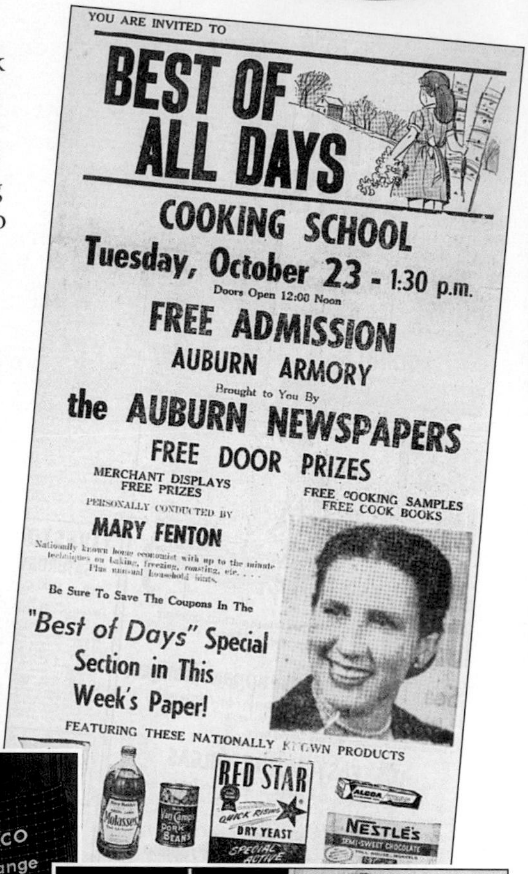

YOU ARE INVITED TO

BEST OF ALL DAYS

COOKING SCHOOL

Tuesday, October 23 - 1:30 p.m.

Doors Open 12:00 Noon

FREE ADMISSION

AUBURN ARMORY

Brought to You By

the AUBURN NEWSPAPERS

FREE DOOR PRIZES

MERCHANT DISPLAYS
FREE PRIZES

FREE COOKING SAMPLES
FREE COOK BOOKS

PERSONALLY CONDUCTED BY

MARY FENTON

Nationally known home economist with up to the minute techniques on baking, freezing, roasting, etc. . . . Plus unusual household hints.

Be Sure To Save The Coupons In The

"Best of Days" Special Section in This Week's Paper!

FEATURING THESE NATIONALLY KNOWN PRODUCTS

RED STAR QUICK RISING DRY YEAST

NESTLE'S SEMI-SWEET CHOCOLATE

IN THE LATE 1940s, Homemaker Schools were staged in appliance dealers' showrooms across the Midwest. Mary Fenton (at right and below) was the first demonstrator to take to the road to conduct these educational events. After 14 years of traveling, Mary decided to plant some roots and moved on to a new career. In 1996, Mary visited current staffer Sunnie Renshaw (far right) at a cooking school in Vacaville, California, where the two enjoyed reminiscing about their travels.

Boy oh Boy—
Just wait 'til you try
HOWDY DOODY'S
FAVORITE TREAT—
9-MINUTE
Marshmallow "Crispy" Squares"

Yes siree, Mom! Make some for the kids tonight! It's so easy — once they taste 'em they'll make 'em for themselves!

THEY'RE SWEET ON EACH OTHER — THEY'RE AT YOUR GROCER'S NOW!

Kellogg's RICE KRISPIES

HOT TIMES IN THE '50s. Elvis captured our hearts, Lucy and Desi made us laugh, and malt shops were "cool" places to be—in more ways than one. Howdy Doody was king of TV land, at least as far as kids were concerned. They knew what time it was—Howdy Doody time, of course! The puppet's product endorsements were a hit, too.

★ ★ ★ That's Entertainment

• Among the most popular family television shows are "The Milton Berle Show", "I Love Lucy", "Dragnet" and "The Adventures of Ozzie and Harriet".

• When singing sensation Elvis Presley appears on "The Ed Sullivan Show", 82.6% of the viewing public tunes in.

• TV quiz shows "Twenty-One", "The $64,000 Question" and "Dotto" captivate America with their "average Joe can get rich" fantasies.

• Drive-in movies peak with 4,062 screens coast to coast.

The 'In' Things

• If you don't have a hula hoop, you're really square.

• Using terms like "make the scene", "later, gator" and "made in the shade" proves your coolness.

• Girls gel, pin and spray their hair (often sleeping on rollers) in search of a natural-curl look.

• Dresses and jumpers are appropriate schoolwear for girls but not slacks or shorts. Dungarees are for playtime only.

Price Check

• The cost to mail a letter jumps from 3¢ to 4¢, the first hike in 26 years.

• Milk costs an average of 66¢ per gallon, and bread is 16¢ per loaf.

• Home-model microwave ovens are introduced, but at $1,300 each, they aren't hot sellers.

• The federal minimum wage increases to $1 per hour.

Play List

• Perry Como scores the first Grammy Award for Best Vocal Performance by a Male with his hit single "Catch a Falling Star".

• The Recording Industry Association of America gives out its first gold album award to the soundtrack from "Oklahoma!"

Food for Thought

• Colonel Sanders showed his pluck by opening Kentucky Fried Chicken, and McDonald's served its first of many customers.

Chapter 4

BREAKFAST & BRUNCH

Rise and shine with these bountiful breakfast recipes guaranteed to get your day off to a mouth-watering start. Turn to these dishes when you're entertaining or to make everyday breakfasts more interesting.

Recipes in this chapter provided courtesy of these past sponsors...

Bisquick
Blue Bonnet
Comstock/Wilderness
Fleischmann's
McCormick
Nabisco
Ore-Ida
Sargento
Stouffer's
Wearever

SOUTHWEST BREAKFAST CASSEROLE

(Pictured at left)

Your family will enjoy this mildly spicy breakfast casserole that offers Southwestern flair. While frozen hash brown potatoes are key to making this meal in a jiffy, hot sausage and zesty pepper Jack cheese provide the palate-pleasing punch.

    1 package (24 ounces) frozen cubed hash
      brown potatoes
    2 tablespoons butter *or* margarine
    2 cups (8 ounces) shredded pepper Jack cheese
  1/4 pound fully cooked hot link sausage,
      sliced into 1/2-inch pieces
    6 eggs, beaten
    1 can (4 ounces) diced green chilies,
      undrained
    1 teaspoon dried oregano
    2 medium tomatoes, sliced
  1/4 cup shredded Parmesan cheese

In a medium skillet, saute hash browns in butter until lightly browned, about 10 minutes. In a bowl, combine hash browns, cheese, sausage, eggs, chilies and oregano. Spoon into a greased 11-in. x 7-in. x 1-1/2-in. baking dish. Bake at 400° for 25 minutes or until potatoes are tender. Arrange tomatoes on top of casserole; sprinkle with Parmesan cheese. If desired, place under broiler until cheese melts, about 2 minutes. **Yield:** 6 servings.

BRUNCH EGGS

Serve this satisfying skillet entree with a fresh fruit compote, hot rolls and coffee to make an easy breakfast or brunch.

    2 medium onions, sliced
    3 tablespoons butter *or* margarine
    3 medium green peppers, thinly sliced
  1/2 cup minced fresh parsley
  1/2 cup water
  1/2 teaspoon salt
  1/4 teaspoon pepper
    3 medium tomatoes, cut into wedges
    6 eggs
  1/2 cup shredded Muenster cheese

In a large skillet, cook onions in butter for 5 minutes. Add green peppers, parsley, water, salt and pepper. Cover and cook, stirring occasionally, about 10 minutes or until liquid evaporates. Add tomato wedges. Make 6 indentations in the vegetable mixture with back of spoon. Break one egg into each indentation. Cover and cook about 4 minutes. Sprinkle with cheese and cook 1-2 minutes longer or until eggs are set. **Yield:** 6 servings.

CHEESY HAM & POTATO FRITTATA

(Pictured below)

A frittata is an Italian-style omelet that usually has the ingredients mixed with the eggs rather than being folded inside as with a French-style omelet. After trying it once, your family will agree that this recipe would be a great Sunday morning tradition.

> 3 tablespoons butter *or* margarine, *divided*
> 1 pound red potatoes, cooked and sliced
> 1-1/2 cups thinly sliced fresh mushrooms
> 1 cup thinly sliced onion
> 1 sweet red pepper, julienned
> 2 cups diced fully cooked ham
> 2 garlic cloves, minced
> 1/4 cup minced fresh parsley *or* basil
> 8 eggs
> Salt and pepper to taste
> 1-1/2 cups (6 ounces) shredded cheddar *or* Swiss cheese

In a large nonstick skillet, melt 2 tablespoons butter over medium-high heat. Brown the potatoes; remove and set aside. In the same skillet, melt the remaining butter; saute the mushrooms, onion, red pepper, ham and garlic over medium-high heat until the vegetables are tender. Add the potatoes and parsley. In a bowl, beat the eggs, salt and pepper. Pour into skillet; cover and cook over medium heat for 10-15 minutes or until eggs are almost set. Sprinkle with cheese. Cover and cook 2 minutes or until eggs are set and cheese is melted. Cut into wedges to serve. **Yield:** 6 servings.

HAM AND CHEESE OMELET ROLL

Smoky ham, gooey cheese and fluffy cooked eggs are encased in homemade yeast dough to create this special loaf. The filling can change with the cook's whim, like the filling of an omelet.

> 7 eggs
> 2 tablespoons butter *or* margarine, *divided*
> 3-1/4 cups all-purpose flour
> 1 tablespoon sugar
> 1 package (1/4 ounce) quick-rise yeast
> 1 teaspoon salt
> 1 cup water
> 2 cups (8 ounces) shredded sharp cheddar cheese, *divided*
> 8 ounces sliced fully cooked ham
> Poppy seeds

In a small bowl, beat 6 eggs. Melt 1 tablespoon butter in a 10-in. nonstick skillet over medium heat; add egg mixture. As eggs set, lift edges, letting uncooked portion flow underneath. When eggs are set, slide omelet onto paper towels; set aside. In a large mixing bowl, combine 2-1/4 cups flour, sugar, yeast and salt. Heat water and remaining butter to 120°-130°. Gradually add to dry ingredients; beat for 2 minutes, scraping bowl occasionally. Stir in enough remaining flour to form a soft dough. Turn onto a floured surface; knead until smooth and elastic, about 6-8 minutes. Cover and let rest 10 minutes. Roll dough to a 12-in. square. Sprinkle 1 cup cheese to within 1/2 in. of edges. Top with ham, omelet and remaining cheese. Roll up, jelly-roll style; pinch seams and ends to seal. Place on a greased baking sheet. Cover and let rise in a warm place until doubled, about 45 minutes. Beat remaining egg; brush over loaf. Sprinkle with seeds. Bake at 400° for 25-30 minutes or until golden brown. Cool on a wire rack for 20 minutes. Serve warm. **Yield:** 1 loaf.

OVERNIGHT FRENCH TOAST

French toast entered American cuisine by way of the Creole cooks in Louisiana. There it was known by its French name, Pain Perdu—meaning lost bread—because it was made from stale bread that otherwise would have gone to waste.

> 5 eggs
> 3/4 cup milk

1/4 teaspoon baking powder
1 tablespoon vanilla extract
1 loaf French bread, cut into 8 thick slices
1 package (16 ounces) frozen unsweetened whole strawberries
4 ripe bananas, sliced
1 cup sugar
1 tablespoon apple pie spice
Cinnamon-sugar

In a bowl, whisk together eggs, milk, baking powder and vanilla. Place bread in shallow dish and pour egg mixture over bread. Cover and refrigerate overnight. Next day, combine strawberries, bananas, sugar and spice. Spoon fruit mixture into a 13-in. x 9-in. x 2-in. baking dish. Place bread in single layer over fruit. Sprinkle with cinnamon-sugar. Bake at 450° for 20-25 minutes. **Yield:** 8 servings.

EGGS ASPARAGUS WITH HOLLANDAISE SAUCE

Hollandaise is a smooth, rich and creamy sauce used to embellish eggs, fish and vegetables. It's usually made in a double boiler to prevent overheating and curdling, but this recipe from 1981 features microwave preparation.

6 egg yolks
4 tablespoons lemon juice
1/2 teaspoon salt
1/4 teaspoon paprika
Dash cayenne pepper
1 cup butter *or* margarine
2 English muffins, split and toasted
1 can (15 ounces) asparagus spears, undrained
4 eggs

In a 4-cup liquid measure, combine egg yolks, lemon juice, salt, paprika and cayenne. Microwave butter on high about 1 minute, just until melted. Allow to cool slightly. Stir yolks vigorously while adding butter in a very thin stream. Microwave on high 45 seconds to 1 minute, stirring vigorously every 15 seconds; set aside. Arrange muffins on serving plates. Heat asparagus spears; drain. Arrange asparagus on muffin halves. Meanwhile, poach eggs. Place one poached egg on each muffin half. Pour sauce over entire sandwich. **Yield:** 4 servings.

QUICK BRUNCH PIZZA

(Pictured above right)

If your family loves pizza, this breakfast variation is one you'll enjoy often. Flavorful ingredients comple-

ment the tender crust. The recipe also makes an excellent appetizer—just cut into smaller slices.

1-1/2 cups biscuit/baking mix
1/3 cup hot water
3 eggs, beaten
1 cup sour cream
1 cup (4 ounces) shredded cheddar cheese
1/2 teaspoon onion salt
4 green onions, sliced
1 cup cubed fully cooked ham

In a bowl, stir biscuit mix and water until soft dough forms. With hands dipped in biscuit mix, press dough on bottom and up sides of a greased 12-in. pizza pan. Bake at 425° for 10 minutes. Stir together eggs, sour cream, cheese, onion salt and green onions; pour over crust. Sprinkle ham over egg mixture. Bake at 350° for 25 minutes or until set. Cool 5 minutes. **Yield:** 6-8 servings.

OPEN-FACE OMELET O'BRIEN

(Pictured above)

Ideal for Sunday brunch, this open-face omelet is an "eggs-cellent" way to start the day.

> 6 tablespoons butter *or* margarine, **divided**
> 3 cups frozen potatoes O'Brien
> 3/4 teaspoon celery salt
> 6 eggs
> 1/4 cup milk
> 1/2 teaspoon salt
Pepper to taste
> 1/2 cup shredded cheddar cheese
> 1/4 cup sliced green onions
Bacon bits

In a 10-in. nonstick skillet over medium heat, melt 3 tablespoons butter. Add potatoes and sprinkle with celery salt. Cook, turning frequently, for about 10 minutes or until potatoes are tender and lightly browned. Remove from skillet and keep warm. In the same skillet, melt remaining butter. In a bowl, beat eggs, milk, salt and pepper; add to the skillet and cook over medium heat. As the eggs set, lift edges, letting uncooked portion flow underneath. When eggs are set, spoon the hot potatoes on top. Garnish with cheese, green onions and bacon bits. Cut into wedges. **Yield:** 4-6 servings.

BAKED EGGS WITH RICE AND CHEESE SAUCE

Weekend houseguests will enjoy waking up to the tempting aroma of this savory breakfast casserole. The addition of cooked rice provides a unique twist.

> 1/2 cup finely chopped green pepper
> 1 cup sliced fresh mushrooms *or*
> 1 can (4 ounces) sliced mushrooms, drained
> 1/4 cup plus 2 tablespoons butter *or* margarine, **divided**
> 3 tablespoons all-purpose flour
> 1 teaspoon salt
> 1/8 teaspoon pepper
> 2 cups milk
> 1 cup (4 ounces) shredded cheddar cheese
> 1 tablespoon chopped chives
> 3 cups cooked rice
> 8 eggs
> 1 cup crushed saltines (about 30 crackers)

In a skillet, cook green pepper and mushrooms in 1/4 cup butter until tender; blend in flour, salt and pepper. Cook, stirring until mixture is bubbly. Add milk; bring to a boil, stirring constantly. Cook until mixture is smooth and thickened. Remove from heat; stir in cheese and chives. Combine 2 cups sauce with cooked rice. Spread rice mixture evenly in a greased 13-in. x 9-in. x 2-in. baking dish. Make 8 indentations in the mixture with the back of a spoon. Break one egg into each indentation. Pour remaining sauce over mixture. Melt remaining butter; combine with crushed saltines. Sprinkle over rice mixture. Bake at 350° for 25-30 minutes or until eggs are cooked to desired doneness. **Yield:** 6-8 servings.

BRUNCH BAKE FLORENTINE

When you see the word "Florentine" in the name of a dish, expect a food made with spinach, often teamed with cheese. This egg casserole provides those classic flavors accented with savory sausage and herbs.

> 1 pound bulk pork sausage
> 1 jar (4 ounces) diced pimientos, drained, **divided**
> 1 package (10 ounces) frozen chopped spinach, thawed, drained
> 1 cup all-purpose flour
> 1/4 cup grated Parmesan cheese
> 1 tablespoon dried minced onion
> 1-1/2 teaspoons Italian seasoning
> 1/2 teaspoon seasoned salt
> 8 eggs
> 2 cups milk
> 1 cup (4 ounces) shredded provolone, mozzarella *or* cheddar cheese

In a skillet, brown sausage; drain. Place in a greased 13-in. x 9-in. x 2-in. baking pan. Top with spinach and half of pimientos. Combine flour, Parmesan cheese and seasonings. In a bowl, beat eggs and milk. Add flour mixture; beat well. Pour over spinach layer. Bake at 425° for 20-25 minutes or until set. Top with remaining pimientos and cheese. Bake for 2-3 minutes or until cheese melts. **Yield:** 10 servings.

BAKED APPLE FRENCH TOAST

(Pictured below)

Sleepyheads in your family will rise and shine when the aroma of this sweet and scrumptious breakfast fills the house. Folks will find this French toast irresistible, so be sure to make plenty. The recipe can easily be doubled.

**1 can (21 ounces) apple *or* blueberry pie
   filling**

3 eggs
1 cup milk
1 teaspoon vanilla extract
**10 slices day-old French bread *or* 8 slices
   day-old cinnamon-raisin bread
   (1/2 inch thick)**
2 tablespoons butter *or* margarine, melted
1 tablespoon sugar
1/8 teaspoon ground cinnamon

Spoon pie filling into a greased 13-in. x 9-in. x 2-in. baking dish. In a bowl, beat eggs, milk and vanilla. Dip bread slices in egg mixture for 1 minute. Arrange 2 rows of bread on top of pie filling, over-lapping slices slightly. Brush bread with melted butter. Sprinkle with sugar and cinnamon. Bake, uncovered, at 350° for 30-35 minutes or until lightly browned. Serve fruit side up. **Yield:** 4-6 servings.

HAM AND CHEESE BRUNCH CASSEROLE

(*Pictured below*)

This tempting strata can be put together the night before guests come to brunch, then baked while the rest of the menu is prepared.

 1 loaf (8 ounces) French *or* Italian bread,
   cut into 3/4-inch cubes
 8 ounces fully cooked ham, cut into
   1/2-inch cubes
1-1/2 cups small broccoli florets
 2 cups (8 ounces) shredded cheddar cheese
 6 eggs
 2 tablespoons Dijon mustard
2-1/2 cups milk
 2 tablespoons butter *or* margarine, melted

Layer half the bread, half the ham, all of the broccoli and half the cheese in a greased 13-in. x 9-in. x 2-in. baking dish. Repeat layers with remaining bread, ham and cheese, pressing lightly. (Dish will be very full.) In a large bowl, combine eggs and mustard. Stir in milk and butter; mix well. Pour evenly over cheese mixture. Let stand 15 minutes or cover and refrigerate up to 24 hours. Remove from the refrigerator 30 minutes before baking. Bake at 350° for 45-50 minutes or until golden brown and set. **Yield:** 8 servings.

QUICHE LORRAINE

Quiche originated in France in the region of Alsace-Lorraine. It's simply a pastry shell filled with a savory custard and other ingredients such as ham, cheese, onions and herbs. This version is the most notable of these savory pies, featuring bits of bacon and Swiss cheese.

 1 pastry shell (9 inches)
 8 bacon strips, cut into 1/2-inch pieces
 1/4 cup chopped green onions
 2 cups (8 ounces) shredded Swiss cheese,
   divided
 6 eggs
 1 cup whipping cream
 1/2 teaspoon salt
Dash of red pepper
Dash of white pepper
 1/8 teaspoon ground nutmeg
Additional ground nutmeg

Bake pastry shell at 400° for 3 minutes; remove from oven and gently prick with a fork. Bake an additional 5 minutes. Meanwhile, cook bacon and onions in a skillet until browned; drain well and sprinkle evenly in pastry shell. Top with 1 cup cheese; set aside. In a bowl, combine eggs, cream, salt, pepper and nutmeg; beat well. Pour mixture into pastry shell; top with remaining cheese. Sprinkle with additional nutmeg. Bake at 350° for 35 minutes or until set. Let stand 10 minutes. **Yield:** 6-8 servings.

BAKED PEACH PANCAKE

This dish makes for a dramatic presentation. Take it right from the oven to the table, fill it with peaches and serve it with bacon or ham.

 2 cups fresh *or* frozen sliced peeled peaches
 4 teaspoons sugar
 1 teaspoon lemon juice
 3 eggs
 1/2 cup all-purpose flour
 1/2 cup milk
 1/2 teaspoon salt
 2 tablespoons butter *or* margarine
Ground nutmeg

In a bowl, combine peaches, sugar and lemon juice; set aside. In a mixing bowl, beat eggs until fluffy. Add

flour, milk and salt; beat until smooth. Place butter in a 10-in. oven-proof skillet; bake at 400° for 3-5 minutes or until melted. Immediately pour batter into hot skillet. Bake for 20-25 minutes or until pancake has risen and is puffed all over. Fill with peach slices and sprinkle with nutmeg. Serve immediately. **Yield:** 4-6 servings.

BAKED FRENCH TOAST

Tempt your taste buds with this fruity baked version of French toast. The luscious escalloped apples add a special flair and will have folks asking for seconds.

   1 package (12 ounces) **frozen escalloped apples,** thawed
   1/3 cup packed **dark brown sugar**
   2 tablespoons **butter** *or* **margarine,** melted
   3 **eggs**
   1 cup **milk**
   1/2 teaspoon **vanilla extract**
   6 to 8 slices **bread** (1 inch thick)

In a 13-in. x 9-in. x 2-in. baking pan, combine apples, brown sugar and butter; mix well. In a medium bowl, whisk together eggs, milk and vanilla. Dip bread into egg mixture; arrange in a single layer on top of apples. Bake at 350° for 35-40 minutes or until bread is firm in center. **Yield:** 4 servings.

or until a knife inserted near the center comes out clean. Allow to stand for 10 minutes before cutting. **Yield:** 6 servings.

HASH BROWN QUICHE

(Pictured above right)

Ham, cheddar cheese and pungent peppers are nestled in a unique hash brown crust to create this morning-meal pleaser. Add some chopped onion or your favorite herb for a bolder flavor.

   3 cups **frozen shredded hash brown potatoes**
   1/3 cup **butter** *or* **margarine,** melted
   1 cup **diced fully cooked ham**
   1 cup (4 ounces) **shredded cheddar cheese**
   1/4 cup **diced green pepper**
   2 **eggs**
   1/2 cup **milk**
   1/2 teaspoon **salt**
   1/4 teaspoon **pepper**

Press hash browns between paper towels to remove excess moisture. Press into the bottom and up the sides of an ungreased 9-in. pie plate. Drizzle with butter. Bake at 425° for 25 minutes. Combine ham, cheese and green pepper; spoon over crust. In a small bowl, beat eggs, milk, salt and pepper. Pour over all. Reduce heat to 350°; bake for 25-30 minutes

BUTTERMILK PECAN WAFFLES

The honeycombed surface of these light nutty waffles is ideal for holding pockets of sweet maple syrup. Waffles are popular not only for breakfast but for dessert as well. These are terrific heaped with fresh strawberries and whipped cream.

   2 cups **all-purpose flour**
   1 tablespoon **baking powder**
   1 teaspoon **baking soda**
   1/2 teaspoon **salt**
   4 **eggs**
   2 cups **buttermilk**
   1/2 cup **butter** *or* **margarine,** melted
   3 tablespoons **chopped pecans**

Combine flour, baking powder, baking soda and salt; set aside. In a mixing bowl, beat eggs until light. Add buttermilk; mix well. Add dry ingredients and beat until batter is smooth. Stir in butter. Pour about 3/4 cup batter onto a lightly greased preheated waffle iron. Sprinkle with a few pecans. Bake according to manufacturer's directions until golden brown. Repeat until batter and pecans are gone. **Yield:** 7 waffles (about 8 inches each).

Chapter 5

SOUPS & SANDWICHES

Nothing beats the classic combination of soup and a sandwich. Here are some savory options you'll find especially enjoyable. Just mix and match to suit your taste.

TOMATO CHICKEN GUMBO

(Pictured at left)

Chock-full of chicken and vegetables, this hearty gumbo is warm and satisfying for lunch or dinner. Why not warm up on a cold day with a bowlful of this robust recipe?

> 6 boneless skinless chicken thighs
> 1 can (14 ounces) chicken broth
> 3 cups water
> 1/2 pound fully cooked smoked sausage links *or* smoked kielbasa, cut into 1/2-inch slices
> 1/2 cup uncooked long grain rice
> 2 cans (8 ounces *each*) tomato sauce
> 1 can (14-1/2 ounces) diced tomatoes with garlic and onion, undrained
> 1 can (11 ounces) whole kernel corn, drained
> 1 medium green pepper, diced

In a shallow baking pan, place chicken. Bake at 400° for 20 minutes; cool slightly. Cut chicken into cubes. In a 6-qt. kettle, bring broth and water to a boil. Add chicken, sausage and rice. Cover; cook over medium heat for 15 minutes. Stir in remaining ingredients; bring to a boil. Cover; cook 5 minutes longer or until rice is tender. **Yield:** 8 servings.

CREAMY FRANKFURTER CORN SOUP

Among the many aliases for frankfurters are hot dogs, wieners and tube steaks. Whatever you call them, the term refers to one of America's favorite sandwiches. This comforting soup that we featured in 1984 blends the flavors of hot dogs and corn in a creamy broth.

> 4 hot dogs, cut into 1/4-inch slices
> 2 tablespoons butter *or* margarine
> 1/4 cup all-purpose flour
> 1 tablespoon dried minced onion
> 2 cups water
> 1 can (11 ounces) Mexicorn, drained
> 1 cup evaporated milk

Saltine crackers

In a skillet, saute hot dogs in butter; stir in flour and onion. Gradually add water, stirring constantly; add corn. Bring to a boil; reduce heat and simmer 15 minutes, stirring occasionally. Stir in evaporated milk. Heat through. Serve with crackers. **Yield:** 4 servings.

HEARTY CHICKEN TORTILLA SOUP

When company comes to visit, this recipe comes in handy since it's so colorful and satisfying. Its zippy flavor gives it Southwestern flair that appeals to all.

>   1 pound boneless skinless chicken breasts, cut up
>   2 cans (14 ounces *each*) chicken broth
>   1/2 cup uncooked long grain rice
>   1 teaspoon ground cumin
>   4 corn tortillas
>   1 can (11 ounces) Mexicorn
>   1 cup chunky salsa
>   1 tablespoon chopped fresh cilantro *or* parsley
>   2 tablespoons lime juice

Spray saucepan with nonstick cooking spray and heat for 1 minute. Add chicken and cook until browned, stirring often. Add broth, rice and cumin. Bring to a boil. Cover and cook over low heat for 20 minutes. Meanwhile, cut tortillas into thin strips and place on a baking sheet. Spray with nonstick cooking spray. Bake at 425° for 10 minutes or until golden. Add corn, salsa, cilantro and lime juice to saucepan and heat through. Garnish with tortilla strips. **Yield:** 6 servings.

BREAKFAST WAFFLE CLUB SANDWICHES

(Pictured above)

Rise and shine to the satisfying flavor this dish offers. Sauteed apples glazed with honey make the topping something special.

>   2 tablespoons butter *or* margarine
>   3/4 cup honey, *divided*
>   2 medium red apples, cored and sliced
>   1/4 cup apple juice
>   8 frozen waffles, toasted
>   8 thin slices deli ham

In a large nonstick skillet, melt butter over medium-high heat; stir in 1/4 cup honey. Add apple slices; cook and stir 4-6 minutes or until apples are lightly browned and crisp-tender. Set aside. In a small saucepan, combine apple juice and remaining honey. Cook over medium heat until heated through. Set aside and keep warm. For each serving, arrange 2 waffles on a serving plate. Place one ham slice on each waffle. Top with one-fourth of apple mixture; drizzle with one-fourth of syrup. **Yield:** 4 servings.

SMOKY PESTO RED-PEPPER CHICKEN POCKETS

Every delicious bite of these pockets is filled with tender chicken breast, roasted red pepper, ripe olives and smoky provolone cheese smothered in a basil-flavored dressing.

>   1 package (about 1 pound) chicken breast tenderloins
>   1 cup water *or* chicken broth
>   1/2 cup sliced green onions
>   1 jar (7 ounces) roasted red peppers, drained and chopped
>   1 can (2-1/4 ounces) sliced ripe olives, drained
>   1 cup diced smoky Provolone cheese
>   1/2 cup prepared pesto sauce
>   1/4 cup mayonnaise
>   2 teaspoons lemon juice
>   4 pita breads (6 inches), halved

In a large skillet, combine chicken and water; bring to a boil. Reduce heat; cover and simmer 5-10 minutes or until internal juices of chicken run clear. Remove chicken; cool slightly and dice. In a medium bowl, combine chicken, green onions, roasted pepper, olives and cheese; mix well. In a small bowl, combine pesto, mayonnaise and lemon juice; mix well. Add pesto mixture to chicken mixture; toss to mix. Spoon mixture evenly into pita halves. Place sandwiches on baking sheet. Bake at 350° for 7-10 minutes or until heated through. **Yield:** 4 servings.

MEDITERRANEAN ONION SOUP

When an extra-special presentation is important, turn to this unique recipe. Not only will you enjoy a steaming bowlful of savory soup...you can eat the container, too! Each portion is served in an edible bowl, shaped from an extra-large onion.

>   6 cups thinly sliced yellow onions (about 3 pounds)
>   2 tablespoons slivered garlic
>   3 tablespoons olive *or* vegetable oil
> 1-1/2 quarts beef broth
>   1 cup red wine *or* additional beef broth
>   1 teaspoon pepper
>   6 extra-large yellow onions
>   1/2 baguette French bread, sliced, toasted
>   6 slices Gruyere *or* Swiss cheese

In a large skillet or kettle, saute sliced onions and garlic in oil until soft and tender. Cover and cook over low heat for 15 minutes. Add broth, wine and pepper; simmer for 30 minutes. Cut off tops and peel off outside skin of extra-large onions. Trim root area, but leave bottoms intact. Place in microwave-safe dish and cover with plastic wrap. Microwave on high for 3-4 minutes. Remove from dish and hollow out center, leaving three outer rings and bottom. Chop the removed onions and add to soup mixture. Fill onion bowls with soup; top with a bread and cheese slice. Broil until cheese is melted. **Yield:** 6 servings.

BROCCOLI SOUP

It's hard to believe that creamy broccoli soups did not gain notable popularity until the 1980s. Now, the majority of restaurants offer this modern classic on their menu. Broccoli is an excellent source of vitamins A and C, as well as calcium, iron and riboflavin.

>   4 cups chopped fresh broccoli
>   2 cans (14 ounces *each*) chicken broth
>   3 medium potatoes, peeled and cut into 1/4-inch slices
>   1 medium onion, sliced
>   1 garlic clove, minced
>   1/8 teaspoon pepper
>   1 cup milk, *divided*
>   2 tablespoons grated Parmesan cheese

In a saucepan, combine the broccoli, broth, potatoes, onion, garlic and pepper. Bring to a boil. Cover and cook over low heat 15 minutes or until the vegetables are tender. Remove from heat. Place half the broth mixture and 1/2 cup milk in a blender or food processor. Cover and process until smooth. Repeat with the remaining broth mixture and remaining milk. Return to pan. Stir in cheese. Heat through. **Yield:** 7 servings.

HEARTY LASAGNA SOUP

(Pictured below)

Nothing chases away the autumn chill like a steaming bowl of this soup. Toasted garlic bread makes the perfect accompaniment should you serve this favorite to lunch guests.

>   1 pound ground beef
>   1/4 teaspoon garlic powder
>   2 cans (14 ounces *each*) seasoned beef broth with onion
>   1 can (14-1/2 ounces) diced tomatoes
>   1/4 teaspoon Italian seasoning
> 1-1/2 cups uncooked mafalda *or* spiral pasta
>   1/4 cup grated Parmesan cheese
> **Additional grated Parmesan cheese, optional**

In a large skillet, cook beef with garlic powder until browned; drain. Add broth, tomatoes and Italian seasoning. Bring to a boil. Stir in pasta. Cook over medium heat for 10 minutes or until pasta is tender. Stir in 1/4 cup cheese. Serve with additional cheese if desired. **Yield:** 4 servings.

DILLED SALMON PITA POCKETS

(Pictured below)

These pita pockets are perfect to pack in your kids' lunch boxes when they can't face another plain sandwich. Or for a refreshing change of pace, serve the salmon salad in cucumber boats. Either way, it's a real treat.

    1 medium cucumber, seeded and chopped
  1/2 cup chopped green *or* sweet red pepper
  1/2 cup chopped red onion
    1 can (14-3/4 ounces) salmon, drained and
      flaked
  2/3 cup plain yogurt
  1/3 cup mayonnaise
    1 tablespoon lemon juice
    2 tablespoons minced fresh parsley *or* 2
      teaspoons dried parsley flakes
    1 teaspoon dill weed
  1/2 teaspoon ground coriander
    3 to 4 pita breads, halved *or* 8 cucumber
      boats
Lettuce leaves, optional

In a mixing bowl, combine cucumber, pepper, onion and salmon. In a separate bowl, blend yogurt, mayonnaise, lemon juice, parsley, dill weed and coriander. Stir dressing into salmon mixture. Serve in pita pockets with lettuce if desired or in cucumber boats. **Yield:** 4 servings.

CHEESY TORTILLA SOUP

This creamy combination really hits the spot whenever you crave a rich flavorful soup. Folks will think you had this dish simmering all day. But convenient canned broth makes it a meal in minutes.

    6 corn tortillas (6 inches)
    1 cup vegetable oil
  1/2 cup chopped onion
    2 garlic cloves, minced
    1 can (14-1/2 ounces) diced tomatoes,
      undrained
    1 pound Mexican process cheese, cubed
    1 can (14 ounces) chicken broth
    1 tablespoon dried cilantro *or* parsley flakes

Cut tortillas in half; slice into 1/4-in. strips. In a 10-in. skillet, cook tortillas in hot oil until crisp but not brown. Remove with slotted spoon; drain on paper towels. Reserve 2 tablespoons oil and place in Dutch oven. Saute onions and garlic in reserved oil until onions are tender. Reduce heat to low. Add tomatoes, cheese, broth and cilantro. Stir until cheese is melted. Divide tortillas among five soup bowls; top with soup. **Yield:** 5 servings.

QUICK FISHERMAN'S CHOWDER

You'll especially enjoy this rich chowder. It's a hearty dish with big chunks of seafood and potatoes in a tempting broth.

    1 can (14-1/2 ounces) diced tomatoes with
      garlic and onion, undrained
    1 can (15 ounces) tomato sauce
    1 can (14 ounces) chicken broth
    1 can (14 ounces) whole new potatoes,
      drained and cubed
    1 celery rib, sliced
    1 pound seafood (halibut *or* red snapper, cut
      in cubes, *or* shelled shrimp *or* scallops)
Chopped fresh parsley, optional

In a large saucepan, combine tomatoes, tomato sauce and broth. Add potatoes and celery to saucepan. Simmer 3 minutes. Stir in seafood; cook

3-5 minutes or until seafood is just cooked. Top with parsley if desired. **Yield:** 4-6 servings.

BUTTERNUT SQUASH SOUP

The sweet orange flesh of a butternut squash is delightful baked, steamed or simmered. Its flavor is associated with autumn. That's why this soup is a perfect starter for all your family's fall feasts.

> 1 medium onion, chopped
> 2 garlic cloves, minced
> 2 tablespoons butter *or* margarine
> 3 medium carrots, diced
> 2 celery ribs, diced
> 1 medium potato, peeled and diced
> 1 butternut squash, peeled, seeded and diced
> 3 cans (14 ounces *each*) chicken broth
> 1/2 cup honey
> 1/2 teaspoon dried thyme
> Salt and pepper to taste

In a large saucepan or Dutch oven, cook onions and garlic in butter until lightly browned, about 5 minutes. Stir in carrots and celery. Cook and stir until tender, about 5 minutes. Stir in potato, squash, broth, honey and thyme. Bring to a boil; reduce heat and simmer 30-45 minutes or until vegetables are tender. Remove from heat and cool slightly. Working in small batches, transfer mixture to blender or food processor; process until smooth. Return pureed soup to saucepan. Season with salt and pepper. Heat through. **Yield:** 6 servings.

FRENCH ONION SOUP

The onion bulb is prized around the world for the magic it makes in a multitude of dishes. This recipe, which has become an American classic, is traditionally topped with toasted bread or croutons and bubbly melted Swiss cheese.

> 4 cups sliced onions
> 1/4 cup butter *or* margarine
> 3 cans (10-1/2 ounces *each*) condensed beef broth, undiluted
> 3 cups water
> 1/8 teaspoon pepper
> 1 teaspoon Worcestershire sauce
> 6 slices French bread, toasted
> 3 cups (12 ounces) shredded Swiss cheese

In a 4-qt. saucepan over medium-high heat, cook onions in butter until tender. Stir in broth, water,

pepper and Worcestershire. Bring to a boil over high heat. Reduce heat to low. Cover; simmer 30 minutes. Ladle soup into six 12-ounce ovenproof bowls; place 1 slice toasted bread on surface of soup in each bowl. Sprinkle 1/2 cup cheese onto each toasted bread slice in soup. Bake at 425° for 10 minutes or just until cheese is melted. **Yield:** 6 servings.

ZESTY JAMAICAN JOE

(Pictured above)

One of the best sandwiches you'll ever taste is this exciting combination that can be cooked up in a matter of minutes.

> 1/2 pound ground beef
> 1 small onion, chopped
> 2 garlic cloves, minced
> 1/8 to 1/4 teaspoon cayenne pepper
> Salt and pepper to taste
> 1 can (14-1/2 ounces) zesty diced tomatoes with jalapeno peppers, undrained
> 1 can (15 ounces) black *or* pinto beans, rinsed and drained
> 1/2 cup diced green pepper
> 3 whole wheat hamburger buns, split

In a skillet, cook beef, onion, garlic and cayenne until beef is no longer pink; drain. Season with salt and pepper. Stir in tomatoes and beans. Cover and cook over medium-low heat for 5 minutes. Stir in green pepper. Cook, uncovered, over medium-high heat for 5 minutes or until thickened, stirring occasionally. Lightly toast buns just before serving. Spoon about 1/2 cup meat mixture over each half bun. Serve open-faced. **Yield:** 3 servings.

SAVORY VEGETABLE RIBOLITTA

(Pictured below)

This Tuscan-style bean and cabbage soup is traditionally thickened with bread such as toasted croutons or crostini, the Italian word for toast. Family and friends are sure to love this delightful hearty soup.

1 cup chopped onion
2/3 cup chopped celery
2/3 cup sliced carrot
2 garlic cloves, finely chopped
2 tablespoons olive *or* vegetable oil
2 cans (19 ounces *each*) white kidney beans, rinsed and drained
1 carton (32 ounces) chicken broth
2 cans (14-1/2 ounces *each*) diced Italian-style tomatoes, undrained
4 cups chopped Savoy cabbage
1/2 cup *each* diced sweet red pepper and zucchini
1/2 teaspoon dried thyme
Toasted croutons *or* crostini*
Shredded Parmesan cheese

In a large saucepan over low heat, cook onion, celery, carrot and garlic in oil until tender, about 5 minutes. Add the beans, chicken broth, tomatoes, cabbage, red pepper, zucchini and thyme. Cook, uncovered, until vegetables are tender and flavors are blended, about 20 minutes. To serve, place croutons or crostini in each soup bowl and ladle soup into the bowl. Sprinkle with cheese. **Yield:** 8 servings. ***Editor's Note:** To prepare crostini, combine 1/2 cup olive oil, 2 cloves minced garlic, 1 teaspoon Italian herb seasoning and a pinch of salt. Cut one loaf of Italian bread into 1-in. slices. Brush oil mixture on one side of bread. Place on baking sheet, coated side up. Bake at 375° for 15 minutes or until lightly toasted.

CHICKEN RAVIOLI SOUPER SUPPER

As the days get shorter and the winds grow colder, enjoy the hearty goodness of this satisfying supper. Ready to serve in just minutes, this "souper" variation of classic ravioli will warm up your clan in no time. Convenient frozen ravioli is the key to this recipe's success.

- 2 **boneless skinless chicken breast halves, cut into bite-size pieces**
- 1 **tablespoon olive *or* vegetable oil**
- 2 **cans (10-1/2 ounces *each*) condensed chicken broth, undiluted**
- 2 **cans (14-1/2 ounces *each*) diced tomatoes with garlic and onion, undrained**
- 2 **small zucchini, diced**
- 1 **package (25 ounces) frozen cheese ravioli**
- 2 **teaspoons dried parsley flakes**

Grated Parmesan cheese

In a Dutch oven, saute chicken in oil for 2 minutes, stirring constantly. Add chicken broth, tomatoes and zucchini; cover and bring to boil. Add frozen ravioli; simmer, uncovered, about 7 minutes or until ravioli reaches desired doneness. Stir in parsley. To serve, ladle into soup bowls; sprinkle with Parmesan cheese. **Yield:** 6 servings.

ETRUSCAN PEASANT SOUP

You'll get rave reviews for this hearty soup that offers a true taste of Italy. Especially delicious, this combination of meat and vegetables is a real crowd-pleaser.

- 1 **pound sweet Italian sausage links, cut into 1/2-inch pieces**
- 1/2 **pound boneless skinless chicken breasts, cut into 1/2-inch pieces**
- 3/4 **cup chopped onion**
- 2 **garlic cloves, minced**
- 1 **tablespoon olive *or* vegetable oil**
- 2 **cups coarsely chopped spinach leaves**
- 1 **can (15 ounces) white kidney beans, rinsed and drained**
- 1 **can (14-1/2 ounces) diced tomatoes with basil, garlic and oregano, undrained**
- 1 **can (14 ounces) chicken broth**
- 1/2 **teaspoon crushed red pepper flakes, optional**
- 2 **tablespoons grated Parmesan cheese**

In a large saucepan or Dutch oven over medium heat, cook sausage, chicken, onion and garlic in oil until sausage is no longer pink. Add spinach, beans, tomatoes, broth and crushed red pepper flakes if desired; bring to a boil. Reduce heat; simmer 20 minutes to blend flavors. Sprinkle individual servings with cheese. **Yield:** 6 servings.

HUEVOS CALIFORNIA WRAPS

(Pictured above)

Wrap sandwiches exploded onto the restaurant scene in the 1990s. Now that fresh tortillas are readily available in supermarkets coast to coast, sandwich wraps are quick and easy to prepare at home as well.

- 2 **tablespoons butter *or* margarine**
- 2 **cups frozen potatoes O'Brien**
- 3/4 **teaspoon chili powder**
- 3/4 **teaspoon salt**
- 4 **eggs, lightly beaten**
- 1/4 **cup salsa *or* taco sauce**
- 1/4 **cup sliced green onions**
- 4 **flour tortillas (8 inches), warmed**

Sour cream, optional

In a large nonstick skillet over medium heat, melt butter. Add potatoes, chili powder and salt; cook until potatoes are tender, about 8 minutes, stirring occasionally. Combine eggs, salsa and onions; add to skillet and cook until eggs are set, stirring occasionally. Spoon egg mixture down center of tortillas. Top with sour cream if desired; roll up. **Yield:** 2 servings.

Chapter 6
CHICKEN & TURKEY

These palate-pleasing poultry recipes feature casseroles, oven entrees, skillet suppers, grilled favorites and more. You and your family are sure to enjoy these enticing entrees.

Recipes in this chapter provided courtesy of these past sponsors...

Almaden	Ore-Ida
Baker's	ReaLemon
Birds Eye	Reynolds
Blue Bonnet	San Giorgio
Campbell's	Sargento
Del Monte	Schilling
Hormel	Stouffer's
Kraft	Sunbeam
Lipton	Swanson
McCormick	Tyson
Nabisco	Wearever

CHEESY CHICKEN FLORENTINE

(Pictured at left)

This easy-yet-elegant recipe combines frozen spinach souffle, cooked rice and seasonings with tender, juicy chicken breasts. It's the perfect entree for evening entertaining or everyday dinners.

- 2 packages (12 ounces *each*) frozen spinach souffle
- 2 cups cooked white rice
- 1 cup milk
- 1 cup (4 ounces) shredded Swiss cheese, *divided*
- 1/4 cup chopped onion
- 2 teaspoons Dijon mustard
- 1/2 teaspoon salt
- 6 boneless skinless chicken breast halves
- 2 tablespoons vegetable oil
- 1 cup fresh bread crumbs
- 2 tablespoons butter *or* margarine, melted

Defrost spinach souffle in microwave on 50% power for 6-7 minutes. In a large bowl, combine spinach souffle, rice, milk, 1/2 cup cheese, onion, mustard and salt; stir well. Transfer to a 13-in. x 9-in. x 2-in. baking dish. Cover and bake at 375° for 25 minutes. Meanwhile, in a large nonstick skillet, saute chicken in oil until both sides are golden brown. Arrange chicken on top of spinach mixture. In a small bowl, combine bread crumbs, butter and remaining cheese; sprinkle over chicken. Bake, uncovered, 25 minutes longer or until spinach mixture is set and chicken juices run clear. **Yield:** 6 servings.

CALIFORNIA CHICKEN

The word "California" is often used to describe recipes that are light and healthy. This simple dish also adds a splash of citrus sunshine. It's terrific cooked on the grill, too!

- 2 tablespoons lemon juice
- 1 tablespoon olive *or* vegetable oil
- 1 tablespoon water
- 2 teaspoons garlic pepper
- 1/2 teaspoon dried basil
- 1/2 teaspoon onion powder
- 1 pound boneless skinless chicken breasts

In a small bowl, combine lemon juice, oil, water, garlic pepper, basil and onion powder. Brush over both sides of chicken. Saute chicken in nonstick skillet until browned and juices run clear. **Yield:** 4 servings.

APPLE CHEDDAR CHICKEN

(Pictured below)

If you're always on the lookout for scrumptious new chicken recipes, you're sure to enjoy this one. Tender chicken breasts are stuffed with cheddar cheese, coated with ground walnuts, then sauteed until golden brown. The savory apple salsa adds a nice crunch.

> 4 boneless skinless chicken breast halves
> 1/4 cup shredded sharp cheddar cheese
> 1/2 teaspoon salt
> 1/4 teaspoon pepper
> 1/2 cup ground walnuts
> 2 tablespoons olive *or* vegetable oil
> 1 cup cinnamon applesauce
> 1/2 cup chopped sweet red pepper
> 2 tablespoons diced green onion
> 1 large tart green apple, cored and diced
> Red *or* green apple slices, optional

Cut a slit in the side of each breast to form a pocket. Stuff each pocket with 1 tablespoon cheese; press to close. Combine salt, pepper and walnuts; coat each breast with mixture. Heat oil in a heavy skillet. Cook chicken for 4-5 minutes per side or until internal juices run clear. Remove to platter; cover and keep warm. In a small saucepan over medium heat, combine applesauce, red pepper and green onion; heat through. Stir in diced apple. Spoon apple mixture over chicken. Garnish with apple slices if desired. **Yield:** 4 servings.

BLACK FOREST CHICKEN AND CABBAGE SKILLET

Potatoes and cabbage have provided nourishment to Germans for generations. Aromatic caraway seeds are also widely used in German cooking, offering a nutty delicate anise flavor.

> 1 pound boneless skinless chicken breast halves *or* thighs
> 1 teaspoon seasoned salt
> 1 small onion, chopped
> 3 medium potatoes, cut into 1/2-inch cubes (about 3-1/2 cups)
> 3 cups coleslaw mix
> 1 teaspoon caraway seeds

Sprinkle chicken with seasoned salt. Spray a 12-in. nonstick skillet with nonstick cooking spray. Heat over medium-high heat. Add chicken. Cover and cook 5 minutes or until lightly browned, turning once. Remove from skillet; set aside. Add onion, potatoes, coleslaw mix and caraway seeds to skillet; mix well, then top with chicken. Cover and cook 10 minutes or until vegetables are tender and internal juices of chicken run clear, stirring occasionally. **Yield:** 4 servings.

BALSAMIC GLAZED CHICKEN

Italian balsamic vinegar, a 1990s newcomer to American kitchens, is made from white grape juice. It gets its dark color and pungent sweetness from aging in wooden barrels over a period of years.

> 1 tablespoon vegetable oil
> 6 chicken thighs, skin removed
> 6 chicken drumsticks, skin removed

3/4 teaspoon pepper
3 garlic cloves, minced
1-1/2 tablespoons tomato paste
1/2 cup chicken broth
2/3 cup balsamic vinegar
1 tablespoon honey
4 tablespoons thinly sliced green onions

In a large skillet, heat oil over medium-high. Season chicken with pepper and cook about 10 minutes or until lightly browned on all sides. Drain and set chicken aside. Saute garlic in the same skillet over medium heat for 2 minutes. Stir in tomato paste and chicken broth, scraping to dissolve any bits on bottom of pan. Increase heat to medium-high; add vinegar and honey; boil rapidly for 3 minutes to reduce liquid to 1 cup. Return chicken to pan; reduce heat to medium. Cook about 30 minutes or until liquid thickens and chicken is done, turning chicken occasionally. Remove chicken to platter. Pour glaze over chicken and sprinkle with green onion. **Yield:** 4 servings.

GRECIAN CHICKEN

Foods cooked in the Greek style typically feature olive oil and a splash of lemon juice. Imported kalamata olives and tangy feta cheese are two more classic Greek ingredients that add flavor to many cooked dishes.

4 bone-in chicken breast halves
3/4 cup olive oil and vinegar salad dressing,
   divided
1 tablespoon lemon peel
2 medium onions, quartered
1/2 cup sliced zucchini
1/2 cup chopped sweet red pepper
1 can (14-1/2 ounces) diced seasoned
   tomatoes, undrained
Salt and pepper
1 cup pitted kalamata olives
1/4 cup crumbled feta cheese

Place chicken in resealable plastic bag. Pour 1/2 cup salad dressing over chicken; close bag and toss to coat well. Drain chicken and place in greased baking dish; discard leftover marinade. Sprinkle chicken with lemon peel. Cook chicken, uncovered, at 350°

for 50-55 minutes. Meanwhile, in a 2-qt. microwave-safe baking dish, combine remaining dressing, onion, zucchini and pepper. Pour tomatoes over mixture. Cover with plastic wrap; vent. Microwave on high, stirring occasionally, for 6-8 minutes or until vegetables are tender. Add salt and pepper; stir well. Stir in olives. Cover and let stand for 2 minutes. Sprinkle with feta cheese. Serve chicken with tomato mixture. **Yield:** 4 servings.

ASIAN CHICKEN STIR-FRY

(Pictured above)

When there's no time to cook, try this great-tasting recipe guaranteed to get you in and out of the kitchen—fast!

1 pound boneless skinless chicken breasts,
   cut into strips
1 tablespoon vegetable oil
1 can (10-3/4 ounces) condensed golden
   mushroom soup, undiluted
1 to 3 tablespoons soy sauce
1/2 to 1 teaspoon garlic powder
1 package (16 ounces) frozen vegetable
   combination, thawed
4 cups hot cooked rice

In a large skillet over medium-high heat, stir-fry chicken in hot oil until chicken is no longer pink and juices evaporate. Add soup, soy sauce and garlic powder. Bring to a boil. Reduce heat to medium. Add thawed vegetables and cook until vegetables are crisp-tender, stirring often. Serve over rice. **Yield:** 4 servings.

No-Fuss Chicken Dinner

(Pictured above)

You'll appreciate this one-dish dinner that cooks in an oven bag. Just pop it in the oven and relax. Then let the wonderful aroma call your family to the table.

   1 tablespoon all-purpose flour
   1 large size oven bag (14 inches x 20 inches)
   1 can (10-3/4 ounces) condensed cream of
      mushroom soup, undiluted
   1 package (9 ounces) frozen cut green beans,
      thawed
1/2 cup condensed chicken broth, undiluted
1/4 teaspoon pepper
   1 can (2.8 ounces) french-fried onions,
      divided
   6 chicken pieces, skin removed
Seasoned salt and pepper, optional

Shake flour in oven bag; place in 13-in. x 9-in. x 2-in. baking pan. Add soup, beans, chicken broth, pepper and half can of onions to oven bag. Squeeze oven bag to blend in flour. Arrange ingredients in an even layer in oven bag. Sprinkle chicken with seasoned salt and pepper. Place chicken in oven bag on top of soup mixture. Sprinkle remaining onions on top of chicken. Close oven bag with nylon tie; cut six 1/2-in. slits in top. Bake at 350° for 45-50 minutes or until chicken is tender. To serve, stir sauce and spoon over chicken. **Yield:** 4 servings.

Frypan Barbecued Chicken

Traditional barbecue is often associated with outdoor cooking. This indoor version made on the stovetop has a from-scratch barbecue sauce that turns plain chicken into a fabulous feast.

   1 cup all-purpose flour
   1 teaspoon salt
1/2 teaspoon chili powder
1/4 teaspoon pepper
   2 broiler/fryer chickens (3 to 4 pounds
      each), cut up
1/3 cup olive *or* vegetable oil
   1 cup ketchup
1/2 cup packed brown sugar
   1 tablespoon dried minced onion
   2 tablespoons Worcestershire sauce
   2 tablespoons prepared mustard
1/4 cup red wine vinegar *or* cider vinegar
1/4 cup water

In a large resealable plastic bag, combine flour, salt, chili powder and pepper. Add chicken, a few pieces at a time, and shake to coat. In a large skillet, brown chicken in hot oil. Meanwhile, in a saucepan, combine ketchup, sugar, onion, Worcestershire, mustard, vinegar and water. Bring to a boil; reduce heat and simmer 5 minutes. Pour sauce over chicken. Cover and simmer, basting occasionally, for 45 minutes or until juices run clear and chicken is tender. **Yield:** 8-12 servings.

Quick Curried Chicken

Curry is a catch-all term that is used to refer to any number of hot, spicy, gravy-based dishes of East Indian origin. You'll favor this saucy supper that's a welcome contrast from your routine menus.

   2 pounds boneless skinless chicken breasts,
      cut into 1-inch cubes
   2 tablespoons vegetable oil
   1 cup water
   1 envelope golden onion soup mix
   1 tablespoon curry powder
1/4 teaspoon garlic powder
   1 cup (8 ounces) plain yogurt
   2 tablespoons all-purpose flour
   1 green pepper, cut in strips
   1 cup pitted dates, snipped
   1 jar (4 ounces) sliced pimientos, drained
Hot cooked rice
Flaked coconut *or* chopped peanuts

In a large skillet, brown chicken in hot oil over high heat. Stir in water, soup mix, curry powder and garlic powder. Cover and simmer for 10 minutes or until chicken juices run clear. Combine yogurt and flour; stir into chicken. Cook until mixture thickens, about 1-2 minutes. Add green pepper, dates and pimientos; simmer for 2 minutes. Serve over rice; garnish with coconut or peanuts. **Yield:** 6-8 servings.

CHICKEN ATHENA

Artichokes date back to ancient Rome, and they remain popular in Mediterranean cooking. In the United States, almost the entire artichoke crop is grown in California's mid-coastal region.

> 1 pound boneless skinless chicken, cubed
> 1 tablespoon olive *or* vegetable oil
> 1 medium onion, coarsely chopped
> 1 can (14-1/2 ounces) diced tomatoes
> 1 jar (6-1/2 ounces) marinated artichoke
>   hearts, undrained
> 1/4 teaspoon dried rosemary
> 1/3 cup crumbled feta cheese

In a skillet over medium-high heat, brown chicken in oil; add onion and cook 2 minutes. Stir in tomatoes, marinade from artichokes and rosemary. Cook over medium heat 10 minutes or until thickened, stirring frequently. Stir in artichoke hearts; heat through. Top with cheese. **Yield:** 4-6 servings.

ORANGE GINGER CHICKEN

Gingerroot is a plant from tropical climates grown for the flesh of its tan gnarled root. Candied ginger is available in the spice section of your supermarket. It's made by cooking chopped ginger in a sugar syrup, then coating the pieces with coarse sugar.

> 1 broiler/fryer chicken (3 pounds), cut up
> Salt and pepper to taste
> 1/4 cup vegetable oil
> 1/2 cup barbecue sauce
> 2 tablespoons all-purpose flour
> 1 cup orange juice
> 2 tablespoons brown sugar
> 1 tablespoon chopped candied ginger
> Dash of hot pepper sauce
> 1 unpeeled orange, sliced
> Hot cooked rice

Season chicken with salt and pepper. In a large skillet, brown chicken in hot oil; drain. Combine barbecue sauce and flour. Add orange juice, brown sugar, ginger and hot pepper sauce; mix well. Pour over chicken. Cover and simmer 30 minutes. Add or-

ange slices; simmer, uncovered, 10 minutes or until chicken juices run clear. Arrange chicken and orange slices over rice. Serve with sauce. **Yield:** 4 servings.

LEMON-TERIYAKI GLAZED CHICKEN

(Pictured below)

Busy cooks appreciate simple yet satisfying main courses to feed their families when time is short. So you'll likely reach for this recipe often. Skillet-cooking keeps the chicken nice and tender, while a blend of seasonings adds fantastic flavor.

> 1/2 cup lemon juice
> 1/2 cup soy sauce
> 1/4 cup sugar
> 3 tablespoons brown sugar
> 2 tablespoons water
> 1-1/2 tablespoons minced garlic
> 3/4 teaspoon ground ginger
> 8 boneless skinless chicken thighs
> Hot cooked rice

Combine first seven ingredients in a large skillet. Cook over medium heat for 3-4 minutes or until sugar dissolves. Add chicken; cook for 30-35 minutes or until chicken juices run clear, turning chicken occasionally. Serve over rice. **Yield:** 4-6 servings.

LOUISIANA CHICKEN & BEANS SKILLET

(Pictured below)

Ready in just 20 minutes, this zippy Cajun dish is absolutely delicious. Adding a dash of hot pepper sauce lets you turn up the heat to suit your family's taste.

1-1/4 pounds boneless skinless chicken thighs *or* breasts, cut into 1-inch pieces
  2 teaspoons Cajun seasoning
  1 medium onion, halved and sliced
  1 tablespoon vegetable oil
  1 can (16 ounces) red kidney beans, rinsed and drained
  1 can (14-1/2 ounces) stewed tomatoes, undrained
  4 cups hot cooked rice
Hot pepper sauce, optional

Sprinkle chicken with Cajun seasoning. In a large skillet over medium-high heat, cook chicken and onion in oil for 5 minutes, stirring frequently. Add beans and tomatoes. Bring to a boil. Reduce heat; cover and simmer 10 minutes or until flavors are blended and internal juices of chicken run clear.

Serve chicken and beans over rice. Sprinkle with hot pepper sauce if desired. **Yield:** 4 servings.

TASTY TURKEY POTPIE

This comforting favorite features chunks of turkey and mixed vegetables in a rich sauce combined in a casserole dish. It's topped with a pastry crust and baked till golden brown.

1/2 cup mayonnaise *or* salad dressing
  2 tablespoons all-purpose flour
  1 teaspoon chicken *or* beef bouillon granules
3/4 cup milk
  3 cans (6-3/4 ounces *each*) chunk white turkey, breast of chicken *or* ham, drained, flaked
  1 package (10 ounces) frozen mixed vegetables, thawed and drained
  1 sheet refrigerated pie pastry

In a 2-qt. saucepan, combine salad dressing, flour and bouillon granules; gradually add milk. Cook, stirring constantly, over low heat until thickened. Stir in turkey and vegetables; spoon into a 1-1/2-qt. casserole. Place pie crust over casserole, pressing edges to seal. Cut several holes in crust. Bake at 375° for 20-25 minutes or until golden brown. **Yield:** 4-6 servings.

GINGERED PEAR CHICKEN AND WALNUTS

Ideal for elegant special-occasion menus, chicken is also an economical choice for family meals. In this dish, you'll note that luscious ripe pears are an appealing complement to poultry.

  4 bone-in chicken breast halves, skin removed
  3 tablespoons butter *or* margarine
1/4 teaspoon salt
  1 can (15 ounces) pear halves, undrained
3/4 cup ginger ale
1/4 cup packed brown sugar
  3 tablespoons soy sauce
  2 teaspoons cornstarch
1/4 cup water
1/4 teaspoon ground ginger
1/4 cup chopped walnuts

In a large skillet, brown chicken in butter about 10 minutes. Sprinkle with salt. Drain pears into a 2-cup glass measure. Set pears aside. If necessary, add water to pear juice to make 3/4 cup. Add ginger ale, brown sugar and soy sauce to juice. Pour over chicken. Cover and cook over medium heat for 25 minutes or until chicken juices run clear, turning occasionally. Remove chicken from skillet; set aside. Combine cornstarch, water and ginger until smooth. Stir into skillet mixture. Bring to a boil; cook and stir for 2 minutes or until thickened. Return chicken to skillet. Cut each pear half into 2 wedges and place around chicken. Spoon sauce over chicken and pears. Sprinkle with nuts. **Yield:** 4 servings.

South of the Border Turkey

Ready in a jiffy, this flavor-packed recipe provides a delightful opportunity to use leftover cooked turkey.

>   **5 tablespoons butter *or* margarine, *divided***
>   **1 large onion, finely chopped**
>   **1 large green pepper, finely chopped**
>   **1 can (14-1/2 ounces) diced tomatoes, undrained**
>   **2 cups diced cooked turkey**
>   **1/2 cup sliced stuffed olives**
>   **1/2 teaspoon salt**
>   **1 teaspoon chili powder**
> **Dash cayenne pepper**
>   **2 cups crushed saltines (about 60 crackers), *divided***
>   **1/2 cup shredded cheddar cheese**

Place 3 tablespoons butter in a 1-1/2-qt. microwave-safe casserole. Microwave on high for 30 seconds. Add onion and green pepper and microwave 6 minutes, stirring after 3 minutes. Add tomatoes and juice, turkey, olives, salt, chili powder and cayenne pepper. Add 3/4 cup saltines; mix well. Sprinkle with remaining saltines and cheese. Dot with remaining butter. Cover and microwave 8 minutes longer, turning after 2 minutes. **Yield:** 6 servings.

Easy Chicken and Pasta

(Pictured above right)

Since this dish combines chicken and pasta, even children love it! The colorful vegetable combination adds a crisp-tender crunch, and the creamy mushroom sauce can't be beat. It's perfect for a quick weeknight meal.

>   **1 pound boneless skinless chicken breasts, cubed**
>   **1 tablespoon vegetable oil**
>   **1 can (10-3/4 ounces) condensed cream of mushroom soup, undiluted**
> **2-1/4 cups water**
>   **1/2 teaspoon dried basil**

>   **1 package (16 ounces) frozen broccoli, cauliflower and carrots combination**
>   **2 cups uncooked spiral pasta**
> **Grated Parmesan cheese**

In an extra-large skillet over medium-high heat, cook chicken in oil until browned, stirring often. Remove chicken from skillet; set aside. Add soup, water, basil and frozen vegetables. Bring to a boil. Add uncooked pasta. Cook over medium heat 10 minutes, stirring often. Return chicken to skillet. Cook 5 minutes or until pasta is done and chicken juices run clear, stirring often. Serve with cheese. **Yield:** 4 servings.

Speedy Cacciatora

Italian for "hunter", cacciatora is an American-Italian term for food that is prepared "hunter-style". Traditionally, onions, tomatoes, various herbs and sometimes wine are used to prepare chicken in this manner. This shortcut version features prepared spaghetti sauce.

>   **8 chicken drumsticks *or* thighs**
>   **1 green pepper, cut into 1/2-inch strips**
>   **1 cup chunky meatless spaghetti sauce**
> **Grated Parmesan cheese**

Place chicken in a 13-in. x 9-in. x 2-in. baking dish. Add green pepper; cover with waxed paper. Microwave on high for 10 minutes, rotating dish once; drain. Spoon sauce over all. Microwave, covered, on high for 5 minutes or until juices of chicken run clear. Let stand 5 minutes. Serve with cheese. **Yield:** 4 servings.

CHICKEN ENCHILADA SKILLET

(Pictured above)

If your family enjoys Southwestern-style recipes, give this one-skillet dish a try. The flavor may remind you of chicken-vegetable enchiladas, but this handy recipe doesn't require the extra time to roll them up. It's also a great meal to keep in mind when you have leftover chicken on hand.

    1 package (16 ounces) frozen broccoli, corn
       and red pepper combination
    1 envelope taco seasoning
    1 can (14-1/2 ounces) diced tomatoes with
       garlic and onion, undrained
    3 cups shredded cooked chicken
    1 cup (4 ounces) shredded Monterey Jack
       cheese
    8 ounces tortilla chips

In a large skillet, combine vegetables, seasoning mix, tomatoes and chicken; bring to a boil over medium-high heat. Cover and cook 4 minutes or until vegetables are cooked and mixture is heated through. Sprinkle with cheese; cover and cook 2 minutes more or until cheese is melted. Serve with chips. **Yield:** 4 servings.

TURKEY TETRAZZINI

Although the name sounds Italian, Chicken Tetrazzini is a thoroughly American dish created in San Francisco early last century in honor of the great opera singer Luisa Tetrazzini.

1-1/2 cups fresh sliced mushrooms
    7 tablespoons butter *or* margarine, *divided*
    6 tablespoons all-purpose flour
1-3/4 cups chicken broth
    1/2 cup whipping cream
    2 egg yolks, lightly beaten
    2 cups cubed cooked turkey
    1/4 cup chopped pimientos
    1/4 cup fresh chopped parsley
    1/4 cup dry white wine *or* additional
       chicken broth
Salt and pepper to taste
    2 tablespoons grated Parmesan cheese
2-1/2 cups uncooked spiral pasta

In a saucepan, cook mushrooms in 1 tablespoon butter until tender. Remove from saucepan; set aside. In same saucepan, melt remaining butter; stir in flour until smooth. Gradually add broth and cream. Cook and stir constantly over medium heat until mixture begins to boil; boil and stir 1 minute. Remove from heat. Add small amount of sauce to egg yolks; blend well. Return egg mixture to sauce mixture; stir until smooth. Add turkey, pimientos, parsley, wine, salt, pepper and reserved mushrooms to sauce; keep warm over low heat. Meanwhile, cook pasta according to package directions; drain. Toss immediately with sauce mixture; top with Parmesan cheese. **Yield:** 4-6 servings.

CHICKEN BREASTS DIJON

The city of Dijon in France has become synonymous with the pale grayish-yellow mustard that hails from that region. Widely used to flavor dishes, Dijon mustard is made from mustard seeds, white wine, unfermented grape juice and various seasonings.

    6 boneless skinless chicken breast halves
    6 slices dried beef
    3 ounces Swiss cheese, cut into 6 sticks
    2 tablespoons butter *or* margarine
    2 tablespoons all-purpose flour
    1/4 teaspoon white pepper
    2/3 cup evaporated milk
    1/2 cup dry white wine *or* chicken broth
    1/4 cup water
    1 tablespoon Dijon mustard
Cooked rice *or* noodles

Pound chicken breasts to 1/4-in. thickness. Place one beef slice and cheese stick down center of each chicken breast; roll up and secure with toothpicks, sealing edges. Melt butter in a large skillet; cook chicken rolls on all sides until golden brown. Cover; simmer 15-20 minutes longer or until chicken juices run clear. Remove chicken rolls to platter; keep warm. Stir flour and pepper into drippings; mix well. Slowly stir in evaporated milk, wine and water. Cook over medium heat, stirring constantly, until mixture comes to a boil and thickens. Remove from heat; stir in mustard. Serve sauce over chicken rolls with rice. **Yield:** 4-6 servings.

CRUNCHY COCONUT CHICKEN

Though Malaysia was the origin of the coconut palm, these trees now grow in the tropics throughout the world. One prolific tree will yield thousands of coconuts during its 70-year lifespan.

> 1 cup flaked coconut
> 13 vanilla wafers, crushed
> 2-1/2 pounds bone-in chicken pieces
> 2 eggs, beaten
> 1/3 cup butter *or* margarine, melted

On a plate, combine coconut and vanilla wafer crumbs. Dip chicken pieces in egg; then coat with coconut mixture. Place in a shallow baking dish; drizzle with butter. Bake at 400° for 1 hour or until chicken juices run clear. **Yield:** 4-6 servings.

COUNTRY CAPTAIN

Now an American classic, Country Captain is said to have taken its name from a British army officer who brought the recipe back from his station in India.

> 1/4 cup all-purpose flour
> 1-1/2 teaspoons salt
> 1/4 teaspoon pepper
> 1 broiler/fryer chicken (3 to 4 pounds), cut up
> 1/2 cup butter *or* margarine
> 1 medium green pepper, cut into strips
> 1 medium onion, sliced
> 1 garlic clove, minced
> 1-1/2 teaspoons curry powder
> 1/2 teaspoon dried thyme
> 1 can (28 ounces) diced tomatoes
> 1/3 cup currants *or* raisins

Combine flour, salt and pepper in a resealable plastic bag. Add chicken pieces, a few at a time; shake to coat with flour mixture. In a large skillet over medium-high heat, brown chicken in butter. Remove chicken; set aside. Add green pepper, onion, garlic, curry powder and thyme to skillet. Cook until onion and green pepper are tender. Return chicken to skillet. Add tomatoes; bring to a boil. Cover and simmer 15 minutes. Add currants and simmer 15 minutes longer or until chicken juices run clear. **Yield:** 4 servings.

HONEY DIJON CHICKEN

(Pictured below)

For an impressive main dish that's not tricky to prepare, try this simple chicken entree. The rich honey-mustard sauce is delicious spooned over rice, while a sprinkling of toasted pecans adds interest to the texture.

> 4 boneless skinless chicken breast halves
> 1 tablespoon butter *or* margarine
> 1 can (10-3/4 ounces) condensed chicken Dijon soup, undiluted
> 1/2 cup milk
> 2 tablespoons honey
> 4 cups hot cooked parslied rice
> 1/4 cup chopped pecans *or* walnuts, toasted

In a large skillet, cook chicken in butter until golden brown. Add soup, milk and honey. Bring to a boil. Cover and cook over low heat for 5 minutes or until chicken is no longer pink. Serve with rice. Sprinkle with pecans. **Yield:** 4 servings.

Fried Chicken Fare

If there is one recipe that inspires more controversy than any other, it's fried chicken. Should it be coated with flour, batter or bread crumbs? Should it be cooked in vegetable oil, bacon fat, butter or lard? Folks disagree on how to make the gravy, if any at all, and even argue over how to cut up the chicken. The team at Tyson chicken has called a truce and encourages cooks to prepare fried chicken whatever way they deem the best. As long as you start with fresh chicken, the end results are sure to be delicious! Here we share three of our favorite recipes…which is your preference?

CRISPY FRIED CHICKEN

This version makes a spicy chicken with a crisp light coating, much like the fried chicken available at takeout stands throughout the country. Home cooks prefer this type for picnics when chicken is served cold.

1-1/2 cups all-purpose flour, *divided*
  1/2 cup Italian salad dressing
    2 pounds bone-in chicken pieces
    1 teaspoon baking powder
    1 teaspoon paprika
  1/2 teaspoon rubbed sage
  1/4 teaspoon salt
  1/4 teaspoon pepper
    1 cup buttermilk
Vegetable oil

In a small bowl, combine 1/2 cup flour and salad dressing to make a paste. Spread mixture all over chicken pieces to coat. Cover; refrigerate overnight. In a pie plate, combine remaining flour, baking powder, paprika, sage, salt and pepper. In another pie plate, place buttermilk. Dip chicken pieces in buttermilk, then in flour mixture. In a 10-in. skillet over medium-high heat, in 1/2-in. hot oil, cook chicken pieces until browned on all sides, carefully turning once. On a wire rack in a jelly-roll pan, arrange chicken pieces in a single layer. Bake at 350° for 50-60 minutes or until chicken is fork-tender. **Yield:** 4-6 servings.

OVEN-FRIED BUTTERMILK CHICKEN

(Pictured above)

Oven-fried chicken is easier to prepare but may not provide the crispness some folks desire. Some cooks prefer to soak the chicken pieces in buttermilk overnight, insisting that it adds flavor and tenderizes the chicken.

  3/4 cup buttermilk
    1 cup all-purpose flour

1-1/2 teaspoons poultry seasoning, optional
1 teaspoon paprika
1/2 teaspoon seasoned salt
1 package of chicken parts (2 breasts, 2 drumsticks, 2 thighs)
1/4 cup butter *or* margarine

Place buttermilk in shallow dish. On waxed paper or plate, mix flour, poultry seasoning if desired, paprika and salt. Dip chicken in buttermilk to coat completely. Dredge in flour mixture to cover completely. Place on clean sheet of waxed paper. In foil-lined 15-in. x 10-in. x 1-in. baking pan, melt butter in a 425° oven for 3-5 minutes or until bubbly. Spread evenly. Place chicken, skin side down, in pan. Bake* chicken at 425° for 30 minutes. Carefully turn chicken over. Bake 30 minutes more or until internal juices of chicken run clear. *Chicken may also be deep-fried (shown in photo at left). To deep fry, heat oil in fryer to 325°. Fry chicken, a few pieces at a time, 10-15 minutes or until deep golden brown, turning occasionally. Drain on paper towels and keep warm in 200° oven. Repeat until all pieces are cooked. **Yield:** 6 servings.

SOUTHERN FRIED CHICKEN WITH CREAM GRAVY

Southern-style recipes season the chicken only with salt and pepper, then make gravy from thickened pan drippings and milk. It's a simple method that has been used for generations.

1/2 cup all-purpose flour
1 teaspoon salt
1/4 teaspoon pepper
2 pounds bone-in chicken pieces
1/4 cup bacon drippings *or* vegetable oil
1-1/2 cups milk *or* half-and-half cream
1 tablespoon chopped fresh parsley
Additional salt and pepper

In a resealable plastic bag, combine flour, salt and pepper. Add chicken a few pieces at a time. Close bag and shake to coat chicken. Repeat with remaining chicken pieces. Reserve 2 tablespoons flour mixture. In a 10-in. skillet over medium-high heat, in hot bacon drippings, cook chicken pieces until well browned on all sides, turning frequently. Reduce heat to low. Cover; cook about 35 minutes until chicken is fork-tender, turning pieces occasionally. Uncover during last few minutes to crisp skin. Remove chicken pieces to warm platter; keep warm. To make gravy: Pour off all but 2 tablespoons drippings from skillet; blend in 2 tablespoons reserved flour mixture. Over medium heat, cook until golden, stirring and scraping bits loose from skillet. Gradually stir in milk; bring to a boil, stirring constantly. Cook 1 minute more. Stir in parsley and season to taste with additional salt and pepper. Spoon gravy over chicken. **Yield:** 4-6 servings.

CAN CHICKENS FLY? They certainly did when ambitious John Tyson (below, right) started shipping poultry interstate. John generally relied on trucks for shipping, but here he loads a plane with a special order in 1946.

CHEESY CHICKEN ENCHILADAS

(Pictured below)

Serve these zesty roll-ups with Spanish rice and refried beans for a dinner the gang is sure to enjoy. Garnish each steamy enchilada with sour cream or guacamole and a sprig of cilantro for added flair.

- 1 pound boneless skinless chicken breasts, cut into 1/2-inch pieces
- 1 envelope taco seasoning
- 1 jar (16 ounces) chunky salsa
- 1 can (15 ounces) black beans, rinsed and drained
- 1 can (8-3/4 ounces) whole kernel corn, drained
- 2 cups (8 ounces) shredded Mexican cheese blend, *divided*
- 1 can (15 ounces) mild enchilada sauce, *divided*
- 8 flour tortillas (6 inches)
- 2 tablespoons sliced ripe olives

Prepare chicken with taco seasoning as directed on package of taco seasoning mix; cool 10 minutes. Stir in salsa, beans, corn and 1 cup cheese. Spread 1/4 cup enchilada sauce on bottom of 13-in. x 9-in. x 2-in. baking dish. Place 2/3 cup chicken mixture down center of each tortilla; roll up. Place in dish, seam side down, on top of sauce. Pour remaining enchilada sauce over tortillas; sprinkle with remaining cheese and the sliced ripe olives. Bake at 375° for 20 minutes or until cheese is melted and filling is hot. **Yield:** 8 servings.

CHICKEN & SNOW PEA SIZZLE

Snow peas are essential in Chinese cooking, as the bright green pods add a delightful crispness to stir-fried dishes. Since they're entirely edible, the French call them mange-tout, or "eat it all".

- 3 teaspoons vegetable oil, *divided*
- 1 cup walnut pieces
- 1 pound boneless skinless chicken breasts, cut into 2-inch strips
- 1/4 pound fresh snow peas
- 2 carrots, cut into 1/2-inch slices
- 1 can (8 ounces) sliced water chestnuts, drained
- 3/4 cup chicken broth
- 2 tablespoons dry white wine *or* additional chicken broth
- 2 tablespoons soy sauce

1 tablespoon cornstarch
1 teaspoon garlic pepper
Hot cooked rice

In a large skillet, heat 2 teaspoons oil; add nuts. Cook, stirring occasionally, for 1 minute. Remove nuts from skillet; set aside. Saute chicken over medium-high heat for 5 minutes; remove and set aside. Add remaining oil; stir-fry snow peas, carrots and water chestnuts for 4-5 minutes. Combine broth, wine, soy sauce, cornstarch and garlic pepper. Pour over vegetables and cook 1-2 minutes or until thickened. Add chicken and walnuts; toss to coat. Serve over rice. **Yield:** 4 servings.

CREAMY PESTO CHICKEN & BOW TIES

(Pictured above)

Since this quick skillet sensation combines chicken and pasta, even children love it! The flavor of the creamy pesto sauce can't be beat. It's perfect for a weeknight.

    3 cups uncooked bow tie pasta
    1 pound boneless skinless chicken breasts,
        cubed
    2 tablespoons butter *or* margarine
    1 can (10-3/4 ounces) condensed
        cream of chicken soup, undiluted
    1/2 cup prepared pesto sauce
    1/2 cup milk

Cook the pasta according to package directions. Drain. Meanwhile, in a large skillet, cook the chicken in butter until browned, stirring often. Add the soup, pesto and milk. Bring to a boil. Cook over low heat for 5 minutes or until internal juices of the chicken run clear. Stir in the pasta and heat through. **Yield:** 4 servings.

ITALIAN-STYLE CHICKEN BREASTS

Sauteed mushrooms and a splash of white wine add interest to these tender boneless chicken breasts. Mozzarella cheese is a popular topper for Italian-style entrees because of its excellent melting properties.

    2 large boneless skinless chicken breast halves
    1/4 cup crushed saltines (about 8 crackers)
    1/4 cup grated Parmesan cheese
    1 egg, well beaten
    1/4 cup butter *or* margarine
    1/4 pound fresh mushrooms, sliced
    1/3 cup dry white wine *or* chicken broth
    2 slices mozzarella cheese

Pound chicken breasts to flatten slightly. Combine saltine crumbs and Parmesan cheese. Coat chicken in crumb mixture, then dip in egg. Return chicken to crumb mixture to coat well. In a large skillet over medium heat, cook chicken in butter until browned on both sides. Place chicken in shallow baking dish. Add mushrooms to skillet; cook until tender, stirring frequently. Stir in wine. Pour mixture over chicken. Cover and bake at 350° for 15 minutes. Uncover; top each chicken breast with once slice of mozzarella cheese. Bake, uncovered, 10 additional minutes. **Yield:** 2 servings.

EASY TURKEY SHEPHERD'S PIE

For most Americans, Thanksgiving wouldn't be complete without the tantalizing taste of turkey. But what do you do with all the leftovers? Here's one tasty idea.

    1 package (22 ounces) frozen mashed
        potatoes
    2-2/3 cups plus 3/4 cup milk, *divided*
    2 cups cubed cooked turkey
    1 can (10-3/4 ounces) condensed cream of
        mushroom soup, undiluted
    1 package (10 ounces) frozen mixed
        vegetables
    2 tablespoons dried minced onion
    1/2 teaspoon Italian seasoning *or* dried thyme
Salt and pepper to taste

Combine potatoes and 2-2/3 cups milk; prepare according to package directions. Meanwhile, in a medium bowl, combine turkey, soup and remaining milk. Stir in vegetables, onion and Italian seasoning. Add salt and pepper. Divide mixture into four 5-in. x 1-1/2-in. tart or potpie pans. Top with prepared potatoes, spreading to edge. Place pans on large baking sheet. Bake at 350° for 25-30 minutes or until bubbly and lightly browned. Serve immediately. **Yield:** 4 servings.

TEXAS-STYLE CORNISH HENS

Cornish game hens are actually miniature chickens, weighing up to 2-1/2 pounds. Each hen is just enough for one serving. They're best broiled, grilled or roasted.

1 teaspoon chili powder, *divided*
1/2 teaspoon salt
1/2 teaspoon garlic powder
4 Cornish game hens (20 ounces *each*)
1/2 cup apple jelly
1/2 cup ketchup
1 tablespoon white vinegar

In a small bowl, combine 1/2 teaspoon chili powder, salt and garlic powder. Rub hens inside and out with seasoning. Tie legs together. Grill hens over medium heat, turning occasionally, for 1 hour or until juices run clear. Meanwhile, in a small bowl, combine jelly, ketchup, vinegar and remaining chili powder. Baste hens frequently with sauce during the last 30 minutes of cooking. **Yield:** 4 servings.

TOMATO BROCCOLI CHICKEN

European explorers carried tomato plants back home from Mexico, but it took some time for tomatoes to gain popularity. It was thought that, like other members of the nightshade family, they were poisonous.

6 boneless skinless chicken breast halves
Salt and pepper to taste
3 tablespoons butter *or* margarine
1/2 cup chopped onion
2 packages (8 ounces *each*) frozen broccoli spears, thawed
1-1/2 teaspoons lemon juice
1/2 teaspoon salt
1/8 teaspoon pepper
3/4 teaspoon dried thyme
3 medium tomatoes, cut into wedges

Season chicken lightly with salt and pepper. Cut into 1/4-in.-wide strips. In a large skillet, cook chicken and onion in butter for 5 minutes or until chicken is no longer pink. Add broccoli, lemon juice, salt, pepper and thyme. Cover and simmer 6 minutes. Add tomatoes and simmer 3-4 minutes longer. **Yield:** 4 servings.

ZESTY CHICKEN DINNER

For easy cleanup, turn to this savory poultry recipe that bakes inside an oven bag. Broccoli and carrots add delightful crisp-tender crunch and color.

1 tablespoon all-purpose flour
1 large size oven bag (14 inches x 20 inches)
1/3 cup Italian salad dressing
4 boneless skinless chicken breast halves
Paprika
2 cups broccoli florets
3 carrots, cut into 2-inch julienne strips
1 to 2 tablespoons sesame seeds, toasted

Shake flour in oven cooking bag; place in shallow 2-1/2-qt. microwave-safe casserole. Add salad dressing; squeeze bag to blend ingredients. Add chicken. Turn bag to coat chicken with dressing. Arrange chicken in single layer. Close bag with nylon tie. Marinate in refrigerator 30 minutes. Open bag; sprinkle chicken with paprika. Place broccoli in center of bag. Arrange chicken around broccoli with thickest portions toward outside. Distribute carrots around chicken. Close bag with nylon tie; cut 6 half-inch slits in top. Microwave on high 9-11 minutes or until chicken is no longer pink, rotating dish after 5 minutes. Let stand in bag 3 minutes. Sprinkle with sesame seeds. **Yield:** 4 servings.

GARDEN RISOTTO WITH CHICKEN

(Pictured at right)

This tasty specialty is a one-dish meal that cooks to perfection. Tender boneless chicken pieces poach in a flavorful mixture of orzo pasta and broccoli florets. Colorful corn adds to the exciting flavor combination.

1 large onion, chopped
3 garlic cloves, minced
2 tablespoons vegetable oil
2 cans (10-1/2 ounces *each*) condensed chicken broth, undiluted
2 cups broccoli florets
1-3/4 cups uncooked orzo pasta
2 boneless skinless chicken breast halves, cut into 1-inch cubes
1 can (15 ounces) whole kernel corn, undrained
1/4 teaspoon salt
1/4 teaspoon pepper
3/4 cup grated Parmesan cheese

In a large nonstick skillet over medium-high heat, cook onion and garlic in oil for 2 minutes. Add broth, broccoli and pasta. Reduce heat to medium; cover and cook for 6 minutes, stirring frequently. Add chicken; cook for 6 minutes. Mix in corn, salt and pepper. Cook for 5 minutes or until chicken is done. Remove pan from heat. Stir in cheese. **Yield:** 4 servings.

CHICKEN PASTA PRIMAVERA

When there's no time to cook, try this great-tasting recipe. A sensational combination of pasta, chicken and vegetables tossed with a creamy easy-to-prepare sauce, it's ready to serve in 30 minutes or less.

  1 package (8 ounces) spaghetti
  1 package (16 ounces) frozen broccoli,
    cauliflower and carrot combination
  1 can (10-3/4 ounces) condensed
    creamy chicken with herbs soup,
    undiluted
  2 tablespoons grated Parmesan
    cheese
1-1/2 cups cubed cooked chicken

In a large saucepan, cook spaghetti according to package directions. Add frozen vegetables for last 5 minutes of cooking time. Drain into colander. In same saucepan, combine soup, cheese, chicken and spaghetti mixture; mix well. Heat through, stirring occasionally. **Yield:** 4 servings.

CHICKEN PESTO MOZZARELLA

(*Pictured above*)

Pesto is an uncooked sauce made with fresh basil leaves, garlic, pine nuts, Parmesan cheese and olive oil. It originated in Genoa, Italy, and although used on a variety of foods, it is a favorite with pasta.

  1 package (8 ounces) linguini *or* spiral pasta
  4 boneless skinless chicken breast halves

Salt and pepper to taste
  1 tablespoon olive *or* vegetable oil
  1 can (14-1/2 ounces) diced tomatoes with
    basil, garlic and oregano, undrained
  1 small onion, chopped
1/3 cup sliced ripe olives
  4 teaspoons pesto sauce
1/4 cup shredded mozzarella cheese

Cook pasta according to package directions; drain. Season chicken with salt and pepper. In a skillet, brown chicken in hot oil over medium-high heat. Add tomatoes, onion and olives; bring to a boil. Cover and cook for 8 minutes over medium heat. Uncover and cook 8 minutes longer or until chicken juices run clear. Spread 1 teaspoon pesto over each breast; top with cheese. Cover and cook until cheese melts. Serve over pasta. **Yield:** 4 servings.

TURKEY CHEESE PUFF

This versatile dish provides a nice way to use up leftovers. Broccoli is paired with turkey and gravy for an irresistible meal-in-one.

  1 package (10 ounces) frozen broccoli spears
  2 cups cubed cooked turkey
  1 can (10-1/2 ounces) chicken gravy
  2 eggs, *separated*
1/4 teaspoon salt
1/4 cup grated Parmesan cheese
1/4 cup slivered almonds

In a saucepan, cook broccoli according to package directions; drain. Transfer to an ungreased 1-1/2-qt. baking dish. Place turkey over broccoli and top with gravy. Bake, uncovered, at 375° for 10 minutes. In a small mixing bowl, beat egg whites and salt until stiff peaks form; set aside. In a separate small mixing bowl, beat egg yolks until thick. Fold egg yolks into egg whites. Gently fold in cheese. Pour mixture over hot turkey and broccoli. Sprinkle with almonds. Bake, uncovered, for 15-20 minutes or until golden brown. **Yield:** 6 servings.

CHICKEN DIVAN

Reaching its peak of popularity in the 1970s, this tempting casserole is ideal for brunches and buffets. The creamy sauce adds a touch of elegance.

  1 cup chopped mushrooms
1/4 cup butter *or* margarine
  3 tablespoons all-purpose flour
1/2 teaspoon salt

1-1/2 cups milk
1 tablespoon dry cooking sherry
1/8 teaspoon ground nutmeg
1 pound fresh broccoli, cut into spears *or*
1 package (10 ounces) frozen broccoli spears, cooked and drained
3 cups cubed cooked chicken *or* turkey
1/4 cup grated Parmesan cheese *or* 1/2 cup shredded cheddar cheese

In a 2-qt. saucepan over medium-high heat, cook mushrooms in hot butter until tender. Stir in flour and salt until blended. Gradually stir in milk; bring to a boil, stirring constantly. Stir in sherry and nutmeg; set aside. In an 11-in. x 7-in. x 2-in. baking dish, place broccoli spears in single layer. Arrange chicken over broccoli. Pour mushroom mixture over all; sprinkle with cheese. Bake at 450° for 15 minutes or until hot. **Yield:** 6 servings.

ONE-DISH CHICKEN AND RICE BAKE

(*Pictured at right*)

This no-fuss meal is prepared in one pan in minutes, then conveniently bakes in the oven. On busy weeknights, you can turn out a delightful dinner for your family in no time. Or present guests with this comforting dish for a satisfying Sunday supper.

1 can (10-3/4 ounces) condensed cream of mushroom soup, undiluted
1 cup water
3/4 cup uncooked long grain rice
1/4 teaspoon paprika
1/4 teaspoon pepper
4 boneless skinless chicken breast halves
Additional paprika and pepper

In a 2-qt. shallow baking dish, mix soup, water, rice, paprika and pepper. Place chicken on rice mixture. Sprinkle with additional paprika and pepper. Cover and bake at 375° for 45 minutes or until chicken juices run clear. **Yield:** 4 servings.

FAMILY CHICKEN DINNER

Just a few simple seasonings are all you need to make chicken moist and tasty. A convenient oven bag prevents the poultry from drying out, plus allows for one-step cleanup.

2 tablespoons all-purpose flour
1 large size oven bag (14 inches x 20 inches)
1 envelope golden onion soup mix

1 cup water
1 package (16 ounces) peeled baby carrots
2 medium red potatoes, cut in small wedges
2-1/2 pounds bone-in chicken pieces, skin removed
Seasoned salt
Paprika

Shake flour in oven bag; place in a 13-in. x 9-in. x 2-in. baking pan. Add onion soup mix and water to oven bag. Squeeze oven bag to blend in flour. Add carrots and potatoes to oven bag. Turn oven bag to coat ingredients with sauce. Sprinkle chicken with seasoned salt and paprika. Arrange chicken in an even layer in oven bag with vegetables around chicken. Close oven bag with nylon tie; cut six 1/2-in. slits in top. Bake at 350° for 55-60 minutes or until chicken juices run clear. **Yield:** 4 servings.

HERBED GAME HENS WITH PASTA

The fragrant leaves of herbs add bold flavor to every-day cooking. Dried herbs have a stronger, more concentrated flavor than fresh herbs, but can quickly lose their pungency. Store dried herbs in an airtight container in a cool dark place for no more than 6 months.

 2 to 3 Cornish game hens (20 ounces *each*),
  split lengthwise
1/4 cup vegetable oil
 3 tablespoons lemon juice
3/4 cup butter *or* margarine, melted
3/4 cup packed fresh parsley
 1 garlic clove, cut in half
1/2 teaspoon salt
 1 teaspoon dried oregano
1/2 teaspoon dried basil
1/2 teaspoon dried thyme
Pepper to taste
 1 package (8 ounces) spaghetti

Place hen halves in large baking pan. Combine oil and lemon juice; pour over hens, coating evenly. Bake at 350° for 1 hour or until internal juices run clear. Meanwhile, in blender or food processor, combine butter, parsley and remaining seasoning ingredients. Blend at high speed until parsley is minced. Divide into two equal parts and set aside. During last 15 minutes of baking, brush both sides of hen halves with half of herb mixture. Prepare spaghetti according to package directions. Drain; toss with remaining herb mixture. Place hen halves on bed of hot cooked spaghetti. **Yield:** 4-6 servings.

GOLDEN CHICKEN AND AUTUMN VEGETABLES

(Pictured below left and on front cover)

Tender chicken in a savory broth is simmered with wholesome sweet potatoes and crisp green beans to create this mouth-watering main dish. It's nice to offer guests an entree that's low in fat yet packed with flavor.

 4 bone-in chicken breast halves, skin removed
 1 cup chicken broth
 1 tablespoon chopped fresh parsley
1/2 teaspoon garlic powder
1/2 teaspoon dried rosemary, crushed
1/4 teaspoon dried thyme
 2 large sweet potatoes, peeled and cut up
 1 box (9 ounces) frozen cut green beans
 or 2 cups fresh whole green beans

In a nonstick skillet over medium-high heat, cook chicken until browned on both sides. Add broth, parsley, garlic powder, rosemary, thyme, potatoes and beans. Bring to a boil. Cover and cook over low heat for 20 minutes or until chicken juices run clear. **Yield:** 4 servings.

PARMESAN FRIED CHICKEN

Many folks find oven-frying more convenient than deep-fat frying. This simple coating results in a delicious down-home chicken feast your family is sure to love.

 2 cups crushed saltines (about 60 crackers)
 1 cup grated Parmesan cheese
 2 teaspoons paprika
1/4 teaspoon pepper
 2 broiler/fryer chickens (3 to 4 pounds *each*),
  cut-up
1-1/3 cups evaporated milk
 1 cup butter *or* margarine, melted

In a large resealable plastic bag or shallow bowl, combine saltines, cheese, paprika and pepper. Dip chicken in evaporated milk, then shake or dredge in saltine mixture. Pour butter into bottom of two 13-in. x 9-in. x 2-in. baking pans to coat. Arrange chicken, skin side down, in baking pans. Bake at 350° for 60-70 minutes or until chicken juices run clear, turning chicken after 30 minutes. **Yield:** 8-10 servings.

CHICKEN PARMESAN

A twist on the traditional, this easy favorite doesn't require dredging or frying, saving time and calories.

        4 boneless skinless chicken breast halves
        2 cans (14-1/2 ounces *each*) Italian-style
            stewed tomatoes
        2 tablespoons cornstarch
        1/2 teaspoon dried oregano *or* dried basil
        1/4 teaspoon hot pepper sauce, optional
        1/4 cup grated Parmesan cheese
Chopped parsley, optional
Hot cooked pasta *or* rice, optional

Slightly flatten each chicken breast half; place in a shallow baking dish. Cover with foil; bake at 425° for 20 minutes. Remove foil; drain. Meanwhile, in a saucepan, combine tomatoes, cornstarch, oregano and pepper sauce if desired. Stir to dissolve cornstarch. Cook, stirring constantly, until thickened. Pour sauce over chicken; top with cheese. Bake, uncovered, 5 minutes longer or until chicken juices run clear. Garnish with parsley; serve with pasta or rice if desired. **Yield:** 4 servings.

CREAMY CHICKEN TETRAZZINI

This rich dish combines cooked spaghetti and bite-size chicken with a sherry-Parmesan cream sauce. Bake until the surface is bubbly and golden brown.

        1 cup sliced mushrooms
        1 small onion, chopped
        1/4 cup butter *or* margarine
        1/4 cup all-purpose flour
        1/2 teaspoon salt
    1-3/4 cups chicken broth
        1 cup half-and-half cream
        2 tablespoons dry cooking sherry
        2 cups cubed cooked chicken *or* turkey
        1/4 cup chopped pimientos
        2 tablespoons chopped parsley
        1 package (8 ounces) spaghetti, cooked and
            drained
        1/2 cup grated Parmesan cheese

In a 2-qt. saucepan over medium-high heat, cook mushrooms and onion in hot butter until tender. Stir in flour and salt until blended. Gradually stir in chicken broth. Cook until mixture boils, stirring constantly. Stir in cream, sherry, chicken, pimientos and parsley; bring to a boil, stirring often. Remove from heat. In a 13-in. x 9-in. x 2-in. baking dish, spread spaghetti. Pour chicken mixture over spaghetti. Top with cheese. Bake at 450° for 15 minutes or until cheese is golden. **Yield:** 6 servings.

ITALIAN HERBED CHICKEN & PASTA

(Pictured above)

Contemporary pasta dishes feature fewer heavy sauces and more vegetables. Seasoned chicken broth keeps the dish moist while adding bold Italian flavor.

        1 can (14 ounces) seasoned chicken broth with
            Italian herbs
        6 sun-dried tomato halves*
        1 pound boneless skinless chicken breasts,
            cut into crosswise strips
        1 tablespoon olive *or* vegetable oil
        2 cups sliced fresh mushrooms
        1 tablespoon all-purpose flour
        1 cup packed coarsely chopped fresh spinach
        4 cups hot cooked tube pasta
Grated Parmesan cheese

Place broth and tomatoes in microwave-safe bowl. Microwave on high for 2 minutes. Let stand 5 minutes. Remove tomatoes; cut up. In a large nonstick skillet, cook chicken in oil until browned, stirring often. Add mushrooms; cook until tender. Stir in flour and cook 1 minute. Add tomatoes and broth. Cook and stir until mixture boils and thickens. Add spinach and pasta. Mix lightly to coat. Serve with cheese. **Yield:** 4 servings. **Editor's Note:** You may substitute 3 chopped plum tomatoes for sun-dried tomatoes. Add with spinach and pasta.

CHICKEN & ARTICHOKE PIZZA WITH TOMATOES

(Pictured above)

Why pop a frozen pizza in the oven when you can serve your family generous slices of this fast and fabulous recipe? Chicken provides an appealing change of pace from the usual beef or pepperoni...and it pairs nicely with the tomatoes and artichokes.

> 3 boneless skinless chicken breasts *or* 4 boneless skinless chicken thighs
> 1 jar (6-1/2 ounces) marinated artichoke hearts, undrained
> 1 to 2 garlic cloves, minced
> 1 prebaked Italian bread shell crust (10 to 16 ounces)
> 2 tablespoons vinaigrette *or* Italian salad dressing, optional
> 4 Italian plum tomatoes, sliced

Salt and pepper to taste

> 1/2 teaspoon dried basil *or* 1 tablespoon fresh basil
> 1-1/2 cups (6 ounces) shredded mozzarella cheese

Cut chicken into 3/4-in. pieces. Drain the artichoke hearts, reserving liquid. Coarsely chop artichokes. In a large nonstick skillet, bring artichoke liquid to a boil over medium-high heat. Cook until most of liquid has evaporated, about 1 minute. Add chicken and garlic to skillet. Cook chicken 3-5 minutes or until internal juices run clear. Stir in artichokes. Remove from heat. Meanwhile, place pizza crust on baking sheet. Brush with dressing if desired. Top evenly with tomato slices. Season with salt and pepper. Top with chicken mixture; sprinkle with basil. Top with cheese. Bake at 425° for 12-17 minutes or until hot and cheese melts. Cut pizza into wedges and serve. **Yield:** 6 servings.

ORIENTAL CHICKEN AND ASPARAGUS

Colorful garden-fresh vegetables and tender chicken combine in this dish to provide a mouth-watering meal that's sure to win rave reviews from your family and guests. The pleasant Asian-style sauce makes it particularly delicious.

> 2 tablespoons cornstarch, *divided*
> 1/2 teaspoon salt
> 6 boneless skinless chicken thighs, cut into strips
> 1/4 pound fresh asparagus spears, cut into 2-inch pieces

1 small sweet red pepper, sliced
1 medium onion, sliced
1 garlic clove, minced
2 tablespoons oyster sauce
1/2 teaspoon sesame oil
1 can (14 ounces) chicken broth
1 can (8 ounces) sliced water chestnuts,
    drained
1/4 cup water
Hot cooked rice

In a medium bowl, combine 1 tablespoon cornstarch and salt. Add chicken and stir to coat. Cover and refrigerate. Spray a large nonstick skillet with nonstick cooking spray. Heat over medium-high heat. Add asparagus; cook, stirring constantly, for 1 minute. Add pepper, onion, garlic, oyster sauce and sesame oil. Cook, stirring frequently, until vegetables are crisp-tender, about 3 minutes. Remove from skillet; set aside. Add chicken to skillet and cook, stirring frequently, about 5 minutes or until juices run clear. Add chicken broth, 1 tablespoon at a time, if needed to prevent over-browning or sticking. When chicken is cooked, add remaining broth and water chestnuts to skillet. Combine remaining cornstarch and water; add to skillet. Cook and stir until sauce is thickened. Return vegetables to skillet and heat. Serve with cooked rice. **Yield:** 4 servings.

CHICKEN & BROCCOLI ALFREDO

(Pictured at right)

This effortless entree combines the familiar flavors of chicken and pasta, draped in a mushroom-Parmesan cream sauce. Colorful broccoli florets round out this super-fast weeknight supper.

1 package (8 ounces) uncooked linguine *or*
    spaghetti
1 cup fresh *or* frozen broccoli florets
2 tablespoons butter *or* margarine
1 pound boneless skinless chicken breasts,
    cubed
1 can (10-3/4 ounces) condensed
    cream of mushroom soup, undiluted
1/2 cup milk
1/2 cup grated Parmesan cheese
1/4 teaspoon pepper
Additional grated Parmesan cheese

Prepare the linguine according to package directions. Add the broccoli during last 4 minutes of cooking time; drain. In a medium skillet over medium-high heat, melt the butter. Add the chicken and cook until no longer pink, stirring often. Add the soup, milk, cheese, pepper and linguine mixture; heat

through, stirring occasionally. Serve with additional cheese. **Yield:** 4 servings.

GRAHAM BAKE CHICKEN

Creator Rev. Sylvester Graham, a United States dietary reformer, touted graham crackers as a health food in the 1830s. While usually associated with sweet desserts, the whole wheat and honey flavored crackers offer a nice complement to chicken as well.

2 broiler/fryer chickens (3 pounds *each*)
    cut up and skin removed
3/4 cup vinaigrette salad dressing
2-1/2 cups graham cracker crumbs
1 tablespoon grated lemon peel
2 teaspoons curry powder
1 teaspoon onion salt
3 tablespoons chopped fresh parsley
2 eggs
2 tablespoons water
1 cup all-purpose flour

In a large non-metallic bowl, combine the chicken and dressing. Marinate in refrigerator for 4-5 hours. Remove the chicken from dressing; pat dry with paper towels. In a shallow dish, combine the cracker crumbs, lemon peel, curry powder, salt and parsley. In a small bowl, beat the eggs with water. Dip the chicken in the flour, coating well, then in the egg mixture and the graham cracker mixture. Place in a greased 13-in. x 9-in. x 2-in. baking pan. Bake at 350° for 40-45 minutes or until chicken juices run clear. **Yield:** 10 servings.

Flashback to the '60s

*T*he times, they are a' changing as the 1960s take shape. Despite all the talk about love and peace and flower power, the decade is marked by civil unrest.

Through it all, the focus on family and home remains strong. Homemaker Schools thrive as they offer women a chance to get together, bond and learn more about cooking.

Average attendance for the 3-hour event is up to 1,000. In some small towns, the only problem is finding a facility large enough to hold the crowd.

Everyone who attends a cooking school receives a free cookbook and has a good time. Dozens win door prizes ranging from bags full of groceries to brand-new appliances.

Many rural women get their first glimpse of the highly touted, new-fangled microwave ovens at the cooking shows. The kitchen marvel win raves, even though it will be more than 10 years before the price comes down enough so that nearly every family can afford one.

TALK ABOUT standing room only. The lines formed early (above) when the Homemaker Schools' Cooking School was in town and every seat was full (below). We're happy to say the same holds true today.

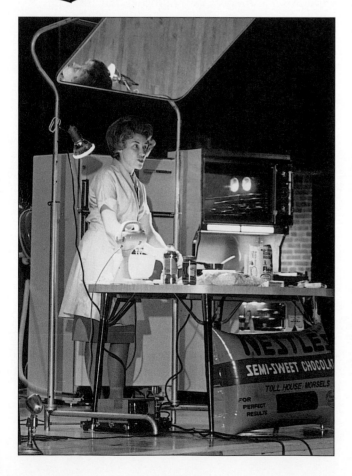

AN OVERHEAD MIRROR (left) ensures the audience can see each step of the recipe that home economist Sandy Bloom is demonstrating. Sandy conducted classes across the Midwest in the 1960s. She returned to the Cooking School in the 1990s and was promoted to executive director.

These Are Foods Sandra Will Be Using at the Cooking School Tomorrow—Get Them at the Economy!

FOOD FASHION FAIR *features*

SANDRA BLOOM

3 Envelopes 17¢   16-oz. Bag 23¢   10-oz. Pkg. 89¢

NESTLES SWEET CHOCOLATE

3 ½-oz. Pkgs. $1.00   11½-oz. Jar 79¢   Lb. 27¢   10-lb. Bag 99¢   Quart Jar White 59

REDEEM YOUR COUPONS HERE!

"The Friendliest Store in Town"

371-9750 **Economy** FOOD MARKET

THE OH-SO-SWEET '60s. The Fab Four's music wowed the world, Sonny & Cher were headed toward stardom, Agent Maxwell Smart didn't quite live up to his last name, grocery prices were much lower (plus the Cooking School got good press) and skirt hems were considerably higher.

Everett Collection

Brown Brothers

★ That's Entertainment

- The "British Invasion" brings the Beatles to America, and just about everyone wants to hold their hands.

- Jed Clampett and his oddball clan strike it rich when "The Beverly Hillbillies" catapults to No. 1 during its first season on television.

- With the hit singles "I Got You, Babe" and "The Beat Goes On", Sonny and Cher become a household name. The next decade they parlay their fame into a comedy show.

- Using outrageous gadgets, including a telephone hidden in the sole of his shoe, bumbling Agent 86 and Fang, canine Agent K-13, fight espionage on the TV show "Get Smart".

The 'In' Things

- With a bit of teasing and a pile of hair-spray, the bouffant hairdo lets young women stand tall early in the decade. But the look falls flat a few years later when Vidal Sassoon introduces the bob cut.

- By saying "Do your own thing, dude," you manage to squeeze two of the decade's most popular catchphrases into one sentence.

- The mini-skirt revolutionizes fashion, thanks to designer Mary Quant. Hemlines range from 4 to 8 inches above the knee.

- For the hottest look, women pair smudgy dark eyes with pale (almost white) lipstick.

Price Check

- The average price of a new home is $17,200.

- A gallon of regular gasoline costs 31¢.

- The price of a gallon of milk breaks the dollar mark by the end of the decade.

- One dollar will buy three Banquet frozen TV dinners. All you need now is a TV tray.

Play List

- Peter, Paul and Mary attract legions of fans with their ballads "Blowin' in the Wind", "Puff the Magic Dragon" and "If I Had a Hammer".

- The Beatles win the Grammy Award for Best New Artist in 1966, while the best performances for male and female go to more traditional acts, Louis Armstrong and Barbra Streisand.

- Soundtracks for such diverse movies as "Goldfinger" and "Mary Poppins" compete with Elvis Presley and the Rolling Stones for top-album status.

Chapter 7

BEEF DISHES

When beef is the featured fare, the entree is sure to capture attention. These meaty specialties will please every palate.

20-MINUTE SAVORY BEEF STEW

(Pictured at left)

Your family will appreciate this saucy entree in the fall and winter when a hearty skillet dinner truly satisfies. The gravy tastes as if it's simmered for hours, though the dish is actually ready in a flash.

> 1 **pound boneless sirloin steak, cut into 1-inch cubes**
> 1 **tablespoon vegetable oil**
> 1 **can (10-3/4 ounces) condensed tomato soup, undiluted**
> 1 **can (10-3/4 ounces) condensed French onion soup, undiluted**
> 1 **tablespoon Worcestershire sauce**
> 1 **package (24 ounces) frozen vegetables for stew**

In a large skillet over medium-high heat, stir-fry beef in hot oil until browned and juices evaporate. Add soups, Worcestershire sauce and vegetables; bring to a boil. Cover and cook over low heat for 10 minutes or until vegetables are tender. **Yield:** 4 servings.

ZESTY ONION MEAT LOAF

The epitome of comfort food, this savory meat loaf is delicious served hot or cold. It's crowned with condensed tomato soup and crispy french-fried onions.

1-1/2 pounds ground beef
> 1 **can (2.8 ounces) french-fried onions, *divided***
> 1 **can (10-3/4 ounces) condensed tomato soup, undiluted, *divided***
> 2 **tablespoons Worcestershire sauce**
> 1/2 **teaspoon Italian seasoning**
> 1/2 **teaspoon salt**
> 1/4 **teaspoon pepper**
> 1 **egg**

Mix together beef, 2/3 cup onions, 1/3 cup soup, Worcestershire sauce, Italian seasoning, salt, pepper and egg. Shape into an 8-in. x 4-in. x 2-in. loaf in a shallow baking dish. Bake at 350° for 1 hour; drain. Spoon remaining soup over meat loaf and top with remaining onions. Bake 5 minutes longer or until onions are golden. **Yield:** 6 servings.

MINI MEAT LOAVES:
Shape meat loaf mixture into five miniature meat loaves; place in a shallow baking dish. Bake at 350° for 30 minutes; drain. Spoon remaining soup over meat loaves and top with remaining onions. Bake 5 minutes longer or until onions are golden. **Yield:** 5 servings.

ZESTY FIESTA BAKE

(Pictured below)

This cheesy casserole has an irresistible home-cooked flavor and a subtle Southwestern kick—perfect for an autumn weeknight meal.

    1 **pound ground beef**
    1 **cup chopped onion**
3/4 **cup mild salsa**
    1 **envelope taco seasoning mix**
1/4 **cup water**
    1 **cup frozen corn**
    1 **can (2-1/4 ounces) sliced ripe olives,**
       drained
    1 **package (8-1/2 ounces) corn bread/**
       muffin mix
1/3 **cup milk**
    1 **egg**
    1 **cup (4 ounces) shredded cheddar cheese**
    1 **can (4 ounces) diced green chilies,**
       undrained

In a large skillet, cook beef and onion until beef is no longer pink; drain. Stir in salsa, seasoning mix and water. Cook over low heat for 5-6 minutes or until mixture thickens. Stir in corn and olives. Spoon into a greased 8-in. square baking dish. Prepare corn bread mix batter according to package directions, using milk and egg. Stir in cheese and chilies. Spread over meat mixture. Bake at 350° for 30-35 minutes or until crust is golden brown. **Yield:** 6 servings.

PIZZA BEEF LOAF

Jazz up traditional meat loaf by adding ingredients with Italian flair. You'll create a memorable meal you'll rely on for years to come.

2/3 **cup crushed saltines (about 20 crackers)**
    1 **medium onion, chopped**
    1 **egg**
    1 **can (8 ounces) tomato sauce**
    1 **teaspoon salt**
1/2 **teaspoon rubbed sage**
1/2 **teaspoon dried oregano**
1/4 **teaspoon garlic powder**
1/8 **teaspoon pepper**
1-1/2 **pounds ground beef**
1/4 **cup ketchup**
1/2 **cup shredded mozzarella cheese**
    6 **stuffed olives, sliced**

In a bowl, combine saltines, onion, egg, tomato sauce, salt, sage, oregano, garlic powder and pepper. Crumble beef over mixture and mix well. Pat into a greased 8-in. x 4-in. x 2-in. loaf pan. Bake, uncovered, at 350° for 1 hour or until meat is no longer pink and meat thermometer reads 160°; drain. Spoon ketchup over loaf; sprinkle with cheese and olives. Return to oven for 5 minutes or until cheese is melted. **Yield:** 6 servings.

ORIENTAL PEPPER STEAK

If your family enjoys bell peppers, get set for a real treat. This inviting entree is ready in a jiffy, and everyone enjoys its full-flavored sauce.

    1 **pound boneless beef round steak, cut**
       into thin strips
    2 **tablespoons vegetable oil**
    1 **envelope onion soup mix**
    2 **cups water,** *divided*
    1 **green pepper, cut into thin strips**
    2 **teaspoons soy sauce**
1/2 **teaspoon ground ginger**
    1 **garlic clove, minced**
    1 **jar (2 ounces) sliced pimientos, drained**
    1 **medium tomato, cut into wedges**
    1 **tablespoon cornstarch**
Hot cooked rice

In a large skillet, brown beef in hot oil; drain. Stir in soup mix and 1-1/2 cups water. Bring to a boil; re-

duce heat and simmer, covered, for 20 minutes. Stir in green pepper, soy sauce, ginger and garlic. Simmer, covered, for 15 minutes or until beef is tender. Stir in pimientos and tomato. Blend cornstarch with remaining water; add to skillet. Bring to a boil; simmer, stirring constantly until sauce is thickened, about 5 minutes. Serve with rice. **Yield:** 4 servings.

GOURMET-STYLE SWISS STEAK

Called smothered steak in England, this dish begins with inexpensive round steak that has been tenderized by pounding. We finish off the dish in a pressure cooker, shaving 2 hours from the typical cooking time.

  2 pounds boneless beef round steak, cut
    into serving pieces
  1 garlic clove, cut in half lengthwise
1/4 cup all-purpose flour
  2 tablespoons paprika
  1 teaspoon salt
1/4 teaspoon pepper
  3 tablespoons vegetable oil
1/4 cup sliced onion
  1 can (4-1/2 ounces) sliced mushrooms,
    drained
1/2 cup water
1/2 cup sour cream

Rub both sides of meat with garlic. Combine flour, paprika, salt and pepper; pound into steak. In pressure cooker, brown meat in hot oil, a few pieces at a time. Combine browned beef with onion, mushrooms and water in pressure cooker. Close cover securely; place pressure regulator on vent pipe. Bring cooker to full pressure over high heat. Reduce heat to medium-high and cook for 15 minutes. (Pressure regulator should maintain a slow steady rocking motion; adjust heat if needed.) Remove from the heat; allow pressure to drop on its own. Place steak on serving platter. Add sour cream to liquid in pressure cooker; heat through. **Yield:** 4-6 servings.

SAUCY STUFFED PEPPERS

(Pictured above right)

This tasty main dish will become a family favorite. The addition of cumin gives the peppers a delightful Southwestern flavor.

  4 medium green, sweet red *or* yellow
    peppers, cut in half lengthwise and seeds
    removed
3/4 pound ground beef

  1 medium onion, chopped
  2 garlic cloves, minced
  1 tablespoon olive *or* vegetable oil
1/2 teaspoon ground cumin
  1 can (8 ounces) tomato sauce
  3 tablespoons ketchup
  2 tablespoons Worcestershire sauce
  1 teaspoon prepared horseradish
1/2 teaspoon salt
1/4 teaspoon pepper
  2 cups cooked white rice
1-1/2 cups (6 ounces) shredded sharp cheddar
    cheese, *divided*
  2 tablespoons chopped fresh parsley

In a large pot of simmering water, cook peppers for 5 minutes. Drain; cool, cut side down, on paper towels. In a large skillet over medium heat, cook ground beef, onion and garlic in hot oil until beef is no longer pink; drain. Stir in cumin; cook and stir 1 minute. Add tomato sauce, ketchup, Worcestershire sauce, horseradish, salt and pepper. Cook 5 minutes, stirring occasionally. Stir in rice and 1 cup cheese. Spoon mixture into pepper halves. Arrange in a 13-in. x 9-in. x 2-in. baking pan. Bake at 350° for 35 minutes. Sprinkle with remaining cheese and parsley before serving. **Yield:** 4 servings.

BEEF AND BACON SHISH KABOBS

(Pictured above)

Nothing says "summer" like shish kabobs sizzling on the outdoor grill. Serve these kabobs over your family's favorite rice or noodles —and don't forget a crisp green salad and some fresh bread.

      1/2 cup steak sauce
      1/4 cup dry sherry *or* beef broth
        2 tablespoons honey
        1 boneless beef sirloin steak (1 pound), cut
          into 1-inch cubes
       20 slices bacon, halved crosswise and
          partially cooked
        1 large onion, cut into wedges
        1 large green *or* sweet red pepper, cut into
          squares
       16 medium mushroom caps
  Hot cooked rice *or* noodles

In a small bowl, blend steak sauce, sherry and honey. Set aside 1/2 cup for basting; cover and refrigerate. Pour remaining marinade into a large resealable plastic bag. Add the steak cubes to bag and turn to coat. Refrigerate 1 hour. Drain and discard marinade. Wrap 1/2 bacon slice around each beef cube. Alternately thread wrapped beef cubes, onion, pepper and mushrooms onto wooden or metal skewers. Grill or broil 6 in. from heat source for 8-10 minutes or until done, turning and brushing occasionally with reserved marinade. Serve immediately with rice or noodles. **Yield:** 4 servings.

BEEF PICKLE LOAF

Avoid menu monotony by adding spark to traditional meat loaf. Chopped pickles and spicy mustard offer a new twist in this pleasing recipe.

        1 egg
        1 cup milk
  1-1/2 teaspoons salt
      1/4 teaspoon pepper
        2 tablespoons spicy brown mustard
      1/4 cup chopped onion
      3/4 cup crushed saltines (about 20 crackers)
        2 pounds ground beef
        1 cup thinly sliced dill *or* sweet pickles
      1/3 cup ketchup

In a large bowl, combine egg, milk, salt, pepper and mustard. Add onion, saltines and beef; mix well. Pat one-half of the beef mixture in a greased 9-in. x 5-in. x 2-in. loaf pan. Top with a layer of pickles. Spoon remaining beef mixture on top of pickle layer. Shape into a loaf. Bake at 350° for 1-1/4 hours or until meat is no longer pink and meat thermometer reads 160°; drain. Spread ketchup on top of loaf. Serve hot or cold. **Yield:** 6-8 servings.

ITALIAN MEAT LOAF PATTIES

Since smaller portions cook more quickly, these tasty loaves bake in just 20 minutes. They're best served over buttered noodles.

> 1 package (12 ounces) extra-wide egg noodles
> 1 tablespoon butter *or* margarine, melted
> 1 can (15-1/2 ounces) sloppy joe sauce, *divided*
> 2 pounds ground beef
> 1 cup seasoned bread crumbs
> 2 eggs, beaten
> 1 tablespoon dried minced onion

Cook noodles according to package directions; drain. Toss in butter; keep hot. Set aside half of sauce. Combine remaining sauce with ground beef, bread crumbs, eggs and onion; mix with fork. On a large greased baking sheet, shape meat mixture into 8 (1 in. thick) oblong patties. Brush reserved sauce over patties. Bake at 375° for 20 minutes or until done. Serve with noodles. **Yield:** 6-8 servings.

LOUISIANA JOE

Take a break from ho-hum sloppy joes by serving this spiced-up version with Cajun flair.

> 1 package (8-1/2 ounces) corn bread/muffin mix
> 1 pound ground beef *or* turkey
> 1 onion, cut into chunks
> 1/2 green pepper, cut into chunks
> 2 garlic cloves, minced
> 1 can (14-1/2 ounces) Cajun stewed tomatoes
> 1 can (8 ounces) tomato sauce

Salt and pepper to taste

Prepare corn bread according to package directions; cut into 6 pieces. In a skillet, cook meat, onion, green pepper and garlic until meat is no longer pink; drain. Stir in tomatoes and tomato sauce. Season with salt and pepper. Simmer for 15 minutes. Serve over corn bread. **Yield:** 6 servings.

TAMALE PIE

This fun and flavorful casserole will please the palates of those who like Tex-Mex cooking. Shredded lettuce, chopped tomatoes, sliced ripe olives and sour cream are ideal accents to round out your meal.

> 1 pound ground beef *or* turkey
> 1 envelope chili seasoning mix
> 1 can (8 ounces) tomato sauce
> 1 can (14 ounces) kidney beans, drained
> 1 package (8-1/2 ounces) corn bread/ muffin mix
> 1/2 cup shredded cheddar cheese

In a large skillet, brown ground beef; drain. Stir in seasoning mix, tomato sauce and beans. Pour into a shallow 2-qt. casserole. Prepare corn bread mix according to package directions. Spread batter over chili mixture. Bake at 350° for 35-40 minutes or until center is firm. Top with cheese. Bake 5 minutes longer or until cheese melts. **Yield:** 6 servings.

ITALIAN BEEF BAKE

For maximum tenderness, chuck roasts must be cooked slowly, as in stewing or braising. You'll surely enjoy the savory goodness of this oven entree.

> 1 boneless beef chuck roast (2 pounds), cut into strips
> 1 envelope onion soup mix
> 1/4 teaspoon salt

Dash pepper

> 1 green pepper, cut into strips
> 1/4 cup chopped onion
> 1 can (14-1/2 ounces) diced tomatoes, undrained
> 1/2 cup beef broth *or* water
> 1 tablespoon steak sauce
> 1 tablespoon cornstarch

Arrange meat in a 13-in. x 9-in. x 2-in baking pan, slightly overlapping strips. Sprinkle with soup mix, salt and pepper. Top with green pepper, onion and tomatoes. Combine broth, steak sauce and cornstarch; pour over meat and vegetables. Cover tightly with foil. Bake at 350° for 2 hours or until meat is tender. **Yield:** 4-6 servings.

QUICK TOMATO MAC 'N' BEEF

(Pictured below)

Try this one-skillet meal that satisfies big appetites with its hearty mix of ingredients. You'll want to serve it often, as it's so convenient—and delicious. Best of all, cleanup is quick, too!

1 pound ground beef
1 cup chopped onion
Salt and pepper to taste
1 can (14-1/2 ounces) diced tomatoes with
 garlic and onion, undrained
1 cup water
1 cup uncooked elbow macaroni
1 cup (4 ounces) shredded cheddar cheese

In a large skillet, cook beef and onion until beef is no longer pink; drain. Season with salt and pepper. Add tomatoes and water; bring to a boil. Stir in macaroni. Cover and simmer 10 minutes or until macaroni is cooked. Stir in cheese. Garnish with green onions and sour cream if desired. **Yield:** 4 servings.

NEW ENGLAND BOILED DINNER

The term "corned" beef comes from the English use of the word "corn", meaning a small particle such as a grain of salt. Turn to this pressure-cooker classic for your next St. Patrick's Day celebration.

1 corned beef brisket with spice packet
 (3-1/2 pounds)
2 cups water
4 medium potatoes, peeled and halved
4 carrots, cut into chunks
8 small white onions
1 small yellow turnip, cut into 4 slices
1 small head green cabbage, quartered
Mustard, optional
Crisp pickles, optional

Place corned beef, contents of spice packet and water in pressure cooker. Close cover securely; place pressure regulator on vent pipe. Bring cooker to full pressure over high heat. Reduce heat to medium-high and cook for 45 minutes. (Pressure regulator should maintain a slow steady rocking motion; adjust heat if needed.) Remove from the heat; allow pressure to drop on its own. Open cooker and add vegetables on top of meat. (Do not fill cooker over 2/3 full.) Replace cover securely. Place pressure regulator on vent pipe. Bring cooker to full pressure over high heat. Reduce heat and cook 5 minutes. Immediately cool according to manufacturer's directions until pressure is completely reduced. Serve with mustard and pickles if desired. **Yield:** 6 servings.

PASTA ITALIANO BAKE

Italian-style entrees remain popular since they're generally economical to prepare yet taste fantastic. A simple side salad is all it takes to round out this flavorful feast.

1 pound ground beef
1/2 cup chopped onion
1/2 cup chopped green pepper
1 garlic clove, minced
1 can (6 ounces) tomato paste
1/2 cup water
1 teaspoon salt
1/2 teaspoon dried oregano
2-1/2 cups medium egg noodles,
 cooked and drained
1/4 cup chopped fresh parsley

1/2 cup mayonnaise *or* salad dressing
3/4 cup grated Parmesan cheese, *divided*
2 eggs, beaten

In a large skillet, brown beef; drain. Add onion, green pepper and garlic; cook until tender. Stir in tomato paste, water, salt and oregano. Cover and simmer 10 minutes. Toss noodles with parsley. In a bowl, combine salad dressing, 1/2 cup of cheese and eggs. Layer noodle mixture, salad dressing mixture and meat mixture in an 11-in. x 7-in. x 2-in. baking dish. Top with remaining cheese. Bake at 350° for 25 minutes or until heated through. **Yield:** 6 servings.

STEAK POTPIE

(Pictured at right)

Quick from-scratch cooking uses handy convenience products to prepare homemade meals in a flash. This down-home dish features canned broth, prepared steak sauce and a colorful frozen vegetable combination to speed up preparation.

1 cup chopped onion
2 tablespoons butter *or* margarine
3 tablespoons all-purpose flour
1-1/2 cups beef broth
1/2 cup steak sauce
3 cups cubed cooked steak (about 1-1/2 pounds)
1 package (16 ounces) frozen broccoli, cauliflower and carrot combination
Pastry for 1 pie crust (9 inches)
1 egg, beaten

In a 2-qt. saucepan over medium-high heat, cook onion in butter until tender. Blend in flour; cook for 1 minute. Add beef broth and steak sauce; cook and stir until mixture thickens and begins to boil. Stir in steak and vegetables. Spoon mixture into an 8-in. square baking dish. Roll out pastry; cut to fit over dish. Seal crust to edge of dish; brush with beaten egg. Cut slits in top of crust to vent. Bake at 400° for 25 minutes or until crust is golden brown. Serve warm. **Yield:** 4 servings.

MEXICALI SPOON BREAD CASSEROLE

The perfect recipe when you're hungry for a main dish with Mexican flavor, this beefy casserole packs a powerful punch. The cheesy spoon bread topping adds a special touch.

1-1/2 pounds ground beef
1 medium onion, chopped
1 can (15 ounces) tomato sauce
1 can (11 ounces) white *or* shoepeg corn, undrained
1 cup sliced ripe olives
1/2 cup chopped green pepper
1 to 2 tablespoons chili powder
1/2 teaspoon garlic powder
1/4 teaspoon pepper
1-1/2 cups milk
1/2 cup yellow cornmeal
1/4 teaspoon salt
1 cup (4 ounces) shredded cheddar cheese
2 eggs, beaten

In a large skillet, cook beef and onion over medium heat until beef is no longer pink; drain. Stir in tomato sauce, corn, olives, green pepper and seasonings. Bring to a boil; reduce heat and simmer 5 minutes. Meanwhile, in a saucepan, combine milk, cornmeal and salt. Bring to a boil over medium heat, stirring constantly; remove from heat. Quickly stir in cheese and eggs. Pour beef mixture into an ungreased 13-in. x 9-in. x 2-in. baking pan. Immediately pour cornmeal mixture over beef mixture. Bake, uncovered, at 350° for 30-35 minutes or until toothpick inserted in topping comes out clean. **Yield:** 6-8 servings.

thermometer reads 140°, 55-60 minutes for medium-rare (150°), 62-65 minutes for medium (160°) and 67-70 minutes for well-done (170°). Let stand 10 minutes before carving. **Yield:** 8-10 servings. **Editor's Note:** After seasoning, the uncooked tenderloin may be wrapped tightly and refrigerated overnight for a more intense flavor.

SPAGHETTI AND MEATBALLS

Nearly every cuisine has its own version of meatballs, from delicate Swedish meatballs to spicy Mexican ones. Perhaps the best-known in this country is Italian. Meatballs and tomato sauce are served over spaghetti.

1-1/2 pounds ground beef
　1/4 cup dried bread crumbs
　1/4 cup grated Parmesan cheese
　1/4 cup finely chopped onion
　1/4 cup milk
　　1 egg, slightly beaten
　　2 tablespoons chopped fresh parsley
　1/2 teaspoon oregano leaves, crushed
　1/2 teaspoon salt
　1/4 teaspoon pepper
　　2 tablespoons vegetable oil
　　2 jars (28 ounces *each*) spaghetti sauce
Hot cooked spaghetti

In a large bowl, combine first 10 ingredients; mix thoroughly. With hands, firmly shape into 1-in. meatballs. In 4-qt. saucepan over medium heat, in hot oil, cook meatballs, 1/4 at a time, until browned on all sides; drain. Return all meatballs to saucepan; pour spaghetti sauce over meatballs. Bring to a boil over high heat. Reduce heat to low. Cover; simmer 15 minutes. Serve over spaghetti. **Yield:** 8 servings.

PEPPERED BEEF TENDERLOIN

(Pictured above)

This peppery, tempting tenderloin is perfect for folks who really savor beef. It's important to let it rest for a few minutes before carving to allow the juices to work through the meat.

　　1 teaspoon dried oregano
　　1 teaspoon paprika
　　1 teaspoon dried thyme
　　1 teaspoon salt
　1/2 teaspoon garlic powder
　1/2 teaspoon onion powder
　1/2 teaspoon pepper
　1/2 teaspoon white pepper
　1/8 to 1/4 teaspoon cayenne pepper
　　1 beef tenderloin (3 pounds)

Combine seasonings and rub over entire tenderloin. Place on a rack in a roasting pan. Bake, uncovered, at 425° until meat is cooked as desired. Allow approximately 45-50 minutes for rare or until a meat

HEARTY BEAN AND CORN BREAD CASSEROLE

Here's a meal that packs a lot of punch. Ground beef brings delicious down-home flavor. Chili beans add just the right amount of spice, and corn bread gives a subtle Southern appeal. No one will walk away from the table hungry when this casserole is the featured fare!

　　1 pound ground beef
　　1 cup chopped onion
　　1 cup chopped green pepper
　　2 cans (16 ounces *each*) hot chili beans,
　　　drained
　　1 can (14-1/2 ounces) diced tomatoes,
　　　undrained

1 egg
2/3 cup milk
1 package (8-1/2 ounces) corn bread/
  muffin mix
1 cup (4 ounces) shredded sharp cheddar
  cheese
Sour cream, black olives, shredded lettuce,
  chopped tomato, sliced green onions and
  picante sauce

In a large skillet, cook ground beef, onion and green pepper until beef is no longer pink; drain. Add beans and tomatoes. Cook over medium heat until bubbly, stirring occasionally. Reduce heat to low; cover and simmer 5 minutes. Pour bean mixture into greased 13-in. x 9-in. x 2-in. baking dish. Beat egg in small mixing bowl. Add milk and corn bread mix; stir until smooth. Spoon corn bread batter over bean mixture and spread evenly. Bake at 400° for 15 minutes or until lightly browned. Remove from oven; sprinkle with cheese. Return to oven for 5 minutes or until cheese is melted and edges are lightly browned. Cool 10 minutes before serving. Serve with your choice of toppings. **Yield:** 8 servings.

MARINATED RIB EYES

(Pictured at right)

Beef wasn't always as popular as it is today. Prior to the Civil War, most Americans preferred pork or chicken. However, shortages of those two meats suddenly made beef popular and very much in demand. Today, tender steaks are all the rage throughout the country.

1/3 cup hot water
3 tablespoons finely chopped onion
2 tablespoons red wine vinegar *or* cider
  vinegar
2 tablespoons olive *or* vegetable oil
2 tablespoons soy sauce
1 teaspoon beef bouillon granules
1 garlic clove, minced
1/2 teaspoon paprika
1/2 teaspoon coarsely ground pepper
2 beef rib eye steaks (about 1 inch thick
  and 12 ounces *each*)

In a bowl, combine the first nine ingredients. Remove 1/2 cup of marinade; cover and refrigerate. Pierce steaks several times on both sides with a fork; place in an 11-in. x 7-in. x 2-in. glass dish. Pour remaining marinade over steaks; turn to coat. Cover and refrigerate overnight. Remove steaks, discarding marinade. Grill, uncovered, over medium-hot heat for 4-8 minutes on each side or until the meat reaches desired doneness (for rare, a meat thermometer should read 140°; medium, 160°; well-done, 170°). Warm reserved marinade and serve with steaks. **Yield:** 2 servings.

BARBECUED SHORT RIBS

These fork-tender ribs turn out perfect every time, and the sauce is wonderfully tangy. Just let them cook as you do household chores, and your home will fill with an incredible aroma.

3-1/2 to 4 pounds beef short ribs
1-1/2 cups water
1 medium onion, sliced
1 tablespoon white vinegar
SAUCE:
1/2 cup ketchup
1/4 cup chopped onion
2 tablespoons lemon juice
2 garlic cloves, minced
1 teaspoon sugar
1/2 teaspoon salt
1/8 teaspoon pepper

In a Dutch oven, combine ribs, water, onion and vinegar; bring to a boil. Reduce heat; cover and simmer for 1 hour, turning ribs occasionally. Drain. Place ribs in a single layer in an ungreased 13-in. x 9-in. x 2-in. baking dish. Combine sauce ingredients; spoon over ribs. Cover and bake at 325° for 1-1/4 hours or until the meat is tender. **Yield:** 4-6 servings.

FRENCH ONION BURGERS

(Pictured above)

Said to have made its first appearance at the St. Louis Louisiana Purchase Exposition in 1904, the hamburger remains one of America's favorite foods. The classic flavor of French onion soup is evident in this tasty burger variation.

  1 pound ground beef
  1 can (10-1/2 ounces) condensed French
     onion soup, undiluted
  4 round hard rolls, split
  4 slices Swiss *or* Gruyere cheese

Shape beef into four 1/2-in.-thick patties. In a medium skillet over medium-high heat, cook patties until browned. Remove patties and drain skillet. Add soup to skillet; bring to a boil. Return patties to skillet. Reduce heat to low. Cover and cook 5 minutes or until patties are no longer pink. Place on four roll halves. Top with cheese and remaining roll halves. Serve with soup mixture for dipping. **Yield:** 4 servings.

SIMPLY DELICIOUS MEAT LOAF

When the winter wind blows cold, there's nothing like sitting down at the dinner table to a steaming plate of homemade meat loaf.

  1/2 cup seasoned bread crumbs
    1 egg, beaten
  1-1/2 pounds ground beef
    1 can (10-3/4 ounces) condensed
      golden mushroom soup, undiluted,
      divided
    1/4 cup water

In a bowl, combine bread crumbs and egg; crumble beef over mixture and mix well. Pat into an ungreased 8-in. x 4-in. x 2-in. loaf pan. Bake at 350° for 30 minutes. Spread half the soup over top of meat loaf. Bake 30 minutes more or until no longer pink and a meat thermometer reads 160°. In a small saucepan, mix 2 tablespoons pan drippings, water and remaining soup. Heat through. Serve with meat loaf. **Yield:** 6 servings.

SAUERBRATEN MEAT LOAF

Sauerbraten is a German specialty made by marinating a beef roast in a sweet-sour sauce for 2 to 3 days before simmering it in the marinade for several hours. The result is an extremely tender roast in a delicious gravy. This popular meat loaf provides sauerbraten flavor in a fraction of the time it takes to prepare the traditional roast.

1-1/4 cups gingersnap cookie crumbs, *divided*
  1/2 cup packed brown sugar
  1/4 cup raisins
    1 can (14 ounces) beef broth
  1/4 cup plus 3 tablespoons cider vinegar,
    divided
  1/2 cup finely chopped onion
  1/2 cup dry bread crumbs
    2 eggs, beaten
    1 teaspoon salt
1-1/2 teaspoons prepared mustard
    2 pounds ground beef

Combine 3/4 cup cookie crumbs, sugar, raisins, broth and 1/4 cup vinegar. Microwave on high for 6-8 minutes, stirring every minute until thickened; set aside. In a bowl, combine onion, bread crumbs, eggs, salt, mustard and remaining cookie crumbs and vinegar. Crumble beef over mixture and mix well. Shape into a loaf. Place in a greased 11-in. x 7-in. x 2-in. baking pan. Pour half of sauce on top of meat. Bake at 350° for 1 hour or until no pink remains and a meat thermometer reads 160°. Serve with remaining sauce. **Yield:** 8 servings.

TOMATO BEEF

After a long day at the office, you'll appreciate coming home to this wholesome beef dish for supper. It offers a light Asian flavor your family is sure to enjoy.

  1 boneless beef sirloin tip roast
    (about 1-1/2 pounds), cut into
    1/2-inch slices

1 tablespoon cornstarch
2 tablespoons vegetable oil, *divided*
3 tablespoons soy sauce
Dash pepper
1/2 teaspoon ground ginger
1 medium green pepper, sliced
1/4 pound fresh mushrooms, sliced
6 green onions, sliced
2 medium tomatoes, cut into wedges

Partially freeze beef slices; cut diagonally in 1/4-in. strips. In a bowl, combine cornstarch, 1 tablespoon oil, soy sauce and pepper. Add beef; toss to coat. Cover and refrigerate several hours or overnight. Drain, reserving marinade. In a large skillet over high heat, stir-fry beef in remaining oil until browned, about 5 minutes. Push to one side of skillet. Add green pepper, mushrooms and onions. Cook until crisp-tender, about 2-3 minutes Stir in tomatoes and reserved marinade; cook 2 minutes. **Yield:** 4 servings.

MEAT LOAVES WITH PEACH SAUCE

Dress up plain meat loaf with a fruity sauce spiced with a touch of cinnamon and ginger.

1/2 cup crushed saltines (about 15 crackers)
1/4 cup chopped green pepper
1/4 cup chopped water chestnuts
1 egg
1 tablespoon soy sauce
1 tablespoon beef bouillon granules
1/4 teaspoon ground ginger
1/4 teaspoon pepper
1 pound ground beef
PEACH SAUCE:
1 can (15-1/4 ounces) sliced peaches, undrained
2 teaspoons beef bouillon granules
6 tablespoons water
2 tablespoons cornstarch
1 tablespoon sugar
1 teaspoon ground cinnamon
1/4 teaspoon ground ginger

In a large bowl, combine the first eight ingredients; crumble beef over mixture and mix well. Shape into 2 loaves and place in a greased shallow baking pan. Bake at 350° for 45 minutes or until no pink remains and a meat thermometer reads 160°. Drain peaches, reserving syrup. Chop peaches into 1/2-in. pieces. In a large saucepan, combine peaches, peach syrup and bouillon. Bring to a boil over medium heat. In a small cup, combine cornstarch and water. Gradually stir into peach mixture. Add sugar, cin-

namon and ginger; cook until thickened. Spoon over baked meat loaves. **Yield:** 4 servings.

SHORTCUT STROGANOFF

(Pictured below)

Reminiscent of traditional beef stroganoff recipes, this quick-and-easy version is one you'll be proud to serve. Slices of tender beef are dressed up in a tangy sauce. The uncooked pasta is simmered right in the sauce to save time and cleanup.

1 pound boneless sirloin steak, thinly sliced into 1/4-inch strips
1 tablespoon vegetable oil
1 can (10-3/4 ounces) condensed cream of mushroom soup, undiluted
1 can (10-3/4 ounces) condensed beef broth, undiluted
1 cup water
2 teaspoons Worcestershire sauce
3 cups uncooked spiral pasta
1/2 cup sour cream

In a large skillet over medium-high heat, stir-fry beef in hot oil until browned and juices evaporate. Add soup, broth, water and Worcestershire sauce; bring to a boil. Stir in pasta. Cook over medium heat for 15 minutes or until done, stirring occasionally. Stir in the sour cream. Heat through. **Yield:** 4 servings.

SAUCY BEEF AND BROCCOLI

(Pictured below)

With tasty tender slices of beef and fresh colorful broccoli, this mouth-watering stir-fry is "a keeper" for busy cooks. You'll appreciate how quick it is to make, and your family will enjoy the soy- and garlic-flavored sauce.

1 pound boneless beef sirloin *or* top round steak (3/4 inch thick)
2 tablespoons vegetable oil, *divided*
2 cups broccoli florets
1/4 teaspoon garlic powder *or* 2 garlic cloves, minced
1 can (10-3/4 ounces) condensed tomato soup, undiluted
2 tablespoons soy sauce
1 tablespoon vinegar
4 cups hot cooked rice

Slice beef into thin strips. In a skillet over medium-high, heat 1 tablespoon oil. Add beef, in two batches, and stir-fry until browned. Set beef aside. Reduce heat to medium. Add remaining oil. Add broccoli and garlic powder; stir-fry until broccoli is crisp-tender. Stir in soup, soy sauce and vinegar. Bring to a boil. Return beef to pan and heat through. Serve over rice. **Yield:** 4 servings.

BEEFY BURRITOS

(Pictured at right)

Flour tortillas are rolled to enclose the savory beef filling central to this dish. Serve with beans and rice plus a selection of garnishes to complete the meal.

- 1 pound ground beef
- 1 medium onion, chopped
- 1 teaspoon chili powder
- 4 cups (16 ounces) shredded cheddar cheese, *divided*
- 12 flour tortillas (8 inches)
- 1 can (10-3/4 ounces) condensed cream of mushroom soup, undiluted
- 1 cup mild *or* medium chunky salsa
- 1 cup milk
- 1 can (4 ounces) diced green chilies, drained

In large skillet, brown beef with onion; drain. Add chili powder; mix well. Spoon 1/4 cup beef mixture and 1/4 cup cheese down center of each tortilla. Roll up; arrange burritos in a greased 13-in. x 9-in. x 2-in. baking dish. In a bowl, combine soup, salsa, milk and chilies; mix well. Pour mixture over burritos in baking dish. Top with remaining cheese. Bake at 350° for 40 minutes or until hot. **Yield:** 6-8 servings.

for 30 minutes or until cheese is melted and sauce is bubbly. Top with shredded lettuce, sour cream and chopped tomatoes if desired. **Yield:** 6 servings.

MEXICAN LASAGNA

Ground beef and flour tortillas are the key ingredients in this layered casserole that has irresistible home-cooked flavor and a subtle kick.

- 1 pound ground beef
- 1/2 cup chopped green pepper
- 1 envelope onion soup mix
- 1 tablespoon chili powder
- 1 can (8 ounces) tomato sauce
- 1 can (6 ounces) tomato paste
- 1/2 cup sliced ripe olives
- 1/4 cup water
- 4 flour tortillas (7 to 8 inches)
- 1 cup (4 ounces) shredded mozzarella cheese
- 1 cup (4 ounces) shredded cheddar cheese,
Shredded lettuce, sour cream and chopped tomatoes, optional

In a large skillet, cook beef and green pepper over medium-high heat until beef is no longer pink; drain. Add soup mix, chili powder, tomato sauce, tomato paste, olives and water. Reduce heat and simmer 5 minutes or until heated through. Cut each tortilla into 4 wedges. Arrange 8 wedges in an 11-in. x 7-in. x 2-in. baking dish. Top with half of the meat mixture and 1/2 cup each of cheeses; repeat layers. Bake at 350°

MINI-MEAT LOAF SUPPER

For a savory twist on a longtime favorite, try these individual meat loaves prepared on the range top.

- 1 small onion, chopped
- 1/2 cup milk
- 1/2 cup dry bread crumbs
- 1 egg, lightly beaten
- 1 teaspoon garlic salt
- 1/2 teaspoon salt
- 1 tablespoon prepared mustard
- 1-1/2 pounds ground beef
- 1 tablespoon vegetable oil
- 4 medium potatoes, cut into 1/2-inch slices
- 1 large onion, cut into 1/2-inch slices
- 4 large carrots, cut into 2-inch julienne strips
- 1 cup dry red wine
Salt and pepper to taste
- 1 package (10 ounces) frozen peas

In a bowl, combine onion, milk, bread crumbs, egg, garlic salt, salt and mustard. Crumble beef over mixture and mix well. Shape mixture into oblong patties. In a large skillet, cook patties in oil until browned. Add potatoes, onion and carrots to skillet and wine. Season with salt and pepper. Cover and simmer 45 minutes. Add peas; cover and simmer 5 minutes. **Yield:** 4 servings.

THREE-MINUTE BEEF KABOB DINNER

When grilling is not an option, here's another delightful method for cooking kabobs. Carrots and cauliflower round out this balanced meal that's ready super fast since it's prepared in a pressure cooker.

    1/2 cup dry red wine *or* beef broth
      1 tablespoon red wine vinegar *or* cider
        vinegar
      1 teaspoon Worcestershire sauce
      1 teaspoon salt
    1/4 teaspoon pepper
    3/4 pound boneless beef sirloin steak, cut into
        1-1/2-inch cubes
    1/2 cup water
      2 medium onions, cut into thirds
      1 green pepper, cut into 8 cubes
    1/2 head cauliflower, broken into florets
      3 medium carrots, cut into 1/2-inch slices
      2 tablespoons butter *or* margarine, softened
    1/2 teaspoon prepared mustard
    1/4 teaspoon salt
    1/8 teaspoon dried oregano
Dash paprika

In a large resealable plastic bag, combine wine, vinegar, Worcestershire sauce, salt and pepper. Add beef to wine mixture; marinate at least 30 minutes. Drain meat, reserving marinade. Place rack and water in pressure cooker. Alternately thread meat, onion and green pepper onto skewers; place on rack in pressure cooker. Pour reserved marinade over kabobs. Place cauliflower beside kabobs on rack; place carrots on top of kabobs. Close cover securely; place pressure regulator on vent pipe. Bring cooker to full pressure over high heat. Reduce heat to medium-high and cook for 3 minutes. (Pressure regulator should maintain a slow steady rocking motion; adjust heat if needed.) Remove from the heat. Immediately cool according to manufacturer's directions until pressure is completely reduced. Arrange on serving platter. Stir together butter, mustard, salt, oregano and paprika; spread on cauliflower. **Yield:** 2 servings.

ITALIAN MEAT PIE

Serving common ingredients in a new way is sure to whet your family's appetite. A steaming wedge of this hearty beef dish is a welcome sight after a hectic day.

SHELL:
    2/3 cup quick-cooking *or* old-fashioned oats
    1/2 cup ketchup
      1 egg
    3/4 teaspoon salt
    1/8 teaspoon pepper
    1/8 teaspoon garlic powder
  1-1/2 pounds ground beef
FILLING:
      2 medium zucchini, sliced *or* 1 package
        (9 ounces) frozen Italian green beans,
        cooked, drained
      1 small onion, thinly sliced
      1 cup (4 ounces) shredded mozzarella
        cheese, *divided*
    1/2 cup ketchup
    1/2 teaspoon dried oregano
    1/2 teaspoon dried basil
      2 tablespoons grated Parmesan cheese

In a large bowl, combine oats, ketchup, egg, salt, pepper and garlic. Crumble beef over mixture and mix well. Press onto bottom and sides of 9-in. pie plate. Bake at 350° for 10 minutes; drain. Combine zucchini, onion, 1/2 cup mozzarella cheese, ketchup and seasonings. Spoon filling into partially baked shell. Top with remaining mozzarella cheese. Sprinkle with Parmesan cheese. Bake at 350° for 20 minutes or until meat is no longer pink. Cut into wedges to serve. **Yield:** 6-8 servings.

HOME-STYLE MEAT LOAF

(Pictured at right)

Make this mouth-watering meal for your family...and don't be surprised if it becomes a regular favorite. Meat loaf is as popular today as ever and the garlic-flavored potatoes will have your crew asking for seconds.

MEAT LOAF:
      1 cup soft bread crumbs
      1 small onion, finely chopped
      1 egg, beaten
    1/4 cup Worcestershire sauce
    1/4 cup ketchup
    1/4 teaspoon salt
Dash pepper
  1-1/2 pounds ground beef
      1 can (2.8 ounces) french-fried onions
POTATOES:
      1 package (22 ounces) frozen mashed
        potatoes
      2 tablespoons minced garlic
      1 tablespoon olive *or* vegetable oil
    1/2 cup whipping cream
    1/4 cup butter *or* margarine
      1 teaspoon dried rosemary, crushed
Salt and pepper to taste

In a bowl, combine the first seven ingredients; crumble beef over mixture and mix well. Shape into a loaf and place in a greased 11-in. x 7-in. x 2-in. baking pan. Bake, uncovered, at 350° for 60 minutes. Sprinkle meat loaf with french-fried onions. Bake an additional 5 minutes or until onions are golden brown. Allow to stand 5 minutes before slicing. Meanwhile, prepare potatoes following package directions. While potatoes are cooking, saute garlic in oil and set aside. Microwave cream and butter on high 1-2 minutes or until butter is melted; add to mashed potatoes. Add garlic and rosemary to mashed potatoes. Season with salt and pepper. Serve potatoes with meat loaf. **Yield:** 6 servings. **Editor's Note:** For an optional meat loaf topping, combine 1/4 cup ketchup and 1 tablespoon Worcestershire sauce. Spoon over meat loaf during last 5 minutes of baking time. Sprinkle topping with french-fried onions. Additional topping may be prepared to serve as sauce for meat loaf.

PAN-SEARED FILET MIGNON WITH ROASTED GARLIC MUSHROOM SAUCE

Filet mignon is the expensive, boneless cut of beef that comes from the small end of the tenderloin. Since it's extremely tender, it should be cooked quickly by broiling, grilling or pan-frying.

    1 can (10-3/4 ounces) condensed
      beef broth, undiluted
  1/2 cup water
  3/4 cup uncooked long grain rice
    1 tablespoon butter *or* margarine
    2 filet mignon steaks (4 to 6 ounces *each*)
    1 cup sliced mushrooms
    1 large onion, chopped
    1 can (10-3/4 ounces) condensed cream of
      mushroom with roasted garlic soup,
      undiluted
  1/2 cup milk
  1/4 cup sliced green onions

In a saucepan, bring broth and water to a boil. Stir in rice. Cover and cook over low heat for 20 minutes or until rice is tender. Meanwhile, heat butter in a skillet. Add steaks and cook 5 minutes. Turn steaks over. Add mushrooms and onion. Cook 5 minutes or until vegetables are tender and steaks have reached desired doneness. Remove steaks. Stir in soup and milk. Heat through. Cut steak into thin slices. Serve steak slices over rice; spoon mushroom sauce over all. Garnish with green onions. **Yield:** 2 servings.

GOOD GRAVY POT ROAST

Pot roast is usually a less tender, inexpensive beef roast that is browned, then braised very slowly in a tightly covered pot. Pot roast can be cooked on the stovetop or in the oven. This version provides plenty of tempting gravy to serve with the roast.

  3/4 cup all-purpose flour
    1 boneless beef chuck roast (about 3-1/2
      pounds)
    3 tablespoons vegetable oil
    1 can (10-3/4 ounces) condensed tomato
      soup, undiluted
    1 can (10-3/4 ounces) condensed cream of
      mushroom soup, undiluted
    1 can (10-3/4 ounces) condensed cheddar
      cheese soup, undiluted
    1 envelope onion soup mix
1-1/2 cups water
Hot cooked mashed potatoes, optional

Place flour in a large bowl or plastic bag. Add chuck roast; dredge or shake to coat. In a Dutch oven, brown roast on all sides in hot oil; drain. In a bowl, combine condensed soups, soup mix and water; mix well. Pour mixture over roast in Dutch oven. Cover and bake at 325° for 3 to 3-1/2 hours or until very tender. Serve pot roast and gravy with mashed potatoes if desired. **Yield:** 8 servings.

TODAY'S EASY BEEF STEW

To avoid messy cleanup, try this hearty stew prepared in a convenient oven bag. It's easy to combine the ingredients and then bake till the beef is tender.

  1/2 cup all-purpose flour
    1 large size oven bag (14 inches x 20 inches)
    1 can (14-1/2 ounces) Italian-style stewed
      tomatoes
    1 envelope onion soup mix
  1/4 teaspoon pepper
    2 pounds beef stew meat, cut into 1-inch
      cubes
    4 carrots, cut into chunks
    4 medium potatoes, quartered

Shake flour in oven cooking bag; place in a 13-in. x 9-in. x 2-in. baking pan. Add tomatoes, soup mix and pepper. Squeeze bag to blend ingredients. Add beef, carrots and potatoes to bag. Turn bag to coat ingredients with sauce. Arrange ingredients in even layer. Close bag with nylon tie; cut six 1/2-inch slits in top. Bake at 325° for 1 hour and 30 minutes or until beef is tender. **Yield:** 4-6 servings.

BEEF TACO SKILLET

On a busy weeknight, turn to this quick skillet dinner to satisfy your hungry brood. It's ready in 20 minutes, leaving more time for family activities.

    1 pound ground beef
    1 can (10-3/4 ounces) condensed tomato
      soup, undiluted
    1 cup chunky salsa *or* picante sauce
  1/2 cup water
    8 flour *or* corn tortillas (6 inches), cut into
      1-inch pieces
    1 cup (4 ounces) shredded cheddar cheese,
      divided

In a skillet, brown beef; drain. Add soup, salsa, water, tortillas and 1/2 cup cheese. Bring to a boil. Cover and cook over low heat for 5 minutes or until hot. Top with remaining cheese. **Yield:** 4 servings.

TACO PIZZA
(Pictured below)

Here's a nice change of pace from traditionally topped pizzas. Best of all, the dough for this festive pizza's crust is prepared in a bread machine. So you "knead" to do very little work!

CRUST:
- 1 cup water (70° to 80°)
- 3 tablespoons vegetable oil
- 1 teaspoon salt
- 2-1/2 cups bread flour
- 1/2 cup cornmeal
- 2 teaspoons bread machine yeast

TOPPING:
- 1 pound ground beef
- 2 teaspoons chili powder
- 1/4 teaspoon salt
- 1 cup mild *or* medium chunky salsa
- 1 can (2-1/4 ounces) sliced ripe olives, drained
- 1-1/2 cups (6 ounces) shredded cheddar cheese
- Shredded lettuce, chopped tomatoes, additional cheddar cheese, taco sauce, sour cream and guacamole, optional

For crust, in bread machine pan, place all ingredients in order suggested by manufacturer. Select dough setting (check dough after 5 minutes of mixing; add 1 to 2 tablespoons of water or flour if needed). Meanwhile, in a large nonstick skillet, cook ground beef over medium-high heat until no longer pink; drain. Season beef with chili powder and salt. Stir in salsa and olives; set aside. When cycle is complete, turn dough onto a lightly floured surface. Roll dough into a 13-in. circle. Transfer to a greased 12-in. pizza pan; form a 3/4-in. rim along edge. Spoon beef mixture onto dough to within 1/2 in. of edge; top with cheese. Bake at 425° on lowest oven rack for 20-25 minutes or until crust is golden brown. Serve hot with additional toppings if desired.
Yield: 1 pizza (8 servings).

Chapter 8

PORK DISHES

You'll find an array of pleasing pork entrees in this handy chapter to create fantastic fare that will spark smiles and appetites. They'll add versatility to your menus year-round.

Recipes in this chapter provided courtesy of these past sponsors...

Birds Eye
Campbell's
Comstock/Wilderness
Del Monte
Fleischmann's
Karo
Kraft
Livingston
Martha White
Nabisco
ReaLemon
Reynolds
Rosetto
Sunbeam
Swanson

FIESTA PORK CHOPS WITH COUSCOUS

(Pictured at left)

When you want to capture the true flavor of Southwestern cooking, reach for this quick recipe. Tender pork chops are simmered in an aromatic, citrus-flavored sauce featuring chunky salsa and golden corn.

> **4 rib pork chops (3/4 inch thick)**
> **Salt and pepper to taste**
> **2 tablespoons vegetable oil**
> **1 can (8 ounces) tomato sauce**
> **1 cup chunky salsa**
> **1 cup whole kernel corn**
> **1/4 cup lemon juice *or* lime juice**
> **1 tablespoon cold water**
> **1 teaspoon cornstarch**
> **Hot cooked couscous**
> **Chopped cilantro *or* parsley, optional**

Sprinkle both sides of chops with salt and pepper. In a large skillet over medium-high heat, cook chops in hot oil for 4 minutes or until brown, turning once; drain. Add tomato sauce, salsa, corn and lemon juice. Bring to a boil. Reduce heat; cover and simmer 6-8 minutes or until chops are no longer pink and juices run clear. Remove chops; keep warm. In a small bowl, combine water and cornstarch; stir into tomato mixture. Cook and stir until thickened and bubbly. Cook and stir 2 minutes longer. Spoon sauce over pork chops and couscous. Garnish with cilantro if desired. **Yield:** 4 servings.

PORK CHOP SKILLET DINNER

Dinner is ready in a flash when you serve this easy-to-make skillet sensation. Crisp-tender broccoli florets add color and vitamins.

> **3 tablespoons all-purpose flour**
> **1/2 teaspoon salt**
> **1/4 teaspoon pepper**
> **4 pork loin chops (1 inch thick)**
> **2 tablespoons butter *or* margarine**
> **1-1/4 cups chicken broth *or* water, *divided***
> **1 medium bunch broccoli, cut into florets (4 cups)**
> **1 cup fresh *or* frozen corn**

In a large resealable plastic bag, combine flour, salt and pepper. Add pork chops, one at a time, and shake to coat. In a large skillet, brown chops in butter. Add 1/2 cup chicken broth. Cover and simmer 10 minutes. Add broccoli, corn and remaining chicken broth to skillet. Cover and simmer 7 minutes longer or until broccoli is crisp-tender and pork is no longer pink. **Yield:** 4 servings.

SPICY LASAGNA TWIRLS

These flavorful pasta twirls are ideal for entertaining, as it's simple to serve individual portions. A crisp tossed salad and garlic bread are easy additions to round out the menu.

- 3/4 pound bulk Italian sausage, cooked, drained
- 1 package (10 ounces) frozen chopped spinach, thawed and well drained
- 1 cup large-curd cottage cheese
- 2 eggs, lightly beaten
- 1 tablespoon dried minced onion
- 3/4 teaspoon salt
- 1/2 teaspoon ground nutmeg
- 1/2 cup grated Parmesan cheese, *divided*
- 1 can (6 ounces) tomato paste
- 3/4 cup dry red wine *or* beef broth
- 1/2 cup water
- 1 garlic clove, crushed
- 1/2 teaspoon Italian seasoning
- 7 lasagna noodles, cooked and drained

In a large skillet, cook the sausage until no longer pink; drain. Stir in the spinach, cottage cheese, eggs, onion, salt, nutmeg and 1/4 cup Parmesan cheese. In a small bowl, blend together the tomato paste, wine, water, garlic and seasoning. Pour half of the wine mixture into a 13-in. x 9-in. x 2-in. baking dish. Spread 1/4 cup sausage mixture on each lasagna noodle. Roll-up jelly-roll style. Stand rolls in baking dish. Pour the remaining wine mixture over noodles. Sprinkle the remaining Parmesan cheese on top. Cover. Microwave on high for 10 minutes, rotating after 5 minutes. Uncover. Microwave on high 2 more minutes. **Yield:** 6 servings.

CRANBERRY PORK ROAST

Guests will rave about this tender pork roast, and you'll love it because it's very little fuss to prepare. The gravy is delicious over creamy mashed potatoes.

- 1 boneless rolled pork loin roast (2-1/2 to 3 pounds)
- 1 can (16 ounces) jellied cranberry sauce

- 1/2 cup sugar
- 1/2 cup cranberry juice
- 1 teaspoon ground mustard
- 1/4 teaspoon ground cloves
- 2 tablespoons cornstarch
- 2 tablespoons cold water

Salt to taste

Place pork roast in a slow cooker. In a medium bowl, mash cranberry sauce; stir in sugar, cranberry juice, mustard and cloves. Pour over roast. Cover and cook on low for 6-8 hours or until meat is tender. Remove roast and keep warm. Skim fat from juices; measure 2 cups, adding water if necessary, and pour into a saucepan. Bring to a boil over medium-high heat. Combine the cornstarch and cold water to make a paste; stir into gravy. Cook and stir until thickened. Season with salt. Serve with sliced pork. **Yield:** 4-6 servings.

POLYNESIAN SWEET-AND-SOUR PORK

The term "sweet-and-sour" is used to describe dishes that have a flavor balanced between sweet and pungent, usually accomplished by combining sugar and vinegar. Here, corn syrup provides the sweetness.

- 1 egg, beaten
- 2 tablespoons all-purpose flour
- 1/2 teaspoon salt

Dash pepper

- 1 pound boneless pork, cut into 1-inch cubes
- 1/4 cup vegetable oil
- 1/3 cup water
- 2 teaspoons chicken bouillon granules
- 1 garlic clove, crushed
- 2 green peppers, diced
- 1 can (20 ounces) pineapple chunks, undrained
- 1/2 cup maraschino cherries, drained
- 1 banana, cut into 1-inch pieces
- 3/4 cup light corn syrup
- 1/3 cup white vinegar
- 2 tablespoons ketchup
- 1/4 cup soy sauce
- 3 tablespoons cornstarch

Hot cooked rice

Beat together egg, flour, salt and pepper. Add pork to batter and mix lightly until each piece is coated. In a large skillet over medium-high heat, cook pork pieces in hot oil until well browned; drain. Add water, bouillon and garlic to pork in skillet. Reduce heat to simmer, cover and cook 15 minutes. Add green peppers. Cover and cook an additional 5 minutes. Drain pineapple, reserving 1/3 cup of syrup. Add pineapple, maraschino cherries and banana to skillet. Combine reserved pineapple syrup, corn syrup, vinegar, ketchup, soy sauce and cornstarch. Add to skillet and cook, stirring constantly until mixture thickens and is hot and bubbly. Serve immediately with cooked rice. **Yield:** 4 servings.

DEEP-DISH HAM AND ONION PIZZA

Why order take-out when this made-from-scratch pizza tastes so much better? You'd better make two, as folks will be back for seconds!

2-3/4 to 3 cups all-purpose flour, *divided*
   1 package (1/4 ounce) quick-rise yeast
   1 teaspoon dried rosemary, crushed
1/2 teaspoon salt
   1 cup water
   3 tablespoons olive *or* vegetable oil, *divided*
   1 egg
   2 medium yellow onions, sliced
1/2 cup thin ham strips
3/4 cup pizza sauce
   1 cup (4 ounces) shredded mozzarella cheese
   1 cup (4 ounces) shredded provolone *or*
      Swiss cheese

In a large mixing bowl, combine 1 cup flour, yeast, rosemary and salt. Heat water to 120°-130°. Gradually add water and 2 tablespoons oil to dry ingredients; beat just until moistened. Stir in egg and enough remaining flour to form a thick batter. Cover and let rest while preparing topping. In a skillet over medium heat, cook onions in remaining oil for 5 minutes. Add ham; cook until onions are golden, stirring occasionally. Cool slightly. With lightly greased hands, spread batter in bottom and 1 in. up sides of a greased 13-in. x 9-in. x 2-in. baking pan. Spread pizza sauce over dough; sprinkle cheeses over sauce. Top with onion mixture. Cover and let rise in a warm place for about 20 minutes. Bake at 400° for 30 minutes or until crust is golden brown. Remove from pan to a wire rack to cool. **Yield:** 1 pizza.

PORK WITH ROASTED PEPPERS & POTATOES

(Pictured at right)

Medallions of tender pork are simmered with potatoes, onions and roasted red peppers in a savory broth to create this mouth-watering meal. Quick and easy, this one-skillet dinner is seasoned with a touch of oregano.

   4 boneless pork chops (1/2 inch thick)
Salt and pepper to taste
   1 tablespoon olive *or* vegetable oil
   4 medium red potatoes, cut into cubes
   1 medium onion, sliced
   1 teaspoon dried oregano
   1 cup chicken broth
1/2 cup diced roasted red peppers

Sprinkle pork chops with salt and pepper. In a large nonstick skillet over medium-high heat, cook chops in oil for 10 minutes or until well browned. Remove chops; set aside. Add potatoes, onion and oregano to skillet. Cook 5 minutes or until browned, stirring occasionally. Add chops, broth and red peppers. Bring to a boil. Cover and cook over low heat for 5 minutes or until meat juices run clear. **Yield:** 4 servings.

ORIENTAL PORK TENDERLOIN PACKETS

Former scouts may recall cooking meals in foil packets over a glowing campfire. In this recipe, the packets are cooked in the oven to seal in exceptional flavor and to allow for swift cleanup.

Heavy-duty aluminum foil
>   1 **pound pork tenderloin, cut into 1/4-inch slices**
>   2 **cups broccoli florets**
>   1 **can (8 ounces) sliced water chestnuts, drained**
>   2 **cups thinly sliced carrots**
>   1 **sweet red pepper, cut in strips**
>   2 **green onions, sliced**
>   1/2 **cup water**
>   4 **teaspoons sesame oil**
>   1 **teaspoon finely chopped fresh gingerroot**

Soy sauce, optional

Tear off four 18-in. x 12-in. sheets of heavy-duty aluminum foil. Center one-fourth of pork, broccoli, water chestnuts, carrots, red pepper and onion on each sheet. Lightly toss ingredients to mix. Combine water, sesame oil and ginger; spoon over prepared ingredients. Bring shorter edges of foil together over food. Fold foil down, allowing space for heat circulation and expansion. Fold in open ends to seal. Place foil packets on baking sheet. Bake at 450° for 18-20 minutes or until pork is done. Using pot holders, transfer packets to dinner plates. To serve, cut an "X" in top of packet; fold foil back. Top with soy sauce if desired. **Yield:** 4 servings.

HUNGARIAN PORK PAPRIKA

Hungarian dishes are often served in a creamy sauce enhanced with sour cream. This dish is simple enough for everyday meals and ideal for company.

>   2 **tablespoons all-purpose flour**
>   1 **tablespoon paprika**
>   1/2 **teaspoon salt**
>   1/4 **teaspoon pepper**
>   1 **pound boneless pork, cut into 1-inch cubes***
>   4 **teaspoons olive *or* vegetable oil**
>   2 **cans (14-1/2 ounces *each*) stewed tomatoes**
>   1/2 **cup sour cream, at room temperature**

Hot cooked noodles, optional
Chopped parsley, optional

In a large plastic bag, combine flour, paprika, salt and pepper. Coat meat with flour mixture. In a skillet, brown meat in oil over medium-high heat.

Stir in tomatoes. Cook, uncovered, over medium heat 20 minutes or until meat is tender, stirring frequently. Remove pan from heat. Remove 1/2 cup sauce mixture from skillet and blend with sour cream. Return mixture to skillet; blend well. (Do not boil.) Serve over hot cooked noodles and garnish with chopped parsley if desired. **Yield:** 4 servings.
***Beef Variation:** 1 pound top sirloin or bottom round steak may be substituted for pork.

MARINATED PORK ROAST

Your family will look forward to this roast, and guests are sure to request the recipe. The flavorful marinade is also delicious on pork chops.

>   1 **tablespoon all-purpose flour**
>   1 **large size oven bag (14 inches x 20 inches)**
>   1 **boneless pork loin roast (3 to 4 pounds)**
>   1/2 **cup soy sauce**
>   1/2 **cup cream sherry**
>   1 **garlic clove, minced**
>   1 **tablespoon ground mustard**
>   1 **teaspoon ground ginger**
>   1 **teaspoon dried thyme**

SAUCE:
>   1 **jar (10 ounces) currant jelly**
>   2 **tablespoons cream sherry**
>   1 **tablespoon soy sauce**

Shake flour in oven bag; place meat in bag and place in 13-in. x 9-in. x 2-in. baking pan. Combine soy sauce, sherry, garlic, mustard, ginger and thyme. Pour in the bag and close bag with nylon tie. Gently turn bag several times to moisten meat. Refrigerate 2-3 hours or overnight, turning several times. Make six 1/2-in. slits in top of bag. Bake at 350° for 1-1/2 hours or until meat thermometer reads 170°. Heat jelly in small saucepan until melted; add sherry and soy sauce. Stir and simmer 2 minutes. Serve with pork roast. **Yield:** 6-8 servings.

TOMATO BACON POMODORO

Pomodoro is Italian for tomato, so dishes described as al pomodoro are served with a tomato sauce. In this delicious dish, crisp bacon adds amazing flavor to the savory sauce.

>   1 **package (19 to 25 ounces) frozen ravioli *or* tortellini**
>   1/2 **pound bacon, finely chopped**
>   1 **tablespoon olive *or* vegetable oil**
>   1/2 **medium onion, diced**
>   1 **garlic clove, minced**

Tomato Basil Pork Chops

1 can (14-1/2 ounces) crushed tomatoes
5 tablespoons tomato paste
2/3 cup chicken broth
1/4 teaspoon dried basil
1/4 teaspoon dried oregano
2 teaspoons chopped fresh parsley
Salt and pepper to taste

Prepare pasta according to package directions. Meanwhile, in a large skillet, cook bacon in olive oil until almost crisp. Add onion and garlic; cook until onions are tender. Stir in the tomatoes, paste, broth, basil, oregano and parsley; simmer for 3 minutes to blend flavors. Season with salt and pepper. Serve over cooked pasta. **Yield:** 4-6 servings.

TASTY TWO-STEP PORK CHOPS

Surprise your family with a homemade meal with no fuss. This ready-in-a-jiffy recipe goes from stovetop to tabletop in 20 minutes. Best of all, there are four exciting variations to keep your menu from becoming dull.

4 boneless pork chops
1 tablespoon vegetable oil
1 can (10-3/4 ounces) condensed cream of
   mushroom soup, undiluted
1/2 cup water

In a large skillet, brown pork chops in hot oil. Add soup and water; cover and simmer until pork is no longer pink. **Yield:** 4 servings.

TOMATO BASIL PORK CHOPS *(Pictured above):*
Reduce water to 1/3 cup. Add 1/2 cup chopped Italian plum tomatoes, 1 tablespoon chopped fresh parsley and 1 teaspoon dried basil or 1 tablespoon fresh basil leaves with soup. Stir in 1 tablespoon butter or margarine before serving.

LEMON THYME PORK CHOPS:
Add 1 tablespoon lemon juice, 1/2 teaspoon dried thyme and 1/4 teaspoon pepper with soup.

PORK CHOPS MORNAY:
Stir 1/3 cup shredded Swiss cheese, 2 tablespoons grated Parmesan cheese and 1/4 teaspoon ground nutmeg into sauce after removing from heat.

ROSEMARY PORK CHOPS:
Brown pork chops in butter or margarine. Add 1/2 cup sliced green onions and cook 2 minutes. Add 1 can cream of mushroom soup with roasted garlic, 1/3 cup water and 1 tablespoon chopped fresh rosemary or 1 teaspoon dried rosemary, crushed. Cover and simmer until pork is no longer pink. Stir in 1/2 cup sour cream before serving.

SMOTHERED MEXICAN PORK CHOPS

(Pictured at left)

Today's pork is leaner and higher in protein than that consumed just 10 years ago. The result is an increased popularity of "the other white meat".

> 4 boneless pork chops (1/2 inch thick)
> 1 tablespoon vegetable oil
> 1 can (14-1/2 ounces) diced tomatoes with garlic and onion, undrained
> 1/2 cup medium chunky salsa
> 1 teaspoon chili powder
> 1 can (16 ounces) black beans, undrained
> 1 package (16 ounces) frozen broccoli, corn and red pepper combination

In a large skillet over high heat, cook pork in oil for 4 minutes on each side or until browned. Add tomatoes, salsa and chili powder; reduce heat to medium. Cover and cook for 5 minutes. Uncover; add beans and vegetables to skillet. Arrange pork on top of vegetables. Cover and cook over medium-high heat for 5 minutes or until pork is no longer pink. **Yield:** 4 servings.

PORK CHOW MEIN

Chow mein is a Chinese-American dish that consists of small pieces of meat and vegetables. The ingredients are often stir-fried separately, then combined in a mild sauce and served over crisp noodles.

> 1 pound boneless pork loin
> 2 garlic cloves, minced
> 4 tablespoons soy sauce, *divided*
> 1 cup chicken broth
> 2 tablespoons cornstarch
> 1/2 to 1 teaspoon ground ginger
> 1 tablespoon vegetable oil
> 1 cup thinly sliced carrots
> 1 cup thinly sliced celery
> 1 cup chopped onion
> 1 cup coarsely chopped cabbage
> 1 cup coarsely chopped fresh spinach

Chow mein noodles *or* hot cooked rice, optional

Cut pork into 4-in. x 1/2-in. x 1/4-in. strips; place in a bowl. Add garlic and 2 tablespoons soy sauce. Cover and refrigerate 2-4 hours. Meanwhile, combine broth, cornstarch, ginger and remaining soy sauce; mix well and set aside. Heat oil in a large skillet or wok on high; stir-fry pork until no longer pink. Remove and keep warm. Add carrots and celery; stir-fry 3-4 minutes. Add onion, cabbage and spinach; stir-fry 2-3 minutes. Stir broth mixture and add to skillet along with pork. Cook and stir until broth thickens, about 3-4 minutes. Serve immediately over noodles if desired. **Yield:** 6 servings.

SAUSAGE SKILLET SUPPER

Fix this satisfying stovetop supper, as everyone will enjoy the wonderful combination of flavors. Tangy barbecue sauce provides a nice complement to the spicy pork sausage.

> 1 pound bulk pork sausage
> 1 can (28 ounces) diced tomatoes, undrained
> 1/2 cup barbecue sauce
> 1/2 cup chopped green pepper
> 1/2 cup chopped onion
> 1/2 cup uncooked long grain rice
> 1/3 cup water
> 1/2 pound process cheese product, sliced

In a large skillet, cook sausage over medium heat until no longer pink; drain. Add tomatoes, barbecue sauce, pepper, onion, rice and water; bring to a boil. Cover. Reduce heat and simmer 25 minutes or until rice is done. Place cheese on top; cover and heat until cheese melts. **Yield:** 6-8 servings.

MOZZARELLA PORK CHOPS

Almost everyone loves one type of cheese or another, whether it's delectably mild and creamy or sharp and crumbly. Mozzarella takes a starring role in many Italian-style favorites, from pizza to lasagna to this tempting pork dish.

> 1 cup crushed saltines (about 30 crackers)
> 1 teaspoon dried oregano
> 4 pork loin chops (1 inch thick)
> 1 egg, beaten
> 3 tablespoons butter *or* margarine
> 1 cup spaghetti sauce
> 1/2 cup dry red wine
> 1 cup (4 ounces) shredded mozzarella cheese

Combine saltines and oregano. Dip chops in beaten egg, then in saltine mixture. In a large skillet, brown pork chops in butter. Arrange chops in a shallow baking dish. Cover and bake at 350° for 20 minutes. Mix spaghetti sauce and wine; pour over

chops and bake, uncovered, for an additional 20 minutes. Sprinkle cheese over top and bake 5 minutes longer or until cheese is melted and slightly brown. **Yield:** 4 servings.

TOMATO-DIJON PORK CHOPS

These moist comforting pork chops come out great every time. Serve over rice or noodles for a complete, fresh-tasting meal.

> 4 pork loin *or* rib chops (3/4 inch thick)
> Salt and pepper to taste
> 1 tablespoon olive *or* vegetable oil
> 1 can (14-1/2 ounces) diced tomatoes with basil, garlic and oregano, undrained
> 1/2 cup dry red wine *or* beef broth
> 1 tablespoon Dijon mustard
> Chopped fresh parsley, optional

Season meat with salt and pepper. In a large skillet over medium-high heat, brown meat in hot oil, about 3 minutes per side; remove from skillet. Drain all but 1 tablespoon fat from skillet. Add tomatoes, wine and mustard to skillet; cook over high heat, stirring occasionally, for 5 minutes or until thickened. Return meat to skillet; spoon tomatoes over meat. Cover and cook over low heat 3 minutes or until meat is no longer pink. Garnish with parsley if desired. **Yield:** 4 servings.

AUTUMN PORK CHOPS

When the weather turns cooler, home cooks turn to heartier recipes to serve their families. These saucy chops are great served over a bed of buttered noodles or with mashed potatoes.

> 4 pork loin *or* rib chops (3/4 inch thick)
> 1 tablespoon vegetable oil
> 1 can (10-3/4 ounces) condensed cream of celery soup, undiluted
> 1/2 cup apple juice *or* water
> 2 tablespoons spicy brown mustard
> 1 tablespoon honey
> Generous dash pepper
> 4 cups hot cooked wide egg noodles

In a skillet over medium-high heat, brown chops on both sides in hot oil for 10 minutes; remove chops and drain skillet. Add soup, apple juice, mustard, honey and pepper to skillet. Bring to a boil. Return chops to pan. Reduce heat to low. Cover and cook 10 minutes or until chops are no longer pink. Serve with noodles. **Yield:** 4 servings.

CHEDDAR HAM PASTA

(Pictured below)

This flavorful dish is well suited for busy everyday dining or casual company fare. The creamy cheese sauce hints of basil, while the tomatoes provide a mild garlic and onion flavor. Your family and friends will love it!

> 12 ounces uncooked spiral pasta
> 1 can (14-1/2 ounces) diced tomatoes with garlic and onion, undrained
> Whole *or* low-fat milk
> 2 tablespoons butter *or* margarine
> 2 tablespoons all-purpose flour
> 1 teaspoon dried basil
> 2 cups (8 ounces) shredded sharp cheddar cheese
> 1-1/2 cups diced fully cooked ham
> Pepper to taste, optional
> Minced fresh parsley, optional

Cook pasta according to package directions; drain. Drain tomatoes, reserving liquid; add milk to liquid to measure 2 cups. Melt the butter in a large saucepan over low heat; stir in flour and basil. Cook over medium heat for 3 minutes, stirring constantly. Stir in milk mixture; cook until thickened, about 3 minutes, stirring constantly. Add cheese; stir until cheese melts. Stir in tomatoes, ham and pasta; heat through. Season with pepper and garnish with parsley if desired. **Yield:** 4 servings.

MEXICAN PORK CHOPS AND BEANS

Salsa, kidney beans and sweet peppers give pork chops a tasty new twist in this easy oven-bag recipe. The meat stays moist and tender in the bag when you bake this family pleaser.

> 2 tablespoons all-purpose flour
> 1 large size oven bag (14 inches x 20 inches)
> 1 cup salsa
> 2 tablespoons lime juice
> 3/4 teaspoon chili powder
> 1/2 teaspoon garlic powder
> 4 pork loin chops (1/2 inch thick)
> 1 can (16 ounces) light red kidney beans, rinsed and drained
> 2 green *or* red sweet peppers, cut into cubes

Shake flour into oven bag; place in a 13-in. x 9- in. x 2-in. baking pan. Add salsa, lime juice, chili powder and garlic powder to bag. Squeeze bag to blend ingredients. Place pork chops in bag. Spoon beans and peppers around pork chops. Close bag with nylon tie; cut six 1/2-in. slits in top. Bake until pork chops are tender and no longer pink, about 35-40 minutes. Let stand in bag 5 minutes. Remove pork chops from bag. Stir beans and peppers. Serve with pork chops. **Yield:** 4 servings.

ROASTED PORK WITH CHERRY SAUCE

A cheery cherry sauce provides a pleasing complement to traditional pork roast in this Sunday dinner favorite.

> 1 boneless pork loin roast (2 to 3 pounds)
> 1 can (21 ounces) cherry pie filling
> 1/2 cup orange juice
> 1/4 cup dry cooking sherry
> 1 tablespoon Dijon mustard
> 1 teaspoon ground cumin
> 1 teaspoon prepared horseradish

Place roast on rack in a shallow baking pan. Insert meat thermometer into thickest part of roast. Bake, uncovered, at 325° for 1-1/4 to 1-3/4 hours or until meat thermometer reads 155°. Meanwhile, combine

remaining ingredients in a medium saucepan. Bring to a boil; reduce heat to low and simmer 15 minutes, stirring occasionally. Brush cherry sauce over roast twice during the last 30 minutes of cooking. Cover roast with foil; let stand 10-15 minutes before slicing. Reheat cherry sauce. Serve sauce with roast. **Yield:** 6-8 servings.

APPLE GLAZED PORK CHOPS

Sweet and tender apple wedges are the perfect accompaniment to tasty pork chops as proven by this awesome autumn entree.

    1 large size oven bag (14 inches x 20 inches)
    1 tablespoon all-purpose flour
    1 envelope onion soup mix
  1/3 cup apple juice
  1/4 cup honey
    4 pork loin chops (1/2 inch thick)
    2 medium apples, cored and cut into wedges

Shake flour in oven bag; place in a 13-in. x 9-in. x 2-in. baking pan. Add soup mix, apple juice and honey to bag; squeeze bag to blend ingredients. Add pork chops and apples to bag. Turn bag to coat ingredients with sauce. Arrange pork chops in an even layer in bag with apples around pork chops. Close bag with nylon tie; cut six 1/2-in. slits in top. Bake at 350° for 35 minutes or until pork chops are tender andno longer pink. Spoon sauce over pork chops and apples. **Yield:** 4 servings.

TERIYAKI PORK KABOBS

(*Pictured above*)

Traditional teriyaki is a Japanese dish of meat that has been marinated in a mixture of soy sauce, sake (rice wine), sugar and ginger before being grilled or stir-fried. In this pleasing kabob recipe, we replaced the sake with beef broth.

    2 tablespoons cornstarch
    1 can (14 ounces) beef broth
    2 tablespoons soy sauce
    1 tablespoon brown sugar
  1/4 teaspoon garlic powder *or* 2 garlic cloves,
        minced
  1/4 teaspoon ground ginger
    1 pound boneless pork loin, cut into 1-inch
        cubes
   12 medium mushrooms
    1 large red onion, cut into 12 wedges
    4 cherry tomatoes
    4 cups hot cooked rice

In a saucepan, mix cornstarch, broth, soy sauce, brown sugar, garlic and ginger until smooth. Cook and stir until mixture boils and thickens. On metal or soaked wooden skewers, alternately thread pork, mushrooms and onion. Grill or broil, uncovered, for 20 minutes or until pork is no longer pink, turning and basting frequently with broth mixture. Place a tomato on each skewer. Bring remaining broth mixture to a boil; simmer 2 minutes. Serve with kabobs and rice. **Yield:** 4 servings.

LOUISIANA PORK CHOPS

(Pictured below)

Hot and pungent pepper flavors are often associated with Louisiana cooking. This simple recipe is ready in a flash, yet packs a powerful punch.

- 1/4 teaspoon *each* black pepper, white pepper and cayenne pepper
- 4 pork chops (3/4 inch thick)
- 1 tablespoon butter *or* margarine
- 1 can (14-1/2 ounces) diced tomatoes with garlic and onion, undrained

Combine peppers. Sprinkle on both sides of pork. In a large skillet, heat butter over medium-high heat. Add pork; cook for 5 minutes. Turn and cook for an additional 4 minutes; drain. Add tomatoes; reduce heat to medium. Cover and cook for 10 minutes or until pork is no longer pink. Remove pork with a slotted spoon to a serving dish; keep warm. Cook sauce until thickened; spoon over pork. **Yield:** 4 servings.

STUFFED CABBAGE ROLLS

Classic cabbage rolls are great to serve on a buffet, as it's easy to serve individual portions. This version is simple to put together—so why not give them a try?

- 12 large cabbage leaves
- 1 pound ground pork
- 1 small onion, finely chopped
- 1 cup cooked rice
- 1 teaspoon prepared mustard

- 1 teaspoon salt, *divided*
- Dash pepper
- 1 can (14-1/2 ounces) diced tomatoes
- 2 tablespoons brown sugar
- 2 tablespoons white vinegar
- 1/2 teaspoon ground allspice
- 1/4 cup cold water
- 2 tablespoons cornstarch

In a 5-qt. Dutch oven, cover cabbage leaves with boiling water; let stand 10 minutes. Drain well. Meanwhile, in a large bowl, thoroughly mix pork, onion, rice, mustard, 1/2 teaspoon salt and pepper. Place about 1/4 cup meat mixture onto each cabbage leaf. Fold in sides to enclose meat mixture and roll up. Secure with toothpicks. In same Dutch oven, place cabbage rolls seam side down. In a medium bowl, combine tomatoes, brown sugar, vinegar, allspice and remaining salt; pour over cabbage rolls. Over medium-high heat, bring to a boil. Reduce heat to low. Cover; simmer 30 minutes or until meat is done. With slotted spoon, remove cabbage rolls to platter and discard toothpicks; keep warm. In a cup, stir 1/4 cup cold water into cornstarch. Add cornstarch mixture to simmering tomato liquid. Cook until mixture boils, stirring constantly. Spoon sauce over cabbage rolls. **Yield:** 12 rolls.

MEXICAN SKILLET

Chili powder is often associated with Mexican cooking. This popular blend contains dried chilies, garlic, oregano, cumin and other seasonings.

- 1 pound ground pork
- 1/2 cup chopped onion
- 1 garlic clove, minced
- 2 teaspoons chili powder
- 1/4 teaspoon salt
- 1 can (14-1/2 ounces) cut green beans, drained
- 1 can (16 ounces) red kidney beans, undrained
- 1/2 pound process cheese product, cubed
- 4 cups shredded lettuce
- 1 large tomato, chopped
- 8 pitted ripe olives, sliced
- 1/2 cup French salad dressing

In a large skillet, brown pork; drain. Add onion, garlic, chili powder and salt; cook until onion is tender. Add green beans and kidney beans to meat mixture; cover and simmer for 10 minutes. Stir in cheese until melted. Place lettuce around meat mixture; top with tomatoes and olives. Drizzle dressing over lettuce. **Yield:** 8 servings.

SWEET-AND-SOUR MEATBALLS

These flavorful meatballs are wonderful over rice but may also be served as an appealing appetizer.

1 egg, beaten
1/4 cup milk
2/3 cup crushed saltines (about 20 crackers)
1/2 teaspoon ground ginger
1/4 teaspoon pepper
3/4 teaspoon salt
1-1/4 pounds ground pork
1/2 cup raisins
2 tablespoons butter *or* margarine
1 can (16 ounces) whole cranberry sauce
1/2 cup barbecue sauce
1/2 cup thin green pepper strips
Hot cooked rice, optional

In a large bowl, combine egg, milk, saltines, ginger, pepper and salt. Add pork and raisins; mix well. Shape meat mixture into 12 round balls and set aside. In a 10-in. skillet over medium heat, cook meatballs in butter until no longer pink; drain. In a small bowl, combine cranberry sauce and barbecue sauce. Pour sauce mixture over meatballs. Cover; reduce heat and simmer 15 minutes. Add green pepper. Cover and simmer an additional 5 minutes. Serve with hot rice if desired. **Yield:** 6 servings.

PORK CHOPS WITH CARAWAY CABBAGE

Each fall, your family will request this hearty skillet supper, featuring complementary pork and cabbage.

4 pork loin chops (3/4 inch thick)
2 tablespoons vegetable oil
1/2 teaspoon pepper
1-1/2 cups finely chopped onion
3 tablespoons butter *or* margarine
6 cups shredded cabbage
2 garlic cloves, minced
3 tablespoons red wine vinegar *or* cider vinegar
1 teaspoon caraway seed
1/2 teaspoon salt

In a skillet over high heat, brown the pork chops in oil; drain. Sprinkle with pepper; remove from skillet. Set aside. In same skillet, saute onion in butter for 1-2 minutes or until tender. Add cabbage, garlic, vinegar, caraway and salt; cook, stirring occasionally, until cabbage wilts. Place chops on top of cabbage. Cover and simmer for 15-17 minutes or until meat is tender. **Yield:** 4 servings.

BAKED HAM STEAK

(Pictured above)

One taste of this recipe and you'll quickly see why ham steaks have become a scrumptious standby in most every kitchen across the country.

2 ham steaks, (1/2 pound *each*), cut in half
1 can (8 ounces) crushed pineapple, drained
1/4 cup packed brown sugar

Line an 11-in. x 7-in. x 2-in. baking pan with aluminum foil. Place ham in pan; top with pineapple. Sprinkle with brown sugar. Bake, uncovered, at 350° for 20-25 minutes or until heated through. **Yield:** 4 servings.

FARMHOUSE PORK AND APPLE PIE

This recipe combines pork and apples nicely to create a comforting main dish. It calls for a bit of preparation, but you and your family will agree that its wonderful flavor makes it well worth the extra effort.

>   1 pound sliced bacon, cut into 2-inch pieces
>   3 medium onions, chopped
>   3 pounds boneless pork, cubed
> 3/4 cup all-purpose flour
> Vegetable oil, optional
>   3 medium tart apples, peeled and chopped
>   1 teaspoon rubbed sage
> 1/2 teaspoon ground nutmeg
>   1 teaspoon salt
> 1/4 teaspoon pepper
>   1 cup apple cider
> 1/2 cup water
>   4 medium potatoes, peeled and cubed
> 1/2 cup milk
>   5 tablespoons butter *or* margarine, *divided*
> Additional salt and pepper
> Minced fresh parsley, optional

Cook bacon in an ovenproof 12-in. skillet until crisp. Remove with a slotted spoon to paper towels to drain. In drippings, saute onions until tender; remove with a slotted spoon and set aside. Dust pork lightly with flour. Brown a third at a time in drippings, adding oil if needed. Remove from the heat and drain. To pork, add bacon, onions, apples, sage, nutmeg, salt and pepper. Stir in cider and water. Cover and bake at 325° for 2 hours or until pork is tender. In a saucepan, cook potatoes in boiling water until tender. Drain and mash with milk and 3 tablespoons butter. Add salt and pepper to taste. Remove skillet from the oven and spread potatoes over pork mixture. Melt remaining butter; brush over potatoes. Broil 6 in. from the heat for 5 minutes or until topping is browned. Sprinkle with parsley if desired. **Yield:** 10 servings.

MAPLE-GLAZED RIBS

(Pictured below left)

Few foods can top the taste of pure maple syrup, but these lip-smacking ribs may be one of them. This main dish is a sure-fire winner.

>   3 pounds pork spareribs, cut into serving-size pieces
>   1 cup maple syrup
>   3 tablespoons orange juice concentrate
>   3 tablespoons ketchup
>   2 tablespoons soy sauce
>   1 tablespoon Dijon mustard
>   1 tablespoon Worcestershire sauce
>   1 teaspoon curry powder
>   1 garlic clove, minced
>   2 green onions, minced
>   1 tablespoon sesame seeds, toasted

Place ribs, meaty side up, on a rack in a greased 13-in. x 9-in. x 2-in. baking pan. Cover pan tightly with foil. Bake at 350° for 1-1/4 hours. Meanwhile, combine the next nine ingredients in a saucepan. Bring to a boil over medium heat. Reduce heat; simmer for 15 minutes, stirring occasionally. Drain ribs; remove rack and return ribs to pan. Cover with sauce. Bake, uncovered, for 35 minutes, basting occasionally. Sprinkle with sesame seeds just before serving. **Yield:** 6 servings.

DELTA SUPPER WITH CORN BREAD TOPPING

(Pictured above right)

When you want to capture the true flavor of Southern cooking, reach for this recipe. Smoked sausage, tomatoes and black-eyed peas make it a hearty meal. And cayenne pepper adds just the right amount of "zip".

>   1 pound smoked sausage, cut into 1-inch pieces
>   1 large onion, cut into thin wedges

2 large green peppers, cut into strips
3 tablespoons vegetable oil, *divided*
1 can (14-1/2 ounces) diced tomatoes,
   undrained
2 cans (16 ounces *each*) black-eyed peas, drained
1 cup self-rising cornmeal mix
1/4 teaspoon cayenne pepper
2/3 cup milk
1 egg, beaten

In a large skillet over medium-high heat, cook the sausage, onion and green pepper in 1 tablespoon oil until vegetables are tender. Stir in tomatoes and peas; reduce heat and simmer for 5 minutes. Pour into a greased 13-in. x 9-in. x 2-in. baking dish. In a small bowl, combine cornmeal mix, cayenne pepper, milk, egg and remaining oil; stir until smooth. Pour over sausage mixture. Bake at 400° for 25-30 minutes or until golden brown. **Yield:** 6-8 servings.

Flashback to the '70s

*I*t's the 1970s and many Midwestern homemakers are dreaming of gold…at least when it came to kitchen appliances.

The plain white refrigerators and stoves of the '60s give way to harvest gold and avocado green. The color splashes into the laundry room, too. There are even some copper-toned ranges, freezers, washers and dryers.

At the Homemaker Schools cooking demonstrations, local sponsors are able to show the newest, coolest appliances to large numbers of women. Work-saving features and spiffy colors help put new appliances on many a woman's wish-list.

Just as the colors expand, so does the territory. The cooking shows, which have been famous in the Midwest for years, branch out and stretch from coast to coast. Thousands more women (and a few men) enjoy the sessions with their fresh ideas, information about recent products, new recipes by the dozens, and good times with friends both old and new.

WITH A LITTLE HELP from the audience, home economist Ruth Anne McKeown (below left) mixes up a treat to share. At right, home economist Del Rae Beerman shops for sponsor products before a cooking show.

Peter Paul
Old Fashioned Cookies 12 Oz. 55¢

Gallon Ice Cream $1.69

HOMING HELPS
Homemakers School
Specials

Axion Laundry Pre-soak . . . . 38-oz. . . . $1.43
Blue Bonnet Margarine . . . . 1-lb. . . . 72¢
Cold Power Laundry Detergent 49-oz. . $1.21
Diamond Walnuts . . . . . . 16-oz. . . . $1.59
Fleischmann's Yeast . . 3 pack . . . . 20¢
Fruit Fresh . . . . . . 5-oz. Can . . . . 99¢
Nabisco Premium Saltine Crackers 1-lb. Box 59¢
Nestea® . . . 3-oz.
Rhodes Frozen Bread Dough 5 - 1-lb. Loaves $1.37
Taster's Choice® $1.29
100% Freeze Dried Coffee 8-oz. $2.61

SPEED QUEEN®
the washer and dryer with the
Silver Lining

150

That's Entertainment

- The "Aloha Satellite Show" starring Elvis Presley is beamed worldwide, and an estimated 1-1/2 billion people tune in.

- Archie Bunker, The Fonz and Laverne & Shirley are among the best-loved TV characters.

- "Jaws" and "The Towering Inferno" ignite a box-office scramble for disaster films. Fans love being scared out of their wits.

- "M*A*S*H", one of the top-grossing films of 1970, spawns a popular TV series that dramatizes the Korean War from the viewpoint of the eccentric staff of a mobile hospital unit.

The 'In' Things

- To look "groovy", today's girl wears hip-hugging, bell-bottom pants, a beaded choker and a pair of brown Earth shoes (with heels lower than the front of the shoe).

- When the stone on your mood ring turns black, friends know to stay away because you're grumpy.

- Velvet hotpants—super-short shorts for women—paired with white go-go boots are all the rage.

Price Check

- A first-class postage stamp costs 6 cents.

- Gasoline, a bargain at 40 cents a gallon in 1970, more than doubles, to 90 cents, by the end of the decade.

- Milk rises to $1.32 per gallon and bread is 24 cents a loaf.

- Over the course of the decade, the cost of a new home goes up 83% and new-car prices double. Income increases only 23%.

Play List

- With the name "John" as the common denominator, singers Elton John, Olivia Newton-John and John Denver debut in 1971, then proceed to crank out hits for years.

- "Love Will Keep Us Together" by The Captain & Tennille is the biggest hit single of 1975. The pair wins a Grammy Award.

- Longtime friends Carly Simon and James Taylor score major hits on the singles chart, including "You're So Vain" for her and "Fire and Ice" for him. They marry.

SUPER '70s.
Archie Bunker's wife, Edith, drove him crazy on "All in the Family", the movie "Jaws" temporarily curbed swimming, bell-bottoms were "cool", Laverne & Shirley's antics gave us the giggles and The Captain & Tennille made beautiful music together.

Chapter 9

FISH & SEAFOOD

Reel in compliments with this fresh catch of succulent seafood entrees. Among these main events, there's something to please every palate, including shrimp, salmon, tuna, crabmeat and more!

Recipes provided courtesy of these past sponsors...

Alaska Salmon
Bertolli
Blue Bonnet
Campbell's
Chicken of the Sea
Kraft
Nabisco
Swanson
Wearever

SHRIMP & VEGETABLE STIR-FRY

(Pictured at left)

Here's a tasty way to enjoy succulent shrimp. In this delicious dish, bite-size pieces of vegetables and seafood are cooked quickly in a minimum amount of fat.

- 3 tablespoons cornstarch
- 1 can (14 ounces) chicken broth
- 1 tablespoon soy sauce
- 1/2 teaspoon sesame oil, optional
- 2 tablespoons vegetable oil, *divided*
- 1 pound medium shrimp, peeled and deveined
- 4 cups cut-up vegetables (thinly sliced carrots, pepper strips, sliced green onions, snow peas, broccoli florets, sliced water chestnuts, etc.)
- 1/2 teaspoon ground ginger
- 1/4 teaspoon garlic powder *or* 2 garlic cloves, minced
- 4 cups hot cooked rice

In a small bowl, mix cornstarch, broth, soy sauce and sesame oil if desired; set aside. Heat 1 tablespoon vegetable oil in skillet. Add shrimp and stir-fry until pink. Remove shrimp from skillet; set aside. Add remaining vegetable oil to skillet. Add vegetables, ginger and garlic; stir-fry until vegetables are crisp-tender. Stir cornstarch mixture; add to skillet. Cook until mixture boils and thickens, stirring constantly. Return shrimp to skillet and heat through. Serve over rice. **Yield:** 4 servings.

CLASSIC TUNA NOODLE CASSEROLE

Before World War I, tuna was seldom served because it was available only at fresh-fish markets. During the war, there was a scarcity of meat, and sardine canners began packing tuna fish. Soon tuna casserole became a standard in the American diet.

- 1 can (10-3/4 ounces) condensed cream of celery soup, undiluted
- 1/2 cup milk
- 2 cups hot cooked medium egg noodles
- 2 cans (6 ounces *each*) tuna, drained and flaked
- 1 cup frozen peas
- 2 tablespoons chopped pimientos, optional
- 2 tablespoons dry bread crumbs
- 1 tablespoon butter *or* margarine, melted

In a 1-1/2-qt. casserole, combine soup and milk; add noodles, tuna, peas and pimientos if desired. Bake at 400° for 20 minutes or until hot; stir. Combine bread crumbs and butter; sprinkle over top. Bake an additional 5 minutes. **Yield:** 4 servings.

BROTHY SHRIMP AND RICE SCAMPI

On restaurant menus, scampi is the term used to describe large shrimp that are seasoned with garlic, brushed with oil or butter, then broiled. This tempting version is served with rice that's been simmered in a seasoned broth.

      2 cans (14 ounces *each*) chicken broth
  3/4 cup uncooked long grain rice
      1 tablespoon olive *or* vegetable oil
      1 pound fresh *or* frozen large shrimp, peeled
          and deveined
      4 garlic cloves, minced
      2 tablespoons lemon juice
      2 green onions, thinly sliced

In a saucepan, bring broth to a boil. Add rice. Cover and cook over low heat for 20 minutes. Heat oil in skillet. Add shrimp and garlic and cook 5 minutes or until done, stirring occasionally. Place shrimp into serving bowls. Stir lemon juice into rice and pour over shrimp. Top with onions. **Yield:** 4 servings.

BALSAMIC GLAZED SALMON

(Pictured below)

Salmon was an important food to many early American Indians. But superstitions prevented members of certain tribes from handling or eating the fish, lest they anger its spirit and cause the fish to leave their waters forever.

      1 tablespoon olive *or* vegetable oil
      4 salmon fillets (6 ounces *each*)
  Lemon-pepper seasoning
      1 can (14 ounces) seasoned chicken broth
          with Italian herbs, *divided*
      3 tablespoons balsamic vinegar
  1-1/2 tablespoons cornstarch
  Hot cooked rice

Heat oil in skillet. Add salmon, skin side up, and cook until browned, about 5 minutes. Turn salmon and season with lemon pepper. Add 1/2 cup broth. Bring to a boil. Cover and cook over low heat for 5 minutes or until fish flakes easily with a fork. Remove salmon and keep warm. Mix remaining broth, vinegar and cornstarch. Add to skillet; cook and stir until mixture boils and thickens. Place rice on serving plate and top with salmon. Spoon sauce over all. **Yield:** 4 servings.

SALMON SUPREME

This jazzy salmon loaf contains pimientos, almonds, mushrooms and more. It's served with a rich cream sauce accented with tasty green olives.

      1 can (4 ounces) mushroom stems and
          pieces, drained
  1/4 cup chopped onion
      5 tablespoons butter *or* margarine, melted,
          divided
      2 cans (14-3/4 ounces *each*) salmon, drained,
          bones and skin removed

1-1/2 cups crushed saltines (about 45 crackers)
   1 jar (4 ounces) sliced pimientos, drained
   1/4 cup chopped almonds
   3 tablespoons chopped parsley
   3 eggs, lightly beaten
   2 teaspoons lemon juice
   3/4 teaspoon tarragon leaves
   1/2 teaspoon salt
Dash pepper
   2 tablespoons all-purpose flour
1-1/2 cups milk
   1/3 cup chopped stuffed olives
   1/4 cup mayonnaise

In a small skillet, cook mushrooms and onion in 3 tablespoons butter until onion is tender. In a large bowl, combine salmon, saltines, pimientos, almonds and parsley. Add mushroom mixture, eggs, lemon juice, tarragon, salt and pepper; mix well. Spoon into a greased 9-in. x 5-in. x 3-in. loaf pan. Bake at 350° for 40-45 minutes or until heated through. Meanwhile, in a small saucepan, combine flour and remaining butter until smooth. Gradually stir in milk. Bring to a boil; cook and stir for 2 minutes or until thickened. Stir in olives and mayonnaise. Serve salmon loaf with sauce. **Yield:** 8 servings.

Fold in crabmeat and pimientos. Pour mixture into a greased 1-1/2-qt. casserole; set aside. Melt remaining margarine; toss with bread crumbs. Sprinkle over casserole. Bake at 400° for 25 minutes or until mixture is hot. **Yield:** 8 servings.

CRAB IMPERIAL

This dish offers a favorite Chesapeake Bay treatment for crab. It is delicious eaten alone or used as a stuffing for fish or other seafood.

   1/2 cup sliced green onions
   1 tablespoon finely chopped green pepper
   6 tablespoons butter *or* margarine, *divided*
   2 tablespoons all-purpose flour
   1 tablespoon lemon juice
   1/2 teaspoon salt
   1/2 teaspoon ground mustard
   1/2 teaspoon Worcestershire sauce
   1 cup milk
   1/4 cup mayonnaise
   1 egg yolk
   1 pound cooked lump crabmeat, picked over
   1 jar (2 ounces) diced pimientos, drained
   1/2 cup fresh bread crumbs

In a 1-qt. saucepan over medium heat, cook green onions and pepper in 4 tablespoons butter until tender. Add flour, lemon juice, salt, mustard and Worcestershire sauce; stir until smooth. Gradually add milk. Cook until mixture boils, stirring constantly. Remove from heat. Stir in mayonnaise. In a small bowl, beat egg yolk with fork; stir in 1/2 cup hot mixture. Add to saucepan, stirring constantly.

FABULOUS FAST SHRIMP

(Pictured above)

America's favorite shellfish, shrimp cook quickly and always draw rave reviews. As a general rule, the larger the shrimp, the higher the price, so feel free to use medium shrimp if you'd like.

   2 celery ribs, chopped
   1/4 cup chopped green pepper
   1/4 cup sliced green onions
   1 tablespoon butter *or* margarine
   1 pound fresh large shrimp, shelled and deveined
   1 can (10-3/4 ounces) condensed cream of chicken *or* 98% fat-free cream of chicken soup, undiluted
   1/2 cup water
Dash cayenne pepper
Hot cooked rice
Paprika

In a large skillet, cook celery, green pepper and green onions in butter until tender. Add shrimp and cook 3-5 minutes or until shrimp turn pink. Add soup, water and cayenne; heat through. Serve over hot cooked rice. Sprinkle with paprika. **Yield:** 4 servings.

FRIED OYSTERS

When King Charles I divided Virginia and gave part to Lord Baltimore to govern, he placed the boundary on the western shore rather than in the center of the Potomac River. Why? So Lord Baltimore's Maryland would control the rights to the rich oyster and crab beds on both sides of the river.

>   1-1/2 cups finely crushed saltines (about 40 crackers)
>   2 eggs
>   2 tablespoons milk
>   1/2 teaspoon celery salt
>   1/8 teaspoon pepper
>   1 quart shucked oysters, drained and patted dry
> Vegetable oil
> Lemon wedges

Place cracker crumbs on a sheet of waxed paper. In a pie plate, beat eggs, milk, celery salt and pepper. Using tongs, dip oysters, one at a time, into egg mixture; coat with crumbs. Let stand on waxed paper 10 minutes. In a 10-in. skillet over medium heat, in 1/2-in. hot oil, fry oysters, a few at a time, 5-7 minutes or until lightly browned, turning once. Drain oysters on paper towels; keep warm until all oysters are cooked. Serve with lemon wedges. **Yield:** 4 servings.

MILANO SHRIMP FETTUCCINE

(*Pictured above*)

In Italian, the word pasta means paste, which refers to the dough made by combining semolina and water. The dough can be shaped into "little ribbons" known as fettuccine, which are thin flat noodles about 1/4-inch wide.

>   4 ounces uncooked spinach *or* egg fettuccine
>   1/2 pound medium shrimp, peeled and deveined
>   1 garlic clove, minced
>   1 tablespoon olive *or* vegetable oil
>   1 can (14-1/2 ounces) diced tomatoes with basil, garlic and oregano, undrained
>   1/2 cup whipping cream
>   1/4 cup sliced green onions

Cook fettuccine according to package directions; drain. Meanwhile, saute shrimp and garlic in oil until shrimp are pink. Stir in tomatoes; simmer 5 minutes. Blend in cream and green onions; heat through. Do not boil. Serve over hot cooked fettuccine. **Yield:** 4 servings.

LOBSTER NEWBURG

This extraordinary entree was created at Delmonico's restaurant in New York City during the late 19th century in honor of a favorite customer. The elegant sauce is often used to enhance other seafood, such as crab, shrimp and scallops.

>   2 green onions, finely chopped
>   1/4 cup butter *or* margarine
>   1 tablespoon all-purpose flour
>   1/2 teaspoon salt
> Generous dash paprika
> Generous dash cayenne pepper
> 1-1/2 cups half-and-half cream
>   2 egg yolks
>   1 pound cooked lobster meat, cut into chunks
>   2 tablespoons dry cooking sherry *or* Madeira wine
> Baked puff pastry shells *or* toast points

In a 3-qt. saucepan over medium-high heat, cook onions in butter until tender. Add flour, salt, paprika and cayenne. Stir until smooth. Gradually stir in cream; bring to a boil, stirring constantly. Remove from heat; set aside. In a small bowl, beat egg yolks slightly; stir in a small amount of the hot mixture.

Add to the saucepan, stirring constantly. Add lobster and cooking sherry. Cook over low heat until hot, stirring constantly. Do not boil. Serve over pastry shells. **Yield:** 6 servings.

CREAMY SEASIDE CASSEROLE

Are you fishing for fast fare to prepare for your family on hurried, hectic days? You'll love this cheesy, quick casserole and will agree it's "reel"-y delicious.

> 1 package (12 ounces) **macaroni shells and cheese dinner**
> 1/4 cup **chopped onion**
> 1/4 cup **chopped sweet red pepper**
> 2 tablespoons **butter** *or* **margarine**
> 1 package (10 ounces) **frozen peas, thawed, drained**
> 1 can (7-3/4 ounces) **salmon, drained, bones and skin removed**
> 1/2 cup **mayonnaise**

Prepare macaroni dinner as directed on package. Saute onion and red pepper in butter. Add to macaroni shells and cheese with peas, salmon and mayonnaise; mix well. Spoon into a 1-1/2-qt. casserole. Cover and bake at 350° for 25 minutes or until heated through. **To Microwave:** Cover with plastic wrap. Microwave on high for 8-10 minutes, turning dish after 5 minutes. **Yield:** 6 servings.

SALMON CROQUETTES

(Pictured at right)

Though the chicken variety of croquettes may be better known, delicate canned salmon is ideal as well. These favorites are fried to a crisp golden brown and served with a tangy tartar sauce.

> 1 can (14-3/4 ounces) **pink salmon, drained, bones and skin removed**
> 1 cup **evaporated milk,** *divided*
> 1-1/2 cups **cornflake crumbs,** *divided*
> 1/4 cup **dill pickle relish**
> 1/4 cup **finely chopped celery**
> 2 tablespoons **finely chopped onion**
> **Oil for deep-fat frying**
> TARTAR SAUCE:
> 2/3 cup **evaporated milk**
> 1/4 cup **mayonnaise**
> 2 tablespoons **dill pickle relish**
> 1 tablespoon **finely chopped onion**

In a medium bowl, combine salmon, 1/2 cup milk, 1/2 cup crumbs, relish, celery and onion; mix well.

With wet hands, shape 1/4 cupfuls into cones. Dip into remaining milk, then into remaining crumbs. Heat oil in a deep-fat fryer to 365°. Fry croquettes, a few at a time, for 2 to 2-1/2 minutes or until golden brown. Drain on paper towels; keep warm. Combine tartar sauce ingredients in a medium saucepan; cook over medium-low heat until heated through and slightly thickened. Serve warm with croquettes. **Yield:** 4-6 servings.

SHRIMP FRIED RICE

This Asian dish is best when prepared with rice that has been cooked and refrigerated for a day before being fried with the other ingredients. It's a tasty way to use up leftovers.

> 1 **egg, lightly beaten**
> 2 tablespoons **butter** *or* **margarine,** *divided*
> 2 **green peppers, cut in strips**
> 1 **red onion, sliced**
> 1 pound **cooked shrimp, peeled and deveined**
> 1 cup **cooked rice**
> 1 **tomato, chopped**
> 2 tablespoons **cornstarch**
> 3/4 cup **chicken broth** *or* **cold water**
> 3 tablespoons **soy sauce**

In a large nonstick skillet, cook and scramble egg in 1 tablespoon butter. Remove egg from skillet, set aside. Melt remaining butter in skillet. Cook peppers and onion in butter until tender. Add shrimp, rice and tomato; mix well. In a small bowl, combine cornstarch, broth and soy sauce; stir into shrimp mixture. Continue cooking until mixture is thickened. Stir in scrambled egg. **Yield:** 4-6 servings.

GREEK GRILLED CATFISH

(*Pictured below*)

The majority of the catfish in today's stores are raised on farms, so home cooks are assured of consistent flavor and quality. The flesh is firm, low in fat and mild in flavor, making it a popular choice at mealtime.

> **6 catfish fillets (8 ounces *each*)**
> **Greek seasoning to taste**
> **4 ounces feta cheese, crumbled**
> **1 tablespoon dried mint**
> **2 tablespoons olive *or* vegetable oil**
> **Fresh mint leaves *or* parsley, optional**
> **Cherry tomatoes, optional**

Sprinkle both sides of fillets with Greek seasoning. Sprinkle each fillet with 1 rounded tablespoon feta cheese and 1/2 teaspoon mint. Drizzle 1 teaspoon olive oil over each. Roll up fillets and secure with toothpicks. Grill over medium heat for 20-25 minutes or until fish flakes easily with a fork. Or, place fillets in a greased baking dish and bake at 350° for 30-35 minutes or until fish flakes easily with a fork. Garnish with mint leaves or parsley and cherry tomatoes if desired. **Yield:** 6 servings.

SOLE WITH CUCUMBER SAUCE

Sliced cucumbers take on a mild pickle flavor as they cook with dill, herbs and sole fillets in this quick and delicious fish dish.

> **2 medium cucumbers, peeled and thinly sliced**
> **1/2 cup chopped green onions**
> **1/4 cup chopped celery**
> **1 tablespoon minced fresh parsley**
> **1 teaspoon dill weed**
> **1 cup chicken broth**
> **4 sole fillets (about 1-1/2 pounds)**
> **2 teaspoons cornstarch**
> **1/2 cup whipping cream**
> **1 teaspoon prepared horseradish**
> **Salt and pepper to taste**

In a large skillet, layer the cucumbers, onions, celery, parsley and dill; add the broth. Top with fillets; bring to a boil. Cover and simmer for 8-10 minutes or until fish flakes easily with a fork. With a slotted spatula, remove fish to a serving platter and keep warm. Combine the cornstarch and cream until smooth; add horseradish, salt and pepper. Stir into the cucumber mixture in the skillet. Simmer for 2 minutes or until thickened. Pour over fish; serve immediately. **Yield:** 4 servings.

OVEN FISH 'N' CHIPS

Enjoy moist, flavorful baked fish with a coating that's as crunchy and golden as the deep-fried variety...plus, crisp, irresistible "fries".

> **2 tablespoons olive *or* vegetable oil**
> **1/4 teaspoon pepper**
> **4 medium baking potatoes (1 pound), peeled**
> **FISH:**
> **1/3 cup all-purpose flour**
> **1/4 teaspoon pepper**
> **1 egg**
> **2 tablespoons water**
> **2/3 cup crushed cornflakes**
> **1 tablespoon grated Parmesan cheese**
> **1/8 teaspoon cayenne pepper**
> **1 pound frozen haddock fillets, thawed**
> **Tartar sauce, optional**

In a medium bowl, combine oil and pepper. Cut potatoes lengthwise into 1/2-in. strips. Add to oil mixture; toss to coat. Place on a greased 15-in. x 10-in. x 1-in. baking pan. Bake, uncovered, at 425° for 25-30 minutes or until golden brown and crisp. Meanwhile, combine flour and pepper in a shallow dish. In a second dish, beat egg and water. In a third dish, combine the cornflakes, cheese and cayenne. Dredge fish in flour, then dip in egg mixture and coat with crumb mixture. Place on a greased baking sheet. Bake at 425° for 10-15 minutes or until fish flakes easily with a fork. Serve with chips and tartar sauce if desired. **Yield:** 4 servings.

SHRIMP SCAMPI

(Pictured at right)

A lively garlic flavor is key to this classic shrimp dish. While it's simple to make, the entree looks fancy enough for company or special occasions.

        8 ounces angel hair pasta
1-3/4 cups chicken broth
        2 garlic cloves, minced
    1/4 teaspoon lemon-pepper seasoning
    1/4 cup chopped green onions, *divided*
    1/4 cup minced fresh parsley, *divided*
        1 pound uncooked shrimp, peeled and
            deveined

Cook pasta according to package directions. Meanwhile, in a large saucepan, combine the broth, garlic, lemon-pepper, 3 tablespoons green onions and 3 tablespoons parsley. Bring to a boil. Add shrimp; cook for 3-5 minutes or until shrimp turn pink. Drain pasta and place in a serving bowl. Top with shrimp mixture and remaining onions and parsley. **Yield:** 4 servings.

ARTICHOKE TUNA TOSS

Your family will love this made-in-minutes medley. The vegetable-and-vermicelli combination appeals to folks' desire for fresh-tasting, healthy foods.

3-1/2 cups water
    1/4 cup butter *or* margarine
        2 packages (4.6 ounces *each*) garlic and olive
            oil vermicelli mix
        1 can (16 ounces) artichoke hearts,
            undrained and quartered
        2 cans (6 ounces *each*) tuna, drained and
            flaked
        1 package (10 ounces) frozen peas
        1 tablespoon olive *or* vegetable oil
        1 tablespoon cider vinegar *or* red wine vinegar
        4 to 6 garlic cloves, minced

In a saucepan, bring water and butter to a boil. Stir in vermicelli with contents of seasoning packets, artichokes, tuna, peas, oil, vinegar and garlic. Return to a boil; cook, uncovered, for 8-10 minutes or until vermicelli is tender. Let stand 5 minutes before serving. **Yield:** 6 servings.

CRUMB-TOPPED SCALLOPS

Scallops are generally classified into two broad groups —bay scallops and sea scallops. East Coast bay scallops are very tiny, averaging 100 per pound. Larger sea scallops measure 1-1/2 inches in diameter and average 30 per pound.

    1/4 cup dry bread crumbs
        1 tablespoon butter *or* margarine, melted
        1 to 2 teaspoons dried parsley flakes
        1 pound sea scallops
        6 fresh mushrooms, quartered
        1 tablespoon white wine *or* chicken broth
1-1/2 teaspoons lemon juice
    1/4 teaspoon dried thyme
    1/8 teaspoon garlic powder
    1/8 teaspoon seasoned salt
    1/8 teaspoon pepper
Lemon wedges, optional

In a small bowl, combine bread crumbs, butter and parsley; set aside. Place scallops and mushrooms in a 9-in. microwave-safe pie plate. Combine wine or broth, lemon juice and seasonings; pour over scallop mixture. Cover and microwave at 50% power for 2 minutes; drain. Sprinkle with crumb mixture. Cover and microwave at 50% power 4-1/2 minutes longer or until scallops are opaque, stirring once. Serve with lemon if desired. **Yield:** 4 servings.

Chapter 10
MEATLESS MARVELS

You won't find meat in these main dishes...but you won't miss it, either! These great entrees have the satisfying, home-cooked flavor your family craves.

Recipes in this chapter provided courtesy of these past sponsors...

Bertolli
Del Monte
Fleischmann's
French's
National Honey Board
Rosetto
Sargento

MOM'S CHEESY MANICOTTI

(Pictured at left)

Next time you're planning a buffet supper, keep this recipe in mind. Make the casserole early in the day or the night before and refrigerate. Remove from the refrigerator 30 minutes before baking. Garlic bread and a tossed salad are the ideal accompaniments.

- 1 package (15 ounces) whole-milk ricotta cheese
- 3/4 cup (6 ounces) shredded Parmesan cheese, *divided*
- 1/2 cup seasoned bread crumbs
- 1/4 cup minced fresh parsley
- 1 egg
- 3 cups (12 ounces) shredded mozzarella cheese, *divided*
- 1 jar (28 ounces) spaghetti sauce, *divided*
- 1 package (8 ounces) manicotti shells, cooked and drained

In a bowl, combine ricotta cheese, 1/2 cup Parmesan, bread crumbs, parsley and egg. Stir in 2 cups mozzarella cheese. Spread 1/2 cup spaghetti sauce in bottom of a 13-in. x 9-in. x 2-in. baking dish. Spoon 1/4 cup ricotta mixture into each manicotti shell; place in baking dish. Pour remaining spaghetti sauce over manicotti; sprinkle with remaining mozzarella and Parmesan cheeses. Bake at 350° for 30 minutes or until cheese is melted and sauce is bubbly. **Yield:** 6 servings.

PASTA IN TOMATO CREAM SAUCE

Draped over tender cooked pasta, this luscious tomato cream sauce is so rich and satisfying, you'll be surprised by how easy it is to prepare.

- 1 package (8 ounces) tube pasta
- 1 can (14-1/2 ounces) diced tomatoes with garlic and onion
- 1/2 cup chopped fresh basil *or* 1 teaspoon dried basil
- 3/4 cup whipping cream
- 1/3 cup grated Parmesan cheese

Cook pasta according to package directions; drain and set aside. In a skillet, cook tomatoes over medium-high heat until thickened, about 5 minutes. Reduce heat; add basil and cream. Heat through. Do not boil. Toss with hot cooked pasta and cheese. Serve immediately. **Yield:** 4 servings.

Monterey Spaghetti

(Pictured below)

An active life calls for a lot of casseroles. It's so nice to have a hearty dish both adults and kids will eat. Topped with cheese and french-fried onions, this tasty casserole will be a hit at your house.

    4 ounces spaghetti, broken into 2-inch pieces
    1 egg
    1 cup (8 ounces) sour cream
    1/4 cup grated Parmesan cheese
    1/4 teaspoon garlic powder
    2 cups (8 ounces) shredded Monterey Jack cheese
    1 package (10 ounces) frozen chopped spinach, thawed and well drained
    1 can (2.8 ounces) french-fried onions, *divided*

Cook spaghetti according to package directions. Meanwhile, in a medium bowl, beat egg. Add sour cream, Parmesan cheese and garlic powder. Drain spaghetti; add to egg mixture with Monterey Jack cheese, spinach and half of the onions. Pour into a greased 2-qt. baking dish. Cover and bake at 350° for 30 minutes or until heated through. Top with re-

maining onions; bake 5 minutes longer or until onions are golden brown. **Yield:** 6-8 servings.

Ravioli Primavera

Frozen ravioli is key to fixing this entree in a flash. For a change of pace, substitute cheese tortellini and vary the type of vegetables you use.

    1 package (25 ounces) frozen cheese ravioli
    2 garlic cloves, minced
    1/4 cup olive *or* vegetable oil
    1 package (16 ounces) frozen Italian-style vegetables
    1/4 cup chicken broth *or* dry white wine
    2 tablespoons chopped fresh parsley
    1/4 teaspoon salt
    1/4 teaspoon pepper
Grated Romano *or* Parmesan cheese

Cook ravioli according to package directions. Meanwhile, in a large skillet over medium heat, cook garlic in oil for 1 minute. Do not brown. Add frozen vegetables; cook for 4 minutes. Add chicken broth; cook for 3 minutes. Stir in parsley, salt and pepper. Cook for 1 minute. Drain cooked ravioli and place on a large platter. Pour vegetable mixture over ravioli. Sprinkle with cheese. **Yield:** 4-6 servings.

Cheese Tomato Pizza

Why order take-out when you can save money by preparing this wholesome pizza at home? Jazz it up by adding some of your favorite toppings.

DOUGH:
3-1/4 cups all-purpose flour
    1 tablespoon sugar
    1 package (1/4 ounce) quick-rise yeast
1-1/2 teaspoons salt
    1 cup water
    2 tablespoons peanut oil
TOPPING:
    1 can (8 ounces) tomato sauce
    1/4 cup tomato paste
    1/2 teaspoon dried oregano
    1/2 teaspoon dried basil
1-1/2 cups (6 ounces) shredded mozzarella and provolone cheese blend
    1/2 cup shredded cheddar cheese
    1/2 cup grated Parmesan cheese

In a large bowl, combine 2 cups flour, sugar, yeast and salt. Heat water and peanut oil until very warm

(120°-130°). Gradually add to dry ingredients. Stir in enough remaining flour to form a soft dough. Turn onto a floured surface. Knead until smooth and elastic, about 8-10 minutes. Cover; let rest 10 minutes. Divide dough in half and shape each half into a ball. Roll each into a 12-in. circle. Place on greased 12-in. pizza pans or baking sheets. Prick dough with fork; let rest 10 minutes. Bake at 450° for 5 minutes. Remove from pans; place on wire cooling racks. In a bowl, combine tomato sauce, tomato paste, oregano and basil; mix well. Spread sauce evenly on each crust; sprinkle with cheeses. Bake on wire racks at 450° for 10 minutes or until done. Cut into wedges and serve immediately. **Yield:** 2 (12-in.) pizzas.

THAI NOODLES AND SNOW PEAS

(Pictured at right)

If you're looking for a fast-to-fix dish that fits today's healthy lifestyle, try this delicious pasta entree. Snow peas and tofu add interest, while the Thai-style dressing adds a unique flavor.

> 1/3 cup rice vinegar
> 1/4 cup honey
> 2 tablespoons peanut butter
> 2 tablespoons soy sauce
> 2 tablespoons vegetable oil
> 1 tablespoon sesame oil
> 2 garlic cloves, minced
> 1/2 teaspoon crushed red pepper flakes
> 1/4 teaspoon ground ginger
> 1 package (15 ounces) extra-firm tofu, drained, pressed and cut into 1/2-inch pieces
> 1 package (9 ounces) fresh Asian-style noodles*
> 4 ounces snow peas, trimmed and diagonally cut
> 1/4 cup chopped fresh cilantro *or* parsley

In a medium bowl, combine the first nine ingredients. Add tofu; marinate for 30 minutes. Cook noodles and snow peas in 3 quarts boiling water for 1-2 minutes or until snow peas are crisp-tender. Rinse with cold water; drain. Place in a large bowl; add tofu and marinade. Toss gently to coat. Add cilantro; toss to coat. **Yield:** 4-6 servings. **Editor's Note:* 1

package (8 ounces) fettuccini, linguine or spaghetti may be substituted for Asian-style noodles. Prepare according to package directions, adding snow peas during the last 2-3 minutes of cooking.

PASTA WITH BLACK OLIVES, WALNUTS AND BASIL

Fresh basil adds bold flavor to this extra-special pasta dish. It's quick to prepare in your food processor, yet tastes like you fussed for hours.

> 2 cups packed fresh basil leaves
> 1 garlic clove, peeled
> 2 tablespoons olive *or* vegetable oil
> 1/4 cup chicken broth
> 1/4 cup coarsely chopped walnuts
> 1 package (1 pound) spiral pasta
> 2 tablespoons coarsely chopped pitted ripe olives
> 1 tablespoon grated Parmesan cheese

Finely chop basil and garlic in food processor. With motor running, add oil in a slow steady stream, then add chicken broth in a slow steady stream. Set aside. In a large skillet, heat walnuts until hot and lightly toasted, stirring occasionally. Cook pasta according to package directions; reserve 1/4 cup of the pasta cooking liquid, then drain pasta. Toss pasta with basil mixture and reserved pasta cooking liquid. Add walnuts, olives and cheese. Toss and serve immediately. **Yield:** 4 servings.

TOPPINGS:
- 1 cup chopped zucchini
- 1 cup sliced fresh mushrooms
- 1/4 cup *each* chopped onion, sweet red and green pepper
- 1 teaspoon olive *or* vegetable oil
- 1-1/4 cups shredded mozzarella cheese

In a mixing bowl, combine the first five ingredients. Add water and oil; beat until smooth. Turn onto a floured surface; knead until smooth and elastic, about 5 minutes. Place in a greased bowl, turning once to grease top. Cover and let rise in a warm place until doubled, about 30 minutes. Punch dough down. Divide in half; roll each portion into a 12-in. circle. Transfer to greased 12-in. pizza pans. Prick dough with a fork. Bake at 400° for 8-10 minutes or until lightly browned. Combine sauce ingredients in a saucepan. Bring to a boil; reduce heat. Simmer, uncovered, for 15-18 minutes, stirring occasionally. In a skillet, saute vegetables in oil until tender. Spread each pizza with 1 cup sauce (refrigerate the remaining sauce for another use). Sprinkle with vegetables and cheese. Bake for 12-15 minutes or until cheese is melted. **Yield:** 2 pizzas (6 slices each).

WHOLE WHEAT VEGGIE PIZZA

(Pictured above)

A wonderful crust layered with herbed tomato sauce and toppings will encourage your family to dig right in to this pleasing pizza.

- 2-1/2 cups all-purpose flour
- 1/2 cup whole wheat flour
- 2 packages (1/4 ounce *each*) quick-rise yeast
- 1 teaspoon garlic powder
- 1/2 teaspoon salt
- 1 cup water (120° to 130°)
- 2 tablespoons olive *or* vegetable oil

SAUCE:
- 1 can (14-1/2 ounces) diced tomatoes, undrained
- 1 tablespoon minced fresh parsley
- 1-1/2 teaspoons sugar
- 1-1/2 teaspoons Italian seasoning
- 1-1/2 teaspoons dried basil
- 1/2 teaspoon garlic powder
- 1/4 teaspoon pepper

TORTELLINI WITH CREAMY ROSEMARY SAUCE

Used in cooking since around 500 B.C., rosemary is native to the Mediterranean area where it still grows wild today. The flavor of its needle-shaped leaves hints of both lemon and lime.

- 1 package (19 ounces) frozen cheese tortellini
- 1 cup sliced mushrooms
- 1/4 cup finely chopped shallots *or* green onions
- 2 tablespoons olive *or* vegetable oil
- 3 tablespoons all-purpose flour
- Dash pepper
- 3/4 cup beef broth
- 3/4 cup half-and-half cream *or* milk
- 1 tablespoon dry sherry, optional
- 1/2 cup toasted walnut pieces
- 2 teaspoons snipped fresh rosemary *or* 1/2 teaspoon dried rosemary, crushed

Prepare tortellini according to package directions. Meanwhile, in a medium saucepan, cook mushrooms and shallots in oil until tender. Stir in flour and pepper. Add beef broth and half-and-half. Cook and stir until thickened and bubbly; cook and stir 1 additional minute. Add sherry if desired. Stir in wal-

nuts and rosemary; heat through. Serve sauce over cooked tortellini. **Yield:** 4-6 servings.

FLORENTINE STUFFED SHELLS

A la Florentine is French for "in the style of Florence", referring to the city in Italy. The term implies the dish will be prepared with spinach. Popeye's obsession with power-packed spinach may come from the fact that it's a rich source of iron as well as vitamins A and C. It tastes great in this pasta entree.

    24 uncooked jumbo pasta shells
     1 package (10 ounces) frozen chopped
       spinach, thawed
     1 egg, beaten
     1 carton (15 ounces) ricotta cheese
 1-1/2 cups (6 ounces) shredded mozzarella
       cheese
   1/3 cup finely chopped onion
     2 garlic cloves, minced
   1/4 teaspoon salt
   1/8 teaspoon ground nutmeg
     2 cups meatless spaghetti sauce
   1/2 cup grated Parmesan cheese

Cook pasta shells according to the package directions. Squeeze spinach to remove as much moisture as possible. Combine spinach, egg, ricotta, mozzarella, onion, garlic, salt and nutmeg; stir to blend well. Stuff shells with spinach mixture, using about 2 tablespoons for each shell. Arrange in a lightly greased 13-in. x 9-in. x 2-in. baking dish. Pour spaghetti sauce over shells. Sprinkle with Parmesan cheese. Cover and bake at 350° for 30 minutes or until hot. **Yield:** 8 servings.

EGG AND CORN QUESADILLA

(Pictured at right)

For a deliciously different breakfast or brunch, try this excellent quesadilla. It's also a good choice for a light lunch or supper. Corn is a natural in Southwestern cooking and a tasty addition to this zippy egg dish.

     1 medium onion, chopped
     1 medium green pepper, chopped
     1 garlic clove, minced
     2 tablespoons olive *or* vegetable oil

     3 cups fresh *or* frozen corn
     1 teaspoon minced chives
   1/2 teaspoon dried cilantro *or* parsley flakes
   1/2 teaspoon salt
   1/4 teaspoon pepper
     4 eggs, beaten
     4 flour tortillas (10 inches)
   1/2 cup salsa
     1 cup (8 ounces) sour cream
     1 cup (4 ounces) shredded cheddar cheese
     1 cup (4 ounces) shredded mozzarella cheese
Additional salsa and sour cream, optional

In a skillet, cook onion, green pepper and garlic in oil until tender. Add the corn, chives, cilantro, salt and pepper. Cook until heated through, about 3 minutes. Stir in eggs; cook until completely set, stirring occasionally. Remove from the heat. Place one tortilla on a lightly greased baking sheet or pizza pan; top with a third of the corn mixture, salsa and sour cream. Sprinkle with a fourth of the cheeses. Repeat layers twice. Top with the remaining tortilla and cheeses. Bake at 350° for 10 minutes or until the cheese is melted. Cut into wedges. Serve with salsa and sour cream if desired. **Yield:** 6-8 servings.

FOUR-CHEESE SPINACH LASAGNA

(Pictured below)

This rich lasagna will become one of your specialties. It's packed with fresh-tasting vegetables like spinach, carrots, red pepper and broccoli. You can serve the colorful casserole to guests, since it's always a huge success.

> 2 cups chopped fresh broccoli
> 1-1/2 cups julienned carrots
> 1 cup sliced green onions
> 1/2 cup chopped sweet red pepper
> 3 garlic cloves, minced
> 2 teaspoons vegetable oil
> 1/2 cup all-purpose flour
> 3 cups milk
> 1/2 cup grated Parmesan cheese, *divided*
> 1/2 teaspoon salt
> 1/4 teaspoon pepper
> 1 package (10 ounces) frozen chopped
> spinach, thawed and well drained
> 1-1/2 cups small-curd cottage cheese
> 1 cup (4 ounces) shredded mozzarella cheese
> 1/2 cup shredded Swiss cheese
> 12 lasagna noodles, cooked and drained

In a skillet, saute the vegetables and garlic in oil until crisp-tender. Remove from the heat; set aside. In a heavy saucepan, whisk the flour and milk until smooth. Bring to a boil; cook and stir for 2 minutes. Reduce heat; add 1/4 cup Parmesan cheese, salt and pepper. Cook 1 minute longer or until cheese is melted. Remove from the heat; stir in spinach. Set 1 cup aside. In a bowl, combine the cottage cheese, mozzarella and Swiss. Spread 1/2 cup of the spinach mixture in a greased 13-in. x 9-in. x 2-in. baking dish. Layer with four noodles, half of the cheese mixture and vegetables and 3/4 cup spinach mixture. Repeat layers. Top with remaining noodles, reserved spinach mixture and remaining Parmesan cheese. Cover and bake at 375° for 35 minutes. Uncover; bake 15 minutes longer or until bubbly. Let stand 15 minutes before cutting. **Yield:** 12 servings.

GARDEN PRIMAVERA PASTA

The Italian phrase alla primavera means "spring style". In cooking, it refers to the use of fresh vegetables to garnish the dish. The vegetables can be either raw or blanched and usually feature a colorful blend of flavors and textures, as in this popular pasta entree.

> 3 cups uncooked bow-tie *or* spiral pasta
> 1 jar (6-1/2 ounces) marinated artichoke
> hearts, undrained
> 1 green pepper, cut into thin strips
> 1 large carrot, cut in julienne strips
> 1 tablespoon vegetable oil
> 1 can (14-1/2 ounces) diced tomatoes with
> garlic and onion
> 1/2 teaspoon dried rosemary, crushed
> 12 pitted ripe olives
> Grated Parmesan cheese

Cook pasta according to package directions; drain. Drain artichokes, reserving marinade. Toss pasta with marinade; set aside. Cut artichoke hearts in half; set aside. In a large nonstick skillet, cook pepper and carrot in hot oil until crisp-tender. Add tomatoes, rosemary and olives. Cook, uncovered, over medium heat for 4-5 minutes or until sauce is thickened. Add artichoke hearts. Serve over pasta with Parmesan cheese. **Yield:** 4 servings.

MUSHROOM QUICHE

Fresh mushrooms and Swiss cheese complement each other in this wonderful dish. Served with fresh fruit, it makes a hearty meal any time of day.

> 1 unbaked pastry shell (9 inches)
> 4 cups sliced fresh mushrooms
> 1 tablespoon butter *or* margarine
> 1 cup (4 ounces) shredded Swiss cheese
> 2 tablespoons all-purpose flour
> 3 eggs, lightly beaten

1-1/4 cups milk
  1 tablespoon minced fresh savory *or* 1
    teaspoon dried savory
1/2 teaspoon salt
1/4 teaspoon pepper

Line unpricked pastry shell with a double thickness of heavy-duty foil. Bake at 425° for 10 minutes or until edges begin to brown. Remove foil; set the crust aside. In a skillet, saute mushrooms in butter. Remove with a slotted spoon; set aside. In a bowl, toss cheese with flour; add eggs, milk, savory, salt and pepper. Stir in mushrooms. Pour into crust. Bake at 350° for 1 hour or until a knife inserted near the center comes out clean. Let stand for 10 minutes before cutting. **Yield:** 6-8 servings.

BLACK BEAN BURRITOS

To shape a burrito, a savory filling is spooned onto a flour tortilla. Then the ends are folded over the filling, and the tortilla is rolled to completely enclose the filling. Burritos may be deep-fried to create a chimichanga, a specialty from Sonora, Mexico.

  3 tablespoons chopped onion
  3 tablespoons chopped green pepper
  1 can (15 ounces) black beans, rinsed and
    drained
  4 flour tortillas (7 inches), warmed
  1 cup (4 ounces) shredded Mexican cheese
    blend *or* cheddar cheese
  1 medium tomato, chopped
  1 cup shredded lettuce
Salsa, optional

In a nonstick skillet coated with nonstick cooking spray, saute onion and green pepper until tender. Add beans; heat through. Spoon about 1/2 cupful off center on each tortilla. Sprinkle with cheese, tomato and lettuce. Fold sides and ends over filling and roll up. Serve with salsa if desired. **Yield:** 4 servings.

CREAMY GARDEN SPAGHETTI

(Pictured above right)

The name of this pasta comes from the Italian word for "strings", since spaghetti is typically long thin strands. Like its cousin macaroni, spaghetti is made from semolina wheat flour and water. Of the hundreds of shapes, sizes and colors of pasta available today, traditional spaghetti continues to be the most popular.

  1/2 pound fresh broccoli, broken into florets
1-1/2 cups sliced zucchini

1-1/2 cups sliced fresh mushrooms
  1 large carrot, sliced
  1 tablespoon olive *or* vegetable oil
  8 ounces uncooked spaghetti
1/4 cup chopped onion
  3 garlic cloves, minced
  2 tablespoons butter *or* margarine
  2 tablespoons all-purpose flour
  2 teaspoons chicken bouillon granules
  1 teaspoon dried thyme
  2 cups milk
1/2 cup shredded Swiss cheese
1/2 cup shredded mozzarella cheese

In a large skillet, saute the broccoli, zucchini, mushrooms and carrot in oil until crisp-tender. Remove from the heat and set aside. Cook spaghetti according to package directions. In another saucepan, saute onion and garlic in butter until tender. Stir in the flour, bouillon and thyme until blended. Gradually add milk. Bring to a boil; cook and stir for 2 minutes or until thickened. Reduce heat to low; stir in cheeses until melted. Add the vegetables; heat through. Drain spaghetti; toss with vegetable mixture. **Yield:** 4 servings.

Chapter 11
SIDE DISHES & CONDIMENTS

Round out your everyday dinners with a tasty condiment or a savory side dish featuring garden-fresh fruits or vegetables, hearty beans, tender pasta or tasty rice.

Recipes in this chapter provided courtesy of these past sponsors...

Blue Bonnet	McCormick
Campbell's	Nabisco
Comstock/Wilderness	Ore-Ida
Del Monte	Reames
Equal	Reynolds
Farmland	Rosetto
French's	Sargento
Fruit-Fresh	Schilling
Heinz	Sunbeam
Karo	Sure-Jell
Kerr	Swanson
Kraft	Wagner's
Martha White	

APPLE SAUSAGE STUFFING

(*Pictured at left*)

The savory aroma and tantalizing taste of this down-home stuffing recipe bring back magical memories of holiday meals shared with family and friends. The unique addition of apple pie filling helps keep the stuffing moist—and delicious.

> 1 pound bulk pork sausage
> 1/4 cup butter *or* margarine
> 1-1/2 cups chopped onion
> 1 cup sliced celery
> 1 can (21 ounces) apple pie filling
> 1 can (14 ounces) chicken broth
> 1/2 cup minced fresh parsley
> 1 package (14 ounces) seasoned stuffing croutons
> 1 cup pecan pieces

In a large skillet, brown sausage; drain. Add butter, onion and celery; cook 2-3 minutes or until vegetables are tender. Stir in pie filling, broth and parsley. In a large bowl, combine stuffing cubes, pecans and apple mixture. Place in a 13-in. x 9-in. x 2-in. baking dish. Bake, uncovered, at 325° for 40 minutes. **Yield:** 10-12 servings.

SCALLOPED POTATOES

In the 16th century, Sir Walter Raleigh helped discredit the poisonous potato superstition when he planted them on his property in Ireland. The Irish knew a good thing when they tasted it, and today grow and consume potatoes in great quantities.

> 6 tablespoons butter *or* margarine
> 6 tablespoons all-purpose flour
> 3 cups milk
> 1 tablespoon beef bouillon granules
> 1 tablespoon dried parsley flakes
> 1/2 teaspoon pepper
> 5 large peeled potatoes, sliced
> 1 medium onion, sliced

In a large saucepan, melt butter; blend in flour. Gradually add milk, bouillon granules, parsley and pepper. Cook over medium heat, stirring constantly, until bouillon granules dissolve and mixture thickens. Stir in potato and onion slices. Spread in a 13-in. x 9-in. x 2-in. baking dish. Bake at 400° for 1 hour or until potatoes are tender. **Yield:** 6-8 servings.

1 teaspoon Worcestershire sauce
1 teaspoon salt
1 teaspoon pepper
1 teaspoon Dijon mustard

Place carrots in a saucepan; add 1 in. of water. Bring to a boil. Cover and simmer for 7 minutes or until tender; drain. In a bowl, combine remaining ingredients; mix well. Stir in carrots. Cover and refrigerate 12 hours or overnight. **Yield:** 12 servings.

BROCCOLI AND CAULIFLOWER RING

A pretty presentation can add spark to everyday vegetables like broccoli and cauliflower. This is a colorful, nutritious blend that you'll enjoy often. It's made in the microwave, which means it's quick and convenient. Sunflower kernels add a pleasant crunch.

   5 cups broccoli florets
   5 cups cauliflowerets
   6 tablespoons water, *divided*
   1 medium tomato, cut into 6 wedges
   3 tablespoons butter *or* margarine
   3 tablespoons sunflower kernels

Place broccoli and cauliflower in a 3-qt. casserole. Sprinkle 4 tablespoons water over vegetables. Cover tightly with plastic wrap, turning back edge to vent. Microwave on high 9-13 minutes or until crisp-tender, stirring after 5 minutes. Drain. Arrange tomato wedges in bottom of 2-qt. glass ring mold, skin side down. Arrange cauliflower and broccoli over tomatoes, pressing to pack firmly. Add remaining water. Cover tightly with plastic wrap, turning back edge to vent. Microwave on high 3 minutes; drain. Invert onto serving plate. Microwave butter and sunflower kernels on high for 2 minutes. Spoon over vegetables. **Yield:** 6-8 servings.

CARROT CRAZIES

(Pictured above)

Here's an easy way to add elegance and flavor to plain carrots. The cool combination of tender carrots, crunchy green peppers and savory onions marinated in a colorful sweet-sour sauce is different and delightful.

   2 pounds carrots, sliced *or* baby carrots
   1 can (10-3/4 ounces) condensed tomato
     soup, undiluted
  24 packets sugar substitute
   1 medium onion, chopped
   1 green pepper, chopped
   3/4 cup red wine vinegar *or* cider vinegar
   1/2 cup vegetable oil *or* olive oil

CHEESE POTATO PUDDING

This tasty side dish offers wonderful from-scratch flavor since it starts with fresh potatoes. It's great served alongside a variety of meat entrees.

   6 baking potatoes, peeled and shredded
   1 medium onion, grated
   3 eggs
   1 teaspoon salt
 3/4 cup all-purpose flour
 1/4 cup vegetable oil
   2 cups (8 ounces) shredded sharp cheddar
     cheese

In a large bowl, combine the potatoes and onion. Stir in the eggs, salt, flour and oil. Stir until well blended. Spread mixture into a greased 13-in. x 9-in. x 2-in. baking dish. Bake at 325° for 1 hour or until brown and crusty. Remove from oven and sprinkle with the cheese. Bake 10 minutes longer or until the cheese is melted. Cut into squares to serve. **Yield:** 12 servings.

Fresh Uncooked Applesauce

Reap a bushel of compliments when you serve this satisfying applesauce. Ideal in autumn, it pairs perfectly with pork. It's also a tasty option for children who don't like the texture of apple slices.

>   5 large apples, peeled, cored and cut into
>   wedges
>   1 tablespoon lemon juice
>   1/3 cup sugar
>   1/2 cup apple juice *or* cider
>   1/4 teaspoon ground cinnamon

In a food processor, combine all ingredients. Cover and process until desired texture. Serve immediately. **Yield:** 4-6 servings.

Refrigerator Cucumber Slices

You and your family will relish every bite of these tangy favorites. They're an enjoyable extra that helps add a special touch to any meal.

>   2 cups white vinegar
>   1 cup water
>   2 cups sugar
>   2 teaspoons salt
>   2 teaspoons celery seed
>   1 teaspoon mustard seed
>   2 garlic cloves, crushed
>   6 cups thinly sliced cucumbers
>   1 cup sliced onions

In a large saucepan, combine the vinegar, water, sugar, salt, celery seed and mustard seed. Bring to a boil, stirring to dissolve sugar. Meanwhile, place one garlic clove each in two hot, sterilized quart jars. Pack the cucumbers and onions into jars, leaving 1/2-in. headspace. Immediately fill the jars with hot vinegar mixture, leaving 1/2-in. headspace. Wipe the jar tops and threads clean. Place lids on jars; screw the bands on firmly. Cool completely before refrigerating. Refrigerate 24 hours to blend flavors. Store in refrigerator for up to 2 months. **Yield:** 2 quarts.

Cheddar-Stuffed Potatoes

(Pictured below)

Whether served as an appetizing side dish or a meal in itself, these tempting potatoes offer stick-to-your-ribs goodness. The picture-perfect presentation makes this dish much more impressive than plain baked potatoes—and they taste better, too!

>   4 large baking potatoes
>   4 bacon strips, diced
>   2 cups small broccoli florets
>   1/2 cup chopped onion
>   1/2 teaspoon salt
>   1/4 teaspoon pepper
> 1-1/2 cups (6 ounces) shredded sharp cheddar
>   cheese, *divided*
> Salsa *or* sour cream, optional

Bake the potatoes at 400° for 55 minutes or until tender; cool for 10 minutes. Meanwhile, in a large skillet, cook bacon until crisp. Remove bacon with slotted spoon; set aside. Drain all but 1 tablespoon drippings. Cook broccoli and onion in drippings over medium-high heat for 8-10 minutes or until tender, stirring occasionally. Cut a thin slice off the top of each potato and discard. Scoop out the pulp, leaving a thin shell. In a bowl, mash pulp with bacon, vegetable mixture, salt and pepper. Stir in 1 cup cheese. Spoon into potato shells. Place in an 11-in. x 7-in. x 2-in. baking dish. Top with remaining cheese. Bake, uncovered, at 400° for 15-20 minutes or until heated through. Serve with salsa or sour cream if desired. **Yield:** 4 servings.

BROCCOLI & GARLIC PASTA

(Pictured below)

This contemporary classic is a great choice when you're looking for a savory side dish or meatless entree packed with bold flavors. Low in fat, this great-tasting recipe is good for you as well.

      1 cup chicken broth
  1/2 teaspoon dried basil
  1/8 teaspoon pepper
      2 garlic cloves, minced
      3 cups broccoli florets
4-1/2 cups hot cooked tube pasta
      1 tablespoon lemon juice
      2 tablespoons grated Parmesan cheese

In a large skillet, combine broth, basil, pepper, garlic and broccoli. Bring to a boil. Cover and cook over low heat for 3 minutes or until broccoli is crisp-tender. Add pasta and lemon juice. Toss to coat. Serve with cheese. **Yield:** 4 servings.

VEGETABLE CASSEROLE

Before the 16th century, celery was used solely as a medicinal herb. Now it's one of the most popular vegetables in the country. Celery is terrific raw for snacking or cooked in soups and stews.

      2 cups sliced celery
  1/2 cup water
  3/4 teaspoon salt, *divided*
3-1/2 tablespoons butter *or* margarine, *divided*

      2 tablespoons all-purpose flour
      1 cup half-and-half cream
      1 chicken bouillon cube
  1/8 teaspoon pepper
Dash ground nutmeg
      2 drops hot pepper sauce
      2 tablespoons chopped pimiento
      1 can (14-1/2 ounces) wax beans, drained
  1/2 cup crushed saltines (about 15 crackers)
  1/3 cup shredded Swiss cheese
  1/2 cup chopped walnuts

In a saucepan, combine the celery, water and 1/2 teaspoon salt. Bring to a boil; simmer 5 minutes or until crisp-tender. Drain and set aside. In the same saucepan, melt 2 tablespoons butter; stir in flour until smooth. Add the cream, bouillon, pepper, nutmeg, pepper sauce and remaining salt. Bring to a boil, stirring constantly. Reduce heat and cook 1 minute. Remove from the heat; stir in the celery, pimiento and beans. Turn into a greased 1-qt. baking dish. Melt remaining butter; toss with cracker crumbs. Add the cheese and walnuts; sprinkle over vegetables. Bake at 400° for 15 minutes or until topping is lightly browned. **Yield:** 6 servings.

SPICED FRUIT COMPOTE

You may be surprised how versatile prepared fruit fillings can be—with a little imagination. This delicious warm compote provides maximum flavor with a minimum of fuss. Topped off with a sweet golden brown biscuit, it is the perfect accompaniment for baked ham or roasted duck.

      2 cans (21 ounces *each*) cherry pie filling
      1 apple, peeled and diced
      1 pear, peeled and diced
      1 orange, peeled, sectioned and halved
  1/4 cup orange juice
  1/4 teaspoon ground cloves
  1/4 teaspoon ground nutmeg
      1 can (12 ounces) refrigerated buttermilk
        biscuits
      1 tablespoon butter *or* margarine, melted
  1/2 teaspoon ground cinnamon
      1 tablespoon sugar

In an ungreased 13-in. x 9-in. x 2-in. baking dish, combine pie filling, fruits, orange juice, cloves and nutmeg; mix well. Microwave on high for 10 minutes, stirring halfway through cooking. Separate dough into 10 biscuits. Place on top of hot fruit mixture. Brush biscuits with melted butter; sprinkle with cinnamon and sugar. Bake at 400° for 13-17 minutes or until biscuits are a deep golden brown. **Yield:** 10 servings. **Editor's Note:** If your microwave does not accommodate a 13-in. x 9-in. x 2-in. baking dish, microwave the fruit mixture in a large microwave-safe bowl, then transfer to a baking dish before topping with biscuits.

MACARONI AND CHEESE

High on most everyone's list of comfort foods, this tasty dish brings to mind fond memories of meals with Mom or Grandma. It's old-fashioned fare that has stood the test of time.

> 1 package (8 ounces) uncooked elbow macaroni
> 1/4 cup butter *or* margarine
> 1/4 cup all-purpose flour
> 1/2 teaspoon salt
> 1/2 teaspoon ground mustard
> 1/4 teaspoon white pepper
> 1/8 teaspoon hot pepper sauce
> 2-1/2 cups milk
> 2 cups (8 ounces) shredded sharp cheddar cheese
> Additional shredded cheddar cheese, optional

Cook macaroni in boiling water according to package directions; drain. In a 2-qt. saucepan over medium heat, melt butter. Stir in flour, salt, mustard, pepper and hot pepper sauce until smooth. Gradually stir in milk; cook until mixture boils, stirring constantly. Stir in cheese. Cook just until cheese is melted, stirring constantly. Add macaroni to sauce. Pour into a greased casserole. Top with additional cheese if desired. Bake at 350° for 30 minutes or until very hot. **Yield:** 6 servings.

ASPARAGUS POLONAISE

French for "in the manner of Poland", vegetables served a la polonaise are sprinkled with chopped hard-cooked egg, parsley and buttered bread crumbs. Try this tempting topping on cauliflower as well.

> 1/2 cup butter *or* margarine
> 1/2 cup crushed saltines (about 15 crackers)
> 1/4 cup fresh minced parsley
> 2 pounds fresh asparagus spears, trimmed, cooked and drained
> 1 tablespoon lemon juice
> 1 hard-cooked egg, chopped

In a skillet, melt butter. Add saltines; cook and stir until saltines are lightly browned. Stir in parsley. Arrange asparagus on serving platter. Sprinkle with lemon juice and egg. Top with saltine mixture. **Yield:** 6-8 servings.

CHEESY GARLIC MASHED POTATOES

(Pictured above)

Since most folks love cheddar cheese and garlic, you'll turn to this tempting side dish frequently. It works well alongside almost any main dish, particularly roasts. The crunchy onion topping adds flavor and provides pleasant eye appeal.

> 4 cups hot prepared mashed potatoes
> 1 can (10-3/4 ounces) condensed cream of chicken soup, undiluted
> 1-1/2 cups (6 ounces) shredded cheddar cheese, *divided*
> 1/8 teaspoon garlic powder
> 1 can (2.8 ounces) french-fried onions

In a large microwave-safe bowl, combine mashed potatoes, soup, 1 cup cheese and garlic powder. Microwave on high for 1-2 minutes or until cheese is melted. Spoon potato mixture into a shallow 2-qt. baking dish. Top with remaining cheese and french-fried onions. Bake at 375° for 5 minutes or until onions are golden brown. **Yield:** 6-8 servings.

Green Bean Bake

Evokes Memories Of Special Times

THE BELOVED "Green Bean Bake" will forever be a traditional holiday favorite. This dish, invented in 1955 by Dorcas Reilly, then-manager of the Campbell's Test Kitchens, remains one of the company's most requested recipes and is a staple at potlucks, family dinners and numerous celebrations. Based on a national survey by Opinion Research Corporation, Campbell's estimates that more than 20 million "Green Bean Bakes" are served on holiday tables each year. Is it a tradition on your family's holiday menu?

GREEN BEAN BAKE

(Pictured above)

1 can (10-3/4 ounces) condensed cream of
   mushroom soup, undiluted
1/2 cup milk
1 teaspoon soy sauce
Dash pepper
4 cups cooked cut green beans
1 can (2.8 ounces) french-fried onions,
   divided

In a 1-1/2-qt. casserole dish, combine the soup, milk, soy sauce, pepper, green beans and 2/3 cup onions. Bake at 350° for 25 minutes or until hot. Stir. Sprinkle with the remaining onions. Bake 5 minutes longer or until the onions are golden brown. **Yield:** 6 servings.

174

ZESTY VEGETABLE MEDLEY

These saucy vegetables are colorful and satisfying. Zippy horseradish adds a surprising flavor that's sure to perk up any meal.

      1/4 cup water
      1/4 teaspoon salt
        1 head cauliflower, broken into florets
        1 medium bunch broccoli, cut into florets
        1 pound carrots, diagonally cut into
          1/2-inch slices
      1/4 cup prepared horseradish
      1/4 cup finely chopped onion
      1/2 teaspoon salt
      1/4 teaspoon pepper
        1 cup mayonnaise
      1/2 cup crushed saltines (about 15 crackers)
        2 tablespoons butter *or* margarine, melted
      1/8 teaspoon paprika

In a 3-qt. baking dish, place water, salt, cauliflower, broccoli and carrots. Cover with plastic wrap and microwave on high for 16-18 minutes, stirring after 8 minutes. Drain. In a small bowl, combine horseradish, onion, salt, pepper and mayonnaise. Pour over vegetables and toss gently to coat. Combine saltines, butter and paprika in separate small bowl. Sprinkle crumb mixture on top of vegetables. Microwave on high for 1-2 minutes, or until bubbly. **Yield:** 12 servings.

ELEGANT CARROTS

Carrots are available year-round, and their low cost and sweet taste make them popular. Substitute fresh baby carrots to cut down on preparation time.

        2 tablespoons butter *or* margarine
      3/4 teaspoon salt
        1 teaspoon brown sugar
      1/2 cup chicken broth *or* water
        6 carrots, sliced 1/2 inch thick
      1/3 cup whipping cream
        1 egg yolk
        2 teaspoons lemon juice
      1/2 cup walnut pieces, toasted

Combine butter, salt, sugar and broth in pressure cooker. Place rack over liquids; add carrots. Close cover securely; place pressure regulator on vent pipe. Bring cooker to full pressure over high heat. Reduce heat to medium-high and cook for 4 minutes. (Pressure regulator should maintain a slow steady rocking motion; adjust heat if needed.) Immediately cool according to manufacturer's directions until pressure is completely reduced. Remove rack. Mix cream and egg yolk until blended. Stir into carrots; heat through. Blend in lemon juice and walnuts. **Yield:** 6 servings.

SPICED PRUNES

These special prunes are great with meats or a cottage cheese salad. Or serve them alone as a breakfast fruit.

        1 pound dried pitted prunes
        2 cups water
        1 teaspoon ground cinnamon
        1 teaspoon ground cloves
      1/2 teaspoon ground ginger
        3 tablespoons lemon juice

In a saucepan over medium heat, combine prunes, water, cinnamon, cloves and ginger; bring to a boil. Remove from the heat; cover and let stand until cool. Stir in lemon juice. **Yield:** 8 servings.

CRUNCHY BROCCOLI CHEESE CASSEROLE

This comforting casserole is great with a roast or chops. It's a simple solution for dressing up plain broccoli.

        1 package (16 ounces) frozen broccoli spears
        1 can (11 ounces) condensed cheddar cheese
          soup, undiluted
      1/2 cup water
      1/3 cup dry bread crumbs
        2 tablespoons butter *or* margarine, melted
        1 tablespoon Salad Supreme Seasoning

Place single layer of broccoli in shallow baking dish. Whisk together soup and water until smooth. Pour over broccoli. Combine bread crumbs, butter and seasoning. Sprinkle over broccoli. Bake at 375° for 20-25 minutes or until broccoli is tender. **Yield:** 4-6 servings.

ITALIAN VEGETABLE TOSS

Summer squash have thin edible skins and soft seeds. The tender flesh has a mild flavor that appeals to all.

        2 medium zucchini, sliced
        2 medium yellow squash, sliced
       10 mushrooms, quartered
        1 tablespoon butter *or* margarine, cubed
        1 tablespoon chopped fresh basil
      1/4 teaspoon pepper
        2 medium tomatoes, cut into wedges
      1/4 cup shredded Parmesan cheese

In a 2-1/2-qt. microwave-safe baking dish, combine zucchini, yellow squash, mushrooms, butter, basil and pepper. Cover with a sheet of wax paper. Microwave on high for 8-10 minutes or until squash is crisp-tender, rotating halfway through cooking time. Add tomato wedges and sprinkle with cheese. Microwave an additional 1-2 minutes or until cheese melts. **Yield:** 4 servings.

Meanwhile, in a large mixing bowl, beat egg yolks until foamy. Add 1/2 cup butter and sugar; mix well. Fold in cottage cheese, carrots, sour cream and noodles. In a small mixing bowl, beat egg whites until stiff; fold into noodle mixture. Place in a greased 2-qt. casserole. Combine bread crumbs and remaining butter. Sprinkle over top. Bake at 350° for 25 minutes or until hot. **Yield:** 8 servings.

HOMEMADE NOODLES

In kitchens across America, noodles are a mainstay. Low in cost, noodles provide a long-lasting feeling of fullness. It's no wonder they're a key ingredient in some of our favorite comfort foods. The difference between noodles and pasta is that in addition to flour and water, noodles contain eggs. Many people use the terms interchangeably, however.

> 1 cup all-purpose flour
> 1 egg
> 1/2 teaspoon salt
> 2 tablespoons milk

In a food processor, combine flour, egg and salt; process until consistency of cornmeal. While processing, gradually add milk. On a floured surface, knead about 20 times. Wrap in plastic wrap and let rest 30 minutes. Divide dough in half. On a floured surface, roll each half to 1/16-in. thickness. Roll up jelly-roll style and cut into 1/4-in. slices. Separate the slices and let rest on a clean towel for at least 1 hour. Cook noodles in boiling salted water until tender, about 12 minutes; drain. **Yield:** 3-4 servings.

GLAZED PINEAPPLE RINGS WITH SWEET POTATO MOUNDS

Rich color, pleasing texture and great taste have given sweet potatoes their delicious reputation. This eye-catching side dish goes particularly well with baked ham, so it's a natural for holiday meals such as Christmas and Easter.

> 1 can (15 ounces) sweet potatoes, drained
> 1/4 cup butter *or* margarine, melted, *divided*
> 1/2 cup light corn syrup
> 1/4 cup packed brown sugar
> 1 can (20 ounces) sliced pineapple, well drained

Mash sweet potatoes. Blend with 1 tablespoon butter; set aside. In a small saucepan, combine syrup, sugar and remaining butter. Cook and stir over medium heat until mixture boils. Remove from heat. Carefully pour into an 11-in. x 7-in. x 2-in. baking

CREAMY CARROT AND NOODLE DELIGHT

(Pictured above)

Noodles are served in every country around the world in some form or another—there are more than 500 known varieties of noodles and pastas in an endless array of flavors, shapes and sizes. Noodles originally came to America from Europe, courtesy of Thomas Jefferson, when he served as U.S. ambassador to France. This rich flavorful side dish is certain to win rave reviews at your house!

> 3 quarts water
> 1 teaspoon salt
> 1 package (12 ounces) frozen home-style egg noodles
> 3 eggs, *separated*
> 1/2 cup plus 2 tablespoons butter *or* margarine, melted, *divided*
> 2 tablespoons sugar
> 1 container (16 ounces) cream-style cottage cheese, undrained
> 2 cups sliced carrots, cooked and drained
> 1 cup sour cream
> 1/2 cup dry bread crumbs

In a Dutch oven, bring water and salt to a boil. Add noodles; cook for 20 minutes or until tender; drain.

dish. Arrange 5 stacks of two pineapple slices each, in hot syrup mixture. Top each set with a mound of sweet potato mixture. Bake at 350° for 30 minutes, basting often with glaze. **Yield:** 5 servings.

HUSH PUPPIES

Hush puppies are a delicious accompaniment to many meals, especially catfish in the South. For stronger flavor, add an additional tablespoon of finely chopped onion and a teaspoon of onion powder to the batter.

>   2 cups self-rising cornmeal mix
>   3 tablespoons self-rising flour
>   1 tablespoon finely chopped onion
> 1-1/4 cups buttermilk
>   1 egg, lightly beaten
> Vegetable oil *or* shortening for deep frying

Combine cornmeal, flour and onion in large mixing bowl. Gradually beat in buttermilk and egg. Set aside for 5 minutes; do not stir. Meanwhile, in a large skillet, heat 1 in. oil over medium-high heat to 400°. Drop small spoonfuls of batter into hot oil. Fry until golden brown, turning occasionally; drain on paper towels. Serve hot. **Yield:** 20 hush puppies.

POTATO-SPINACH STRATA

(Pictured at right)

Perfect as an elegant side dish or meatless luncheon entree, this layered recipe is a unique way to serve frozen hash brown potatoes. Top with spaghetti sauce for an extra burst of flavor.

>   1 package (10 ounces) frozen chopped
>   spinach, thawed and well drained
>   2 cups (16 ounces) small-curd cottage cheese
> 1/4 cup chopped onion
>   2 teaspoons Italian seasoning
> 1/2 teaspoon garlic salt
> 1/4 teaspoon pepper
> 1/8 teaspoon ground nutmeg, optional
>   1 package (26 ounces) frozen shredded
>   hash brown potatoes, *divided*
> Salt and paprika to taste, optional
> 1/2 cup shredded mozzarella cheese
> 1/2 cup shredded cheddar cheese
>   1 jar (15 ounces) spaghetti sauce, heated

Combine the spinach, cottage cheese, onion and seasonings; mix well and set aside. Season potatoes with salt and paprika if desired. Layer half of the potatoes in the bottom of a 9-in. springform pan or 2-qt. casserole; spread cottage cheese mixture over pota-

toes. Top with remaining potatoes. Sprinkle with cheeses. Bake at 375° for 40-45 minutes or until heated through. Top each serving with spaghetti sauce. **Yield:** 6 servings.

SWEET POTATO CUPS

These cinnamon-laced sweet potatoes get a sweet accent from brown sugar. It's a unique side dish to serve on a Thanksgiving buffet.

>   1 can (15 ounces) cut sweet potatoes,
>   drained and mashed
>   1 jar (7 ounces) marshmallow creme
> 1/4 cup packed brown sugar
>   1 teaspoon salt
> 1/2 teaspoon ground cinnamon
>   1 can (11 ounces) mandarin oranges, drained

In a small mixing bowl, combine the sweet potatoes, marshmallow creme, brown sugar, salt and cinnamon; beat until light and fluffy. Fold in the oranges. Spoon mixture into foil-lined muffin cups. Bake at 350° for 20 minutes or until heated through. **Yield:** 8 cups.

ESCALLOPED SWEET POTATOES

When buying fresh sweet potatoes, choose those that are small to medium in size with smooth, unbruised skin. Store in a dark, dry, cool place—but don't refrigerate. Sweet potatoes should be used within 1 week of purchase.

> 3 medium sweet potatoes, cooked, peeled and halved lengthwise
> 1 unpeeled orange, thinly sliced
> 2 unpeeled apples, thinly sliced

SYRUP:
> 1/2 cup water
> 2 tablespoons maple syrup
> 2 tablespoons orange juice
> 2 tablespoons pineapple juice
> 2 tablespoons brown sugar
> 1 tablespoon butter *or* margarine

TOPPING:
> 3 tablespoons crushed saltines
> 2 tablespoons brown sugar
> 1 tablespoon butter *or* margarine
Marshmallow creme
> 3 maraschino cherries, halved

Arrange the sweet potatoes in a 9-in. square baking pan. Top with oranges and apples. In a small saucepan, combine the syrup ingredients and bring to a boil. Pour over fruit. In a bowl, combine the saltines, sugar and butter. Sprinkle over fruit. Bake at 350° for 20 minutes. Spoon a dollop of marshmallow creme onto center of each potato. Bake an additional 10 minutes or until lightly browned. Garnish with cherries. **Yield:** 6 servings.

STIR-FRY VEGETABLE MEDLEY

Though stir-frying is associated with Asian cooking, this recipe is an American concoction—without soy sauce, ginger and the like. It will blend nicely with a variety of entrees.

> 1 medium onion, thinly sliced
> 2 carrots, diagonally sliced
> 1 bunch broccoli, cut into florets
> 1/2 head cauliflower, cut into florets
> 3 tablespoons vegetable oil
> 1 jar (4 ounces) sliced pimientos, drained
> 1 cup pitted ripe olives
> 3/4 teaspoon garlic salt
> 3/4 teaspoon dried oregano
> 1/2 teaspoon pepper
> 1/2 teaspoon sugar
> 2 tablespoons water

In a large skillet over high heat, cook onion, carrots, broccoli and cauliflower in hot oil 3-4 minutes,

stirring often. Add pimientos, olives, seasonings, sugar and water. Cover and cook 3-4 minutes, stirring occasionally, until vegetables are crisp-tender. **Yield:** 8-12 servings.

BARBECUED BAKED BEANS

If you like the flavor of homemade baked beans but don't have the time to make them, why not try this recipe instead. A simple sauce dresses up canned beans in a hurry. These beans will become a mainstay at your summer cookouts.

> 1 package (16 ounces) sliced bacon
> 1 can (16 ounces) pork and beans, undrained
> 1 can (16 ounces) butter beans, undrained
> 1 can (15 ounces) kidney beans, undrained
> 3/4 cup packed brown sugar
> 2/3 cup barbecue sauce
> 1/3 cup ketchup
> 2 teaspoons cider vinegar
> 1 teaspoon ground mustard

Cook bacon until crisp; drain. Crumble and place in a mixing bowl. Add remaining ingredients to bacon; mix well. Pour into a 2-qt. casserole. Bake, uncovered, at 350° for 45 minutes or until hot. **Yield:** 8-10 servings.

DILLED CARROTS

Dill plants grow to a height of 3 feet and have feathery green leaves called dill weed. The distinctive flavor of dill is wonderful in creamy sauces and dressings. It goes especially well with mild-flavored vegetables such as carrots.

> 8 carrots, sliced 1/2 inch thick
> 1 teaspoon salt
> 3/4 cup water
> 1/4 cup milk
> 2 tablespoons butter *or* margarine
> 1/2 teaspoon dill weed
> 1/4 teaspoon ground nutmeg

In a 2-qt. saucepan, combine carrots, salt and water. Bring to a boil. Cover and simmer until carrots are tender, about 15 minutes; drain. Stir in milk, butter, dill weed and nutmeg. **Yield:** 6-8 servings.

NACHO POTATO TOPPER

(Pictured above)

Meat-and-potato meals are staples in kitchens everywhere. But sometimes, ordinary "taters" need a little spark. This zesty topper adds just the right amount of Mexican flair to perk up baked potatoes.

>   **1 can (10-3/4 ounces) condensed cheddar
>   cheese soup, undiluted**
>   **1/2 cup chunky salsa**
>   **4 hot baked potatoes, split**

In a small saucepan, mix soup and salsa. Cook over low heat, stirring often, until heated through. Serve over potatoes. **Yield:** 4 servings.

CHEESY BROCCOLI POTATO TOPPER

(Pictured above)

The delicious duo of broccoli and cheese blends nicely with potatoes to create a savory side dish.

>   **1 can (10-3/4 ounces) condensed cheddar
>   cheese soup, undiluted**
>   **1 cup cooked broccoli florets**
>   **4 hot baked potatoes, split**

Stir soup in can until smooth. Place hot potatoes on a microwave-safe plate. Carefully fluff potatoes with a fork. Top each potato with broccoli florets; spoon soup over potatoes. Microwave on high for 4 minutes or until hot. **Yield:** 4 servings.

Special Spuds…One Potato, Two Potato…

AMERICANS have long been enamored with potatoes. Over the past 50 years, both a beloved children's toy (Mr. Potato Head) and a '60s disco dance (The Mashed Potato) have been named after the tater. Why?

Spuds are the most popular veggie in the U.S., beating out tomatoes by more than two to one. They're cheap and filling, plus they star in many of our favorite comfort foods.

On average, potatoes are served at one out of every three meals Americans eat. So it's no surprise that recipes evolved quickly past the basic baked, mashed and fried varieties.

Soon, hash browns and Tater Tots became common ingredients in family meals. Delicious yet easy casseroles, like the three below from Ore-Ida, followed. With frozen potatoes, the recipes go together in a snap.

In a bowl, combine the potatoes, soup, sour cream, 1-3/4 cups of cheddar cheese and Parmesan cheese. Transfer to a greased 3-qt. baking dish. Sprinkle with remaining cheddar cheese. Bake, uncovered, at 350° for 40-45 minutes or until bubbly and cheese is melted. Let stand for 5 minutes before serving. **Yield:** 10 servings.

CHEESY HASH BROWN BAKE

(Pictured above)

This casserole is great for busy moms because it can be prepared ahead of time. It's creamy and comforting.

- 1 package (30 ounces) frozen shredded hash brown potatoes, thawed
- 2 cans (10-3/4 ounces *each*) condensed cream of potato soup, undiluted
- 2 cups (16 ounces) sour cream
- 2 cups (8 ounces) shredded cheddar cheese, *divided*
- 1 cup grated Parmesan cheese

PIZZA TOT HOT DISH

(Pictured above right)

You'll need just seven basic ingredients to make this effortless casserole. If you cook for just two, you can divide it into two smaller casserole dishes—one for dinner now and one to freeze for later. Take the frozen casserole from the freezer and thaw in the refrigerator overnight before baking as directed.

- 1 pound ground beef
- 1 medium green pepper, chopped
- 1 medium onion, chopped
- 1 can (10-3/4 ounces) condensed tomato with roasted garlic and herbs soup, undiluted
- 1 jar (4-1/2 ounces) sliced mushrooms, drained
- 2 cups (8 ounces) shredded mozzarella cheese
- 1 package (32 ounces) frozen Tater Tots

In a skillet, cook the beef, pepper and onion until meat is no longer pink; drain. Add soup and mushrooms. Transfer to a greased 13-in. x 9-in. x 2-in.

baking dish. Top with cheese and potatoes. Bake, uncovered, at 400° for 30-35 minutes or until golden brown. **Yield:** 6-8 servings.

COUNTRY-STYLE HASH BROWN CASSEROLE

For dinner on the double, serve this popular casserole with your favorite easy-to-prepare entree.

>   1 package (26 ounces) frozen cubed *or* shredded hash brown potatoes, thawed
> 1-1/2 cups (6 ounces) shredded pepper-Jack cheese
>   1 can (10-3/4 ounces) condensed cream of chicken soup, undiluted
>   1 cup (8 ounces) sour cream
>   1/2 cup chopped onions
>   1 jar (2 ounces) diced pimientos, drained
>   1/2 teaspoon salt
>   1 cup fresh bread crumbs
>   2 tablespoons butter *or* margarine, melted
>   1 can (2.8 ounces) french-fried onions

In a large bowl, combine first seven ingredients; mix well. Spread into an ungreased 11-in. x 7-in. x 2-in. baking dish. Toss bread crumbs with butter; sprinkle over casserole. Bake at 350° for 30 minutes or until bread crumbs are golden brown and mixture is bubbly. Sprinkle french-fried onions over casserole. Bake 5 minutes longer or until onions are golden. **Yield:** 6 servings.

STUFFED BUTTERNUT SQUASH

Here's a meal-in-one squash idea. Ham, mustard, apples and brown sugar go so well with butternut squash.

>   3 small butternut squash (about 1-1/2 pounds *each*)
>   2 cups cubed fully cooked ham
>   1 cup soft bread crumbs
>   1/2 cup shredded tart apple
>   1/4 cup packed brown sugar
>   2 tablespoons prepared mustard

Cut squash in half lengthwise; discard seeds. Place squash, cut side down, in a 15-in. x 10-in. x 1-in. baking pan. Fill pan with hot water to a depth of 1/2 in. Bake, uncovered, at 350° for 30 minutes. Combine remaining ingredients. Turn squash cut side up; stuff with ham mixture. Cover stem end with foil to prevent drying. Bake at 350° for 30 minutes or until squash is tender. **Yield:** 6 servings.

PARMESAN PEAS

When you're pressed for time, you'll find this tasty medley is fast to fix thanks to the wholesome goodness of frozen peas.

>   2 packages (10 ounces *each*) frozen peas
>   1 can (4 ounces) sliced mushrooms, drained
>   6 green onions, sliced *or* 1/4 cup chopped onion
>   1/4 cup dried parsley flakes
>   1/2 teaspoon salt
>   1/4 teaspoon pepper
>   1/2 cup grated Parmesan cheese
>   1/3 cup butter *or* margarine, melted

Combine all ingredients in an 11-in. x 7-in. x 2-in. microwave-safe baking dish; stir gently to mix. Cover and microwave on high for 12 minutes or until peas are done, stirring occasionally. **Yield:** 6 servings.

SKILLET CINNAMON APPLE RINGS

Red cinnamon candies give bright color and zing to these tender apples. The rings are great served with pork entrees.

>   3/4 cup red-hot cinnamon candies
>   2 cups water
>   2 large apples

In a 10-in. skillet, dissolve candies in water over medium-high heat. Core apples and cut crosswise in 1/2-in. rings; add to skillet. Reduce heat and simmer gently until apples are transparent but not soft. Cool in syrup before serving. **Yield:** 4 servings.

1 package (22 ounces) frozen mashed
  potatoes
2 tablespoons minced garlic
1 tablespoon olive *or* vegetable oil
1/2 cup whipping cream
1/4 cup butter *or* margarine
1 teaspoon dried rosemary, crushed
Salt and pepper to taste

Prepare potatoes according to package directions. While potatoes are cooking, cook garlic in oil until soft; set aside. Microwave cream and butter on high 1 minute or until butter is melted; add to mashed potatoes. Add garlic and rosemary. Season with salt and pepper. **Yield:** 6 servings.

YAMS WITH DATES AND WALNUTS

Walnuts and cinnamon top this no-fuss autumn side dish that cooks in the microwave. The rich chopped dates add a touch of sweetness.

2 large yams *or* sweet potatoes (about 1-3/4
  pounds), peeled, thinly sliced
1/2 cup pitted dates, snipped *or* chopped dates
2 tablespoons water
1 tablespoon butter *or* margarine
1/2 cup walnut pieces
Ground cinnamon

Spread half of the yams in a 2-qt. microwave-safe dish. Sprinkle with dates. Top with the remaining yams; add the water. Dot with butter. Cover; microwave on high 7 minutes. Top yams with nuts; sprinkle with cinnamon. Microwave an additional 3-4 minutes or until the yams are tender. Let stand, covered, for 5 minutes. **Yield:** 4 servings.

HERBED GARDEN VEGETABLES

(Pictured above)

The subtle seasonings in this recipe let the garden goodness of broccoli, cauliflower and peppers shine through. And "micro-cooking" helps lock in the vegetables' vitamins and nutrients.

2 cups broccoli florets
2 cups cauliflowerets
1/2 sweet red pepper, cut into strips
1 teaspoon dried basil
3 tablespoons water
1 tablespoon butter *or* margarine

In a 2-qt. microwave-safe baking dish, place broccoli, cauliflower and pepper strips. Sprinkle with basil and water. Dot with butter. Cover with a sheet of wax paper. Microwave on high for 4-6 minutes or until vegetables are crisp-tender. **Yield:** 4 servings.

GARLIC MASHED POTATOES

Throughout the centuries, garlic's medicinal claims have included a cure for toothaches, open wounds, consumption and evil spirits. All we know for certain is this: these creamy garlic-flavored potatoes are a sure cure for hunger, especially when paired with a meaty main course.

SWISS VEGETABLE MEDLEY

Swiss-style cheeses taste good on sandwiches and salads. Since they have excellent melting properties, they're terrific for topping vegetable casseroles as well. This dish gets added flavor and crunch from french-fried onions.

1 can (10-3/4 ounces) condensed cream of
  mushroom soup, undiluted
1/3 cup sour cream
1/4 teaspoon pepper
1 package (16 ounces) frozen broccoli,
  cauliflower and red pepper combination
1 can (2.8 ounces) french-fried onions,
  divided
1 cup (4 ounces) shredded Swiss cheese,
  divided

In 2-qt. shallow baking dish, combine soup, sour cream and pepper; stir until well blended. Add vegetables, 2/3 cup french-fried onions and 1/2 cup cheese; mix well. Cover; bake at 350° for 30 minutes or until heated through and vegetables are tender. Stir. Sprinkle with remaining cheese and onions. Bake 5 minutes or until onions are golden brown. **Yield:** 6 servings.

BARBECUED LIMA BEANS

These pale green, plump-bodied beans were named for Lima, Peru, where they were first found as early as 1500. There are two distinct varieties of lima beans— the baby lima and the Fordhook. Either kind will work well in this saucy recipe. Even folks who usually say "no" to lima beans enjoy this dish.

- 1/2 cup ketchup
- 1/3 cup dark corn syrup
- 2 tablespoons chopped onion
- 1 tablespoon white vinegar
- 2 teaspoons ground mustard
- 1/2 teaspoon salt
- 1/8 teaspoon hot pepper sauce
- 2 packages (10 ounces *each*) frozen lima beans

In a 10-in. skillet, combine all ingredients. Cover; bring to a boil over medium heat, stirring occasionally. Simmer over low heat 15 minutes or until beans are tender. **Yield:** 6 servings.

SKILLET BEANS AND PASTA TOSS

(Pictured at right)

This splendid side dish is the perfect complement to both casual suppers and special-occasion meals. Tender green beans and bright red tomatoes add pretty color to tender-cooked pasta. This tasty dish is an attractive addition to your table.

- 1/2 cup chopped onion
- 1/4 teaspoon dried rosemary, crushed
- 1 tablespoon olive *or* vegetable oil
- 1 can (14-1/2 ounces) cut green beans, undrained
- 1 can (14-1/2 ounces) diced tomatoes with basil, garlic and oregano, undrained
- 1 cup uncooked spiral *or* tube pasta

In a large skillet, cook onion and rosemary in oil for 3 minutes. Drain beans, reserving liquid; pour liquid into skillet. Add tomatoes; bring to a boil. Cook, uncovered, over medium heat for 5 minutes.

Stir in pasta. Reduce heat; cover and cook about 12 minutes. Add beans; cook an additional 5 minutes or until pasta is tender. **Yield:** 4 servings.

ALMOND VEGETABLE TOPPING

This nutty topping provides an easy way to jazz up plain vegetables. It's excellent over cooked green beans, sliced carrots or cauliflower.

- 1/2 cup butter *or* margarine, softened
- 1/4 cup sliced almonds
- 1 tablespoon honey
- 1 drop almond extract

In a small bowl, blend all ingredients. Cover and store in refrigerator. Serve on hot cooked vegetables. **Yield:** 3/4 cup.

POTATO-STUFFED PEPPERS

(Pictured below)

Dress up everyone's favorite everyday mashed potatoes by serving individual portions in green or sweet red pepper halves. Cheese and a sprinkling of paprika add the perfect finishing touch to this microwave recipe.

1 package (22 ounces) frozen mashed
   potatoes
2 cups milk
2 tablespoons butter *or* margarine
1 envelope ranch salad dressing mix
Pepper to taste

4 medium green *or* sweet red peppers
1 cup (4 ounces) shredded cheddar cheese
Paprika

Prepare potatoes with milk and butter according to package directions. Stir in dressing mix and season with pepper; set aside. Cut peppers in half lengthwise; do not remove the tops. Remove stems and seeds. Place in an ungreased microwave-safe 13-in. x 9-in. x 2-in. baking dish. Cover and microwave on high for 5 minutes. Spoon potatoes into pepper halves. Cover and microwave on high for 3-4 minutes or until peppers are tender. Sprinkle with cheese and paprika. **Yield:** 8 servings.

Italian-Style Pasta Toss

This robust pasta salad is reminiscent of the delectable qualities found in a traditional Italian antipasto. The easy-to-fix frozen tortellini marinates in a zesty dressing to create a lip-smacking sensation that stands out from ordinary pasta salads.

      1 package (19 to 25 ounces) frozen cheese
         tortellini *or* ravioli
      2 green onions, sliced
      2 carrots, thinly sliced
      1 green pepper, chopped
      1 jar (6-1/2 ounces) marinated artichoke
         hearts, undrained
      1 can (about 15 ounces) large ripe olives,
         drained
      1 can (14-1/2 ounces) diced tomatoes with
         garlic and onion
      1 package (about 2 ounces) sliced
         pepperoni, separated into slices
      1 bottle (8 ounces) Italian *or* Caesar salad
         dressing
   Grated Parmesan cheese

Cook pasta according to package directions. Meanwhile, in a large bowl, combine remaining ingredients except cheese; toss. Drain pasta. Add to vegetable mixture; toss gently. Serve immediately or refrigerate and serve cold. Sprinkle with cheese just before serving. **Yield:** 4-6 servings.

Golden Carrots

The best carrots are young and slender. If you buy carrots with the green tops, remove them as soon as possible because they rob the carrots of moisture and vitamins.

      3 tablespoons butter *or* margarine
      1 pound medium carrots, sliced 1/2 inch
         thick
   1/4 teaspoon salt
   1/4 teaspoon ground ginger
   1/4 cup minced fresh parsley

In a saucepan, melt butter; add carrots, salt and ginger. Cover and cook until crisp-tender, about 15 minutes. Toss in parsley. **Yield:** 6-8 servings.

Apple Mallow Sweet Potato Bake

Thanksgiving is not complete without a marshmallow-topped sweet potato casserole. The addition of apples and pecans provides a new way to enjoy this side dish.

   1/2 cup packed brown sugar
   1/2 teaspoon ground cinnamon
      2 medium apples, peeled and sliced
   1/3 cup chopped pecans
      1 can (2 pounds, 8 ounces) cut sweet
         potatoes, drained
   1/4 cup butter *or* margarine
      2 cups miniature marshmallows

Combine brown sugar and cinnamon. Toss mixture with apples and pecans. Alternate layers of apple mixture and sweet potatoes in 1-1/2-qt. casserole. Dot with butter. Cover. Bake at 350° for 35-40 minutes. Sprinkle marshmallows over sweet potatoes and apples. Broil until lightly browned. **Yield:** 6-8 servings.

Pan-Fried Onion Slices

(Pictured above)

Onions come in a wide array of sizes, shapes and flavors. Some popular varieties are Bermuda, Spanish, Vidalia and Walla Walla, all of which will work well in this savory recipe.

      2 large onions (10 to 12 ounces *each*),
         peeled and sliced 1/2 inch thick
      1 to 2 tablespoons vegetable oil
      4 tablespoons grated Parmesan cheese
   1/4 teaspoon dried oregano
   Pepper to taste

In a skillet, cook onion in oil 8-10 minutes or until onions are tender, turning halfway through cooking time. Sprinkle with cheese, oregano and pepper; heat until cheese is melted. **Yield:** 4 servings.

ASPARAGUS ONION CASSEROLE

(Pictured below)

Round out your everyday dinners and special-occasion meals with this down-home side dish featuring garden-fresh asparagus. Topped with a savory cheese sauce and toasted bread crumbs, this is a recipe you can rely on time after time.

> 1 pound fresh asparagus, cut into 1-inch pieces *or* 2 packages (10 ounces *each*) frozen cut asparagus, thawed
> 1 medium onion, sliced
> 5 tablespoons butter *or* margarine, *divided*
> 2 tablespoons all-purpose flour
> 1 cup milk
> 1 package (3 ounces) cream cheese, cubed
> 1 teaspoon salt
> 1/8 teaspoon pepper
> 1/2 cup shredded cheddar cheese
> 1 cup soft bread crumbs

In a skillet, cook the asparagus and onion in 1 tablespoon butter until crisp-tender, about 8 minutes. Transfer to an ungreased 1-1/2-qt. baking dish. In a saucepan, melt 2 tablespoons butter. Stir in flour until smooth; gradually add milk. Bring to a boil; cook and stir for 2 minutes or until thickened. Reduce heat. Add cream cheese, salt and pepper; stir until cheese is melted. Pour over vegetables. Sprinkle with cheddar cheese. Melt remaining butter; toss with bread crumbs. Sprinkle over casserole. Bake, uncovered, at 350° for 35-40 minutes or until heated through. **Yield:** 4-6 servings.

BROCCOLI AND NOODLES SUPREME

Dress up your main meal of chicken, beef or turkey with this creamy side dish. It's true comfort food that folks will rave about. Best of all, it cooks in one pan so there's little mess and no fuss.

> 3 cups uncooked medium egg noodles
> 2 cups broccoli florets
> 1 can (10-3/4 ounces) condensed cream of chicken soup, undiluted
> 1/2 cup sour cream
> 1/3 cup grated Parmesan cheese
> 1/8 teaspoon pepper

Prepare noodles according to package directions. Add broccoli during last 5 minutes of cooking time; drain. In the same pan, combine soup, sour cream, cheese, pepper and noodle mixture; mix well. Heat through. **Yield:** 5 servings.

IRISH HERBED POTATOES

St. Patrick's Day is a favorite holiday because everything is so festive, especially the food. The day's menu would hardly be complete without these tasty "green" potatoes speckled with parsley, chives and dill.

> 2-1/2 pounds potatoes, peeled and cut into wedges
> 1/2 cup butter *or* margarine, melted
> 1 tablespoon lemon juice
> 1/4 cup chopped fresh parsley
> 3 tablespoons chopped fresh *or* dried chives
> 3 tablespoons chopped fresh dill *or* 3 teaspoons dill weed
> 1/8 teaspoon salt
> 1/8 teaspoon pepper

In a saucepan, cook potatoes in boiling salted water until tender; drain. Combine remaining ingredients; pour over potatoes and toss to coat. Serve immediately. **Yield:** 8-10 servings.

GARLIC AU GRATIN TOMATOES

You'll likely reach for this recipe when you have a bumper crop of tomatoes. The distinctive taste of garlic nicely enhances the vine-ripened vegetable.

> 8 medium tomatoes
> 1-1/2 cups soft bread crumbs

2 to 4 garlic cloves, minced
1/2 cup grated Parmesan cheese
1/3 cup chopped fresh parsley
1/2 teaspoon salt
1/4 teaspoon pepper
1/3 cup olive *or* vegetable oil

Cut a thin slice from the top of each tomato. Scoop out the pulp, leaving a 1/2-in.-thick shell. Invert tomatoes onto paper towels to drain. Meanwhile, in a bowl, combine bread crumbs, garlic, cheese, parsley, salt and pepper. Stuff tomatoes; place in a greased shallow baking dish. Drizzle with oil. Bake, uncovered, at 400° for 15-20 minutes or until stuffing is lightly browned. **Yield:** 4-6 servings. **Editor's Note:** To make appetizers, stuff 48 cherry tomatoes with crumb mixture; bake for 8-10 minutes.

SANTA FE POTATO PANCAKES

(Pictured above)

Whip up these patties to serve alongside your favorite grilled meat. The subtle Mexican seasonings enhance the mild potato flavor to create a special dish.

    1 package (26 ounces) frozen shredded hash brown potatoes
    1 cup (4 ounces) shredded pepper-Jack cheese
1/2 cup sour cream
1/2 cup milk
    2 eggs

1/4 cup sliced green onions
1/2 teaspoon salt
1/2 teaspoon pepper
1/2 teaspoon ground cumin
1/4 cup all-purpose flour
    3 tablespoons vegetable oil
Additional sour cream, optional

Combine the first nine ingredients; let stand for 10 minutes. Stir in flour. In a large skillet, drop 1/4 cupfuls mixture into hot oil. Cook over medium-high heat 6 minutes or until golden, turning once. Drain on paper towels. Serve with sour cream if desired. **Yield:** 4 servings.

STEWED TOMATO CORN RELISH

You'll "relish" the flavor this simple salsa-type mixture adds to baked chicken and grilled steaks. Make it a day or two in advance so the flavors can blend.

    1 can (14-1/2 ounces) stewed tomatoes, drained
    1 can (15-1/4 ounces) whole kernel corn, drained
    1 large green pepper, diced
1/2 cup Italian salad dressing
    1 teaspoon dried basil *or* 1 tablespoon chopped fresh basil

Coarsely chop tomatoes. Add corn and green pepper. Toss with dressing and basil. Store in the refrigerator. **Yield:** 4 cups.

You'll be proud to fill your freezer and pantry with these blue-ribbon favorites.

ONE ADVANTAGE of gardening is the abundance of fresh fruits and vegetables that result directly from your efforts. Over the years, home cooks have created dozens of jelly and jam recipes that allow us to preserve this tasty bounty for year-round enjoyment. Whether you're an experienced "canner" or giving freezer jams a try for the first time, you'll find these fruity selections easy to prepare. Your family will appreciate the homemade goodness.

Rinse clean plastic containers and lids with boiling water. Dry thoroughly. Wash strawberries and remove stems. Crush strawberries thoroughly, one layer at a time. Measure exactly 2 cups prepared fruit into a large bowl. Stir in sugar. Let stand 10 minutes, stirring occasionally. In a small saucepan, mix water and pectin. Bring to a boil over high heat, stirring constantly. Continue boiling and stirring for 1 minute. Stir pectin mixture into fruit. Stir constantly until sugar is dissolved and no longer grainy, about 3 minutes. (A few sugar crystals may remain.) Fill all containers quickly to within 1/2 in. of tops. Wipe off top edges of containers; quickly cover with lids. Let stand at room temperature 24 hours. Jam is ready to use. Store in refrigerator up to 3 weeks or freeze up to 1 year. Thaw in refrigerator. **Yield:** 6 (1 cup) containers.

Editor's Note: Any one of the following can be added to strawberries before the sugar: 1/2 cup slivered almonds, chopped pecans, pumpkin or sunflower kernels or pine nuts (toasted, if desired); 1/4 cup dry white vermouth or sherry wine; 2 tablespoons orange-flavored liqueur; 1 tablespoon finely chopped crystallized ginger; 2 teaspoons almond extract; 1 tablespoon grated lemon, lime or orange peel; 1/4 cup mashed ripe banana and 1 tablespoon lemon juice.

30-MINUTE STRAWBERRY FREEZER JAM

(Pictured above)

At the start of summer, supermarkets, produce stands and pick-your-own farms are overflowing with vine-ripened strawberries. Why not preserve that fresh-picked flavor to enjoy throughout the year?

    1 quart fully ripe strawberries
    4 cups sugar
    3/4 cup water
    1 package (1-3/4 ounces) powdered
      fruit pectin

BLUEBERRY FREEZER JAM

Whether served on toast, muffins or crackers, homemade freezer jam is an enjoyable extra that adds sweetness to your menu.

    2-1/2 pints fully ripe blueberries
    5-1/4 cups sugar
      3/4 cup water
        1 package (1-3/4 ounces) powdered
          fruit pectin

Rinse clean plastic containers and lids with boiling water. Dry thoroughly. Wash blueberries and remove stems. Crush blueberries thoroughly, one layer at a time. Measure exactly 3 cups prepared fruit into a large bowl. Stir in sugar. Let stand 10 minutes, stirring occasionally. In a small saucepan, mix water and pectin. Bring to a boil over high heat, stirring constantly. Continue boiling and stirring for 1 minute. Stir pectin mixture into fruit mixture. Stir constantly until sugar is dissolved and no longer grainy, about 3 minutes. (A few sugar crystals may remain.) Fill all containers quickly to within 1/2 in. of tops. Wipe off top edges of containers; quickly cover with lids. Let stand at room temperature 24 hours. Jam is now ready to use. Store in refrigerator up to 3 weeks or freeze extra containers up to 1 year. Thaw in refrigerator. **Yield:** 7 (1 cup) containers.

RASPBERRY-PEACH FREEZER JAM

Achieve maximum flavor with minimum labor by preparing quick and easy freezer jams. The fruity combination of raspberries and peaches is sure to please.

1-1/2 pints fully ripe red raspberries
1-1/4 pounds fully ripe peaches
    7 cups sugar
    3/4 cup water
    1 package (1-3/4 ounces) powdered
      fruit pectin

Rinse clean plastic containers and lids with boiling water. Dry thoroughly. Crush raspberries thoroughly, one layer at a time. (Press half of pulp through a sieve to remove some of the seeds if desired.) Measure exactly 2 cups prepared raspberries into a large bowl. Peel peaches and remove pits. Finely chop or grind fruit. Measure exactly 1-1/2 cups prepared peaches into bowl with raspberries. Stir in sugar. Let stand 10 minutes, stirring occasionally. In a small saucepan, mix water and pectin. Bring mixture to a boil over high heat, stirring constantly. Continue boiling and stirring for 1 minute. Stir pectin mixture into fruit mixture. Stir constantly until sugar is dissolved and no longer grainy, about 3 minutes. (A few sugar crystals may remain.) Fill all containers quickly to within 1/2 in. of tops. Wipe off top edges of containers; quickly cover with lids. Let stand at room temperature 24 hours. Jam is now ready to use. Store in refrigerator up to 3 weeks or freeze extra containers up to 1 year. Thaw in refrigerator. **Yield:** 7 (1 cup) containers.

LEMON-ORANGE FREEZER JELLY

Satisfying citrus provides sweet-tart flavor to this tempting jelly. Jellies are firmer than jams since they are made with fruit juice rather than crushed fruit.

    2 cups orange juice
  1/4 cup fresh lemon juice
4-1/2 cups sugar
    3/4 cup water
    1 package (1-3/4 ounces)
      powdered fruit pectin

Rinse clean plastic containers and lids with boiling water. Dry thoroughly. Pour orange and lemon juices into a large bowl. Stir in sugar. Let stand 10 minutes, stirring occasionally. In a small saucepan, mix water and pectin. Bring mixture to a boil over high heat, stirring constantly. Continue boiling and stirring for 1 minute. Stir pectin mixture into juice mixture. Stir constantly until sugar is dissolved and no longer grainy, about 3 minutes. (A few sugar crystals may remain.) Fill all containers quickly to within 1/2 in. of tops. Wipe off top edges of containers; quickly cover with lids. Let stand at room temperature 24 hours. Jelly is now ready to use. Store in refrigerator up to 3 weeks or freeze extra containers up to 1 year. Thaw in refrigerator. **Yield:** 5 (1 cup) containers.

SPICED STRAWBERRY JAM

During the summer, many country cooks put up jars of jam destined to be slathered on homemade bread. The addition of spices makes this recipe especially good.

    2 quarts fully ripe strawberries
  1/2 teaspoon ground allspice
  1/2 teaspoon ground cinnamon
  1/2 teaspoon ground cloves
    7 cups sugar
    1 package (1-3/4 ounces) powdered
      fruit pectin

Wash strawberries and remove stems. Crush strawberries thoroughly, one layer at a time. Measure exactly 4-1/2 cups into 6 or 8 qt. saucepan; add spices. Mix fruit pectin into fruit. Place over high heat and stir until mixture comes to a full boil. Immediately add sugar and stir. Bring to a full rolling boil and boil 1 minute, stirring constantly. Remove from heat; skim off foam with metal spoon. Ladle quickly into hot jars, filling to within 1/4 in. of top. Cover and process in boiling water bath for 5 minutes. **Yield:** 9 (8 ounce) jars.

HOT VEGETABLE PLATE

(Pictured below)

A creamy mustard sauce adds spark to an interesting lineup of vegetables in this pleasing fall side dish. You'll receive plenty of compliments regarding the special presentation.

> 1 medium kohlrabi
> 1 medium turnip
> 1 small rutabaga
> 4 medium carrots, halved crosswise
> 4 medium leeks (white portion only), sliced
> 12 fresh cauliflowerets

MUSTARD SAUCE:

> 1/4 cup butter *or* margarine
> 2 tablespoons all-purpose flour
> 1/4 teaspoon salt, optional

Pinch pepper

> 1 cup milk
> 1 to 2 teaspoons Dijon mustard

Peel kohlrabi, turnip and rutabaga; cut into 1/4-in. slices. Halve the kohlrabi and turnip slices; quarter the rutabaga slices. Place all vegetables in a large saucepan and cover with water; cook until crisp-tender. Meanwhile, melt the butter in a small saucepan; stir in the flour. Bring to a boil; cook and stir for 2 minutes. Add salt if desired and pepper. Gradually add the milk; cook and stir until mixture boils. Reduce the heat; cook and stir for 1 minute or until thickened. Remove from heat; stir in the mustard. Drain vegetables; serve with warm mustard sauce. **Yield:** 8 servings.

NUTTY BARLEY BAKE

A lot of people have never seen barley in anything but soup. This tasty and distinctive harvest dish is so good that even if you double the recipe, you'll still wind up with an empty dish.

> 1 medium onion, chopped
> 1 cup medium pearl barley
> 1/2 cup slivered almonds *or* pine nuts
> 1/4 cup butter *or* margarine
> 1/2 cup minced fresh parsley
> 1/4 cup thinly sliced green onions
> 1/4 teaspoon salt
> 1/8 teaspoon pepper
> 2 cans (14 ounces *each*) beef broth

Additional parsley, optional

In a skillet over medium heat, saute onion, barley and nuts in butter until barley is lightly browned. Stir in parsley, green onions, salt and pepper. Transfer to a greased 2-qt. baking dish. Stir in broth. Bake, uncovered, at 350° for 1 hour and 15 minutes or until the barley is tender and the liquid is absorbed. Sprinkle with parsley if desired. **Yield:** 6 servings.

HOLIDAY CRANBERRY CHUTNEY

A chunky chutney like this one makes a lovely gift in a decorated jar. It's great served as an appetizer with crackers or alongside a main dish.

> 1 package (12 ounces) fresh *or* frozen
>   cranberries

1-1/4 cups sugar

> 3/4 cup water
> 1 large tart apple, chopped
> 2 teaspoons ground cinnamon
> 1 teaspoon ground ginger
> 1/4 teaspoon ground cloves

In a saucepan, combine all ingredients; bring to a boil, stirring constantly. Reduce heat; simmer for 15-20 minutes or until apple is tender and mixture thickens. Cool completely. Store in the refrigerator. Serve over cream cheese with crackers or as a condiment with pork, ham or poultry. **Yield:** 3 cups.

HERB-BUTTERED CORN

(Pictured above)

It's no wonder that people love the taste of fresh corn on the cob. For a flavorful, different way to serve sweet corn, try this recipe.

1/2 cup butter *or* margarine, softened
1 tablespoon minced fresh chives
1 tablespoon minced fresh dill
1 tablespoon minced fresh parsley
1/2 teaspoon dried thyme
1/4 teaspoon salt
Dash garlic powder
Dash cayenne pepper
10 ears fresh corn, husked and cooked

In a bowl, combine first eight ingredients; mix well. Spread over each ear of corn. **Yield:** 10 servings.

CHEESY CORN SPOON BREAD

Homey and comforting, this custard-like side dish will be a much-requested recipe at potlucks and holiday dinners. The jalapeno pepper adds just the right "bite".

1 medium onion, chopped
1/4 cup butter *or* margarine
2 eggs
2 cups (16 ounces) sour cream
1 can (15-1/4 ounces) whole kernel corn, drained
1 can (14-3/4 ounces) cream-style corn
1/4 teaspoon salt
1/4 teaspoon pepper
1 package (8-1/2 ounces) corn bread/muffin mix
1 medium jalapeno pepper, minced*
2 cups (8 ounces) shredded cheddar cheese, *divided*

In a skillet, saute onion in butter until tender; set aside. In a bowl, beat the eggs; add sour cream, both cans of corn, salt and pepper. Stir in corn bread mix just until blended. Fold in sauteed onion, jalapeno and 1-1/2 cups of cheese. Transfer to a greased shallow 3-qt. baking dish. Sprinkle with the remaining cheese. Bake, uncovered, at 375° for 35-40 minutes or until a toothpick inserted near the center comes out clean; cool slightly. **Yield:** 12-15 servings. ***Editor's Note:** When cutting or seeding hot peppers, use rubber or plastic gloves to protect your hands. Avoid touching your face or eyes.

CONTINENTAL ZUCCHINI

Zucchini are plentiful, and people often joke about using them up before they multiply! Sharing zucchini—and zucchini recipes—is a good-neighbor policy.

> 1 tablespoon vegetable oil
> 1 pound zucchini (about 3 small), cubed
> 1 to 2 garlic cloves, minced
> 1 jar (2 ounces) chopped pimientos, drained
> 1 can (15-1/2 ounces) whole kernel corn, drained
> 1 teaspoon salt, optional
> 1/4 teaspoon lemon-pepper seasoning
> 1/2 cup shredded mozzarella cheese

Heat oil in a large skillet. Saute zucchini and garlic for 3-4 minutes. Add pimientos, corn, salt if desired and lemon-pepper; cook and stir for 2-3 minutes or until zucchini is tender. Sprinkle with cheese and heat until cheese is melted. **Yield:** 6 servings.

LEMONY ACORN SLICES

(Pictured above)

This style of preparation is a nice change from simple baked acorn squash. With the skins on the slices and a lemony syrup drizzled over them, this side dish looks as good as it tastes.

> 2 large acorn squash (about 2-1/4 pounds *each*)
> 1 cup plus 2 tablespoons water, *divided*
> 1/2 cup sugar
> 2 tablespoons lemon juice
> 1 tablespoon butter *or* margarine
> 1/4 teaspoon salt
> 1/8 teaspoon pepper
> **Lemon wedges and fresh mint, optional**

Wash squash. Cut in half lengthwise; remove and discard the seeds and membrane. Cut each half crosswise into 1/2-in. slices; discard ends. Place slices in a large skillet. Add 1 cup of water; bring to a boil. Reduce heat; cover and simmer for 20 minutes or until tender. Meanwhile, in a heavy saucepan, combine sugar and remaining water. Cook over medium heat until sugar melts and syrup is golden, stirring occasionally. Remove from the heat; carefully add lemon juice, butter, salt and pepper. Cook and stir over low heat until butter melts. Place squash on a serving plate; top with the syrup. Garnish with lemon and mint if desired. **Yield:** 6 servings.

ORANGE-KISSED BEETS

Pickled beets and Harvard beets are two traditional ways to serve this garnet-red vegetable. For a change of pace, try this sweet tangy sauce, which nicely complements sliced beets.

> 1/3 cup orange juice
> 2 tablespoons light brown sugar
> 1 tablespoon butter *or* margarine
> 1/2 teaspoon cornstarch
> 1/8 teaspoon ground ginger
> 1/8 teaspoon salt
> 1/8 teaspoon pepper
> 1 can (8-1/4 ounces) sliced beets, drained
> 2 tablespoons golden raisins
> **Strips of orange peel**

In a saucepan over medium heat, cook and stir the orange juice, brown sugar, butter, cornstarch, ginger, salt and pepper until thick. Add the beets and raisins; heat through. Garnish with orange peel. **Yield:** 2 servings.

CORN AND BACON CASSEROLE

Corn is a wonderfully versatile vegetable. Everything on the plant can be used: the husks for tamales, the kernels for food, the stalks for fodder. It's also the foundation of many by-products, including cornmeal, corn oil, cornstarch, corn syrup and laundry starch.

    6 bacon strips
  1/2 cup chopped onion
    2 tablespoons all-purpose flour
    2 garlic cloves, minced
  1/2 teaspoon salt
  1/2 teaspoon pepper
    1 cup (8 ounces) sour cream
3-1/2 cups fresh *or* frozen whole kernel corn
    1 tablespoon chopped fresh parsley
    1 tablespoon chopped fresh chives

In a large skillet, cook bacon until crisp. Drain, reserving 2 tablespoons of drippings. Crumble bacon; set aside. Saute onion in drippings until tender. Add flour, garlic, salt and pepper. Cook and stir until bubbly; cook and stir 1 minute more. Remove from the heat and stir in sour cream until smooth. Add corn, parsley and half of the bacon; mix well. Pour into a 1-qt. baking dish. Sprinkle with remaining bacon. Bake, uncovered, at 350° for 20-25 minutes or until heated through. Sprinkle with chives. **Yield:** 6-8 servings.

VEGETABLE NOODLE CASSEROLE

If you're looking for a filling side dish, this recipe fits the bill. It combines nutritious vegetables and hearty noodles in a delectable cream sauce. Serve this casserole at potlucks and family gatherings. It'll get passed around until the pan is scraped clean.

    1 can (10-3/4 ounces) condensed cream of
      chicken soup, undiluted
    1 can (10-3/4 ounces) condensed cream of
      broccoli soup, undiluted
1-1/2 cups milk
    1 cup grated Parmesan cheese, *divided*
    3 garlic cloves, minced
    2 tablespoons dried parsley flakes
  1/2 teaspoon pepper
  1/4 teaspoon salt
    1 package (16 ounces) wide egg noodles,
      cooked and drained
    1 package (16 ounces) frozen broccoli,
      cauliflower and carrot blend, thawed
    2 cups frozen corn, thawed

In a bowl, combine the soups, milk, 3/4 cup Parmesan cheese, garlic, parsley, pepper and salt; mix well. Add the noodles and vegetables; mix well. Pour into a greased 13-in. x 9-in. x 2-in. baking dish. Sprinkle with the remaining Parmesan. Cover and bake at 350° for 45-50 minutes or until heated through. **Yield:** 12-14 servings.

ASPARAGUS WITH ORANGE SAUCE

(Pictured below)

This dish offers an inspiring taste of spring. A light, creamy orange sauce drapes the tender asparagus making a tempting treat for the whole family.

    2 pounds fresh asparagus, trimmed
  1/4 cup plain nonfat yogurt
    2 tablespoons mayonnaise
    2 tablespoons orange juice
    1 teaspoon grated orange peel
Dash cayenne pepper
Orange slices and additional orange peel,
  optional

Place asparagus and a small amount of water in a skillet; bring to a boil. Cook for 6-8 minutes or until crisp-tender. Meanwhile, combine yogurt, mayonnaise, orange juice, peel and cayenne. Drain asparagus; top with orange sauce. Garnish with orange slices and peel if desired. **Yield:** 8 servings.

Chapter 12

COOKIES & BARS

You'll make your family's day when you offer a pretty platter stacked with tempting bars and brownies or a cookie jar brimming with fresh-baked treats.

Recipes in this chapter provided courtesy of these past sponsors...

Baker's
Blue Bonnet
Crisco
Diamond Walnuts
Dromedary
Eagle Brand
Hershey's
Karo
Kraft
Mounds
Nestea
Nestlé
Planter's
Reese's
Sunsweet
Taster's Choice

CHOCOLATE MORSEL PASTRY COOKIES

(Pictured at left)

These crisp pastry cookies may look difficult, but they're really a snap to prepare—thanks to the use of frozen puff pastry dough. The flaky pinwheels encase a layer of sweetened cream cheese and creamy chocolate morsels. For the best flavor, serve shortly after baking.

> 1 package (17-1/2 ounces) frozen puff pastry sheets, thawed
> 1 package (8 ounces) cream cheese, softened
> 3 tablespoons sugar
> 1-3/4 cups (11-1/2 ounces) milk chocolate morsels, *divided*

On a lightly floured surface, roll one puff pastry sheet into a 14-in. x 10-in. rectangle. In a small bowl, combine cream cheese and sugar until smooth. Spread half of cream cheese mixture over puff pastry, leaving 1-in. border on one long side. Sprinkle with half of the morsels. Roll up starting at long side covered with cream cheese. Seal end by moistening with water. Repeat with remaining ingredients. Refrigerate for 1 hour. Line baking sheets with waxed paper or lightly grease. Cut rolls crosswise into 1-in.-thick slices. Place cut side down on prepared baking sheets. Bake at 375° for 20-25 minutes or until golden brown. Cool on baking sheets for 2 minutes; remove to wire racks to cool completely. **Yield:** 2 dozen.

DEEP-DISH BROWNIE

The addition of baking powder makes these tempting brownies a bit more cake-like than some fudgy brownie recipes. If you wish to gild the lily, top them with chocolate frosting.

> 3/4 cup butter *or* margarine, melted
> 1-1/2 cups sugar
> 1-1/2 teaspoons vanilla extract
> 3 eggs
> 3/4 cup all-purpose flour
> 1/2 cup baking cocoa
> 1/2 teaspoon baking powder
> 1/2 teaspoon salt

Blend butter, sugar and vanilla in a medium mixing bowl. Add eggs; beat well with spoon. In a small bowl, combine flour, cocoa, baking powder and salt. Gradually add to egg mixture; beat well. Spread into a greased 8-in. square baking pan. Bake at 350° for 40-45 minutes or until brownie begins to pull away from edges of pan. Cool. **Yield:** 16 squares.

TOFFEE BITS TRIANGLES

(Pictured below)

Cutting these bar cookies into triangles gives them a more festive appearance but with far less work than is required for cutout cookies. Rich and buttery, the semisweet chocolate layer provides an ideal complement to the sweet, toffee-flavored cookie.

    1 cup butter *or* margarine, softened
    1 cup packed light brown sugar
    1 teaspoon vanilla extract
    1 egg yolk
    2 cups all-purpose flour
1-3/4 cups (10 ounces) English toffee bits *or*
      brickle bits, *divided*
    1 package (12 ounces) semisweet
      chocolate chips

In a large mixing bowl, beat butter on medium speed until creamy. Beat in brown sugar, vanilla and egg

yolk until well mixed. Stir in flour and 1 cup toffee bits. Press into an ungreased 15-in. x 10-in. x 1-in. baking pan. Bake at 350° for 18-20 minutes or until lightly brown. Immediately sprinkle baking pieces over top. Let stand until softened, about 5 minutes; spread evenly. Sprinkle remaining toffee bits over top. Refrigerate 10 minutes or until chocolate is set. Cut into 3-in. squares; cut each square into 4 triangles. **Yield:** 5 dozen.

DOUBLE-CHOCOLATE BROWNIES

You'll go nuts over these heavenly bars. For a special-occasion dessert, top each brownie with a generous scoop of ice cream and drizzle with chocolate syrup.

    1 package (12 ounces) semisweet chocolate
      chips, *divided*
  1/2 cup butter *or* margarine
1-1/2 cups sugar
1-1/4 cups all-purpose flour
    1 teaspoon vanilla extract
  1/2 teaspoon baking powder
  1/4 teaspoon salt
    3 eggs
    1 cup coarsely chopped nuts
Ice cream
Chocolate syrup

In a large microwave-safe bowl, combine 1 cup chocolate chips and butter. Microwave on high for 1 to 1-1/2 minutes or until smooth when stirred. Stir in sugar, flour, vanilla, baking powder, salt and eggs until smooth. Stir in nuts and remaining chocolate chips. Spread into a greased 13-in. x 9-in. x 2-in. baking pan. Bake at 350° for 30-35 minutes or until center is set. Cool in pan on wire rack. Cut into squares. Serve with ice cream and chocolate syrup. **Yield:** 12-15 servings.

LEMON BARS

Lemons add a welcome sweet-tart flavor to a variety of foods and beverages. At the supermarket, select lemons that are plump, firm and heavy for their size.

    1 cup butter *or* margarine, softened
  1/2 cup confectioners' sugar
2-1/4 cups all-purpose flour, *divided*
    4 eggs
    2 cups sugar
    1 teaspoon baking powder
    1 tablespoon grated lemon peel
  1/4 cup lemon juice
Additional confectioners' sugar

In a large mixing bowl, beat butter, confectioners' sugar and 2 cups flour at medium speed until well mixed. Press mixture into 13-in. x 9-in. x 2-in. baking pan. Bake at 350° for 15-20 minutes or until golden. Meanwhile, in the same bowl, beat eggs with sugar at medium speed until well mixed. Beat in remaining flour, baking powder, lemon peel and lemon juice until smooth; pour over baked layer. Bake 25-30 minutes longer or until lightly browned. Cool slightly in pan on wire rack; sprinkle with confectioners' sugar. Cool completely; cut into bars. **Yield:** 36 bars.

TWO GREAT TASTES COOKIES

Developed in 1890 and promoted as a health food at the 1904 St. Louis World's Fair, peanut butter is a blend of ground shelled peanuts, vegetable oil and a small amount of salt. The flavors of chocolate and peanut butter taste so good together, they are often teamed in popular desserts.

  3/4 cup butter *or* margarine, softened
    1 cup sugar
  1/2 cup packed brown sugar
    1 teaspoon vanilla extract
    2 eggs
    2 cups all-purpose flour
    1 teaspoon baking soda
    1 cup peanut butter chips
    1 cup semisweet chocolate chips *or* milk
      chocolate chips

In a large mixing bowl, cream butter, sugars and vanilla until light and fluffy. Add eggs; beat well. Combine flour and baking soda; add to creamed mixture. Beat well. Stir in peanut butter chips and chocolate chips. Drop by teaspoonfuls onto ungreased baking sheet. Bake at 350° for 10-12 minutes or until lightly browned. Cool slightly; remove from baking sheet onto wire rack. Cool completely. **Yield:** 5 dozen.

PECAN-TOPPED CHOCOLATE COCONUT COOKIES

(Pictured above right)

When you want to bake a cookie with a little more flair, reach for this recipe. These mouth-watering bites make such an appealing sight on your table that no one will be able to eat just one.

  2/3 cup butter *or* margarine
  3/4 cup sugar

    1 egg
1-1/2 teaspoons vanilla extract
1-1/3 cups all-purpose flour
  1/3 cup baking cocoa
  1/4 teaspoon baking powder
  1/4 teaspoon baking soda
  1/8 teaspoon salt
  1/2 cup flaked coconut
About 48 large pecan halves
CHOCOLATE GLAZE:
    2 tablespoons sugar
    2 tablespoons water
  1/2 cup semisweet chocolate chips

In a large mixing bowl, beat butter, sugar, egg and vanilla until light and fluffy. In a separate bowl, stir together flour, cocoa, baking powder, baking soda and salt; add to butter mixture with coconut, beating until well blended. Cover; refrigerate about 1 hour. Shape dough into 1-in. balls. Place on an ungreased baking sheet. Bake at 350° for 8-10 minutes or until almost set. Remove from baking sheet to wire rack. Cool completely. To make glaze, stir together sugar and water in a small saucepan. Cook over medium heat, stirring constantly until mixture boils and sugar is dissolved. Remove from heat; immediately add chocolate chips, stirring until melted. Cool to spreading consistency. Frost each cookie and top with a pecan half. **Yield:** 4 dozen (1/2 cup glaze).

Toll House Cookies

The Most Popular Cookie in America Was Invented by Accident At a Massachusetts Inn. Thank You, Ruth Wakefield.

IN THE 1700s, a toll house was a place where travelers paid toll, changed horses and enjoyed delicious home-cooked meals. Some 200 years later, an old toll house near Whitman, Massachusetts caught the eye of Ruth and Kenneth Wakefield. They bought it and turned it into a lodge.

In honor of the building's past, Ruth named the lodge "Toll House Inn" and impressed her guests with luscious homemade meals. She modified recipes from colonial times to make them even better.

One day Ruth was mixing up her usual Butter Drop Do cookies when she got an inkling to try something new. She cut a bar of Nestlé semisweet chocolate into tiny bits and added them to the dough.

Ruth thought the bits would melt, creating a chocolate-flavored dough. Instead, the pieces held their shape, softening to a creamy texture.

Ruth served the cookies anyway. Inn-goers—and just about everyone who's tried them since—loved the cookies. They became so popular that the recipe was printed in several New England newspapers, and sales of Nestlé semisweet chocolate bars soared.

Ruth agreed to let Nestlé print her recipe on the chocolate-bar wrapper. As part of the agreement, Ruth got all the chocolate she could use for the rest of her life.

Nestlé eventually scored the bars and packaged them with special choppers to make it easier to turn bars to bits. In 1939, Nestlé began selling tiny pieces of chocolate called "morsels" in a ready-to-use package complete with the recipe for Toll House Cookies.

TOLL HOUSE CHOCOLATE CHIP COOKIES

1 cup butter *or* margarine, softened
3/4 cup sugar
3/4 cup packed brown sugar
1 teaspoon vanilla extract
2 eggs
2-1/4 cups all-purpose flour
1 teaspoon baking soda
1 teaspoon salt
1 package (12 ounces) semisweet chocolate morsels
1 cup chopped nuts, optional

In a large mixing bowl, cream butter, sugars and vanilla. Beat in eggs, one at a time; mix well. In a small bowl, combine flour, baking soda and salt; gradually add to creamed mixture and mix well. Stir in morsels and nuts if desired. Drop by rounded tablespoonfuls 2 in. apart on ungreased baking sheets. Bake at 375° for 9-11 minutes or until golden brown. Cool for 2 minutes before removing to wire racks to cool completely. **Yield:** 5 dozen.

PAN COOKIE VARIATION:
Prepare dough as directed above. Spread dough into a greased 15-in. x 10-in. x 1-in. baking pan. Bake at 375° for 20-25 minutes or until golden brown. Cool in pan on wire rack. Cut into bars. **Yield:** 4 dozen.

TRIPLE-LAYER BROWNIES

These scrumptious brownies get dressed with gooey marshmallows and a pleasing layer of peanut butter and crisp rice cereal. Mix up a batch for a special gathering or when you just want to treat yourself.

        2 cups sugar
        2 cups all-purpose flour
      2/3 cup baking cocoa
        1 teaspoon baking powder
      1/2 teaspoon salt
      3/4 cup cold butter *or* margarine
        4 eggs
        2 teaspoons vanilla extract
    2-1/2 cups miniature marshmallows
        1 package (10 ounces) peanut butter chips
        2 tablespoons shortening
        3 cups crisp rice cereal

In a bowl, combine sugar, flour, cocoa, baking powder and salt. Cut in butter with pastry blender until mixture resembles coarse crumbs. Lightly beat eggs and vanilla. Add to dry mixture; beat until blended. Spread batter into a greased 13-in. x 9-in. x 2-in. baking pan. Bake at 350° for 25 minutes; remove from oven. Sprinkle marshmallows evenly over brownies, covering entire surface; return to oven. Bake for an additional 5 minutes; remove from oven. Cool in pan 10 minutes. Microwave chips and shortening on high for 1 minute; stir. If necessary, microwave for additional 15-second intervals until chips are melted. Add rice cereal; stir until thoroughly coated. Immediately spread over top of marshmallows. Cool completely in pan on wire rack. Cut into bars. **Yield:** 32 bars.

OATMEAL SCOTCHIES

(Pictured at right)

An old-fashioned favorite, these classics are packed with butterscotch morsels. You can vary the baking time if you prefer chewy or crisp cookies.

    1-1/4 cups all-purpose flour
        1 teaspoon baking soda
      1/2 teaspoon ground cinnamon
      1/2 teaspoon salt
        1 cup butter *or* margarine, softened
      3/4 cup sugar
      3/4 cup packed brown sugar
        2 eggs
        1 teaspoon vanilla extract *or* grated peel
          of 1 orange
        3 cups quick *or* old-fashioned oats
        1 package (11 ounces) butterscotch morsels

In a small bowl, combine flour, baking soda, cinnamon and salt. In a large mixing bowl, beat butter, sugars, eggs and vanilla until fluffy. Gradually beat in flour mixture. Stir in oats and morsels. Drop by rounded tablespoons onto ungreased baking sheets. Bake at 375° for 7-8 minutes for chewy cookies, 9-10 minutes for crisp cookies. Cool on baking sheets for 2 minutes; remove to wire racks to cool completely. **Yield:** 4 dozen.

HOPSCOTCH

Kids will be happy to help with these yummy no-bake cookies that gained popularity in the 1960s. Today, most cooks will choose to melt the morsels in a microwave instead of a double boiler.

      1/2 cup peanut butter
        1 cup butterscotch morsels
        1 can (3 ounces) chow mein noodles
        2 cups miniature marshmallows

Place peanut butter and butterscotch morsels in a double boiler. Heat over hot (not boiling) water until morsels are melted, stirring until smooth. Add noodles and marshmallows; toss until coated. Drop by teaspoonfuls onto waxed paper-lined baking sheet. Chill until firm. **Yield:** 4 dozen.

CHOCOLATE CARAMEL BARS

(Pictured below)

Who can resist the gooey goodness of caramel and chocolate? These light melt-in-your-mouth pleasures make for sweet snacking anytime! Your family will rave about their moist, satisfying flavor.

1-3/4 cups plus 3 tablespoons all-purpose flour, *divided*
1-3/4 cups quick-cooking oats
   1 cup packed brown sugar
1/2 teaspoon baking soda
1/4 teaspoon salt
1/2 cup Lighter Bake baking fat replacement
1/4 cup vegetable oil
   1 cup semisweet chocolate chips
3/4 cup fat-free caramel ice cream topping

In a mixing bowl, combine 1-3/4 cups flour, oats, brown sugar, baking soda and salt. Add Lighter Bake and oil; stir with fork until evenly moist and crumbly. Reserve 1 cup crumb mixture for topping. Press remaining crumb mixture evenly onto bottom of a 13 in. x 9 in. x 2 in. baking pan coated with nonstick cooking spray. Bake at 350° for 15 minutes; cool 10 minutes. Sprinkle with chocolate chips. Stir 3 tablespoons flour into caramel topping. Drizzle over chocolate to within 1/4 in. of edges. Sprinkle with reserved crumbs. Bake 15 minutes or until edges are golden. Cool; cut into bars. **Yield:** 3 dozen.

PECAN MINI KISSES CUPS

These unique cookies are sure to be crowd pleasers, so why not bake a batch for your next get-together? A rich cream cheese-based dough lines the bottom of mini-muffin cups and is topped off with a luscious filling, chocolate baking pieces and crunchy pecans.

1/2 cup butter *or* margarine, softened
   1 package (3 ounces) cream cheese, softened
   1 cup all-purpose flour
   1 egg
2/3 cup packed light brown sugar
   1 tablespoon butter *or* margarine, melted
   1 teaspoon vanilla extract
Dash salt
  72 mini kisses chocolate baking pieces, *divided*
1/2 cup coarsely chopped pecans

In a medium bowl, beat butter and cream cheese until blended. Add flour; beat well. Cover; refrigerate 1 hour or until firm enough to handle. In a small bowl, stir together egg, brown sugar, melted butter, vanilla and salt until well blended. Shape chilled dough into 24 balls (1 in. each); press balls onto bottom and up sides of ungreased miniature muffin cups (1-3/4 in. in diameter). Place 2 mini kisses in each cup. Spoon about 1 teaspoon pecans over mini kisses. Fill each cup with egg mixture. Bake at 325° for 25 minutes or until filling is set. Lightly press 1 mini kiss in center of each cookie. Cool in pan on wire rack. Remove from pan. **Yield:** 2 dozen.

CHOCOLATE CLOUDS

Light as a feather, these tempting treasures are sure to satisfy your sweet tooth. Chocolate chunks are hidden within these irresistible meringue cookies.

   3 egg whites
1/8 teaspoon cream of tartar
3/4 cup sugar
   1 teaspoon vanilla extract
   2 tablespoons baking cocoa
1-3/4 cups semisweet chocolate chunks *or* 2 cups semisweet chocolate chips

In a large mixing bowl, beat egg whites and cream of tartar until soft peaks form. Gradually add sugar and vanilla, beating until stiff peaks hold, sugar is dissolved and mixture is glossy. Sift cocoa onto egg white mixture; gently fold just until combined. Fold in chocolate chunks. Drop by heaping tablespoonfuls onto parchment paper or foil-lined baking sheet. Bake at 300° for 35-45 minutes or just until dry. Carefully peel cookies off paper; cool completely on wire rack. Store covered at room temperature. **Yield:** 2-1/2 dozen.

DREAM BARS

Wonderfully moist and chewy with coconut and nuts, these treats are winners with kids and adults alike. The crust is buttery rich.

CRUST:
> 1 cup all-purpose flour
> 1/2 cup packed brown sugar
> 1/2 cup cold butter *or* margarine

FILLING:
> 2 eggs, lightly beaten
> 1 cup packed brown sugar
> 1 teaspoon vanilla extract
> 2 tablespoons all-purpose flour
> 1/2 teaspoon salt
> 1 cup flaked coconut
> 1 cup chopped walnuts

In a small bowl, combine flour and brown sugar; cut in butter until crumbly. Pat into a 13-in. x 9-in. x 2-in. baking pan. Bake at 350° for 10 minutes. Meanwhile, in a mixing bowl, beat eggs and brown sugar; stir in vanilla. Combine flour and salt; add to egg mixture. Fold in coconut and walnuts. Spread over baked crust. Return to oven and bake 20-25 minutes longer or until golden brown. Cool in pan on a wire rack. **Yield:** about 32 servings.

CRUNCHY PEANUT BRICKLE BARS

(Pictured above right)

Make your family's day by serving a pretty platter stacked with these tempting bars. The crisp crust complements the rich peanut butter-toffee topping perfectly. It's a recipe to rely on when you need a sweet snack or dessert for a crowd.

> 2 cups quick-cooking oats
> 1-1/2 cups all-purpose flour
> 1 cup chopped dry-roasted peanuts
> 1 cup packed brown sugar

> 1 teaspoon baking soda
> 1/2 teaspoon salt
> 1 cup butter *or* margarine, melted
> 1 can (14 ounces) sweetened condensed milk
> 1/2 cup peanut butter
> 1 package (10 ounces) English toffee bits *or* 7-1/2 ounces almond brickle chips

In a large bowl, combine oats, flour, peanuts, sugar, baking soda and salt; stir in butter until crumbly. Reserve 1-1/2 cups crumb mixture; press remaining mixture on bottom of greased 15-in. x 10-in. x 1-in. jelly roll pan. Bake at 375° for 12 minutes. In a small mixing bowl, beat condensed milk and peanut butter until smooth; spread evenly over prepared crust to within 1/4 in. of edge. In a medium bowl, combine reserved crumb mixture and English toffee bits. Sprinkle evenly over peanut butter mixture; press down firmly. Bake at 375° for 20 minutes or until golden brown. Cool completely on wire rack. Cut into bars. Store loosely covered at room temperature. **Yield:** 48 bars.

HIGH-PROTEIN ENERGY BARS

Bars cookies are easy to make because the dough is simply spread in the pan and baked. These snacks will provide a boost of energy as they're loaded with nutritious ingredients.

> 1/2 cup butter *or* margarine, softened
> 1 cup packed brown sugar
> 2 eggs
> 1 teaspoon vanilla extract
> 1/3 cup baking cocoa
> 1/4 cup milk
> 1 cup whole wheat flour
> 1/4 cup nonfat dry milk powder
> 1/4 cup wheat germ
> 1/2 teaspoon baking powder
> 1/4 teaspoon baking soda
> 1-2/3 cups peanut butter chips
> 1/2 cup raisins

In a large mixing bowl, cream butter, brown sugar, eggs and vanilla until fluffy. Blend in cocoa and milk; add wheat flour, milk powder, wheat germ, baking powder and baking soda. Beat until ingredients are thoroughly combined; fold in chips and raisins. Spread mixture evenly into a greased 13-in. x 9-in. x 2-in. baking pan. Bake at 350° for 30-35 minutes or until mixture begins to pull away from sides of pan. Cool completely in pan. **Yield:** 16 bars.

BLACK AND WHITE TEA COOKIES

It's fun to gather a group of friends for a weekend before the holidays and do nothing but bake cookies. These pretty spritz cookies will look nice in the goody baskets you give as gifts.

> 1 cup (6 ounces) semisweet chocolate morsels
> 1 cup butter *or* margarine, softened
> 1 cup sugar
> 1 package (3 ounces) cream cheese, softened
> 1 teaspoon vanilla extract
> 1 egg
> 2-1/2 cups all-purpose flour
> 1 teaspoon baking powder
> 1/2 teaspoon salt
> 2 teaspoons water

In a small microwave-safe bowl, microwave morsels on high for 1 minute; stir. Microwave at additional 10- to 20-second intervals, stirring until smooth; set aside. In a large mixing bowl, cream butter, sugar, cream cheese and vanilla. Beat in egg. In a small bowl, combine flour, baking powder and salt; gradually add to mixture in mixing bowl. Cover and chill

1 hour or until firm. Divide the dough in half; stir melted morsels and water into one half, leaving other half plain. Form plain dough into 3/4-in. balls. Place on an ungreased baking sheet. Flatten with bottom of a glass dipped in flour. Using a cookie press fitted with the disk of your choice, press chocolate dough onto each plain cookie. Bake at 375° for 8-10 minutes. Cool on a wire rack. **Yield:** 5 dozen.

CHOCOLATE-PEANUT BUTTER CRISPIES

Instead of the typical melted marshmallows, this clever recipe calls for melted chocolate and peanut butter chips. With crisp rice cereal and nuts, these bars taste almost like candy.

> 1 cup semisweet chocolate chips *or* milk chocolate chips
> 1 cup peanut butter chips
> 2 tablespoons vegetable oil
> 1-1/2 cups crisp rice cereal
> 1/2 cup chopped dates, chopped nuts *or* flaked coconut

In a medium microwave-safe bowl, microwave the chocolate chips, peanut butter chips and oil on high for 1 minute; stir. If necessary, microwave at additional 15-second intervals, stirring after each heating, just until chips are melted when stirred. Add cereal and dates; stir until well blended. Spread into a foil-lined 8- or 9-in. square baking pan. Cover; refrigerate until firm. Cut into bars. **Yield:** 3 dozen bars.

PINEAPPLE DROP COOKIES

For a little variation, try these tropical-tasting cookies. Studded with walnuts and raisins, these drop cookies will quickly become a family favorite.

> 1-3/4 cups plus 2 tablespoons all-purpose flour
> 1 teaspoon baking powder
> 1/2 teaspoon baking soda
> 1/2 teaspoon salt
> 1/2 cup shortening
> 1 cup packed brown sugar
> 1 egg
> 1 teaspoon vanilla extract
> 3/4 cup drained crushed pineapple
> 3/4 cup chopped walnuts
> 1/2 cup raisins

In a bowl, combine flour, baking powder, baking soda and salt; set aside. In a large mixing bowl, cream shortening. Add sugar, egg and vanilla, beating until well blended. Add pineapple; mix well. Stir in dry ingredients, walnuts and raisins. Drop by rounded teaspoonfuls onto ungreased baking sheet. Bake at 375° for 12-15 minutes or until lightly browned. **Yield:** 3-1/2 dozen.

CHOCOLATE-ALMOND BARS

(Pictured below)

This recipe is elegant enough to serve for dessert, yet casual enough to take on a picnic. Whatever the occasion, folks are sure to love the chocolate-almond flavor.

> 2 **cups all-purpose flour**
> 3/4 **cup butter** *or* **margarine, softened**
> 1/3 **cup packed brown sugar**
> 4 **eggs**
> 3/4 **cup light corn syrup**
> 3/4 **cup sugar**
> 2 **tablespoons butter** *or* **margarine, melted**

> 1/2 **teaspoon almond extract** *or* **1/4 cup amaretto liqueur**
> 1 **tablespoon cornstarch**
> 2 **cups sliced almonds**
> 1 **package (12 ounces) semisweet chocolate morsels,** *divided*

In a large mixing bowl, beat flour, 3/4 cup butter and brown sugar until crumbly. Press into a greased 13-in. x 9-in. x 2-in. baking pan. Bake at 350° for 12-15 minutes or until golden brown. In a medium bowl with a wire whisk, beat eggs, corn syrup, granulated sugar, melted butter, almond extract and cornstarch. Stir in almonds and 1-2/3 cups morsels. Spoon over hot crust; spread evenly. Bake for 25-30 minutes or until center is set. Cool in pan on wire rack. Place remaining morsels in a heavy-duty plastic bag. Microwave on high for 30-45 seconds; knead. Microwave at additional 10- to 20-second intervals, kneading until smooth. Cut tiny corner from bag; squeeze to drizzle chocolate over bars. Refrigerate for a few minutes to firm chocolate before cutting into bars. **Yield:** 2-1/2 dozen.

Magic Cookie Bars

Do You Believe in Magic? A Civil War Staple Helps Create Dessert in a Wink.

IT'S BEEN more than 145 years since Gail Borden unveiled Eagle Brand Sweetened Condensed Milk. Unlike fresh milk, the canned variety didn't require refrigeration or spoil quickly without it. Therein lied its "magic".

A blend of whole milk and pure cane sugar, Borden's invention became a household item during the Civil War. Homemakers found that the milk plus a few other simple ingredients created rich desserts with minimal effort.

In 1931, the company offered $25 for quick and easy, fool-proof recipes using the milk. More than 80,000 recipes poured in.

Today, the product is still a favorite among bakers. Apparently they've discovered how sweet it is! The timeless recipe for Magic Cookie Bars is the proof.

MAGIC COOKIE BARS

   1/2 **cup butter** *or* **margarine, melted**
1-1/2 **cups graham cracker crumbs**
    1 **can (14 ounces) sweetened condensed milk**
    1 **package (6 ounces) semisweet chocolate chips**
1-1/3 **cups flaked coconut**
    1 **cup chopped nuts**

Pour butter evenly into the bottom of a 13-in. x 9-in. x 2-in. baking pan. Sprinkle crumbs over butter; pour sweetened condensed milk over crumbs. Top with remaining ingredients; press down firmly. Bake at 350° for 25-30 minutes or until lightly browned. Cool. Chill if desired. Cut into bars. Store loosely covered at room temperature. **Yield:** 2 dozen.

VARIATIONS:
SEVEN-LAYER MAGIC COOKIE BARS:
Add 1 package (6 ounces) butterscotch chips after chocolate chips.

DOUBLE-CHOCOLATE MAGIC COOKIE BARS: Increase chocolate chips to 1 package (12 ounces).

RAINBOW MAGIC COOKIE BARS: Add 1 cup plain candy-coated chocolate pieces after chocolate chips.

MAGIC PEANUT COOKIE BARS: Omit chocolate chips. Add 2 cups chopped chocolate-covered peanuts.

MINT BARS: Add 1/2 teaspoon peppermint extract and 4 drops green food coloring with sweetened condensed milk. Proceed as directed.

MOCHA BARS: Add 1 tablespoon instant coffee and 1 tablespoon chocolate-flavored syrup to sweetened condensed milk. Proceed as directed.

PEANUT BUTTER BARS: Beat 1/3 cup peanut butter with sweetened condensed milk. Proceed as directed.

MAPLE BARS: Combine 1/2 to 1 teaspoon maple flavoring with sweetened condensed milk. Proceed as directed.

Chewy Chocolate Chip Granola Brownies

If you enjoy granola as a snack or as a cereal with milk, you're sure to love these chewy bars. Vary the recipe by adding chopped nuts or substituting your favorite dried fruit for the raisins.

1/4 cup butter *or* margarine
1/4 cup shortening
1 cup packed brown sugar
1 egg
1 teaspoon vanilla extract
1-1/3 cups all-purpose flour
1/2 teaspoon baking soda
1/2 teaspoon salt
1/2 teaspoon ground cinnamon
1/4 cup milk
1-2/3 cups granola cereal
1 cup raisins
1 cup flaked coconut
1 cup semisweet chocolate chips

Cream butter, shortening, brown sugar, egg and vanilla in large mixing bowl until light and fluffy. Combine flour, baking soda, salt and cinnamon; add alternately with milk to creamed mixture. Stir in cereal, raisins, coconut and chips. Spread batter evenly in a foil-lined 15-in. x 10-in. x 1-in. baking pan. Bake at 350° for 20-25 minutes or until edges are golden brown. Cool completely on wire rack. Invert pan and peel off foil; cut into bars. **Yield:** 4 dozen.

Frosted Banana Bars

(Pictured at right)

Make these moist bars whenever you have ripe bananas on hand, then store them in the freezer to share later at a potluck. With creamy frosting and big banana flavor, this treat is a real crowd-pleaser.

1/2 cup butter *or* margarine, softened
2 cups sugar
3 eggs
1-1/2 cups mashed ripe bananas (about 3 medium)
1 teaspoon vanilla extract
2 cups all-purpose flour
1 teaspoon baking soda
Pinch salt
FROSTING:
1/2 cup butter *or* margarine, softened
1 package (8 ounces) cream cheese, softened

4 cups confectioners' sugar
2 teaspoons vanilla extract

In a mixing bowl, cream butter and sugar. Beat in eggs, bananas and vanilla. Combine the flour, baking soda and salt; add to creamed mixture and mix well. Pour into a greased 15-in. x 10-in. x 1-in. baking pan. Bake at 350° for 25 minutes or until cake springs back in center when lightly touched. Cool. For frosting, cream butter and cream cheese in a mixing bowl. Gradually add confectioners' sugar and vanilla; beat well. Spread over bars. **Yield:** 3 dozen.

Caramel Nut Crisps

With caramels, coconut and nuts, this no-bake cookie has something for everyone. The whole family will agree this recipe is a real winner.

1 package (14 ounces) caramels
3 tablespoons water
2 cups crisp rice cereal
1 cup corn flakes
1-1/2 cups flaked coconut
1 cup chopped nuts

Combine caramels and water in a microwave-safe bowl. Microwave on high for 3 minutes or until caramels are melted, stirring every 30 seconds. Add cereals, coconut and nuts; toss until well coated. Drop by rounded teaspoonfuls onto greased baking sheet; let stand until firm. **Yield:** 3-1/2 dozen.

CHEERY CHERRY COOKIES

(Pictured below)

With a glass of ice-cold milk, a couple of cherry cookies really hit the spot for dessert or as a snack. The coconut and bits of cherries provide a fun look and texture.

- 1 cup packed brown sugar
- 3/4 cup butter *or* margarine, softened
- 1 egg
- 2 tablespoons milk
- 1 teaspoon vanilla extract
- 2 cups all-purpose flour
- 1/2 teaspoon salt
- 1/2 teaspoon baking soda
- 1/2 cup chopped maraschino cherries, well drained
- 1/2 cup chopped pecans
- 1/2 cup flaked coconut

In a large mixing bowl, cream brown sugar, butter, egg, milk and vanilla. In another bowl, combine flour, salt and baking soda. Gradually add to creamed mixture. Fold in cherries, pecans and coconut. Drop by teaspoonfuls onto ungreased baking sheets. Bake at 375° for 10-12 minutes or until golden brown. **Yield:** 4 dozen.

COFFEE BRITTLE COOKIES

Instant coffee lends a unique flavor to these almond-topped delights. Be sure to bake them in the correct size pan; otherwise the baking time and texture of the cookie may be affected.

- 1 cup butter *or* margarine, softened
- 2 teaspoons instant coffee granules
- 1 teaspoon salt
- 1 teaspoon vanilla extract
- 1/2 teaspoon almond extract
- 1 cup sugar
- 2 cups all-purpose flour
- 1 cup semisweet chocolate chips
- 1 cup finely chopped almonds

In a large mixing bowl, combine butter, coffee granules, salt, vanilla and almond extract. Gradually beat in sugar. Add flour and chocolate chips; mix well. Press into an ungreased 15-in. x 10-in. x 1-in. baking pan. Sprinkle almonds over top. Bake at 375° for 25 minutes or until set. Cool; break into irregular pieces. **Yield:** 3 dozen.

GRANOLA SNACK BARS

Granola provides plenty of vitamins, minerals and fiber, but its enduring popularity is also due to its wonderful flavor. Children will surely enjoy these sensational snack bars chock-full of raisins and nuts.

- 3-1/2 cups quick-cooking *or* old-fashioned oats
- 1 cup raisins
- 1 cup chopped nuts
- 2/3 cup butter *or* margarine, melted
- 1/2 cup packed brown sugar
- 1/3 cup corn syrup
- 1 egg, beaten
- 1/2 teaspoon vanilla extract
- 1/2 teaspoon salt

Toast oats in a large shallow baking pan at 350° for 12-15 minutes or until golden brown. Combine oats and remaining ingredients; mix well. Press firmly into a 13-in. x 9-in. x 2-in. baking pan. Bake at 325° for 30-35 minutes or until golden brown. Cool; cut into bars. **Yield:** 2 dozen bars.

ORANGE DATE SOFTIES

Orange juice and peel add a slight citrus twist to these wonderful drops. The down-home aroma as they bake is a wonderful way to welcome family home.

- 1 package (8 ounces) chopped dates
- 1/2 cup packed brown sugar

1/2 cup butter *or* margarine
1/2 cup orange juice
  1 teaspoon grated orange peel
  2 eggs
1-1/4 cups all-purpose flour
  1 teaspoon salt
3/4 teaspoon baking soda
  1 cup butterscotch morsels
  1 cup chopped walnuts

In a saucepan, combine dates, sugar, butter, orange juice and orange peel. Cook over low heat about 10 minutes or until slightly thickened, stirring occasionally. Cool 15 minutes. Add eggs; beat well. Stir together flour, salt and baking soda; gradually add to date mixture. Stir in morsels and nuts. Drop by rounded tablespoonfuls 2 in. apart onto ungreased baking sheet. Bake at 375° for 10 minutes or until lightly browned. Remove to wire rack to cool. **Yield:** 3 dozen.

PEANUT BUTTER FUDGE BROWNIE BARS

(Pictured above right)

These moist chocolate brownies are topped with creamy peanut butter fudge. They're so delicious, you'll never make ordinary brownies again!

1-1/2 cups butter *or* margarine, melted, *divided*
1-1/2 cups sugar
  2 eggs
  1 teaspoon vanilla extract
1-1/4 cups all-purpose flour
  2/3 cup baking cocoa
  1/4 cup milk
1-1/4 cups chopped pecans, *divided*
  1 package (10 ounces) peanut butter chips
  1 can (14 ounces) sweetened condensed milk
  1/4 cup semisweet chocolate chips

In a large bowl, combine 1 cup melted butter, sugar, eggs and vanilla; beat well. Add flour, cocoa and milk; beat until blended. Stir in 1 cup pecans. Pour into a greased 13-in. x 9-in. x 2-in. baking pan. Bake at 350° for 25-30 minutes or just until edges begin to pull away from sides of pan. Cool completely in pan on wire rack. In a medium saucepan over low heat, combine remaining butter and peanut butter chips, stirring constantly. Stir in sweetened condensed milk until smooth; pour over baked layer. Place chocolate chips in a small microwave-safe bowl. Microwave on high for 45 seconds; stir. If necessary, microwave an additional 15 seconds at a time, stirring after each heating, just until chips are melted. Drizzle bars with melted chocolate; sprinkle with remaining pecans. Refrigerate 1 hour or until firm. Cut into bars. **Yield:** 2 dozen.

HONEY OATMEAL CHEWIES

Honey is widely used as a bread spread and as a sweetener in various baked goods. The delicate fragrance and flavor of honey enhances these old-fashioned oatmeal cookies.

1-1/4 cups butter-flavored shortening
  1 cup sugar
  2/3 cup packed brown sugar
  1/4 cup honey
  1 egg
  1/4 cup milk
  1 teaspoon vanilla extract
2-1/2 cups all-purpose flour
  1 teaspoon baking soda
  1/2 teaspoon salt
  1 cup quick-cooking oats
  1 cup flaked coconut
  1 cup chopped dates
  1/2 cup wheat germ, optional
  1/3 cup chopped walnuts

In a large mixing bowl, cream shortening, sugars, honey, egg, milk and vanilla until light and fluffy. In another bowl, combine flour, baking soda and salt; mix into creamed mixture. Stir in oats, coconut, dates, nuts and wheat germ if desired. Drop by teaspoonfuls onto ungreased baking sheet. Bake at 350° for 11-12 minutes for soft cookies, 13-14 minutes for crisp cookies. Remove to wire rack to cool. **Yield:** 6 dozen.

Flashback to the '80s

*T*he winds of change blow all the way around the world in the 1980s. Relations between the U.S. and the Soviets warm, with presidents Ronald Reagan and Mikhail Gorbachev meeting to talk peace. On Nov. 9, 1989, the Berlin Wall comes down.

On the home front, Ted Turner launches Cable News Network, personal computers become available for the home and office, cellular phone networks debut and the first test tube baby is born. The title "super moms" is coined for women who juggle family, home and career.

Cooking Schools continue to gain popularity, selling out auditoriums with up to 2,000 seats in mere hours.

PROBABLY no one conducted more Cooking Schools over the years than Joyce Siefering (above). She hosted shows from the early 1970s through the mid-1990s. Then, as well as now, the auditoriums were always packed (below right). Pat Wade (far right) joined the Homemaker Schools in the late 1980s, demonstrating recipes throughout the Northeast. Today, she's the operations manager at the home office in Wisconsin.

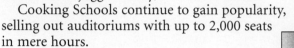

Everett Collection

Ewing Galloway

Everett Collection

Everett Collection

Ewing Galloway

ENTERTAINING '80s.
Teens dance in the streets in the movie "Fame", Lena Horne wins a Grammy, acid-washed jeans are hip, Princess Diana's look spawns copycats, Coke goes through some painful changes and remote-control TVs are everywhere.

That's Entertainment

• Movies such as "Fame", "Dirty Dancing", "The Rose" and "Purple Rain" spawn mega-hit singles.

• Madonna influences fashion as well as music, as girls seek the fishnet stockings, bustiers and cross necklaces of their idol.

• Lena Horne earns a Grammy Award in 1981 for "The Lady and Her Music Live on Broadway".

The 'In' Things

• Teenage girls strive to look cool in vibrant blue eye shadow and matching mascara.

• Jeans take a beating—literally—acid-washed and sand-blasted jeans are hip.

• Lady Diana haircuts become the rage after Britain's Prince Charles announces his intention to marry Diana Spencer.

• The casual blazer with T-shirt shown on TV's "Miami Vice" goes over big with teens and young men.

• The battle of the sexes gets a new weapon—the remote control. In 1985, more TV sets are sold with remotes than without.

Price Check

• A first-class postage stamp increases from 15¢ to 25¢ over the course of the decade.

• Gasoline prices break the dollar-per-gallon mark—and stay there.

• A gallon of milk costs over $2 by 1980.

• The average new car can still be bought for well under $10,000 by the end of the decade. The average price is $8,243.

Food for Thought

• Paul Newman shows he can "act" like a businessman, launching Newman's Own natural foods line with his personal salad dressing recipe. All profits go to charity.

• Coca-Cola falls flat with the announcement that it will replace its time-tested formula with New Coke, a sweeter beverage aimed at a younger audience. Soon after, Classic Coke is reborn.

• On opposite ends of the weight-watching scale, Stouffer's Lean Cuisine and Ben & Jerry's ice cream both debut.

Chapter 13

CAKES & CHEESECAKES

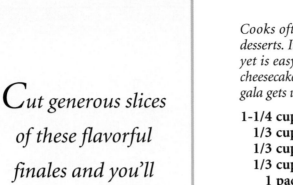

*C*ut generous slices of these flavorful finales and you'll receive rave reviews, for it seems nothing satisfies a craving for something sweet like a pleasing portion of cake.

Recipes in this chapter provided courtesy of these past sponsors...

Baker's
Bisquick
Campbell's
Comstock/Wilderness
Cool Whip
Equal
Hershey's
Jell-O
Keebler
Nestea
Nestlé
Taster's Choice

CHOCOLATE PEANUT BUTTER CHEESECAKE

(Pictured at left)

Cooks often choose cheesecake for special-occasion desserts. It offers a rich flavor and elegant appearance, yet is easy to prepare. When planning a party, make cheesecake a day or two ahead, then refrigerate until the gala gets underway.

1-1/4 cups graham cracker crumbs
  1/3 cup plus 1/4 cup sugar, *divided*
  1/3 cup cocoa
  1/3 cup butter *or* margarine, melted
    1 package (10 ounces) peanut butter chips
    3 packages (8 ounces *each*) cream cheese, softened
    1 can (14 ounces) sweetened condensed milk
    4 eggs
    2 teaspoons vanilla extract
DRIZZLE:
    2 tablespoons butter *or* margarine
    2 tablespoons baking cocoa
    2 tablespoons water
    1 cup confectioners' sugar
  1/2 teaspoon vanilla extract
Whipped topping
Milk chocolate kisses

In a bowl, combine graham cracker crumbs, 1/3 cup sugar, cocoa and butter; press into bottom of a 9-in. springform pan. Microwave peanut butter chips on high for 1 minute; stir. If needed, microwave at additional 15-second intervals, stirring after each heating, just until chips are melted. In a large mixing bowl, beat cream cheese and remaining sugar until fluffy. Gradually beat in milk and melted chips until smooth. Add eggs and vanilla; beat well. Pour over crust. Bake at 300° for 60-70 minutes or until center is almost set. Remove from oven. With knife, loosen cake from sides of pan. Cool. Remove sides of pan. To prepare drizzle, in a small saucepan, melt butter over low heat; add cocoa and water. Cook and stir until slightly thickened. Do not boil. Cool slightly. Gradually add confectioners' sugar and vanilla, beating with whisk until smooth. Drizzle over cake. Garnish with whipped topping and chocolate kisses. Refrigerate until serving. **Yield:** 12 servings.

SWIRLED CHEESECAKE TRIANGLES

(Pictured below)

These luscious cheesecake bars are easy to make, yet so rich and creamy that folks will think you fussed for hours. A combination of peanut butter and milk chocolate morsels is the key to their fantastic flavor.

       2 cups graham cracker crumbs
   1/2 cup butter *or* margarine, melted
1-1/3 cups sugar, *divided*
       2 packages (8 ounces *each*) cream cheese,
         softened
   1/4 cup all-purpose flour
       1 can (12 ounces) evaporated milk
       2 eggs
       1 tablespoon vanilla extract
       1 cup (6 ounces) peanut butter and milk
         chocolate morsels

In a medium bowl, combine graham cracker crumbs, butter and 1/3 cup sugar; press onto bottom of un-greased 13-in. x 9-in. x 2-in. baking pan. In a large mixing bowl, beat cream cheese, flour and remaining sugar until smooth. Gradually beat in evaporated milk, eggs and vanilla. In a microwave-safe bowl, microwave morsels on medium-high power for 1 minute; stir. Microwave at additional 10- to 20-second intervals, stirring until smooth. Stir 1 cup cream cheese mixture into chocolate. Pour remaining cream cheese mixture over crust. Pour chocolate mixture over cream cheese mixture. Swirl mixtures with spoon, pulling plain cream cheese mixture up to surface. Bake at 325° for 40-45 minutes or until set. Cool completely in pan on wire rack; refrigerate until firm. Cut into triangles. **Yield:** 30 triangles.

PEACH-TOFFEE SHORTCAKES

Fragrant fruit and crunchy toffee bits accent delectable shortcakes that are crowned with caramel-flavored whipped cream.

2-1/3 cups biscuit/baking mix
   1/2 cup milk
       3 tablespoons brown sugar
       3 tablespoons butter *or* margarine, melted
1-1/2 cups whipping cream
   1/4 cup caramel ice cream topping
       2 tablespoons confectioners' sugar
       2 bars (1.4 ounces *each*) chocolate-covered
         toffee, crushed
       2 to 3 peaches, cut into 1/2-inch pieces

In a bowl, combine biscuit mix, milk, brown sugar and butter; stir until soft dough forms. Place dough on surface dusted with biscuit mix. Gently roll in biscuit mix to coat. Shape into ball; knead gently 8-10 times. Roll dough 1/2 in. thick. Cut with 3-in. round cutter dipped into biscuit mix. Place on ungreased baking sheet. Bake at 425° for 8-11 minutes or until golden brown. Cool 10 minutes. Meanwhile, in a chilled medium bowl, beat whipping cream, caramel topping and confectioners' sugar until stiff. Stir in crushed toffee bars and peaches. Split each shortcake crosswise. Fill and top shortcakes with topping. **Yield:** 6 servings.

TOMATO SOUP CAKE

This moist spice cake was first made with canned tomatoes, but the tomatoes were replaced by soup in the 1920s, not long after Campbell's introduced condensed tomato soup into the marketplace.

       2 cups all-purpose flour
1-1/3 cups sugar
       4 teaspoons baking powder
       1 teaspoon baking soda
1-1/2 teaspoons ground allspice
       1 teaspoon ground cinnamon
   1/2 teaspoon ground cloves
       1 can (10-3/4 ounces) condensed tomato soup,
         undiluted

1/2 cup shortening
2 eggs
1/4 cup water
Confectioners' sugar

In a large mixing bowl, measure all ingredients except confectioners' sugar. Beat at low speed until well mixed, constantly scraping bowl. Beat on high for 4 minutes, scraping bowl occasionally. Pour into greased and floured 10-in. fluted tube pan. Bake at 350° for 1 hour or until toothpick inserted in cake comes out clean. Cool in pan on wire rack 10 minutes. Remove from pan; cool completely. Sprinkle with confectioners' sugar. **Yield:** 16 servings.

BLACK FOREST MINI CHEESECAKES

When desserts are labeled "Black Forest", you can expect a combination of chocolate and cherry flavors. These single-serving-size cheesecakes will add a touch of elegance to the end of your meal.

18 to 24 vanilla wafers
2 packages (8 ounces *each*) cream cheese, softened
1-1/4 cups sugar
1/3 cup baking cocoa
2 tablespoons all-purpose flour
3 eggs
1 cup sour cream
1/2 teaspoon almond extract
FILLING:
1 cup sour cream
2 tablespoons sugar
1 teaspoon vanilla extract
1 can (21 ounces) cherry pie filling, chilled

Place each wafer in bottom of foil-lined cups. In a mixing bowl, beat cream cheese until smooth. Add sugar, cocoa and flour; blend. Beat in eggs. Stir in sour cream and extract. Fill each cup almost full with cheese mixture. Bake at 350° for 15-20 minutes or just until set. Remove from oven; cool 5-10 minutes. For filling, combine sour cream, sugar and vanilla. Spread heaping teaspoonful on top of each cup. Cool completely in pans; chill thoroughly. Garnish with dollop of cherry pie filling just before serving. **Yield:** 18-24 servings.

PEACH PRALINE SPICE CAKE

(Pictured above right)

Studded with crunchy pecans, this yummy dessert is an awesome way to end an autumn feast.

CAKE:
1 package (18-1/4 ounces) spice cake mix
2 to 3 teaspoons ground cinnamon
2 to 3 teaspoons ground cloves
2 to 3 teaspoons ground allspice
1/8 teaspoon pepper
1 can (21 ounces) peach pie filling
1 cup pecan pieces
GLAZE:
1 cup packed brown sugar
3/4 cup butter *or* margarine
2 tablespoons honey *or* light corn syrup
1 teaspoon ground cinnamon
1 teaspoon ground allspice
1 teaspoon ground nutmeg
2/3 cup whipping cream
1 cup pecan pieces
Fresh sliced peaches, optional
Whipped cream

In a mixing bowl, combine cake mix and spices. Prepare cake mix according to package directions. Stir in pie filling and pecans. Spoon batter into a greased and floured 13-in. x 9-in. x 2-in. baking pan. Bake at 350° for 45-50 minutes or until a toothpick inserted near the center comes out clean. For glaze, in a saucepan over medium heat, combine brown sugar and butter. Bring to a boil; reduce heat to low and simmer 2 minutes. Add honey and simmer 2 minutes longer. Add the spices and cream; bring to a boil and simmer 2 minutes. Remove from heat and stir in pecans. Serve with cake. Top with sliced peaches if desired and whipped cream. **Yield:** 12-15 servings.

a boil over medium heat. Cook and stir for 2 minutes. Remove from the heat; stir in vanilla. Cool to lukewarm. Gradually beat in confectioners' sugar until the frosting reaches desired spreading consistency. Frost cupcakes. **Yield:** 1-1/2 to 2 dozen.

CALICO APPLE CAKE

The applesauce in this tempting snack cake contributes both flavor and moisture. It's a particular favorite of children, since it's studded with chocolate morsels and raisins.

>   2 cups all-purpose flour
>   1 teaspoon baking soda
>   1 cup semisweet chocolate morsels
>   2 eggs
>   1 cup applesauce
> 1/2 cup butter *or* margarine, softened
> 3/4 cup sugar
>   1 teaspoon salt
>   1 teaspoon ground cinnamon
> 1/2 teaspoon ground nutmeg
> 1/2 cup raisins
> 1/2 cup chopped walnuts

Combine flour and baking soda; add chocolate morsels; set aside. In a large mixing bowl, beat eggs, applesauce, butter, sugar and spices until smooth. Gradually add flour mixture; beat until well-blended. Fold in raisins and walnuts. Spread evenly in a greased 13-in. x 9-in. x 2-in. baking pan. Bake at 350° for 40 minutes or until a toothpick inserted near the center comes out clean. Cool in pan on a wire rack. **Yield:** 24 squares.

ZUCCHINI CUPCAKES

(Pictured above)

You'll love these irresistible spice cupcakes with creamy caramel frosting. They're such a scrumptious dessert, you'll forget you're eating your vegetables, too!

>   3 eggs
> 1-1/3 cups sugar
> 1/2 cup vegetable oil
> 1/2 cup orange juice
>   1 teaspoon almond extract
> 2-1/2 cups all-purpose flour
>   2 teaspoons ground cinnamon
>   2 teaspoons baking powder
>   1 teaspoon baking soda
>   1 teaspoon salt
> 1/2 teaspoon ground cloves
> 1-1/2 cups shredded zucchini
> CARAMEL FROSTING:
>   1 cup packed brown sugar
> 1/2 cup butter *or* margarine
> 1/4 cup milk
>   1 teaspoon vanilla extract
> 1-1/2 to 2 cups confectioners' sugar

In a mixing bowl, beat eggs, sugar, oil, orange juice and extract. Combine next six ingredients; add to the egg mixture and mix well. Add zucchini and mix well. Fill greased or paper-lined muffin cups two-thirds full. Bake at 350° for 20-25 minutes or until cupcakes test done. Cool for 10 minutes; remove to a wire rack to cool completely. For frosting, combine brown sugar, butter and milk in a saucepan; bring to

MINI CHIP STREUSEL CAKE

Since it doesn't have any frosting, this cake is easily eaten on the run. If you pack lunches for your family, treat them to a generous slice of this cake.

MINI CHIP STREUSEL:
>   3/4 cup packed brown sugar
>   1/4 cup cold butter *or* margarine
>   1/4 cup all-purpose flour
>   1/4 teaspoon salt
>   1/4 teaspoon ground cinnamon
>   1 cup chopped walnuts
>   3/4 cup miniature semisweet chocolate chips
CAKE:
>   1/2 cup butter *or* margarine
>   1 cup sugar
>   3 eggs

1 teaspoon vanilla extract
1 cup sour cream
2 cups all-purpose flour
1 teaspoon baking powder
1 teaspoon baking soda
1/4 cup miniature semisweet chocolate chips

In a small mixing bowl, combine brown sugar, butter, flour, salt and cinnamon; stir until crumbly. Mix in nuts. Reserve one cup of nut streusel for bottom. Stir chips into remaining nut streusel; set aside. For coffee cake batter, cream butter and sugar in a large mixing bowl. Add eggs; blend on low speed. Stir in vanilla and sour cream. Combine flour, baking powder and baking soda; add to batter, stirring until well mixed. Sprinkle reserved 1 cup streusel mixture into bottom of well-greased and floured 10-in. fluted tube pan. Spread one-third of batter in pan; sprinkle with half of streusel. Repeat layers, ending with batter on top. Bake at 350° for 55-60 minutes or until cake tests done. Cool in pan 10 minutes before inverting onto serving plate. Melt 1/4 cup chips in small saucepan; drizzle over cake. **Yield:** 10 to 12 servings.

CHOCOLATE CHERRY CREAM-FILLED LOG

(Pictured at right)

This spectacular dessert can't be topped when your family is calling for something sweet to eat. Folks will think you fussed all day.

    4 eggs, *separated*
    1/2 cup plus 1/3 cup sugar, *divided*
    1 teaspoon vanilla extract
    1/3 cup baking cocoa
    1/2 cup all-purpose flour
    1/4 teaspoon baking powder
    1/4 teaspoon baking soda
    1/8 teaspoon salt
    1/3 cup water
Confectioners' sugar
    1 can (21 ounces) cherry pie filling *or* topping, *divided*
1-1/2 cups whipped topping
CHOCOLATE GLAZE:
    2 tablespoons butter *or* margarine
    2 tablespoons baking cocoa
    2 tablespoons water
    1 cup confectioners' sugar
    1/2 teaspoon vanilla extract

Line a 15-in. x 10-in. x 1-in. baking pan with aluminum foil; generously grease foil. In a large mixing bowl, beat egg whites until foamy; gradually add 1/2 cup sugar, beating until stiff peaks form. In a small mixing bowl, beat egg yolks and vanilla on high speed for about 3 minutes. Gradually add remaining sugar; continue beating for 2 minutes. Combine cocoa, flour, baking powder, baking soda and salt; add to egg yolk mixture alternately with water on low speed, beating just until batter is smooth. Gradually fold chocolate mixture into egg whites; spread evenly in baking pan. Bake at 375° for 12-15 minutes or until the top springs back when touched lightly in the center. Immediately loosen cake from edges of pan; invert on towel sprinkled with confectioners' sugar. Carefully remove foil. Immediately roll cake in towel starting from narrow end; place on wire rack to cool. Combine 1 cup pie filling and whipped topping; mix well. Unroll cake; remove towel. Spread with filling; reroll cake. For glaze, melt butter over low heat; add cocoa and water, stirring until smooth and slightly thickened. Do not boil. Remove from heat; cool slightly. Gradually blend in sugar and vanilla. Glaze cake; chill. Just before serving, spoon 1/2 cup pie filling over cake. Serve with remaining pie filling. **Yield:** 10-12 servings.

PASTEL CAKE

(Pictured below)

Showstopping cakes are a must at any celebration. This quick-to-mix recipe is hard to resist. The addition of colorful sprinkles makes it especially appealing to kids.

- 1 package (18-1/4 ounces) white cake mix
- 1 package (3 ounces) lime gelatin
- 1 package (3 ounces) orange gelatin
- 2 cartons (8 ounces *each*) whipped topping, thawed

Line two greased 9-in. round cake pans with waxed paper. Prepare cake mix according to package directions using water, eggs and oil. Divide batter equally between 2 bowls. Add lime gelatin to one bowl and orange gelatin to the other bowl. Stir until well blended. Pour each color batter into a prepared cake pan. Bake at 350° for 28-30 minutes or until a toothpick inserted in the center comes out clean. Cool 15 minutes; remove from pans. Cool completely on wire racks. Place lime-flavored cake layer on serving plate; spread with 1/2 carton of the whipped topping. Top with orange-flavored cake layer. Frost top and sides of cake with remaining whipped topping. Refrigerate at least 1 hour or until ready to serve. Store cake in the refrigerator. **Yield:** 12 servings.

FOUR-LAYER PASTEL CAKE:

Slice each cake layer in half horizontally. Layer alternating flavors of cake with whipped topping. Frost top and sides of cake with whipped topping.

GINGERBREAD

Gingerbread is a cake that is traditionally served without a frosting. A dollop of whipped cream or lemon sauce is all you need to garnish this old-fashioned treat.

- 1/4 cup butter *or* margarine, softened
- 1/2 cup packed dark brown sugar
- 1/2 cup dark molasses
- 1 egg
- 2 cups all-purpose flour
- 1/2 teaspoon salt
- 1-1/2 teaspoons baking powder
- 1/2 teaspoon baking soda
- 2 teaspoons ground ginger
- 1 teaspoon ground cinnamon
- 1 cup sour milk*

In a large mixing bowl, cream butter at medium speed until light and fluffy. Gradually beat in brown sugar and molasses until well combined. At low speed, beat in egg until well mixed. In a medium bowl, combine flour, salt, baking powder, baking soda, ginger and cinnamon. Add dry ingredients alternately with milk to creamed mixture, mixing well after each addition. Turn into a greased 9-in. square pan. Bake at 350° for 35-40 minutes until toothpick inserted near center comes out clean. Cool in pan on wire rack 30 minutes. Cut into squares. **Yield:** 9 servings. ***Editor's Note:** To make 1 cup sour milk, measure 1 tablespoon vinegar into a 1-cup measure. Fill measure to 1-cup mark with milk.

Rich Chocolate-Peanut Butter Cake

(Pictured at right)

How about a luscious layer cake topped with creamy milk chocolate-peanut butter frosting? This simple-to-prepare cake contains peanut butter and milk chocolate morsels that add nice texture to the baked cake.

> 2 cups all-purpose flour
> 1-3/4 cups sugar
> 2/3 cup baking cocoa
> 1-1/2 teaspoons baking powder
> 1-1/2 teaspoons baking soda
> 1/2 teaspoon salt
> 1 cup milk
> 1 cup water
> 1/2 cup vegetable oil
> 2 eggs
> 2 teaspoons vanilla extract
> 1 package (11 ounces) peanut butter and milk chocolate morsels, *divided*

FROSTING:
> 1 package (8 ounces) cream cheese, softened
> 1 teaspoon vanilla extract
> 1/8 teaspoon salt
> 3 cups confectioners' sugar
> 1 bar (2 ounces) semisweet baking chocolate, grated *or* made into curls

In a large mixing bowl, combine flour, sugar, cocoa, baking powder, baking soda and salt. Add milk, water, oil, eggs and vanilla; blend until moistened. Beat for 2 minutes (batter will be thin). Pour into two greased and floured 9-in. round cake pans. Sprinkle 1/3 cup morsels over each cake. Bake at 350° for 25-30 minutes or until toothpick inserted in the center comes out clean. Cool in pans on wire racks for 10 minutes; remove to wire racks to cool completely. In a small microwave-safe bowl, microwave remaining morsels on medium-high for 1 minute; stir. Microwave at additional 10- to 20-second intervals, stirring until smooth. In a small mixing bowl, beat cream cheese, melted morsels, vanilla and salt until light and fluffy. Gradually beat in confectioners' sugar. Spread frosting between layers and on top and sides of cake. Garnish with chocolate curls before serving. **Yield:** 10-12 servings.

Black Forest Chocolate Cheesecake

This classic chocolate cheesecake draped with ruby-red cherry pie filling is sure to impress.

> 1-1/4 cups graham cracker crumbs
> 3/4 cup baking cocoa, *divided*
> 1-1/2 cups sugar, *divided*
> 1/2 cup butter *or* margarine, melted
> 2 packages (8 ounces *each*) cream cheese, softened
> 1 cup sour cream
> 3 eggs
> 2-1/2 teaspoons almond extract, *divided*
> 1 cup cold whipping cream
> 1/4 cup confectioners' sugar
> 1 can (21 ounces) cherry pie filling, chilled

In a bowl, combine the cracker crumbs, 1/4 cup cocoa, 1/4 cup sugar and butter. Press mixture firmly onto the bottom of 9-in. springform pan. In a large mixing bowl, beat the cream cheese, sour cream and 1-1/4 cups sugar until smooth. Add 1/2 cup cocoa, eggs and 2 teaspoons extract; beat just until blended. Pour over crust. Bake at 350° for 45-50 minutes or until center is almost set; remove from oven to wire rack. Cool for 30 minutes. With a knife, loosen the cake from side of pan. Cool completely; remove side of pan. Cover; refrigerate. Beat cream, confectioners' sugar and 1/2 teaspoon extract; beat until stiff. Just before serving, spread or pipe whipped cream around top edge of cheesecake; fill center with pie filling. Cover and refrigerate leftovers. **Yield:** 12 servings.

Holiday Poke Cake

It's not paint-by-number, but it's almost as much fun. Who says you have to be a grownup all the time?

MAKING a poke cake is a lot like coloring with bright crayons at the same time you're baking. It's…fun.

Is it juvenile? No, but it might make you feel like a kid again, and there's nothing wrong with that. If you do have children in your life, they're guaranteed to love it, too.

Poke cakes are a Jell-O creation from the 1960s. The recipe gives you the flexibility to create masterpieces to match the season or your mood.

If you desire dessert on a hot summer day, try lemon gelatin for a cake that looks like sunshine yet refreshes and cools. Show your spirit on Independence Day with one blazing red layer and one berry blue.

Planning a party before or after a big game? Create a poke cake using your favorite team's colors.

If it's raining, create your own rainbow. The only thing standing between you and a fun time in the kitchen (and a good dessert later on) is your imagination. Oh, go ahead. Why not?

HOLIDAY POKE CAKE

Not Christmastime yet? Celebrate another holiday. Near Valentine's Day, try two shades of red gelatin. For St. Patty's Day, stick with lime for both layers.

- **2 baked round white cake layers, completely cooled (8 or 9 inches *each*)**
- **2 cups boiling water, *divided***
- **1 package (3 ounces) any flavor red gelatin**
- **1 package (3 ounces) lime gelatin**
- **1 carton (8 to 12 ounces) frozen whipped topping, thawed**

Place cake layer, top sides up, in two clean round cake pans. Pierce layers with large fork at 1/2-in. intervals. In a small bowl, stir 1 cup boiling water into red gelatin. In a separate small bowl, stir 1 cup boiling water into lime gelatin. Stir gelatin mixtures at least 2 minutes or until completely dissolved. Carefully pour red gelatin over one cake layer. Pour lime gelatin over second cake layer. Refrigerate cake layers for at least 3 hours. Dip 1 cake pan in warm water for 10 seconds; unmold onto serving plate. Spread with about 1 cup whipped topping. Unmold second cake layer; carefully place on top of first layer. Frost top and sides of cake with remaining whipped topping. Refrigerate at least 1 hour or until serving. **Yield:** 12 servings.

MINI CHIP CARROT CAKE

When shredding the carrots for this cake, use a very fine grater so the carrots will almost disappear as the layers bake. The cream cheese glaze is the perfect complement to carrot, apple-nut or spice cakes.

 3/4 cup whole wheat flour
 3/4 cup all-purpose flour
 3/4 cup sugar
 1/2 cup packed brown sugar
1-1/4 teaspoons baking soda
 2 teaspoons ground cinnamon
 1/2 teaspoon salt
 3 eggs
 3/4 cup vegetable oil
1-1/2 teaspoons vanilla extract
 2 cups shredded carrot
 1 cup miniature semisweet chocolate chips
 1/2 cup chopped walnuts

GLAZE:
 1 package (3 ounces) cream cheese, softened
1-1/2 cups confectioners' sugar
 1 tablespoon milk
 1 teaspoon vanilla extract

In a large mixing bowl, combine flours, sugar, brown sugar, baking soda, cinnamon and salt. Beat eggs, oil and vanilla in small bowl. Add to dry ingredients; blend. Stir in carrot, chips and walnuts. Pour into a well-greased and floured 10-in. fluted tube pan or 13-in. x 9-in. x 2-in. baking pan. Bake at 350° for 45-50 minutes for tube pan or 35-40 minutes for 13-in. x 9-in. x 2-in. baking pan or until cake tests done. Cool in tube pan for 10 minutes before removing to a wire rack. For glaze, beat cream cheese until smooth in small bowl. Blend in confectioners' sugar, milk and vanilla. Beat until pouring consistency. Pour over cooled cake. **Yield:** 12-16 servings.

FILLED CHOCOLATE CUPCAKES

(Pictured at right)

Long a favorite of kids, cupcakes can make adults smile, too! Whether you choose the traditional coconut filling or the creamy cherry variation, these mini cakes will take center stage at your next get-together.

FILLING:
 1 package (8 ounces) cream cheese, softened
 1/3 cup sugar
 1 egg
 1/8 teaspoon salt
 1 cup sweetened coconut flakes
 1/2 cup semisweet chocolate chips

BATTER:
 3 cups all-purpose flour
 2 cups sugar
 2/3 cup baking cocoa
 2 teaspoons baking soda
 1 teaspoon salt
 2 cups water
 2/3 cup vegetable oil
 2 tablespoons white vinegar
 2 teaspoons vanilla extract
Additional sweetened coconut flakes

To prepare filling, in a small bowl, beat cream cheese, sugar, egg and salt until smooth and creamy. Stir in coconut and chocolate chips; set aside. To prepare batter, in a large bowl, stir together flour, sugar, cocoa, baking soda and salt. Add water, oil, vinegar and vanilla; beat on medium speed for 2 minutes. Fill paper or foil-lined muffin tins 2/3 full with chocolate batter. Spoon 1 tablespoon filling into the center of each cupcake. Lightly sprinkle each cupcake with additional coconut. Bake at 350° for 20 to 25 minutes or until a toothpick inserted in cake portion comes out clean. Cool completely. **Yield:** 2-1/2 dozen.

CHOCOLATE-CHERRY VARIATION:
Prepare filling as directed above, but eliminate coconut. Add 3/4 cup cherry pie filling to filling mixture. Add 1/2 teaspoon almond extract to filling if desired. To serve, spoon remaining pie filling over baked cupcakes.

Mocha Nut Upside-Down Cake

This recipe uses cake flour, which is sold in a 2-pound box and produces a very fine texture. Serious bakers will want to keep a box handy for the recipes that call for it. To substitute all-purpose flour, use 7/8 of a cup, or 1 cup minus 2 tablespoons.

    10 tablespoons butter *or* margarine, *divided*
   1/4 cup packed light brown sugar
   2/3 cup light corn syrup
2-1/2 teaspoons instant coffee granules, *divided*
   1/4 cup whipping cream
     1 cup chopped walnuts
1-3/4 cups cake flour, sifted
     2 teaspoons baking powder
     2 teaspoons salt
1-1/2 cups sugar
     2 eggs, *separated*
     3 squares (1 ounce *each*) unsweetened
       chocolate, melted
     1 teaspoon vanilla extract
     1 cup milk

In a small saucepan over medium heat, melt 4 tablespoons butter. Stir in brown sugar; heat until bubbly. Stir in corn syrup and 1/2 teaspoon coffee granules; bring to a boil, stirring constantly. Add nuts. Pour into a generously greased 10-in. tube pan (mixture will be thin); set aside. In a small bowl, combine flour, baking powder and salt. Beat remaining butter in large mixing bowl until soft. Gradually add sugar. Beat in egg yolks, chocolate and vanilla until well blended. Add flour mixture, alternately with milk, beginning and ending with flour. In a small mixing bowl, beat egg whites until stiff; fold into cake batter. Spoon batter evenly over nut mixture in pan. Bake at 350° for 45 minutes or until toothpick inserted in center comes out clean. Cool in pan for 5 minutes before inverting onto a serving plate. Serve warm. **Yield:** 12 servings.

Pick-Up Cake

Family and friends will be grateful you took the time to make them a special treat. Best of all, this cake is easy to eat on the go with no mess.

   1/3 cup hot water
     1 package (8 ounces) chopped dates
   1/2 cup butter *or* margarine
   1/3 cup sugar
     2 eggs
     1 cup all-purpose flour
     1 teaspoon baking soda
   1/2 teaspoon salt

     1 cup vanilla wafer crumbs
      (about 16 wafers)
   1/2 cup chopped walnuts

Pour hot water over chopped dates in a small bowl; mix well. Let stand 30 minutes. In a mixing bowl, beat butter and sugar until creamy. Add eggs, one at a time, beating until light. Combine flour, baking soda and salt; stir in wafer crumbs. Stir into butter mixture until well blended. Stir in date mixture; blend well. Pour into a greased 9-in. square baking pan. Sprinkle walnuts evenly over top; press in lightly. Bake at 350° for 30 minutes or until a toothpick inserted near the center comes out clean. Cool in pan on wire rack. **Yield:** 12 servings.

Maple Pumpkin Cheesecake

(Pictured at right)

If you're tired of plain cheesecake, try this unique flavor. The spectacular pumpkin filling is lightly spiced with cinnamon and nutmeg, reminiscent of classic pumpkin desserts. A rich maple glaze garnished with crunchy pecans provides a pretty crown.

1-1/4 cups graham cracker crumbs
   1/4 cup sugar
   1/4 cup butter *or* margarine, melted
     3 packages (8 ounces *each*) cream cheese,
      softened
     1 can (14 ounces) sweetened condensed
      milk
     1 can (15 ounces) solid-pack pumpkin
     3 eggs
     1 cup maple syrup, *divided*
1-1/2 teaspoons ground cinnamon
     1 teaspoon ground nutmeg
     1 cup whipping cream
   1/2 cup chopped pecans0

In a small bowl, combine crumbs, sugar and butter; press firmly on bottom of a 9-in. springform pan. In a large mixing bowl, beat cream cheese on medium speed until fluffy. Gradually beat in condensed milk until smooth. Add pumpkin, eggs, 1/4 cup syrup, cinnamon and nutmeg; mix well. Pour into springform pan. Bake at 300° for 1 hour and 15 minutes or until center is almost set. Cool on a wire rack for 10 minutes. Carefully run a knife around edge of pan to loosen; cool 1 hour longer. Refrigerate overnight; remove sides of pan. In a saucepan, combine cream and remaining syrup. Boil rapidly for 15-20 minutes or until thickened, stirring occasionally. Stir in pecans. Cool. Spoon over cheesecake before serving. **Yield:** 20 servings.

plastic wrap. Freeze for 10 minutes or until firm but pliable. Meanwhile, line two baking sheets with foil; mark two 8-in. diameter circles on each. Place one patty in center of each circle; press with fingers into marked circles. Bake at 350° for 10-12 minutes or until almost set; cool on foil. In a mixing bowl, combine remaining cocoa mixture and whipping cream; beat until stiff. Place 1 cookie on serving plate; place small chocolate pieces around the outside edge of cookie. Spoon one-fourth of cream mixture in center; gently spread out to chocolate pieces. Repeat layers with remaining cookies, cream mixture and chocolate pieces, ending with cream. Place remaining chocolate pieces over top of torte. Cover; refrigerate 6 hours or until filling has softened cookies. **Yield:** 10 servings.

MINI KISSES COOKIE TORTE

(Pictured above)

This luscious torte is fun to make. Rich mocha-flavored whipped cream is slathered between chocolaty cookie layers to create this special treat.

>   1 cup sugar
> 1/2 cup baking cocoa
> 1/2 cup water
> 1/3 cup shortening
>   1 tablespoon instant coffee granules
> 1/4 teaspoon ground cinnamon
>   1 package (11 ounces) pie crust mix
> 2-1/2 cups cold whipping cream
>   1 package (10 ounces) semisweet
>   chocolate baking pieces, *divided*

In a large microwave-safe bowl, place sugar, cocoa, water, shortening, coffee granules and cinnamon. Microwave on high for 1 minute; stir. Continue microwaving, at 30-second intervals, until mixture is smooth and creamy when stirred with a wire whisk. Remove 3/4 cup of mixture; set aside remaining mixture. In a bowl, combine 3/4 cup cocoa mixture and pie crust mix; blend until smooth. Shape into a ball; cut into 4 pieces. Shape into patties; wrap in

DAFFODIL CAKE

This delicate marble sponge cake is noted for its remarkable lightness. It depends on beaten egg whites for its characteristic texture. Make sure that the pan is not greased. In ungreased pans, the batter will cling to the sides and rise together.

>   1 cup sifted cake flour
> 1/2 cup sugar, *divided*
>   4 egg yolks
> 1/2 teaspoon lemon extract
> 10 egg whites, at room temperature
>   1 teaspoon cream of tartar
> 1/2 teaspoon salt
> 3/4 cup sugar
> 1/2 teaspoon vanilla extract

Sift flour and 1/2 cup sugar together 3 times; set aside. In a mixing bowl, beat egg yolks at high speed 4 minutes or until thick and lemon-colored. Add lemon extract; beat at medium speed an additional 5 minutes or until thick. Set aside. In a mixing bowl with clean beaters, beat egg whites until foamy. Add cream of tartar and salt; beat until soft peaks form. Gradually add 3/4 cup sugar; continue beating until stiff peaks form. Sprinkle one-fourth of flour mixture over egg whites; gently fold in flour mixture. Repeat until all of flour mixture has been added. Divide egg white mixture in half. Fold vanilla into half of egg white mixture. Gently fold beaten egg yolks into remaining egg white mixture. Pour half of yellow mixture into an ungreased 10-in. tube pan, then gently add half of white mixture. Repeat procedure with remaining mixtures. Gently swirl batters with a knife to create marble effect. Bake at 350° for 45-50 minutes or until cake springs back when lightly touched. Invert pan carefully. Let cake cool in pan 40 minutes. Loosen cake from sides of pan using a narrow metal spatula; remove from pan. **Yield:** One 10-inch cake.

Cocoa-Cream Cheese Frosting

For weekday treats or special-occasion desserts, this chocolaty frosting will add a fabulous final touch to any homemade or store-bought cake. It's rich, creamy and delectable.

> 3 packages (3 ounces *each*) cream cheese, softened
> 1/3 cup butter *or* margarine
> 6 cups sifted confectioners' sugar
> 1 cup baking cocoa
> 5 to 7 tablespoons half-and-half cream

Blend together cream cheese and butter in a large mixing bowl. Combine confectioners' sugar and cocoa; gradually add to cheese mixture. Blend in cream. **Yield:** about 5 cups.

Apricot Walnut Swirl Cake

(Pictured at right)

This tasty recipe is light on fat and calories but full of flavor. In fact, friends and family won't know they're eating healthier unless you tell them. You'll love the magic swirl that forms when the batter is layered with the pretty apricot-nut filling.

> 2-1/3 cups reduced-fat biscuit/baking mix
> 12 packets sugar substitute
> 2/3 cup fat-free milk
> 2 tablespoons margarine, melted
> 1 egg
> 1/3 cup fat-free sour cream
> FILLING:
> 1/2 cup plus 1/3 cup light apricot preserves *or* apricot spreadable fruit, *divided*
> 18 packets sugar substitute
> 4 teaspoons ground cinnamon
> 1/2 cup chopped walnuts

In a medium bowl, combine baking mix and sugar substitute; mix in milk, margarine, egg and sour cream. Spread 1/3 of the batter in a greased and floured 8-in. fluted tube pan. In a small bowl, combine 1/2 cup preserves and remaining filling ingredients; mix well. Spoon half the filling over batter. Repeat layers, ending with batter. Bake at 375° for 25 minutes or until coffee cake is browned on the top and toothpick inserted in center comes out clean.

Cool in pan for 5 minutes before removing to wire rack to cool 5-10 minutes. Spoon remaining preserves over the top of coffee cake; serve warm. **Yield:** 12 servings.

Coconut Cheesecake Cups

Coconut adds wonderful texture to these tempting individual desserts. For added embellishment, top with extra maraschino cherries, fresh berries or a dollop of sour cream or whipped topping.

> 12 vanilla wafers
> 1 package (8 ounces) cream cheese, softened
> 1/2 cup sugar
> 2 eggs
> 2 tablespoons all-purpose flour
> 1 teaspoon almond extract
> 1-1/3 cups flaked coconut, *divided*
> 6 maraschino cherries, halved, optional

Place wafers, flat side down, in paper-lined muffin cups. In a large mixing bowl, beat cream cheese until smooth. Gradually beat in sugar and continue beating until light and fluffy. Add eggs, one at a time, beating well after each addition. Blend in flour and extract; stir in 2/3 cup coconut. Spoon into cups, filling three-fourths full. Top with remaining coconut. Place a cherry half into center of each cup if desired. Bake at 325° for 30 minutes or until filling is set. Cool on wire rack. Serve cooled or chilled. Store in the refrigerator. **Yield:** 12 servings.

CHOCOLATE RASPBERRY CHEESECAKE

(*Pictured below*)

Luscious cheesecake is an excellent way to bring a meal to a magnificent conclusion. Nestled in a crumb crust, the plump raspberries and creamy chocolate accent the custard-like cheesecake perfectly. Make sure everyone saves room for this dessert.

  2 packages (3 ounces *each*) cream cheese, softened
  1 can (14 ounces) sweetened condensed milk
  3 tablespoons lemon juice
  1 teaspoon vanilla extract
  1 egg
  1 cup fresh *or* frozen raspberries
  1 chocolate crumb crust (9 inches)
  1 bar (2 ounces) semisweet baking chocolate
1/4 cup whipping cream
Additional fresh raspberries optional

In a mixing bowl, beat cream cheese, sweetened condensed milk, lemon juice and vanilla until smooth. Add egg; beat on low speed just until combined. Arrange raspberries on bottom of pie crust. Place pie crust on a baking sheet. Slowly pour cheesecake mix- ture over fruit. Bake at 350° for 30-35 minutes or un- til center is almost set. Cool on wire rack. In a small saucepan, combine chocolate and whipping cream. Cook and stir over low heat until thickened and smooth. Remove from heat. Top cheesecake with chocolate glaze; chill. Garnish with fresh raspberries if desired. **Yield:** 8 servings.

CHOCOLATE PEPPERMINT LOG

Greek mythology claims that mint was once the nymph Mentha. She angered Pluto's wife, who turned her into this aromatic herb.

  4 eggs, *separated*
1/2 cup sugar
  1 teaspoon vanilla extract
1/3 cup sugar
1/3 cup baking cocoa
1/2 cup all-purpose flour
1/4 teaspoon baking powder
1/4 teaspoon baking soda
1/8 teaspoon salt
1/3 cup water
Confectioners' sugar
PEPPERMINT FILLING:
  1 cup whipping cream, chilled
1/4 cup confectioners' sugar
1/4 cup finely crushed peppermint candy *or*
      1/2 teaspoon mint extract
Red food coloring
CHOCOLATE GLAZE:
  2 tablespoons butter *or* margarine
  2 tablespoons baking cocoa
  2 tablespoons water
  1 cup confectioners' sugar
1/2 teaspoon vanilla extract

Line a 15-in. x 10-in. x 1-in. baking pan with alu- minum foil; generously grease foil. In a large mix- ing bowl, beat egg whites until foamy; gradually add 1/2 cup sugar; beat until stiff peaks form. In a small mixing bowl, beat egg yolks and vanilla on high about 3 minutes; gradually add 1/3 cup sugar; con- tinue beating for 2 minutes. Combine cocoa, flour, baking powder, baking soda and salt; add to egg yolk mixture alternately with water on low, beating just

until batter is smooth. Gradually fold chocolate mixture into egg whites; spread evenly in baking pan. Bake at 375° for 12-15 minutes, or until top springs back when touched lightly in center. Immediately loosen cake from edges of pan; invert on towel sprinkled with confectioners' sugar. Carefully remove foil. Immediately roll cake in towel starting from short end; place on wire rack to cool. In a small mixing bowl, beat cream until slightly thickened. Add sugar and candy and a few drops of red food coloring; beat until stiff. Unroll cake; remove towel. Spread with peppermint filling; reroll cake. To prepare glaze, over low heat, melt butter; add cocoa and water, stirring until smooth and slightly thickened. Do not boil. Remove from heat; cool slightly. Gradually blend in sugar and vanilla. Drizzle over cake. **Yield:** 10-12 servings.

GLAZED LEMON BUNDT CAKE

(Pictured above right)

A sunny lemon-flavored cake is just the dessert to brighten up any gloomy day. Lemon peel provides a nice zing in every bite. A light glaze gives the golden cake a delicate crust. Watch this dessert disappear at your next gathering.

>   1 cup butter *or* margarine, softened
>   2 cups sugar
>   4 eggs
> 1-1/2 teaspoons lemon extract
> 1-1/2 teaspoons vanilla extract
>   3 cups all-purpose flour
>   2 teaspoons baking powder
>   1/2 teaspoon salt
>   1 cup milk
>   1 tablespoon grated lemon peel

GLAZE:
>   1/4 cup lemon juice
>   1 tablespoon water
>   1/2 teaspoon lemon extract
>   3/4 cup sugar

In a mixing bowl, cream butter and sugar. Add the eggs, one at a time, beating well after each addition. Beat in extracts. Combine flour, baking powder and salt; add to the creamed mixture alternately with milk. Stir in lemon peel. Pour into a greased and floured 10-in. fluted tube pan. Bake at 350° for 60-70 minutes or until a toothpick inserted near the center comes out clean. Cool for 10 minutes; invert onto a wire rack. Cool 10 minutes longer. Place rack on waxed paper. Combine glaze ingredients; drizzle over the warm cake. Cool completely before serving. **Yield:** 12-16 servings.

SPICED TEA CAKE

Tea is native to China, where it grew wild until the Chinese discovered that the leaves helped flavor the flat taste of the water they boiled to prevent illness. The instant tea used in this recipe is simply brewed tea that has been dehydrated and granulated.

CAKE:
>   1 package (18-1/4 ounces) yellow cake mix
>   1/2 cup sugar
>   1 tablespoon unsweetened lemon-flavored iced tea mix
>   1 teaspoon ground cinnamon
>   1/2 teaspoon ground cloves
>   1 cup orange juice
>   3/4 cup butter *or* margarine, melted
>   4 eggs

GLAZE:
>   1 tablespoon butter *or* margarine
>   2 tablespoons packed brown sugar
>   2 tablespoons milk
>   3/4 cup confectioners' sugar
>   1/4 cup chopped walnuts

In a large mixing bowl, combine cake ingredients. Beat 2 minutes on high. Pour into a greased and floured 10-in. fluted tube pan. Bake at 350° for 50-60 minutes or until a toothpick inserted near the center comes out clean. Cool in pan 15 minutes; turn onto a serving plate. In a saucepan over low heat, melt butter; remove from heat. Stir in brown sugar and milk. Blend in confectioners' sugar until smooth. Spoon over cake; sprinkle with walnuts. **Yield:** 12-16 servings.

BUTTERSCOTCH PUMPKIN CAKE

(Pictured above)

A nip in the air will stimulate your sweet tooth for an autumn treat. This spectacular cake will fit the bill. It's not frosted—simply serve with the wonderful butterscotch sauce on the side.

   1 package (11 ounces) butterscotch morsels,
     divided
   2 cups all-purpose flour
1-3/4 cups sugar
   1 tablespoon baking powder
1-1/2 teaspoons ground cinnamon
   1 teaspoon salt
   1/2 teaspoon ground nutmeg
   1 cup solid-pack pumpkin
   1/2 cup vegetable oil
   3 eggs
   1 teaspoon vanilla extract
Confectioners' sugar, optional
   1/3 cup evaporated milk

In a small microwave-safe bowl, microwave 1 cup morsels on medium-high power for 1 minute; stir. Microwave at additional 10- to 20-second intervals, stirring until smooth. Cool to room temperature. In a medium bowl, combine flour, sugar, baking powder, cinnamon, salt and nutmeg. In a large bowl, stir together melted morsels, pumpkin, oil, eggs and vanilla with a wire whisk. Stir in flour mixture. Spoon batter into a greased 10-in. fluted tube pan.

Bake at 350° for 40-50 minutes or until toothpick inserted in cake comes out clean. Cool in pan on wire rack for 30 minutes; remove to wire rack to cool completely. Sprinkle cake with confectioners' sugar if desired. In a medium heavy-duty saucepan, heat evaporated milk over medium heat just to a boil; remove from heat. Add remaining morsels; stir until smooth. Return to heat. Stirring constantly, bring mixture just to a boil. Cool to room temperature. Stir before serving. Serve cake with butterscotch sauce. **Yield:** 12-16 servings.

POUND CAKE

Pound cake was originally made with a pound each of butter, sugar, eggs and flour, thus its name. It required a strong arm to beat air into the batter, since no leavening was added. This version is designed to work with an electric mixer. It may be flavored with vanilla extract, citrus peel or almond extract if you desire.

   1 cup butter *or* margarine, softened
1-2/3 cups sugar
   1 teaspoon vanilla extract
   1/2 teaspoon ground mace *or* nutmeg
   6 eggs, at room temperature
   2 cups all-purpose flour

In a large mixing bowl on medium speed, cream butter until light and fluffy. Gradually beat in sugar, vanilla and mace until well mixed, constantly scraping bowl. Beat in eggs, one at a time, beating well after each addition. Gradually beat in flour. Turn into two greased and floured 8-in. x 4-in. x 2-in. loaf pans. Bake at 300° for 55-60 minutes or until toothpick inserted in center comes out clean. Cool in pans on wire rack 10 minutes. Remove from pans to wire rack; cool completely. **Yield:** 16 servings. **Editor's Note:** Pound cake can be baked in a greased and floured 10-in. tube pan. Bake at 300° for 1-1/2 hours or until a toothpick inserted near the center comes out clean.

CARROT CAKE

Perhaps the health-food movement of the 1970s helped spur the interest in carrot cake. Whatever the cause, this tempting treat is now enjoyed from coast to coast.

   2 cups all-purpose flour
   2 cups sugar
   1/2 teaspoon salt
   1 teaspoon baking soda
   2 teaspoons ground cinnamon

3 eggs
1-1/2 cups vegetable oil
  2 cups finely grated carrots
  1 teaspoon vanilla extract
  1 cup well-drained crushed pineapple
  1 cup flaked coconut
  1 cup chopped nuts, *divided*
CREAM CHEESE FROSTING:
  2 packages (3 ounces *each*) cream cheese,
    softened
  3 cups confectioners' sugar
  6 tablespoons butter *or* margarine, softened
  1 teaspoon vanilla extract

In a mixing bowl, combine first five ingredients. Add eggs, oil, carrots and vanilla; beat until combined. Stir in pineapple, coconut and 1/2 cup nuts. Pour into a greased 13-in. x 9-in. x 2-in. baking pan. Bake at 350° for 50-60 minutes or until cake tests done. Cool. Combine frosting ingredients in a small bowl; mix until well blended. Frost cooled cake. Sprinkle with remaining nuts. Store in refrigerator. **Yield:** 12-16 servings.

SPICED PINEAPPLE UPSIDE-DOWN CAKE

(Pictured at right)

Bake this beautiful cake in a large iron skillet. We guarantee your family and friends will thoroughly enjoy this old-fashioned dessert.

1-1/3 cups butter *or* margarine, softened,
    divided
  1 cup packed brown sugar
  1 can (20 ounces) pineapple slices, drained
  10 to 12 maraschino cherries
  1/2 cup chopped pecans
1-1/2 cups sugar
  2 eggs
  1 teaspoon vanilla extract
  2 cups all-purpose flour
  2 teaspoons baking powder
  1/2 teaspoon baking soda
  1/2 teaspoon salt
  1/2 teaspoon ground cinnamon
  1/2 teaspoon ground nutmeg
  1 cup buttermilk

In a small saucepan, melt 2/3 cup of butter; stir in brown sugar. Spread in the bottom of an ungreased heavy 12-in. skillet or a 13-in. x 9-in. x 2-in. baking pan. Arrange pineapple in a single layer over sugar mixture; place a cherry in the center of each slice. Sprinkle with pecans and set aside. In a mixing bowl, cream sugar and remaining butter. Beat in eggs and

vanilla. Combine the dry ingredients; add alternately to batter with buttermilk, mixing well after each addition. Carefully pour over the pineapple. Bake at 350° for 40 minutes for skillet (50-60 minutes for baking pan) or until a toothpick inserted near the center comes out clean. Immediately invert onto a serving platter. **Yield:** 12 servings.

DOUBLE-CHOCOLATE SNACK CAKE

"Chocoholics" will love this extra-special treat that's quick to stir together. Serve a generous slice with a tall glass of cold milk.

1-2/3 cups all-purpose flour
  1 cup packed brown sugar
  1/4 cup baking cocoa
  1 teaspoon baking soda
  1/4 teaspoon salt
  1 cup water
  1/3 cup vegetable oil
  1 teaspoon white vinegar
  3/4 teaspoon vanilla extract
  1/2 cup semisweet chocolate chips

In a large mixing bowl, stir together flour, brown sugar, cocoa, baking soda and salt. Add water, oil, vinegar and vanilla; beat until smooth. Pour batter into a greased and floured 8-in. square baking pan. Sprinkle chips over top. Bake at 350° for 35-40 minutes or until a toothpick inserted near center comes out clean. Cool in pan on wire rack; cut into squares. **Yield:** 8 servings.

ORANGE BLISS CHEESECAKE

(*Pictured below*)

A subtle orange-flavored filling contrasts nicely with a chocolate-crumb crust. Family and friends will comment on the wonderful flavor and color.

>   1 cup chocolate wafer crumbs
>   3 tablespoons butter *or* margarine, melted
> 1/2 cup orange juice
>   1 envelope unflavored gelatin
>   3 packages (8 ounces *each*) cream cheese, softened
> 3/4 cup sugar
>   1 cup whipping cream, whipped
>   1 tablespoon grated orange peel
> **Mini chocolate chips and sliced orange wedges, optional**

Combine crumbs and butter; press onto the bottom of an ungreased 9-in. springform pan. Bake at 350° for 10 minutes. Cool. In a saucepan, combine orange juice and gelatin; let stand for 5 minutes. Cook and stir over low heat until the gelatin dissolves. Cool for 10 minutes. Meanwhile, in a mixing bowl, beat cream cheese and sugar until light and fluffy; gradually add gelatin mixture. Beat on low until well mixed. Chill until partially set, about 3-5 minutes (watch carefully—mixture will set up quickly). Gen-

tly fold in whipped cream and orange peel. Spoon into the crust. Chill for 6 hours or overnight. Just before serving, run a knife around edge of pan to loosen. Remove sides of pan. Garnish with chocolate chips and oranges if desired. **Yield:** 8-10 servings.

COCOA MARBLE CHEESECAKE

This fast-to-fix dessert features chocolate and plain cheesecake batters that are swirled together and nestled in a prepared crumb crust. The smooth, creamy texture is sure to please.

>   2 packages (8 ounces *each*) cream cheese, softened
>   1 cup sugar, *divided*
>   2 tablespoons cornstarch
>   2 eggs, slightly beaten
>   1 teaspoon vanilla extract
> 1/3 cup baking cocoa
>   1 graham cracker crust (9 inches)

Beat cream cheese, 3/4 cup sugar and cornstarch in large mixing bowl until smooth. Beat in eggs and vanilla. Measure 1 cup batter; set aside. Combine cocoa and remaining sugar; beat cocoa mixture into remaining 2 cups batter in bowl until well blended. Pour half of the plain batter over crust. Top with half of the chocolate batter; repeat layers. Cut through batter with a knife to swirl the chocolate. Bake at 350° for 30-35 minutes or until center is firm. Cool completely on wire rack. Refrigerate 4 hours or overnight. **Yield:** 12 servings.

CARROT DATE CUPCAKES

These moist spice cupcakes are great for breakfast or an afternoon snack. For added sweetness and convenience, frost the tops with ready-to-spread icing.

>   2 cups all-purpose flour
>   2 teaspoons ground cinnamon
>   1 tablespoon ground nutmeg
>   1 teaspoon baking powder
> 1/2 teaspoon salt
> 3/4 cup packed brown sugar
>   2 eggs, beaten
> 1/2 cup vegetable oil

1/2 cup milk
2 cups shredded carrots
1/2 cup chopped dates

In a large bowl, combine flour, cinnamon, nutmeg, baking powder and salt. Add brown sugar, eggs, oil and milk; stir just until dry ingredients are moistened. Stir in carrots and dates. Fill greased or paper-lined cups three fourths full. Bake at 400° for 20-25 minutes or until toothpick inserted in center comes out clean. Cool 5 minutes; remove from pan. **Yield:** 12 cupcakes.

HOT FUDGE PUDDING CAKE

(Pictured at right)

Chocolate fans will cheer for this decadent dessert. As the rich cake bakes, a luscious fudge sauce is created in the bottom of the pan.

1-1/4 cups sugar, *divided*
1 cup all-purpose flour
7 tablespoons cocoa, *divided*
2 teaspoons baking powder
1/4 teaspoon salt
1/2 cup milk
1/3 cup butter *or* margarine, melted
1-1/2 teaspoons vanilla extract
1/2 cup packed light brown sugar
1-1/4 cups hot water
Whipped topping, optional

In a bowl, stir together 3/4 cup sugar, flour, 3 tablespoons cocoa, baking powder and salt. Stir in milk, butter and vanilla; beat until smooth. Pour batter into an ungreased 8-in. or 9-in. square baking pan. Stir together remaining sugar, brown sugar and remaining cocoa; sprinkle mixture evenly over batter. Pour hot water over top; do not stir. Bake at 350° for 35 to 40 minutes or until center is almost set. Let stand 15 minutes; spoon into dessert dishes, spooning sauce from bottom of pan over top. Garnish with whipped topping if desired. **Yield:** 8 servings.

TAKE-ALONG CARROT CAKE

Since it's baked in a rectangular dish, this nutty spice cake is easy to serve at picnics and potlucks. Satisfying cream cheese frosting glazes the top of this surefire winner.

1-1/2 cups all-purpose flour
3/4 cup sugar
1/2 cup packed brown sugar 
1-1/4 teaspoons baking soda
2 teaspoons ground cinnamon
1/2 teaspoon salt
3 eggs
3/4 cup butter *or* margarine, melted
1-1/2 teaspoons vanilla extract
2 cups shredded carrots
1 package (10 ounces) peanut butter chips
1/2 cup chopped walnuts
FROSTING:
1/4 cup butter *or* margarine
1 package (3 ounces) cream cheese, softened
2 cups confectioner's sugar
1 teaspoon vanilla extract
Chopped walnuts, optional

In a large bowl, combine flour, sugars, baking soda, cinnamon and salt. In a small bowl, beat eggs, butter and vanilla. Add to dry ingredients and blend. Stir in carrots, chips and walnuts. Pour into a greased and floured 13-in. x 9-in. x 2-in. baking dish. Bake at 350° for 35-40 minutes or until a toothpick inserted near the center comes out clean. Cool. Cream butter and cream cheese until light and fluffy. Slowly beat in confectioner's sugar until smooth; stir in vanilla. Spread on cooled cake. Garnish with walnuts if desired. **Yield:** 12-15 servings.

PERFECTLY-CHOCOLATE CHOCOLATE CAKE

(Pictured below)

This luscious cake topped with creamy chocolate buttercream frosting continues to be an all-time favorite dessert. The simple-to-prepare batter may also be baked as an elegant three-layer cake or a batch of moist chocolaty cupcakes—the choice is up to you.

        2 cups sugar
    1-3/4 cups all-purpose flour
      3/4 cup baking cocoa
    1-1/2 teaspoons baking powder
    1-1/2 teaspoons baking soda
        1 teaspoon salt
        2 eggs
        1 cup milk
      1/2 cup vegetable oil
        2 teaspoons vanilla extract
        1 cup boiling water

PERFECTLY-CHOCOLATE ONE-BOWL FROSTING:
      1/2 cup butter *or* margarine
      2/3 cup baking cocoa
        3 cups confectioners' sugar
      1/3 cup milk
        1 teaspoon vanilla extract

Grease and flour two 9-in. round baking pans. In a large bowl, combine sugar, flour, cocoa, baking powder, baking soda and salt. Add eggs, milk, oil and vanilla; beat on medium speed for 2 minutes. Stir in boiling water (batter will be thin). Pour batter into prepared pans. Bake at 350° for 30-35 minutes or until a toothpick inserted in center comes out clean. Cool 10 minutes; remove from pans to wire racks. Cool completely. For frosting: In a medium microwave-safe bowl, melt butter. Stir in cocoa. Alternately add confectioners' sugar and milk, beating to spreading consistency. Add a small amount of additional milk if needed. Stir in vanilla. Frost cake. **Yield:** 10-12 servings.

ONE CAKE PAN:

Grease and flour a 13-in. x 9-in. x 2-in. baking pan. Pour batter into prepared pan. Bake 35-40 minutes. Cool completely. Frost. **Yield:** 10-12 servings.

THREE-LAYER CAKE:

Grease and flour three 8-in. round baking pans. Pour batter into prepared pans. Bake 35-40 minutes. Cool 10 minutes; remove from pans to wire racks. Cool completely. Frost. **Yield:** 10-12 servings.

BUNDT CAKE:

Grease and flour a 12-cup bundt pan. Pour batter into prepared pans. Bake 50-55 minutes. Cool 15 minutes; remove from pans to wire racks. Cool completely. Frost. **Yield:** 10-12 servings.

CUPCAKES:

Line muffin cups (2-1/2 in. in diameter) with paper bake cups. Fill cups 2/3 full with batter. Bake 22-25 minutes. Cool completely. Frost. **Yield:** 2-1/2 dozen.

OH-SO-WACKY COCOA CUPCAKES

Children will enjoy helping parents with this wacky recipe. All the ingredients are measured into one bowl, then quickly mixed together. Add your favorite frosting to top these chocolaty cupcakes.

1-1/2 cups all-purpose flour
   1 cup sugar
   3 tablespoons baking cocoa
  1/2 teaspoon salt
   1 teaspoon baking soda
   3 tablespoons butter *or* margarine
   1 tablespoon vanilla extract
   1 tablespoon white vinegar
   1 cup cold water

In a large mixing bowl, mix all ingredients until combined. (Do not over mix.) Fill greased or paper-lined cups two-thirds full. Bake at 350° for 15-20 minutes. Cool. **Yield:** 12-14 cupcakes.

GERMAN CHOCOLATE CAKE

This spectacular cake is not frosted. Each layer is spread with a coconut-pecan filling to create a showstopping dessert. To save time, the cake can be baked days before and frozen until you're ready to assemble and serve it.

  1/4 cup baking cocoa
  1/2 cup boiling water
   1 cup plus 3 tablespoons butter *or*
      margarine, softened
2-1/4 cups sugar
   1 teaspoon vanilla extract
   4 eggs
   2 cups all-purpose flour
   1 teaspoon baking soda
  1/2 teaspoon salt
   1 cup buttermilk *or* sour milk*
FROSTING:
   1 can (14 ounces) sweetened condensed
      milk
   3 egg yolks, lightly beaten
  1/2 cup butter *or* margarine
   1 teaspoon vanilla extract
1-1/3 cups sweetened coconut flakes
   1 cup chopped pecans

Grease and flour three 9-in. round baking pans. In a small bowl, stir together cocoa and water until smooth. In a large mixing bowl, beat butter, sugar and vanilla until light and fluffy. Add eggs, one at a time, beating well. Stir together flour, baking soda and salt; add to butter mixture alternately with chocolate mixture and buttermilk, beating just enough to blend. Pour batter into prepared pans.

Bake at 350° for 25-30 minutes or until top springs back when touched lightly. Cool 5 minutes; remove from pans to wire racks. Cool completely. For frosting, in a medium saucepan, stir together condensed milk, egg yolks and butter. Cook over low heat, stirring constantly, until mixture is thickened and bubbly. Remove from heat; stir in vanilla, coconut and pecans. Cool to room temperature. Spread between layers and over top and sides of cake. **Yield:** 10-12 servings. *****Editor's Note:** To sour milk, use 1 tablespoon white vinegar plus enough milk to equal 1 cup.

MARBLED PUMPKIN CHEESECAKE

This excellent cheesecake is a celebration of fall flavors. The tastes of pumpkin, cinnamon and nutmeg come together in the rich cheesecake that's studded with tiny bits of chocolate.

1-1/4 cups graham cracker crumbs
  1/4 cup butter *or* margarine, melted
   1 cup plus 2 tablespoons sugar, *divided*
   1 package (12 ounces) semisweet
      chocolate mini morsels, *divided*
   3 packages (8 ounces *each*) cream cheese,
      softened
  1/4 cup packed brown sugar
   1 can (15 ounces) solid-pack pumpkin
   4 eggs
  1/2 cup evaporated milk
   2 tablespoons cornstarch
  3/4 teaspoon ground cinnamon
  1/8 teaspoon ground nutmeg

In a medium bowl, combine graham cracker crumbs, butter and 2 tablespoons sugar. Press onto bottom of greased 9-in. springform pan. Sprinkle with 1-1/3 cups morsels. In a medium microwave-safe bowl, microwave remaining morsels on high for 45 seconds; stir. Microwave at additional 10- to 20-second intervals, stirring until smooth; cool to room temperature. In a large mixing bowl, beat cream cheese, brown sugar and remaining sugar until smooth; beat in pumpkin. Beat in eggs, evaporated milk, cornstarch, cinnamon and nutmeg. Remove 1 cup pumpkin mixture; stir into melted chocolate. Pour remaining pumpkin mixture into crust. Spoon chocolate-pumpkin mixture over top; swirl with a knife. Bake at 325° for 1 hour. Turn oven off; allow cheesecake to stand in oven for 30 minutes. Remove from oven; run knife around edge of cheesecake. Refrigerate immediately for 2-3 hours or until firm. Remove side of pan. Garnish as desired. **Yield:** 12-16 servings.

Chapter 14

PIES & TARTS

Any way you slice it, enticing pies and tempting tarts are sure to bring your everyday dinners and special-occasion suppers to a tantalizing conclusion.

Recipes in this chapter provided courtesy of these past sponsors...

Baker's
Bertolli
Bisquick
Blue Bonnet
Comstock/Wilderness
Cool Whip
Eagle Brand
Equal
Hershey's
Honey Maid
Jell-O
Karo
Pillsbury
Ready Crust
Royal
Nabisco
Nestlé

ALMOND MACAROON CHERRY PIE

(Pictured at left)

Mouth-watering cherries star in this luscious pie. Baked in a delicate pastry crust, the filling is topped with a crunchy streusel featuring coconut and almonds.

- 1 can (21 ounces) cherry pie filling
- 1 teaspoon lemon juice
- 1/2 teaspoon ground cinnamon
- 1/4 teaspoon salt, *divided*
- 1 unbaked pastry shell (9 inches)
- 1 cup flaked coconut
- 1/2 cup sliced almonds
- 1/4 cup sugar
- 1/4 cup milk
- 1 teaspoon butter *or* margarine, melted
- 1/4 teaspoon almond extract
- 1 egg, beaten

In a large bowl, combine pie filling, lemon juice, cinnamon and 1/8 teaspoon salt; spoon into pastry shell. Bake at 400° for 20 minutes; remove from oven. In a medium bowl, combine remaining salt and all remaining ingredients; mix well. Carefully spoon around the edges over fruit mixture. Return to the oven; bake 15-20 minutes longer or until crust and topping are golden brown. Cover pie with foil during last 5-10 minutes of baking to prevent excess browning if desired. **Yield:** 8 servings.

NO-BAKE PUMPKIN PIE

When the Colonists arrived in North America, they found the Native Americans growing and harvesting pumpkins for food. This large fruit was happily embraced by the new Americans and subsequently became a Thanksgiving tradition.

- 1 envelope unflavored gelatin
- 2 tablespoons cold water
- 1/4 cup boiling water
- 1-1/2 teaspoons ground cinnamon
- 1/2 teaspoon ground ginger
- 1/4 teaspoon ground cloves
- 3/4 cup sugar
- 2 teaspoons vanilla extract
- 1 cup milk
- 1 can (15 ounces) solid-pack pumpkin
- 1 graham cracker crust (9 inches)

In a blender, place gelatin and cold water; let stand to soften gelatin. Pour in boiling water; blend on low to dissolve gelatin. Add spices, sugar, vanilla and milk; blend on low to mix. Add pumpkin and blend on medium until smooth and well combined. Pour into crust. Chill 3 hours or until set. **Yield:** 6-8 servings.

EASY BANANA SOUR CREAM PIE

Grown in warm, humid tropics, bananas are picked and shipped green. Contrary to nature's norm, they are one fruit that develops better flavor when ripened after being picked.

1-2/3 cups graham cracker crumbs
   1/4 cup sugar
   1/4 cup butter *or* margarine, melted
   1/4 teaspoon ground cinnamon
    1 package (3.4 ounces) instant vanilla pudding mix
    1 cup (8 ounces) sour cream
    1 cup milk
    2 medium bananas, thinly sliced

In a medium bowl, combine crumbs, sugar, butter and cinnamon. Reserve 1/4 cup crumb mixture for topping. Press remaining crumbs into bottom and up sides of a 9-in. pie plate. In a large mixing bowl, combine pudding mix, sour cream and milk. Beat on low speed for 1-2 minutes or until well blended. Spread half of pudding mixture into crust; top with bananas. Spoon remaining pudding mixture over bananas. Top with reserved crumbs. Chill before serving. **Yield:** 8 servings

FLUFFY LEMON BERRY PIE

(Pictured above)

This extraordinary no-bake pie is a fast and foolproof make-ahead recipe. It's the perfect choice when you don't want to heat up the kitchen. A creamy lemon filling is accented with juicy berries.

    4 ounces cream cheese, softened
1-1/2 cups cold milk
    2 packages (3.4 ounces *each*) instant lemon pudding mix
    1 carton (8 ounces) frozen whipped topping, thawed
    1 shortbread *or* graham cracker crust (9 inches)
    1 cup blueberries, raspberries *or* sliced strawberries

In a large mixing bowl, beat the cream cheese until smooth. Gradually beat in milk until well blended. Add pudding mixes. Beat 2 minutes or until smooth. Stir in half of the whipped topping. Spoon into the crust. Top with remaining whipped topping. Refrigerate 3 hours or until set. Garnish with berries. **Yield:** 8 servings.

SHOOFLY PIE

The origin of this pie's name is the subject of several stories. One is that this dandy Pennsylvania Dutch dessert is so sweet that one must shoo away the flies as the pie cools on the windowsill. Another says the pie was created to attract flies away from other foods. Neither story is as appetizing as the pie itself.

1-1/2 cups all-purpose flour
   1/2 cup packed light brown sugar
   1/4 teaspoon salt
   1/4 teaspoon ground cinnamon
   1/8 teaspoon ground cloves
   1/8 teaspoon ground ginger
   1/8 teaspoon ground nutmeg
   1/4 cup butter *or* margarine
    1 cup boiling water
   1/2 cup dark molasses
1-1/2 teaspoons baking soda
    1 egg, lightly beaten
    1 unbaked pastry shell (9 inches)

In a large bowl, combine flour, brown sugar, salt, cinnamon, cloves, ginger and nutmeg. Cut in butter with pastry blender or 2 knives until mixture resembles coarse crumbs; set aside. In a bowl, combine water, molasses and baking soda; beat in egg. Spread a fourth of the crumb mixture into pastry shell. Pour a third of the molasses mixture over the crumbs. Repeat layers, ending with crumb mixture. Bake at 450° for 10 minutes. Reduce temperature to 350° and bake an additional 15-20 minutes or until set. Cool on a wire rack. **Yield:** 8 servings.

CHOCOLATE MOUSSE AND PRALINE PIE

This tempting dessert stars a sugary pecan layer topped with a rich and airy chocolate mousse. It's all nestled in a homemade chocolate crumb crust.

CRUST:
1-1/2 cups vanilla wafer crumbs
   6 tablespoons baking cocoa
   1/3 cup confectioners' sugar
   6 tablespoons butter *or* margarine, melted
PRALINE LAYER:
   1/3 cup butter *or* margarine
   1/4 cup packed brown sugar
   1 tablespoon sugar
   1 tablespoon cornstarch
   2 tablespoons water
   2/3 cup chopped pecans
CHOCOLATE MOUSSE:
   1 teaspoon unflavored gelatin
   1 tablespoon cold water
   2 tablespoons boiling water
   1/2 cup sugar
   1/4 cup baking cocoa
   1 cup whipping cream, chilled
   1 teaspoon vanilla extract
Whipped cream
Pecan halves

For crust, combine crumbs, cocoa and confectioners' sugar; stir in butter. Press into bottom and up sides of a 9-in. pie plate. Bake at 350° for 10 minutes; cool on wire rack. For praline layer, melt butter; remove from heat and stir in brown sugar. Blend sugar and cornstarch; add with water to brown sugar mixture. Cook over medium heat, stirring constantly, until bubbly. Remove from heat; stir in pecans. Pour into crust; refrigerate (do not cover). Meanwhile, sprinkle gelatin over cold water; let stand 1 minute to soften. Add boiling water; stir until gelatin is completely dissolved and mixture is clear. In a small mixing bowl, combine sugar, cocoa, whipping cream and vanilla. Beat until stiff; add gelatin mixture and beat just until blended. Carefully spread over praline layer. Chill several hours. Garnish with whipped cream and pecan halves. **Yield:** 6-8 servings.

NO-BAKE CRANBERRY WALNUT PIE

(Pictured below)

The luscious pudding-based filling is complemented by a tangy cranberry-walnut layer. Simply assemble, then chill until serving time. Garnish with whipped topping and additional walnuts to add to its appeal.

1-1/4 cups cold milk
   2 packages (3.4 ounces *each*) instant cheesecake pudding mix
   1/2 teaspoon grated lemon peel
   1 carton (8 ounces) frozen whipped topping, thawed, *divided*
   1 graham cracker crust (9 inches)
   1 can (16 ounces) whole-berry cranberry sauce, *divided*
   1/2 cup toasted chopped walnuts, *divided*

Pour milk into a large bowl. Add pudding mixes and lemon peel. Beat with a wire whisk for 1 minute (mixture will be thick). Gently stir in half of the whipped topping. Spread half of the pudding mixture into crust. Spread half of the cranberry sauce over pudding mixture. Sprinkle with half of the walnuts. Spread the remaining pudding mixture over walnuts. Refrigerate 4 hours or until set. Garnish with the remaining cranberry sauce, whipped topping and walnuts. **Yield:** 8 servings.

WHITE CHOCOLATE STRAWBERRY PIE

(Pictured below)

This spectacular pie can be whipped up in a jiffy, so keep it in mind next time you need a showstopping dessert. "Wow!" is what folks will say when you set this pie on the table. It's fun to serve since it's attractive, not overly sweet and bursting with fresh flavor.

    1 box (6 ounces) white baking bars, *divided*
    2 tablespoons milk
    1 package (3 ounces) cream cheese, softened
1/3 cup confectioners' sugar
    1 teaspoon grated orange peel
    1 cup whipping cream, whipped
    1 graham cracker crust (9 inches)
    2 cups sliced fresh strawberries

In a double boiler or microwave, melt 4 ounces of baking bars with milk. Cool to room temperature.

Meanwhile, beat cream cheese and sugar in a mixing bowl until smooth. Beat in orange peel and melted chocolate. Fold in whipped cream. Spread into crust. Arrange strawberries on top. Melt the remaining baking bar; drizzle over berries. Refrigerate for at least 1 hour. Store in the refrigerator. **Yield:** 8 servings.

MAGIC LIME PIE

This luscious lime pie can be made at a moment's notice with ingredients you can easily keep on hand. Serve up generous slices after a variety of meals.

    1 graham cracker crust (9 inches)
    1 can (14 ounces) sweetened condensed milk
1/2 cup lime juice
Green food coloring, optional
    1 cup whipping cream

In a large bowl, combine sweetened condensed milk, lime juice and 3 drops food coloring if desired. Stir until well blended. In a small mixing bowl, beat cream until stiff peaks form. Fold half of whipped cream into milk mixture. Pour into crumb crust. Top with remaining whipped cream. Chill. **Yield:** 8 servings.

QUICK SPICED FRUIT TART

It's a pleasure to serve this festive fruit-topped tart because it tastes as good as it looks. The crust is laced with aromatic spices including cinnamon, cloves and ginger, which complement the berries.

    1 can (14 ounces) sweetened condensed milk
    1 can (6 ounces) frozen orange juice concentrate, thawed
1/2 cup sour cream
1/2 cup butter *or* margarine, softened
1/4 cup packed brown sugar
3/4 cup all-purpose flour
1/2 cup finely chopped walnuts
    1 teaspoon ground cinnamon
1/4 teaspoon ground cloves
1/8 teaspoon ground ginger
Assorted fresh fruit (sliced bananas, orange segments, sliced strawberries, blueberries, raspberries, sliced kiwi fruit, etc.)
Additional chopped walnuts, optional

In a bowl, combine condensed milk, orange juice concentrate and sour cream; mix well. Chill. In a large mixing bowl, beat butter and brown sugar until fluffy; mix in flour, walnuts and spices until thoroughly blended. Press dough onto a greased 12-in. pizza pan, forming rim around edge. Prick with a fork. Bake at 375° for 5-7 minutes or until lightly browned. Cool. Spoon filling evenly onto crust. Arrange fruit on top. Garnish with additional walnuts if desired. Chill before serving. **Yield:** 10-12 servings.

PUMPKIN CREAM PIE

The pumpkin is a member of the gourd family, which includes winter squash, watermelon and muskmelon. Its orange flesh has a mild sweet flavor that's prized in pies, muffins and quick breads, especially in the fall. Sour cream, cream cheese and marshmallows make this pumpkin pie something special.

- 1 **package (3 ounces) cream cheese, softened**
- 1 **package (3.4 ounces) instant vanilla pudding mix**
- 3/4 **cup milk**
- 1 **cup (8 ounces) sour cream**
- 1 **graham cracker crust (9 inches)**
- 3/4 **cup solid-pack pumpkin**
- 1 **teaspoon pumpkin pie spice**
- 1 **cup miniature marshmallows**

In a small mixing bowl, whip cream cheese; set aside. In a separate bowl, beat pudding mix, milk and sour cream for 1 minute. Combine 1/4 cup pudding mixture with cream cheese; spread in bottom of crust. Stir pumpkin and spice into remaining pudding mixture; pour over cream cheese mixture. Top with marshmallows. Broil for 1-1/2 minutes or until lightly browned. Refrigerate 2 hours. **Yield:** 8 servings.

APPLE TART

(Pictured above right)

As a change of pace, folks will enjoy this wonderful tart instead of traditional apple pie. Soon after baking, the tart is inverted onto a serving plate to show off the tender apples crowning the top.

- 1 **cup sugar,** *divided*
- 2 **tablespoons all-purpose flour**
- 1/2 **teaspoon ground cinnamon**
- 6 **medium baking apples, peeled and thinly sliced**
- 1 **tablespoon butter** *or* **margarine**
Pastry for a single-crust pie

In a small skillet, heat 3/4 cup sugar, stirring constantly until it is liquefied and just golden. Remove from the heat and quickly pour into a 10-in. pie

plate; set aside. In a small bowl, combine flour, cinnamon and remaining sugar. Arrange half of the apples in a single layer in a circular pattern in pie plate. Sprinkle with half of the sugar mixture. Arrange half of the remaining apples in a circular pattern over sugar; sprinkle with the remaining sugar mixture. Place remaining apples over all, keeping the top as level as possible. Dot with butter. Roll out pastry to 9 in.; place over apples, pressing gently to completely cover. Do not flute. Bake at 400° for 50 minutes or until golden brown and apples are tender. As soon as tart comes out of the oven, carefully invert onto a large serving plate and remove pie plate. Cool. **Yield:** 8 servings.

GRAHAM CRACKER CRUST

If you don't have a prepared graham cracker pie crust on hand, you can quickly make your own. It's easy to dress up this simple mixture by adding your favorite spice or a few tablespoons of finely chopped nuts.

1-2/3 cups graham cracker crumbs
   1/4 cup sugar
   1/3 cup butter *or* **margarine, softened**

Combine graham cracker crumbs, sugar and butter. Press onto the bottom and up the sides of an ungreased 9-in. pie plate. Bake at 375° for 8 minutes or until crust is lightly browned. Cool on a wire rack. **For No-Bake Crust:** Do not bake. Cover and refrigerate 30 minutes before using. **Yield:** 1 crust (9 inches).

sheet; pour batter into crust. Bake at 350° for 45 minutes or until set. Cool on wire rack. In a small microwave-safe bowl, combine cream and remaining vanilla and morsels. Microwave on medium-high for 1-1/2 minutes; stir. Microwave at additional 10- to 20-second intervals, stirring until smooth. Cut pie into wedges; top with ice cream. Spoon sauce over ice cream and pie. **Yield:** 8 servings.

Frozen Fluffy Strawberry Pie

Guests' eyes will light up at the sight of this pretty pink make-ahead pie. The sensational strawberry flavor is especially refreshing in summer.

> 1 **package (3 ounces) cream cheese, softened**
> 1 **can (14 ounces) sweetened condensed milk**
> 1-1/2 **cups pureed fresh *or* unsweetened frozen strawberries**
> 3 **tablespoons lemon juice**
> 1 **cup whipping cream, whipped**
> 1 **graham cracker crust (9 inches)**
> **Fresh strawberries, optional**

In a large bowl, beat cream cheese until fluffy; beat in condensed milk. Stir strawberries and lemon juice into cream cheese mixture. Fold in whipped cream. Pour into crust (mixture should mound slightly). Freeze 4 hours or until firm. Before serving, garnish with fresh strawberries if desired. Return leftovers to freezer. **Yield:** 8 servings.

Fudgy Coconut-Nut Pie

Rich and satisfying, this dessert is a real crowd-pleaser. You'll love the combination of creamy cocoa, moist coconut and crunchy nuts.

> 6 **tablespoons butter *or* margarine, melted**
> 1 **cup sugar**
> 1/3 **cup baking cocoa**
> 3 **eggs, slightly beaten**
> 1 **teaspoon vanilla extract**
> 3/4 **cup flaked coconut**
> 1/2 **cup coarsely chopped nuts**
> 1 **shortbread pie crust (9 inches)**
> **Sweetened whipped cream, optional**
> **Toasted coconut, optional**
> **Additional chopped nuts, optional**

In a bowl, combine butter, sugar and cocoa until smooth. Add eggs and vanilla; blend well. Stir in coconut and nuts. Pour into crust. Place on baking sheet. Bake at 350° for 35-40 minutes or until fill-

Peanut Butter-Chocolate Brownie Pie

(*Pictured above*)

This luscious dessert combines the popular flavors of chocolate and peanut butter. Served with a scoop of your favorite ice cream, this brownie pie will make a fabulous finale for a family meal.

> 1/2 **cup baking cocoa**
> 1/2 **cup all-purpose flour**
> 1/4 **teaspoon salt**
> 2 **eggs**
> 1-1/4 **teaspoons vanilla extract, *divided***
> 1 **cup sugar**
> 1/2 **cup butter *or* margarine, melted**
> 1 **package (11 ounces) peanut butter and milk chocolate morsels, *divided***
> 1 **chocolate crumb crust (9 inches)**
> 2/3 **cup whipping cream**
> **Vanilla *or* chocolate ice cream**

In a small bowl, combine cocoa, flour and salt. Beat eggs and 1 teaspoon vanilla in a small mixing bowl; blend in sugar and butter. Add cocoa mixture; blend well. Stir in 3/4 cup morsels. Place crust on baking

ing is set. Cool on wire rack. Garnish with whipped cream, coconut or nuts if desired. **Yield:** 8 servings.

VANILLA WAFER CRUST

It's easy to prepare a crumb crust from scratch. Simply place the wafers in a heavy-duty resealable plastic bag, then seal the bag, pushing out as much air as possible. Press a rolling pin over the bag, crushing the cookies into fine crumbs. Combine the crumbs with the remaining ingredients and pat into your favorite pie plate.

 42 **vanilla wafers, finely crushed**
  2 **tablespoons sugar**
 1/3 **cup butter *or* margarine, melted**

Combine wafer crumbs and sugar. Stir in butter. Press mixture onto the bottom and up the sides of an ungreased 9-in. pie plate. Bake at 375° for 8-10 minutes or until lightly browned. Cool on a wire rack. **Yield:** 1 crust (9 inches).

FROZEN CHOCOLATE CHEESECAKE TART

Put a flavorful finishing touch on a special meal by serving this irresistible chocolate dessert. It offers an overwhelming rich flavor and appearance which is beyond compare.

2-1/4 **cups crushed chocolate cream-filled sandwich cookies (about 22 cookies)**
 1/3 **cup butter *or* margarine, melted**
FILLING:
  2 **packages (8 ounces *each*) cream cheese, softened**
 1/3 **cup confectioners' sugar**
 1/3 **cup whipping cream**
  1 **teaspoon vanilla extract**
  3 **cups vanilla chips, melted and cooled**
 1/2 **cup miniature semisweet chocolate chips**
Chocolate curls, optional

In a small bowl, combine the cookie crumbs and butter. Press onto the bottom and up the sides of a greased 9-in. fluted tart pan with a removable bottom. Cover; place in freezer, being careful not to push up on the removable pan bottom. Freeze for at least 1 hour. In a mixing bowl, beat the cream cheese and sugar until smooth. Add the cream, vanilla and melted vanilla chips; beat for 3 minutes. Stir in the chocolate chips; pour over crust. Cover and freeze for 8 hours or overnight. Uncover and re-

frigerate 3-4 hours before serving. Garnish with chocolate curls if desired. Refrigerate leftovers. **Yield:** 12 servings.

TEXAS PECAN PIE

(Pictured below)

Pecans are grown almost exclusively in North America and mostly in the Southern states. This sinfully rich nut pie is a true classic that is especially popular in the Deep South.

  1 **cup light corn syrup**
  1 **cup packed dark brown sugar**
 1/4 **teaspoon salt**
 1/3 **cup butter *or* margarine, melted**
  1 **teaspoon vanilla extract**
  3 **eggs, lightly beaten**
1-1/2 **cups pecan halves**
  1 **unbaked pastry crust (9 inches)**
Whipped topping

In a large bowl, combine syrup, brown sugar, salt, butter and vanilla. Beat in eggs. Add pecans. Pour into pie crust. Bake at 350° for 45 minutes or until set. Cool on a wire rack. Serve with a dollop of whipped topping. **Yield:** 6 servings.

Making and Shaping Single- and Double-Crust Pie Pastry

1 Combine flour and salt in a bowl. With a pastry blender or two knives, cut in shortening until the mixture is the size of small peas.

2 Sprinkle 1 tablespoon of cold water at a time over the mixture and gently mix with a fork. Repeat until all the dough is moist, using only as much water as necessary to moisten the flour.

3 Shape into a ball. (For a double-crust pie, divide dough in half so that one ball is slightly larger than the other.) On a floured surface or floured pastry cloth, flatten the ball (the larger one, if making a double-crust pie) into a circle, pressing together any cracks or breaks.

4 Roll with a floured rolling pin from the center of the dough to the edges, forming a circle 2 in. larger than the pie plate. The dough should be about 1/8 in. thick.

5 To move pastry to the pie plate, roll up onto the rolling pin. Position over the edge of pie plate and unroll. Let the pastry ease into the plate. Do not stretch the pastry to fit. For a single-crust pie, trim pastry with a kitchen shears to 1/2 in. beyond plate edge; turn under and flute as in step 8. For a double-crust pie, trim pastry even with the edge. For a lattice-crust pie, trim pastry to 1 in. beyond plate edge. Either bake the shell or fill according to recipe directions.

6 For a double-crust pie, roll out second ball into a 12-in. circle about 1/8 in. thick. With a knife, cut several slits in dough to allow steam to escape while baking. Roll up onto the rolling pin; position over filling.

7 With kitchen shears, trim top crust to 1 in. beyond plate edge. Fold top crust over bottom crust.

8 To flute the edge as shown at left, place your thumb on the inside of the crust and your other thumb and index finger on the outside of the crust. Press the dough to seal.

PASTRY PIE CRUSTS

Making a pie crust is easy if you follow the numbered steps and photos on the opposite page. The amount of water needed to moisten the dough will vary from day to day, depending on the humidity in the air. Many cooks wrap the dough in plastic wrap and refrigerate it for 30 minutes after Step 3. The resting time makes it easier to roll out the dough. When rolling out pastry, mend any cracks by wetting your fingers with water and pressing the dough back together.

SINGLE-CRUST PIE
1-1/4 cups all-purpose flour
   1/2 teaspoon salt
   1/3 cup shortening
    4 to 5 tablespoons cold water

Follow steps 1 through 5 for single-crust pie on opposite page. Fill or bake shell according to recipe directions. **Yield:** 1 pastry shell (9 or 10 inches).

DOUBLE-CRUST PIE
   2 cups all-purpose flour
   3/4 teaspoon salt
   2/3 cup shortening
    6 to 7 tablespoons cold water

Follow steps 1 through 8 for double-crust pie on opposite page. Bake according to recipe directions. **Yield:** pastry for double-crust pie (9 or 10 inches).

LAYER-AFTER-LAYER LEMON PIE

If you're running short on time, this pie is a breeze to make because it takes advantage of a prepared graham cracker crust. Cool and refreshing, its lemon flavor is a fitting finale on a hot summer day.

   1/3 cup strawberry jam
    1 graham cracker crust (9 inches)
    4 ounces cream cheese, softened
    1 tablespoon sugar
    2 cartons (8 ounces *each*) whipped topping, thawed, *divided*
1-1/2 cups cold milk
    2 packages (3.4 ounces *each*) instant lemon pudding mix

Spread jam in crust. In a mixing bowl, beat cream cheese and sugar until smooth. Gently stir in a fourth of the whipped topping. Spread over jam layer. Pour milk into a large bowl. Add pudding mixes. Beat with a wire whisk for 2 minutes or until well blended. Gently stir in a fourth of the whipped topping. Spread over cream cheese layer. Refrigerate 4 hours or until set. Garnish with the remaining whipped topping. **Yield:** 8 servings.

CHEESY CHERRY PIE

(Pictured above)

Family and friends will savor every mouth-watering morsel of this cherry-topped cheese pie. Poured into a prepared chocolate crumb crust, it bakes in just 40 minutes. A classic sour cream and ruby red cherry topping provides a burst of flavor and color.

    2 packages (8 ounces *each*) cream cheese, softened
   1/2 cup plus 2 tablespoons sugar, *divided*
    2 eggs
   1/4 teaspoon almond extract
    1 chocolate crumb *or* graham cracker crust (9 inches)
   1/2 cup sour cream
   1/2 teaspoon vanilla extract
    1 can (21 ounces) cherry pie filling
White candy coating curls, optional

In a mixing bowl, beat cream cheese, 1/2 cup sugar, eggs and almond extract until smooth and fluffy. Pour into crust. Bake at 325° for 35-40 minutes or until set. In a bowl, combine sour cream, vanilla and remaining sugar. Gently spread over top of pie. Bake an additional 5 minutes. Cool to room temperature and refrigerate. Top with pie filling before serving. Garnish with candy coating curls if desired. **Yield:** 10 servings.

BUTTERMILK PIE

Just a bite of this old-fashioned treat will take you back to the days when homemade pies were a routine part of many mealtime menus. You'll flip over the creamy custard filling.

    3 cups sugar
    6 tablespoons all-purpose flour
1-1/2 cups buttermilk, *divided*
    5 eggs
    1/2 cup butter *or* margarine, melted
    2 teaspoons vanilla extract
    2 unbaked pastry shells (9 inches *each*)
    1 cup chopped pecans, optional

In a bowl, combine sugar, flour and 3/4 cup buttermilk. Add eggs and remaining buttermilk; mix well. Stir in the butter and vanilla. Divide evenly among pie shells. Top with pecans if desired. Bake at 425° for 10 minutes. Reduce heat to 350°; bake 25-30 minutes longer or until a knife inserted near the center comes out clean. Cool completely. Store in the refrigerator. **Yield:** 12-16 servings.

AMBROSIA CHEESE PIE

(Pictured below)

Here's a refreshing no-bake pie that you can prepare in a jiffy. Simply assemble, then chill until serving time. Flaked coconut and fruity garnishes on top hint at the delicious flavor inside this light and fluffy dessert.

    1 package (8 ounces) cream cheese, softened
    1/2 cup confectioners' sugar

    1/4 cup orange juice
    1 can (15 ounces) mandarin orange
       segments, drained
1-1/4 cups flaked coconut, *divided*
    1/2 cup sour cream
    1 carton (8 ounces) frozen whipped
       topping, thawed
    1 graham cracker crust (9 inches)
    1 can (8 ounces) pineapple chunks, drained

In a large mixing bowl, beat cream cheese, confectioners' sugar and orange juice until fluffy. Set aside 8 orange segments for garnish; fold remaining segments into cheese mixture until slightly broken up. Stir in 1 cup coconut and sour cream. Reserve 1 cup whipped topping for garnish; fold remaining topping into filling. Spoon into crust. Refrigerate until set, about 3 hours. Garnish with reserved whipped topping, remaining coconut, orange segments and pineapple chunks. **Yield:** 8 servings.

FRUIT COCONUT CRUMB PIE

Chock-full of strawberries, banana slices and pineapple, a wide slice of this festive pie is a great end to a delicious meal. Your family will savor every forkful.

    1 package (10 ounces) frozen sweetened
       sliced strawberries, thawed
    1 medium banana, sliced
    1 can (20 ounces) pineapple chunks, drained
    1/2 cup flaked coconut
    1 tablespoon lemon juice
    1/4 cup sugar
    3 tablespoons quick-cooking tapioca
    1/4 teaspoon salt
    1 unbaked pastry shell (9 inches)
TOPPING:
    1 cup vanilla wafer crumbs (about 16 wafers)
    3 tablespoons all-purpose flour
    3 tablespoons brown sugar
    3 tablespoons butter *or* margarine
    1/4 cup chopped walnuts

Drain strawberries, reserving 1/4 cup syrup. Mix strawberries, banana, pineapple, coconut, lemon juice and reserved strawberry syrup. Combine sugar, tapioca and salt; mix into fruits. Turn into pastry shell. For topping, combine wafer crumbs, flour and brown sugar in a small bowl; cut in butter until crumbly. Stir in nuts. Sprinkle over fruit; cover loosely with aluminum foil. Bake at 375° for 25 minutes. Remove aluminum foil; bake an additional 20-25 minutes or until crust is brown. Cool on a wire rack. **Yield:** 8 servings.

PEANUT BUTTER CHIP BANANA PIE

If you love traditional banana cream pie and the flavor of peanut butter, this dynamite recipe combines the two for a doubly delicious dessert.

   1/3 cup sugar
   1/3 cup cornstarch
   1/4 teaspoon salt
2-1/4 cups milk
   2 egg yolks
   1 package (10 ounces) peanut butter chips
   1 teaspoon vanilla extract
   2 medium ripe bananas
   1 graham cracker crust (9 inches)
Whipped topping, optional

In a heavy saucepan, combine sugar, cornstarch and salt; stir in milk. Cook and stir over medium heat until thick and bubbly. Remove from heat. Beat egg yolks. Stir 1 cup hot mixture into yolks; return to pan. Cook and stir over medium heat until gently boiling; cook and stir 2 minutes more. Add peanut butter chips and vanilla; stir until mixture is smooth. Cool. Slice bananas; place in bottom of crust. Cover with filling. Press plastic wrap onto pie filling. Chill 3-4 hours. Remove plastic wrap. Garnish with whipped topping if desired. **Yield:** 8 servings.

EASY CHEESY APPLE PIE

Everyone who tries this tempting dessert will comment on how nicely the buttery cheddar cheese complements the tart apple filling.

   1 cup all-purpose flour
   1/4 cup quick-cooking oats
1-1/2 teaspoons sugar
   1/2 teaspoon salt
   1/3 cup butter *or* margarine, melted
   1/4 cup cold milk
   1 package (3 ounces) cook-and-serve
      vanilla *or* coconut cream pudding mix
   6 cups sliced peeled tart apples (about 4
      large)
   1/2 cup shredded cheddar cheese
TOPPING:
   1/3 cup all-purpose flour

   1/3 cup sugar
   1/4 cup quick-cooking oats
   3 tablespoons butter *or* margarine, softened

In a bowl, combine flour, oats, sugar, salt, butter and milk. Press onto bottom and sides of 9-in. pie plate. In a large bowl, combine pudding mix and apples; spoon into crust. Sprinkle with cheese. For topping, combine flour, sugar and oats. Cut in butter until crumbly. Sprinkle over cheese and apples. Bake at 350° for 40-45 minutes or until light brown and apples are tender. Serve warm. **Yield:** 8 servings.

COUNTRY PEACH TART

(Pictured above)

This fruity finale can be put together in a flash, so keep it in mind next time you need a dessert in a hurry. It's bursting with fresh peach flavor.

Pastry for single-crust pie (9 inches)
   1 tablespoon all-purpose flour
   8 packets sugar substitute
   4 cups sliced peeled fresh peaches *or* frozen
      peaches, thawed
Ground nutmeg

On a floured surface, roll pastry into a 12-in. circle; transfer to an ungreased baking sheet. Combine flour and sugar substitute; sprinkle over peaches and toss. Arrange peaches on pastry, leaving a 2-in. border around edge of pastry. Sprinkle peaches lightly with nutmeg. Fold in edge of pastry. Bake at 425° for 30 minutes or until crust is browned and fruit is tender. Cool on a wire rack. **Yield:** 8 servings.

BANANA SPLIT TARTS

Say the words "banana split" and you'll likely bring smiles to the faces of kids and grown-ups alike. Here we've given a new twist to the traditional toppings. Strawberry yogurt is spooned over ripe banana slices nestled in individual tart shells. For added fun, top these tempting tarts with a dollop of whipped topping and a drizzle of chocolate syrup—and don't forget the cherry on top!

> 1 package (6 count) individual graham cracker tart shells
> 1 medium ripe banana
> 1 cup (8 ounces) strawberry yogurt
> Red food coloring, optional
> 1 can (8 ounces) pineapple tidbits, drained
> Whipped topping
> Chocolate syrup and maraschino cherries, optional

Arrange tart shells on a serving platter. Thinly slice banana into bottom of crusts. Add 1-2 drops food coloring to yogurt if desired. Stir yogurt; spoon over banana. Spoon pineapple over yogurt layer. Garnish tarts with a dollop of whipped topping. Garnish with chocolate syrup and cherries if desired. Refrigerate until serving time. **Yield:** 6 servings.

PEANUT BUTTER PRALINE PIE

Traditional peanut butter pie gets tweaked in this tasty version. A chocolate crumb crust holds a pleasing praline layer veiled with a rich peanut butter pudding.

CRUST:
1-1/2 cups vanilla wafer crumbs
> 6 tablespoons baking cocoa
> 1/3 cup confectioners' sugar
> 6 tablespoons butter *or* margarine, melted

FILLING:
> 1/3 cup butter *or* margarine
> 1/4 cup packed brown sugar
> 2 tablespoons sugar
> 1 tablespoon cornstarch
> 2 tablespoons water
> 1/2 cup chopped pecans
> 1 package (3 ounces) cook-and-serve vanilla pudding mix
> 2 cups milk
> 1 package (10 ounces) peanut butter chips
> 1 cup whipped topping

Additional whipped topping, optional
Chopped pecans, optional

Combine wafer crumbs, cocoa, confectioners' sugar and butter. Press onto the bottom and up the sides of an ungreased 9-in. pie plate. Bake at 350° for 10 minutes. Cool on a wire rack. For filling, melt butter in small saucepan; remove from heat. Stir in brown sugar. Thoroughly combine sugar and cornstarch; add with water to brown sugar mixture. Stir constantly over medium heat until bubbly; remove from heat and stir in pecans. Pour into cooled crust; refrigerate, uncovered, until set. Combine pudding mix and milk in medium saucepan, stirring constantly over medium heat until mixture boils; remove from heat. Immediately add chips; stir until melted and well-blended. Place plastic wrap directly onto surface of pudding mixture; refrigerate 1 hour. Stir; fold in 1 cup whipped topping. Carefully spread over filling. Place plastic wrap directly onto pudding mixture; chill overnight. Remove plastic wrap. If desired, garnish with whipped topping and pecans just before serving. **Yield:** 6 to 8 servings.

COCONUT PEACH CRUNCH PIE

This spectacular pie is sure to satisfy your family's sweet tooth. Peach fruit filling is spooned into a prepared shortbread crust, then sprinkled with a coconut streusel topping. When baked to a golden brown, the results are picture-perfect.

> 1 shortbread crust (9 inches)
> 1 egg yolk, beaten
> 1 can (21 ounces) peach pie filling
> 1 cup flaked coconut
> 1/2 cup all-purpose flour
> 1/2 cup sugar
> 1/4 cup butter *or* margarine, melted
> 1/4 cup wheat germ

Brush bottom and sides of crust with egg yolk; set on a baking sheet. Bake at 350° for 5 minutes or until light brown. Spoon pie filling into crust. In a small bowl, combine coconut, flour, sugar, butter and wheat germ. Mix until well blended. Spread over fruit filling. Bake on baking sheet for 30-35 minutes or until filling is bubbly and topping is light brown. Cool on a wire rack. **Yield:** 6-8 servings.

WALNUT PUMPKIN PIE

(Pictured above)

A slice of this extraordinary pumpkin pie will bring your holiday feast to a lip-smacking conclusion! Its crunchy walnut streusel is a pleasant surprise that family and friends are sure to appreciate. You may want to bake more than one since everyone will be asking for seconds!

> 1 can (15 ounces) **solid-pack pumpkin**
> 1 can (14 ounces) **sweetened condensed milk**
> 1 **egg**
> 1-1/4 teaspoons **ground cinnamon,** *divided*
> 1/2 teaspoon *each* **ground ginger, nutmeg and salt**
> 1 **graham cracker crust (9 inches)**
> 1/2 cup **packed brown sugar**
> 2 tablespoons **all-purpose flour**
> 2 tablespoons **cold butter** *or* **margarine**
> 3/4 cup **chopped walnuts**

In a mixing bowl, combine pumpkin, milk, egg, 3/4 teaspoon cinnamon, ginger, nutmeg and salt; mix well. Set crust on a baking sheet; pour filling into crust. Bake at 425° for 15 minutes; remove pie from oven. Reduce oven temperature to 350°. In a small bowl, combine sugar, flour and remaining cinnamon; cut in butter until crumbly. Stir in walnuts. Sprinkle walnut mixture evenly over pie. Bake 40 minutes longer or until knife inserted near the center comes out clean. Cool on a wire rack. **Yield:** 8 servings.

CINNAMON RICOTTA PIE

(Pictured above)

Similar to traditional Italian ricotta pies, this satisfying dessert is not overly sweet. No one can resist the yummy combination of fresh berries and creamy ricotta cheese.

PASTRY:
1-1/2 cups all-purpose flour
  1/4 cup sugar
  1/2 teaspoon ground cinnamon
  1/4 teaspoon salt
  1/4 cup light olive oil
FILLING:
  1/2 cup sugar
    2 tablespoons cornstarch
  1/8 teaspoon ground cinnamon
    1 carton (15 ounces) part-skim ricotta
      cheese
    2 egg whites
    1 teaspoon vanilla extract
    1 cup strawberries
    1 cup raspberries

In a large bowl, combine the flour, sugar, cinnamon and salt. Stir in olive oil. With fingertips, blend until crumbly. Shape into a ball; flatten slightly. Wrap with plastic wrap and refrigerate 15 minutes. Roll out pastry between two sheets of lightly floured waxed paper to fit a 9-in. pie plate. Transfer pastry to pie plate. Trim pastry to 1/2 in. beyond edge of pan; flute edges. Refrigerate. For filling, in a large bowl, combine sugar, cornstarch and cinnamon. Stir in ricotta, egg whites and vanilla until blended. Pour into prepared pastry. Bake at 375° for 45-50 minutes or until filling is just set in center. Cool on a wire rack. Refrigerate for several hours. Serve with fresh berries. **Yield:** 8 servings.

CHOCOLATE CHIP PIE

This dessert delights chocolate lovers and travels very well to a potluck dinner or other gatherings. It's guaranteed to make someone feel special.

    2 eggs
  1/2 cup all-purpose flour
  1/2 cup sugar
  1/2 cup packed brown sugar
  3/4 cup butter *or* margarine, softened
    1 cup (6 ounces) semisweet chocolate
      morsels
    1 cup chopped nuts
    1 unbaked deep-dish pastry shell
      (9 inches)*
Sweetened whipped cream *or* ice cream

In a large mixing bowl, beat eggs on high speed until foamy. Beat in flour, sugars and butter. Stir in morsels and nuts. Spoon into pastry shell. Bake at 325° for 55-60 minutes or until knife inserted halfway between outside edge and center comes out clean. Cool on wire rack. Serve warm with whipped cream. **Yield:** 8 servings. ***Editor's Note:** If using a frozen pie shell, use deep-dish style, thawed completely. Bake on a baking sheet and increase baking time slightly.

IMPOSSIBLY EASY FRENCH APPLE PIE

Call it old-fashioned, comforting, mouth-watering and easy to make—all those descriptions fit this crustless apple pie. It bakes up golden brown with a nutty crumb topping. For an added treat, crown each serving of this glorious dessert with a scoop of vanilla or caramel ice cream.

    1 cup biscuit/baking mix, *divided*
  1/4 cup chopped nuts
  1/4 cup packed brown sugar
    3 tablespoons butter *or* margarine, *divided*
    3 cups sliced peeled apples
    1 teaspoon ground cinnamon
  1/4 teaspoon ground nutmeg
  1/2 cup sugar
  1/2 cup milk
    2 eggs

In a bowl, combine 1/2 cup biscuit mix, nuts and brown sugar. Cut in 2 tablespoons butter until mixture resembles coarse crumbs; set aside. In a bowl, combine apples, cinnamon and nutmeg; spread into a greased 9-in. pie plate. In a bowl, combine sugar, milk, eggs and remaining butter and biscuit mix; stir until smooth. Pour over apples. Sprinkle with crumb mixture. Bake at 325° for 40-45 minutes or until knife inserted in the center comes out clean. Cool 5 minutes. **Yield:** 6 servings.

CHOCOLATE CHEESE PIE

This impressive pie only looks like you fussed, since it's quite easy to prepare. Your family will gobble it up quickly. For variety, use a chocolate crumb crust and garnish with chocolate curls.

>   **2 packages (one 8 ounces, one 3 ounces)**
>   **cream cheese, softened**
>   **3/4 cup sugar**
>   **1/4 cup baking cocoa**
>   **2 eggs**
>   **1 teaspoon vanilla extract**
>   **1/2 cup whipping cream**
>   **1 graham cracker crust (9 inches)**

In a large mixing bowl, combine cream cheese and sugar; blend well. Beat in cocoa, scraping sides of bowl and beaters; beat in eggs and vanilla. Add cream; blend well. Pour into crust. Bake at 350° for 40 minutes (center will be soft but will set upon cooling). Cool on a wire rack; chill for several hours or overnight. **Yield:** 8 servings.

EASY CHOCOLATE COCONUT CREAM PIE

Extra-speedy to prepare, this pudding pie blends the popular flavors of chocolate and coconut. To increase the coconut flavor, lightly toast the coconut before adding it to this recipe. Save a tablespoon to garnish the top of the pie.

>   **1 package (3.4 ounces) vanilla cook-and-serve**
>   **pudding mix**
>   **1/2 cup sugar**
>   **1/4 cup baking cocoa**
> **1-3/4 cups milk**
>   **1 cup flaked coconut**
>   **1 pastry shell (9 inches), baked**
>   **2 cups whipped topping**

In a large microwave-safe bowl, combine pudding mix, sugar and cocoa. Stir in milk until blended. Microwave at high for 6 minutes or until mixture boils and is thickened and smooth, stirring every 2 minutes with wire whisk. Cool 5 minutes; stir in coconut. Pour into crust. Cool; refrigerate 6 hours or until firm. Top with whipped topping. **Yield:** 8 servings.

LUSCIOUS LEMONADE PIE

(Pictured below)

This refreshing lemon pie looks quite elegant for a springtime dinner, yet requires little effort. Guests will never suspect they're eating a quick-and-easy dessert.

>   **1 envelope whipped topping mix**
>   **1/2 cup cold milk**
>   **1/2 teaspoon vanilla extract**
>   **3/4 cup lemonade concentrate**
>   **1 can (14 ounces) sweetened condensed**
>   **milk**
>   **1 graham cracker crust (9 inches)**
>   **1 to 2 cups assorted fresh berries**
> **Whipped topping, optional**

In a mixing bowl, prepare whipped topping mix with milk and vanilla according to package directions. Stir in lemonade concentrate and condensed milk; mix well. Pour into pie crust. Cover; freeze for at least 2 hours. Top with berries. Garnish with whipped topping if desired. **Yield:** 8 servings.

FRESH BLUEBERRY TARTS

These attractive individual treats deliver a burst of blueberry flavor. You'll also appreciate their quick and easy convenience.

> 1 package (8 ounces) cream cheese, softened
> 1/4 cup packed light brown sugar
> 1 package (6 count) individual graham cracker tart shells
> 2 cups fresh blueberries, *divided*
> 3 tablespoons sugar
> 1 teaspoon fresh lemon juice
> 1 teaspoon grated lemon peel

In a bowl, beat cream cheese and brown sugar until smooth. Spread in tart shells. In another bowl, mash 3 tablespoons blueberries with sugar, lemon juice and peel. Add remaining berries and toss. Spoon into tarts. Chill for 1 hour. **Yield:** 6 servings.

HOLIDAY MINT PIE

(Pictured below)

Sure to solicit praise, this delightful dessert has the classic flavor of grasshopper pie. It's cool and creamy, yet the crumbled mint cookies add an enjoyable texture.

> 1 package (8 ounces) cream cheese, softened
> 1/3 cup sugar
> 1 carton (12 ounces) whipped topping, thawed, *divided*
> 3 drops green food coloring
> 1 cup chopped grasshopper cookies
> 1 chocolate crumb crust (9 inches)
> Mint leaves *and/or* chocolate leaves, optional

In a large mixing bowl, mix the cream cheese and sugar at medium speed until well blended. Fold in 3 cups whipped topping, food coloring and cookies. Spoon into crust. Refrigerate at least 3 hours or until set. Garnish with the remaining whipped topping. Decorate with mint and chocolate leaves if desired. **Yield:** 8 servings.

RAISIN NUT PIE

It's hard to imagine, but about half of the world's raisin supply comes from California. In the most basic terms, a raisin is simply a grape that has been sun-dried or dehydrated mechanically. Their wholesome goodness shines through in this pie.

> 3 eggs
> 3/4 cup dark corn syrup
> 2/3 cup packed light brown sugar
> 1/4 cup butter *or* margarine, melted
> 1 teaspoon vanilla extract
> 1/4 teaspoon salt
> 1 cup raisins
> 1/2 cup chopped pecans *or* walnuts
> 1 unbaked pastry shell (9 inches)
> Whipped cream *or* ice cream, optional

In a medium bowl, beat eggs. Add corn syrup, brown sugar, butter, vanilla and salt; mix well. Stir in raisins and nuts. Transfer into pastry shell. Bake at 400° for 35 minutes or until center is almost set. Cool on wire rack. Serve with whipped cream or vanilla ice cream if desired. **Yield:** 8 servings.

FUDGY PECAN PIE

This pie may look too good to eat—but don't let that stop you! Encased in a flaky pastry crust, the nutty chocolate filling is hard to resist.

1/3 cup butter *or* margarine, melted
2/3 cup sugar
1/3 cup baking cocoa
  3 eggs
  1 cup light corn syrup
1/4 teaspoon salt
  1 cup chopped pecans
  1 unbaked pastry shell (9 inches)
Whipped topping and pecan halves, optional

Combine butter, sugar and cocoa, stirring until well blended; set aside. In a bowl, beat eggs slightly; stir in syrup and salt. Add cocoa mixture; blend well. Stir in pecans. Pour into pastry shell. Bake at 375° for 45-50 minutes or until set. Cool on a wire rack. Cover; let stand about 8 hours before serving. Garnish with whipped topping and pecan halves if desired. **Yield:** 8 servings.

FUDGY MOCHA PECAN PIE:

Dissolve 1 teaspoon instant coffee granules in 1 teaspoon hot water; add to mixture with syrup and salt.

BLACK WALNUT PIE

This rich dessert, which is similar to traditional pecan pie, will be a favorite for years to come.

  1 cup light corn syrup
1/2 cup packed brown sugar
1/2 cup plus 1 tablespoon sugar, *divided*
  3 tablespoons butter *or* margarine
  3 eggs
  1 cup chopped black walnuts

  1 tablespoon all-purpose flour
  1 unbaked pastry shell (9 inches)

In a saucepan, combine the corn syrup, brown sugar and 1/2 cup sugar; bring to a boil. Remove from the heat; stir in butter until melted. In a mixing bowl, beat eggs. Gradually stir in hot mixture; mix well. Add walnuts. Combine flour and remaining sugar; sprinkle over bottom of pastry shell. Pour walnut mixture into shell. Bake at 350° for 45-50 minutes or until browned. **Yield:** 6-8 servings.

APPLE CREAM PIE

(Pictured above)

When an appealing apple pie is just what you want, try this classic recipe. Whipping cream adds a luscious richness while a sprinkle of cinnamon provides flavor.

  4 cups sliced peeled tart apples
  1 unbaked pastry shell (9 inches)
  1 cup sugar
  1 cup whipping cream
  3 tablespoons all-purpose flour
Ground cinnamon

Place apples in pastry shell. Combine sugar, cream and flour; pour over the apples. Sprinkle with cinnamon. Bake at 400° for 10 minutes. Reduce heat to 375°; bake for 35-40 minutes or until pie is set in center. Cover crust edges with foil during the last 15 minutes if needed. Cool on a wire rack. Serve warm or cover and refrigerate. **Yield:** 6-8 servings.

1 can (20 ounces) crushed pineapple
1 cup sugar
1/4 cup all-purpose flour
1 tablespoon lemon juice
1 tablespoon butter *or* margarine, melted
1/4 teaspoon salt
Pastry for double-crust pie (9 inches)
3/4 cup flaked coconut
1/2 cup confectioners' sugar
1/4 teaspoon vanilla extract

Drain pineapple, reserving 1 tablespoon juice for glaze. In a medium bowl, combine pineapple, sugar, flour, lemon juice, butter and salt; mix well and set aside. Line a 9-in. pie pan with the bottom pastry. Sprinkle with coconut. Spread pineapple mixture over coconut. Top with remaining pastry; flute edges and cut slits in top. Bake at 400° for 35-40 minutes or until golden brown. Cool 20 minutes on a wire rack. Meanwhile, for glaze, combine confectioners' sugar, vanilla and reserved pineapple juice until smooth. Spread over the top of warm pie. Serve warm or at room temperature. **Yield:** 6-8 servings.

PEACHY RHUBARB PIE

(Pictured above)

If you enjoy pies with fruity combinations, this one is sure to tempt your taste buds. The lattice crust shows off the pretty hues of golden peaches and rosy rhubarb.

1 can (8-1/2 ounces) sliced peaches
2 cups chopped fresh *or* frozen rhubarb, thawed and drained
1 cup sugar
1/4 cup flaked coconut
3 tablespoons quick-cooking tapioca
1 teaspoon vanilla extract
Pastry for double-crust pie (9 inches)
1 tablespoon butter *or* margarine

Drain peaches, reserving syrup; chop the peaches. Place peaches and syrup in a bowl; add rhubarb, sugar, coconut, tapioca and vanilla. Line a 9-in. pie plate with the bottom pastry. Add filling; dot with butter. Top with remaining pastry or a lattice crust; flute edges. If using a full top crust, cut slits in it. Bake at 350° for 1 hour or until crust is golden brown and filling is bubbly. **Yield:** 6-8 servings.

GLAZED PINEAPPLE PIE

With its unique glaze, this pie is a tropical treat that goes over well anytime. It also cuts nicely, so it makes a pretty presentation on your table.

CHOCOLATE PEPPERMINT PIE

This delightful frozen dessert will satisfy a chocolate lover's craving. Keep the recipe handy since it's great for summertime celebrations.

1 quart chocolate-chocolate chip ice cream, softened
1 chocolate crumb crust (9 inches)
1 package (6 ounces) chocolate-covered peppermint candies
1 cup whipping cream, *divided*

Spoon ice cream into crust. Freeze until firm, about 2 hours. Meanwhile, in a small saucepan, heat the candies with 3-4 tablespoons of cream; stir until smooth. Cool. Whip the remaining cream; spoon over ice cream. Drizzle with half of the chocolate-peppermint sauce. Serve slices with the remaining sauce. **Yield:** 6-8 servings.

TRADITIONAL PUMPKIN PIE

Though most families enjoy two or three different desserts at their holiday dinner, one of them must be pumpkin pie. Otherwise, it just wouldn't be Thanksgiving!

1 can (16 ounces) solid-pack pumpkin

1 can (14 ounces) sweetened condensed milk
2 eggs
1 teaspoon ground cinnamon
1/2 teaspoon ground ginger
1/2 teaspoon ground nutmeg
1/2 teaspoon salt
1 unbaked pastry shell (9 inches)

In a large mixing bowl, combine all ingredients except pastry shell; mix well. Pour into pastry shell. Bake at 425° for 15 minutes. Reduce oven temperature to 350°; continue baking 35-40 minutes or until knife inserted 1 inch from edge comes out clean. Cool. Garnish as desired. **Yield:** 8 servings.

BLUEBERRY PIE

This scrumptious pie is easy to assemble, but folks will rave about the impressive results. The plump fresh berries are juicy and sweet in this delectable summertime treat.

1 pastry shell (9 inches), baked
5 cups fresh blueberries, *divided*
3/4 cup sugar, *divided*
2 tablespoons cornstarch
1/4 teaspoon ground cinnamon
Dash salt
1/2 cup water
1 tablespoon butter *or* margarine
Whipped cream

In a large bowl, toss 2 cups blueberries and 1/4 cup sugar; set aside. In a 2-qt. saucepan, combine remaining sugar, cornstarch, cinnamon, salt and water. Stir in remaining blueberries and butter. Over medium heat, bring to a boil, stirring constantly. Cook 2 minutes more or until thickened and clear. Pour hot mixture over reserved berries and sugar mixture in bowl; stir just to combine. Pour the blueberry mixture into cooled crust. Cover; refrigerate at least 6 hours. Garnish with whipped cream. **Yield:** 8 servings.

STRAWBERRY MERINGUE PIE

(Pictured at right)

This dessert is quite simple, so don't be put off by the long directions. It's elegant-looking and provides a perfect ending for any occasion.

1/3 cup finely crushed saltines (about 12
     crackers), *divided*
3 egg whites
1/4 teaspoon cream of tartar

1/8 teaspoon salt
1 cup sugar
1 teaspoon vanilla extract
1/2 cup chopped pecans, toasted
1 package (4 ounces) German sweet
     chocolate
2 tablespoons butter *or* margarine
1 cup whipping cream
2 tablespoons confectioners' sugar
4 cups fresh strawberries, halved

Sprinkle 2 tablespoons of cracker crumbs into a greased 9-in. pie plate. In a mixing bowl, beat egg whites, cream of tartar and salt until soft peaks form. Gradually add sugar and continue beating until stiff peaks form. Fold in vanilla, pecans and remaining cracker crumbs. Spread meringue onto the bottom and up the sides of the prepared pan. Bake at 300° for 45 minutes. Turn off oven and do not open door; let cool in oven overnight. In a small saucepan over low heat, melt chocolate and butter, stirring constantly. Drizzle over shell. Let stand at least 15 minutes or until set. Top with berries. Whip cream and confectioners' sugar until soft peaks form; spoon over berries. **Yield:** 6-8 servings.

Flashback to the '90s

*T*echnology takes the nation on a great ride in the 1990s—and the Cooking School gets an electronic upgrade. At home, many folks are buying personal computers and linking up to the Internet to chat via E-mail. Cell phone sales skyrocket, and few can claim they're out of touch. Phones are ringing everywhere, it seems.

Onstage at Cooking Schools, huge video screens make certain everyone in the audience can see exactly what the home economist is demonstrating.

In December 1995, Reiman Publications buys Homemaker Schools, partnering a well-known national cooking school with the largest food magazine in the nation. *Taste of Home*, with more than 4 million subscribers, is the flagship of Reiman's 10 national magazines.

The Cooking School continues to grow. The Recipe Collection for each season is expanded from a pamphlet to a four-color cookbook in magazine format. At the end of the decade, Homemaker Schools officially takes the name "Taste of Home Cooking School".

TWO onstage big-screen video monitors (above) ensure everyone in the audience at a Cooking School can see. Shows are typically a family affair—with moms, grandmas and daughters (top right). Before the show (right), sponsors often provide displays, literature and product samples. Each attendee gets a goodie bag that includes a free cookbook. Although the lines are sometimes long (below) to get into a show, the folks are always friendly.

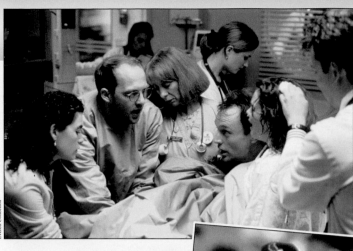

NEW FOR THE '90s.
"ER" becomes Thursday night "must-see" TV, Mark McGwire sets a new home run record, Johnny Carson retires, everybody wants to have "Friends", Spam goes "lite" and "Mad About You" hits TV's top 10.

That's Entertainment

• "ER" and "NYPD Blue" are among the hottest TV dramas. Comedies "Mad About You" and "Seinfeld" also rank regularly in Nielsen's top 10.

• After more than 30 years as host of "The Tonight Show", Johnny Carson retires in May 1992.

• Our national pastime gets a new hero when Mark McGwire hits home run No. 62, breaking Roger Maris' record.

• Bob Newhart ends his decades-long run on television, most recently in a self-titled sitcom.

The 'In' Things

• The television show "Friends" hooks a whole new generation on coffee shops, and Jennifer Aniston's hairdo as "Rachel" is copied by thousands of young women from coast to coast.

• Fanny packs, small pouches that buckle around the waist, briefly eclipse purses as the main way to keep ID, cash and keys handy.

• Pants favored by teens become so baggy that they often slip down, revealing the tops of underwear. Add a flannel shirt for the "grunge" look.

Price Check

• The cost of a first-class stamp jumps from 25¢ to 29¢ on Feb. 1, 1991, and then to 32¢ on Jan. 1, 1995.

• A gallon of gas and a dozen eggs cost $1.16 each in 1995. Eggs get cheaper but gas goes up toward the end of the decade.

• The average cost of a new home is $158,700.

Play List

• "Candle in the Wind", a tribute by Elton John to the late Princess Diana of Wales, is the top song of 1997, the year she dies.

• Cher stages her umpteenth comeback, and the single "Believe" hits No. 1 on the pop chart in 1999.

Food for Thought

• Milk gets its own publicity campaign, with a number of high profile white-mustachioed sports and movie stars asking, "Got Milk?"

• Hormel comes out with Spam Lite, a leaner version of the canned classic.

Chapter 15

JUST DESSERTS

254

Why not freshen your repertoire of delicious desserts with one of these sensational sweets? These tempting morsels are destined to become family favorites year-round.

Recipes in this chapter provided courtesy of these past sponsors...

Blue Bonnet
Comstock/Wilderness
Dromedary
Eagle Brand
Equal
Hershey's
Jet-Puffed
Kraft Marshmallows
Minute Tapioca
Nestlé
Pecan Valley
Reynolds
Sunbeam
Taster's Choice

HOLIDAY TRUFFLES

(Pictured at left)

Satisfy your sweet tooth with these tantalizing chocolate treats. Whether prepared on the stovetop or in the microwave oven, their creamy, smooth texture will please even the most discriminating palate. By using an assortment of toppings, you can offer guests a variety of flavors.

> **3 cups (18 ounces) semisweet chocolate chips**
> **1 can (14 ounces) sweetened condensed milk**
> **1 tablespoon vanilla extract**
> **Finely chopped toasted nuts, flaked coconut *and/or* baking cocoa**

In a heavy saucepan over low heat, melt chips and milk. Remove from the heat; stir in vanilla. Chill 3 hours or until firm. Shape into 1-in. balls; roll in nuts, coconut or cocoa. Chill 1 hour or until firm. Store covered at room temperature or in the refrigerator. **Yield:** about 6 dozen.

MICROWAVE INSTRUCTIONS:
In a large microwave-safe bowl, combine chips and milk. Microwave on high for 3 minutes, stirring after 1-1/2 minutes. Stir until smooth. Proceed as directed.

BASIC DESSERT CREPES

These delightful crepes may be filled with fresh fruit, whipped cream, pudding, ice cream or pie filling. Use your imagination to create something new for your clan. Syrups or sauces may be drizzled over the top to add a different finishing touch.

> **1/2 cup milk**
> **1/2 cup water**
> **4 eggs**
> **1 teaspoon vanilla extract**
> **2 tablespoons butter *or* margarine, melted**
> **1 cup all-purpose flour**
> **2 teaspoons sugar**
> **1/2 teaspoon salt**

In a mixing bowl, combine milk, water, eggs, vanilla and butter. In a separate bowl, combine the flour, sugar and salt; add to milk mixture and mix well. Cover and refrigerate for 1 hour. Heat a lightly greased 8-in. nonstick skillet; pour 2 tablespoons batter into the center of skillet. Lift and tilt pan to evenly coat bottom. Cook until top appears dry; turn and cook 15-20 seconds longer. Remove to a wire rack. Repeat with remaining batter, adding butter to skillet as needed. When cool, stack crepes with waxed paper or paper towels in between. **Yield:** 18 crepes.

CREAMY RASPBERRY DESSERT

Do-ahead and delicious, this dessert is a favorite because of its pretty color, creamy texture and terrific flavor. A light, no-bake filling makes it easy. Try garnishing with fresh berries for a pretty look.

>   1 cup graham cracker crumbs
>   3 tablespoons sugar
> 1/4 cup butter *or* margarine, melted
> **FILLING:**
>   1 package (10 ounces) frozen raspberries, thawed
> 1/4 cup cold water
>   1 envelope unflavored gelatin
>   1 package (8 ounces) cream cheese, softened
> 1/2 cup sugar
>   1 cup whipping cream, whipped
> **Whipped cream and fresh raspberries**

Combine crumbs, sugar and butter. Press onto the bottom of an 8-in. or 9-in. springform pan. Bake at 350° for 10 minutes. Cool. Meanwhile, for filling, drain raspberries and reserve juice. Set berries aside. In a small saucepan, combine juice, cold water and gelatin. Let stand for 5 minutes. Cook and stir over low heat until gelatin dissolves. Remove from the heat; cool for 10 minutes. In a mixing bowl, beat cream cheese and sugar until blended. Add berries and gelatin mixture; beat on low until thoroughly blended. Chill until partially set. Watch carefully, as mixture will set quickly. By hand, gently fold in whipped cream. Spoon into the crust. Chill for 6 hours or overnight. Just before serving, run a knife around edge of pan to loosen. Remove sides of pan. Garnish with whipped cream and fresh raspberries. **Yield:** 10 servings.

CHERRY MACAROON PARFAITS

(Pictured above)

There's no better way to beat the summer heat than with a cool parfait. Keep this recipe in mind when unexpected company drops by or you just want to treat your family. It's as speedy as it is elegant.

>   1 package (3.4 ounces) instant vanilla pudding mix
>   3 cups cold milk
>   1 can (21 ounces) cherry pie filling
> 1/4 teaspoon almond extract
>   6 macaroon cookies, crumbled
> **Whipped topping, optional**

In a bowl, prepare pudding with milk according to package directions. In a small bowl, combine pie filling and almond extract. Alternate layers of pudding, crumbled cookies and fruit filling in parfait or dessert dishes. Garnish with whipped topping if desired. **Yield:** 6 servings.

BANANA SPLIT TRIFLE

Eyes will light up when you present this spectacular dessert. Each spoonful contains the luscious goodness of creamy pudding, vanilla wafers, juicy fruits and chewy coconut.

>   2 packages (3.4 ounces *each*) instant banana cream *or* vanilla pudding mix
>   3 cups cold milk
>   1 carton (16 ounces) vanilla yogurt
>   36 vanilla wafers
>   2 firm bananas, sliced
>   1 can (20 ounces) crushed pineapple, well drained
> 1/2 cup halved maraschino cherries, drained
>   1 cup flaked coconut

In a large mixing bowl, combine pudding mix and milk; beat 1 minute. Add yogurt; beat until smooth and thickened. Spoon 1-1/2 cups pudding mixture into a 2-qt. serving bowl. Top with 9 wafers and half of the banana slices. Top with half of the pineapple, cherries and coconut. Repeat all layers. Top with remaining pudding mixture. Place remaining wafers around edge of bowl. **Yield:** 8 servings.

BLUEBERRY COBBLER

Cobbler is best served warm about 45-60 minutes after removing from the oven. If desired, pour a little half-and-half cream over each serving.

        2 cans (14 ounces *each*) blueberries,
            undrained
        1 cup plus 1 tablespoon sugar, *divided*
    1/4 cup quick-cooking tapioca
    1/4 teaspoon salt
    1/2 teaspoon grated lemon peel
        2 tablespoons butter *or* margarine
    1/4 cup water
        1 cup biscuit/baking mix
    1/4 teaspoon ground cinnamon

Drain blueberries, reserving 1-1/2 cups liquid. Combine 1 cup sugar, tapioca and salt in a saucepan. Add blueberries, reserved liquid and lemon peel; let stand 5 minutes. Cook and stir over medium heat until mixture comes to a boil. Pour into a 9-in. square baking dish; dot with butter. In a bowl, stir water into biscuit mix; drop by teaspoonful onto hot blueberry mixture. Mix remaining sugar and cinnamon; sprinkle over top. Bake at 425° for 20-25 minutes or until filling is bubbly and a toothpick inserted in topping comes out clean. **Yield:** 8 servings.

CHOCOLATE AND
PEANUT BUTTER DIPPED APPLES

(Pictured at right)

You'll draw raves when you present a platter of these deliciously dipped apples at your next family gathering. These festive apples will add a tempting new twist to your next Halloween menu.

    10 to 12 medium apples, stems removed
    10 to 12 wooden ice cream sticks
        1 cup semisweet chocolate chips
        1 package (10 ounces) peanut butter chips,
            divided

        1/4 cup plus 2 tablespoons shortening (no substitutes), *divided*

Line a tray with wax paper. Wash apples; dry thoroughly. Insert wooden stick into each apple; place on prepared tray. In a medium microwave-safe bowl, combine chocolate chips, 2/3 cup peanut butter chips and 1/4 cup shortening. Microwave on high for 1 minute; stir. If necessary, microwave on high for an additional 30 seconds at a time or just until chips are melted when stirred, stirring after each heating. Dip bottom three-fourths of each apple into mixture. Twirl and gently shake to remove excess; return to prepared tray. In a small microwave-safe bowl, combine remaining 1 cup peanut butter chips and remaining 2 tablespoons shortening. Microwave on high for 30 seconds; stir. If necessary, microwave on high for an additional 15 seconds at a time or just until chips are melted when stirred, stirring after each heating. Spoon over the top of each apple, allowing to drip down sides. Refrigerate until serving. **Yield:** 10-12 servings.

WARM CARAMEL APPLE TOPPING

(Pictured below)

This versatile caramel topping is bound to become a most-requested recipe at your home. It deliciously captures the fabulous flavor of fall.

> 1 can (21 ounces) apple pie filling
> 1/2 cup caramel ice cream topping
> 1/3 cup orange juice
> 1/8 teaspoon ground nutmeg
> 1 quart vanilla ice cream *or* 6 slices pound cake
> Salted peanuts, optional

In a saucepan over low heat, simmer the pie filling, caramel topping, orange juice and nutmeg for 5 minutes or until heated through. Serve warm over ice cream or pound cake. Top with peanuts if desired. **Yield:** 2 cups topping (about 6 servings).

CHERRY TRIFLE

Trifle is a traditional English dessert containing layers of cake, pudding or custard and fruit or jam. Often it's topped with whipped cream and sprinkled with nuts. You'll love this cheery cherry version.

> 1 package (3.4 ounces) instant vanilla pudding mix
> 2 cups cold milk
> 1 loaf (10-3/4 ounces) frozen pound cake, thawed
> 1/4 cup orange juice
> 1 can (21 ounces) cherry pie filling, *divided*
> 1-1/2 cups whipped topping, *divided*
> 1/2 cup sliced almonds, toasted

Prepare pudding with milk according to package directions; let stand 5 minutes. Cut cake into 1/4-in. slices; brush slices with orange juice. Line bottom and sides of 2-qt. serving bowl or trifle dish with a third of the cake slices. Layer one half of the pudding, one third of the pie filling, one half of the whipped topping and one third of the cake slices. Repeat layers of cake, pudding and pie filling. Spread remaining whipped topping over top. Spoon remaining pie filling into center, leaving a 1-in. border. Sprinkle almonds around edge. Cover and refrigerate at least 4 hours or overnight. **Yield:** 8 servings.

BROWNIE PEANUT BUTTER CUPS

Children will adore these chocolaty brownie treats studded with colorful peanut butter candies. They're best served with a tall glass of cold milk.

> 1/3 cup creamy peanut butter
> 1/4 cup reduced-fat cream cheese, softened
> 2 tablespoons sugar
> 1 egg
> 1 package fudge brownie mix (13-inch x 9-inch pan size)
> 1/2 cup Reese's Pieces

In a small mixing bowl, beat together peanut butter, cream cheese, sugar and egg; set aside. Prepare brownie mix according to package directions. Place 1 heaping teaspoon of peanut butter mixture in the center of each foil-lined muffin cup. Fill cups half full with brownie batter. Sprinkle Reese's Pieces over brownie batter. Bake at 350° for 25 minutes; do not overbake. Cool in pan for 5 minutes before removing to a wire rack. **Yield:** 18 servings.

PEANUT BUTTER CHOCOLATE FUDGE

Homemade candy is fun to make, serve and give as a gift, especially around the holidays. Once you taste this foolproof fudge, you'll never buy the expensive store-bought variety again.

2 cups peanut butter chips, *divided*
1/2 cup butter *or* **margarine,** *divided*
1/2 cup baking cocoa
1 teaspoon vanilla extract
4-1/2 cups sugar
1 jar (7 ounces) marshmallow creme
1 can (12 ounces) evaporated milk

Place 1 cup peanut butter chips in a medium bowl; set aside. In a medium microwave-safe bowl, microwave 1/4 cup butter for 30 seconds or until melted. Stir in cocoa until smooth. Add remaining peanut butter chips and vanilla; set aside. In a heavy 4-qt. saucepan, combine sugar, marshmallow creme, evaporated milk and remaining butter. Cook and stir over medium heat until mixture comes to a full rolling boil 5 minutes, stirring constantly. Remove from heat. Immediately add 3 cups hot mixture to reserved peanut butter chips. Add remaining hot mixture to cocoa mixture. Stir both mixtures until smooth. Immediately spread peanut butter mixture into a foil-lined 13-in. x 9-in. x 2-in. baking pan. Spread cocoa mixture on top of peanut butter layer. Refrigerate for 2 hours or until firm. Lift from pan; remove foil. Cut into squares. **Yield:** 10 dozen.

Pecan Delights

(Pictured above right)

Just about everyone loves chocolate-covered turtles, so you'll find this recipe well worth the time in the kitchen. Why not make several batches and pack some pretty seasonal tins for gifts?

2-1/4 cups packed brown sugar
1 cup butter *or* **margarine**
1 cup light corn syrup
1/8 teaspoon salt
1 can (14 ounces) sweetened condensed milk
1 teaspoon vanilla extract
1-1/2 pounds pecan halves
1 cup (6 ounces) semisweet chocolate chips
1 cup milk chocolate chips
2 tablespoons shortening

In a large saucepan, combine the first four ingredients. Cook over medium heat until the brown sug-

ar is dissolved. Gradually add milk and mix well. Continue cooking until candy thermometer reads 248° (firm-ball stage). Remove from heat; stir in vanilla until blended. Fold in the pecans. Drop by tablespoons onto a greased waxed paper- or parchment-lined baking sheet. Chill until firm. Melt chocolate chips and shortening in a microwave-safe bowl or double boiler. Drizzle over each cluster. Cool. **Yield:** about 4 dozen.

Cherries and Chocolate Fudge

If you're making fudge for the first time or are in a hurry, this recipe is for you! It's surprisingly quick and easy to make, taking just minutes in the microwave.

1 can (14 ounces) sweetened condensed milk
1 package (12 ounces) semisweet chocolate chips
1/2 cup chopped almonds
1/2 cup chopped candied cherries
1 teaspoon almond extract

In a large microwave-safe bowl, combine milk and chips; microwave on high for 1-1/2 minutes; stir. Microwave at additional 10- to 20-second intervals, stirring until chips are melted and smooth. Stir in almonds, cherries and almond extract. Spread evenly in a foil-lined 9-in. square baking pan. Cover with plastic wrap and chill 2 hours or until firm. Lift from pan; remove foil. Cut into squares. **Yield:** 5 dozen.

erate at least 30 minutes before serving. Sprinkle with toffee bits. Garnish with sweetened whipped cream if desired. **Yield:** 8 servings.

FOR CHOCOLATE MOUSSE PIE:

Spoon mousse into a 9-in. graham cracker pie crust. Refrigerate about 3 hours. Garnish as desired.

FOR CHOCOLATE MOUSSE TORTE:

Cut a frozen pound cake (10-3/4 ounces) horizontally to make 3 or 4 layers. Place bottom layer on a serving plate. Spread with mousse. Repeat layering. Cover top and sides of torte with remaining mousse. Refrigerate about 2 hours or until serving. Garnish as desired.

BAKED APPLES

When the autumn winds begin to blow, this wonderfully easy recipe is a cinch to prepare. If you prefer, bake the apples earlier in the day and reheat in the microwave just until warm.

> 6 large tart apples
> 2 tablespoons lemon juice
> 1 cup chopped dates
> 1/2 teaspoon ground cinnamon
> 1/4 cup water
> 1 cup maple syrup

Core apples and remove a 1-in. strip of peel around top of each to prevent apples from splitting. Brush tops and inside with lemon juice. In a small bowl, combine dates and cinnamon; fill the center of each apple with mixture. Place filled apples in a 2-qt. baking dish. Pour water in bottom of dish. Pour syrup over apples. Bake at 350° for 45-50 minutes or until apples are tender, spooning syrup mixture over apples occasionally during baking. **Yield:** 6 servings.

MAGIC MOUSSE

(Pictured above)

Decadent desserts create magic at the end of a meal! Chocolate lovers will enjoy this delightfully sweet mousse. It has a unique melt-in-your-mouth texture that people can't seem to resist. Plus, it's no fuss to fix and impressive to serve.

> 1 envelope unflavored gelatin
> 2 tablespoons cold water
> 1/4 cup boiling water
> 1 cup sugar
> 1/2 cup baking cocoa
> 2 cups cold whipping cream
> 2 teaspoons vanilla extract

English toffee bits *or* brickle bits
Sweetened whipped cream, optional

In a small bowl, sprinkle gelatin over cold water; let stand 2 minutes to soften. Add boiling water; stir until gelatin is completely dissolved and mixture is clear. Cool slightly. In a large mixing bowl, mix sugar and cocoa; add whipping cream and vanilla. Beat on medium speed, scraping bottom of bowl occasionally, until stiff peaks form. Pour in gelatin mixture; beat until well blended. Spoon into dessert dishes. Refrig-

TOLL HOUSE FAMOUS FUDGE

When you get the urge for a piece of candy, why not make your own? This rich and creamy fudge can be made with semisweet, milk chocolate or butterscotch morsels, so choose your favorite flavor. To make the recipe even more special, substitute cashews or macadamia nuts for the pecans.

1-1/2 cups sugar
  2/3 cup evaporated milk
    2 tablespoons butter *or* margarine
  1/4 teaspoon salt
    2 cups miniature marshmallows
1-1/2 cups semisweet chocolate morsels *or* 1-3/4 cups milk chocolate morsels *or* 1-2/3 cups butterscotch morsels

1 teaspoon vanilla extract
1/2 cup chopped pecans *or* walnuts, optional

In a medium heavy-duty saucepan, combine the sugar, evaporated milk, butter and salt. Bring mixture to a boil over medium heat, stirring constantly. Boil, stirring constantly, for 4-5 minutes. Remove from heat. Stir in the marshmallows, morsels, vanilla and nuts if desired. Stir vigorously for 1 minute or until the marshmallows are melted. Pour into a foil-lined 8-in. square baking pan; refrigerate for 2 hours or until firm. Lift from pan; remove foil. Cut into squares. **Yield:** 5 dozen.

LIGHTNING MICROWAVE FUDGE

This candy recipe is easy and ready in a flash. The kids could help by lining the pan with foil, measuring ingredients and stirring the fudge until smooth.

3-2/3 cups confectioners' sugar
1/2 cup baking cocoa
1/2 cup butter *or* margarine, cut into pieces
1/4 cup milk
1 tablespoon vanilla extract
1/2 cup chopped nuts, optional

In a large microwave-safe bowl, combine the sugar, cocoa, butter and milk; microwave on high for 2-3 minutes or until butter is melted. Stir until mixture is smooth. Stir in the vanilla and nuts if desired; blend well. Spread mixture evenly in a foil-lined 8-in. square baking pan. Chill for several hours or until firm. Lift from pan; remove foil. Cut into squares. **Yield:** 5 dozen.

CHERRY DESSERT TOPPING

You can serve this ruby-red dessert sauce over ice cream, angel food cake or pound cake with tasty results. It's also an outstanding filling for Basic Dessert Crepes on page 255.

1 can (16 ounces) water-packed pitted red
    sour cherries
1/2 cup sugar
4-1/2 teaspoons quick-cooking tapioca
1/8 teaspoon salt

Drain cherries, reserving liquid and adding water if necessary to equal 3/4 cup. Combine sugar, tapioca and salt in saucepan. Add cherries and measured liquid; let stand 5 minutes. Cook and stir over medium heat until mixture comes to a full boil, about 6-8 minutes. Let stand 20 minutes to thicken. Serve warm or chilled. **Yield:** 1-1/2 cups.

CHOCOLATE CHERRY SQUARES

(Pictured below)

Many dessert lovers agree that nothing can top the tempting combination of chocolate and cherries. And with this simple recipe, you can present your family and friends with that delicious duo in a flash.

1 cup butter *or* margarine, softened
1-3/4 cups sugar
1/2 teaspoon vanilla extract
1/4 teaspoon almond extract
4 eggs
2 cups all-purpose flour
6 tablespoons baking cocoa
1 can (21 ounces) cherry pie filling, *divided*
Confectioners' sugar, optional

In a large mixing bowl, beat butter, sugar and extracts. Add eggs; beat on medium speed for 2 minutes. Combine flour and cocoa; gradually add to butter mixture, beating until blended. Spread batter in a greased 13-in. x 9-in. x 2-in. baking pan. Spoon 12 dollops of pie filling over batter in three rows of four, using about 1 tablespoon per dollop. Bake at 350° for 30-35 minutes or until top springs back when touched lightly in center. Cool; sprinkle with confectioners' sugar if desired. Cut into squares; serve with remaining pie filling. **Yield:** 12 servings.

CRANBERRY APPLE CRISP

(*Pictured below*)

An attractive and unique dessert, this crisp is also a popular side dish served with pork or poultry.

> 3 cups peeled and sliced tart apples
> 2 cups fresh cranberries
> 36 packets sugar substitute, *divided*
> 1/3 cup all-purpose flour
> 1/4 cup chopped pecans
> 1/4 cup butter *or* margarine, melted

In an ungreased 9-in. pie plate, combine apples, cranberries and 24 packets sugar substitute. In a separate bowl, combine flour, pecans, butter and remaining sugar substitute. Sprinkle mixture over the top of the apples and cranberries. Bake at 350° for 50 minutes or until bubbly and lightly browned. **Yield:** 8 servings.

CHOCOLATE YOGURT CREAM PUDDING

Light and luscious, this low-fat chocolate dessert tastes as good as it looks. Its silky texture is hard to resist.

> 1 cup sugar
> 1/3 cup baking cocoa
> 1 envelope unflavored gelatin
> 1-1/3 cups 2% milk
> 2 cups reduced-fat vanilla yogurt
> 1 teaspoon vanilla extract
> Raspberries *or* sliced fresh strawberries

In a saucepan, combine sugar, cocoa and gelatin. Gradually stir in milk; let stand 5 minutes. Cook over medium heat, stirring constantly, until mixture comes to boil and gelatin is dissolved. Cool slightly. Add yogurt and vanilla; blend gently until well combined. Pour into dessert dishes. Refrigerate 6 hours or until set. Top with fruit. **Yield:** 8 servings.

HILL 'N' DALE CANDY

For munching or gift-giving, this chocolate snack is chock-full of fluffy marshmallows and crunchy nuts. If you prefer clusters, drop mixture by teaspoonfuls onto waxed paper, then chill until set.

> 1 cup (6 ounces) semisweet chocolate
> morsels
> 1 cup butterscotch morsels
> 2 cups miniature marshmallows
> 1 cup chopped walnuts

In a large microwave-safe bowl, microwave chocolate and butterscotch morsels on medium-high for 1-1/2 minutes; stir. Microwave at additional 10- to 20-second intervals, stirring until smooth. Add marshmallows and walnuts; stir. Spread evenly into a buttered and foil-lined 8-in. square baking pan. Chill for 1 hour or until firm. Turn out of pan and remove foil. Cut into 1-in. squares. **Yield:** 2 dozen.

CARAMEL-GLAZED FLAN

(Pictured at right)

Elegant caramel flan is a custard baked over caramelized sugar. When the cooked and cooled flan is inverted onto a serving platter, the delicious caramel sauce runs over the flan. Though the dessert looks impressive, it's actually rather easy to prepare.

- 3/4 cup sugar
- 4 eggs
- 1-3/4 cups water
- 1 can (14 ounces) sweetened condensed milk
- 1/2 teaspoon vanilla extract
- 1/8 teaspoon salt

In a heavy skillet over medium-low heat, cook sugar, stirring constantly, until melted and caramel-colored. Pour into a 9-in. round dish or baking pan, tilting to coat bottom completely. In a medium bowl, beat eggs; stir in water, condensed milk, vanilla and salt. Pour over caramelized sugar; set pan in larger pan. Fill larger pan with 1-in. hot water. Bake at 350° for 55-60 minutes or until center is just set (mixture will jiggle). Remove dish from larger pan to a wire rack; cool for 1 hour. Refrigerate several hours or overnight. To unmold, run a knife around edge and invert onto a large rimmed serving platter. **Yield:** 8 servings.

COFFEE-SCOTCH FUDGE

Butterscotch is a blend of butter and brown sugar, making it a popular choice for cookies, ice cream toppings, candies and frosting. This fudge is highlighted with a splash of coffee, providing a pleasing flavor combination.

- 2 cups butterscotch morsels
- 1 tablespoon instant coffee granules
- 1 teaspoon boiling water
- 2/3 cup sweetened condensed milk
- 1/2 cup chopped salted peanuts

In a large microwave-safe bowl, microwave the morsels on medium-high for 1-1/2 minutes; stir. Microwave at additional 10- to 20-second intervals, stirring until smooth; set aside. In a small bowl, dissolve the coffee granules in boiling water. Add the condensed milk and mix well. Blend the coffee mixture into melted morsels. Stir in peanuts. Pour into a lightly greased, foil-lined 8-in. square baking pan. Refrigerate for 1 hour or until firm. Lift from pan; remove foil. Cut into 1-in. squares. Keep refrigerated until serving. **Yield:** 5 dozen.

CREAMY DOUBLE-DECKER FUDGE

The combination of chocolate and peanut butter creates a taste sensation that's hard to beat. This pretty candy will add a festive touch to your cookie and candy tray during the holidays.

- 1 cup peanut butter chips
- 1 can (14 ounces) sweetened condensed milk, *divided*
- 1 teaspoon vanilla extract, *divided*
- 1 cup (6 ounces) semisweet chocolate chips

In a bowl, combine peanut butter morsels and 2/3 cup condensed milk. Microwave on high for 1 to 1-1/2 minutes or until morsels are melted and mixture is smooth when stirred. Stir in 1/2 teaspoon vanilla; spread evenly into a foil-lined 8-in. square baking pan. Microwave remaining condensed milk and chocolate morsels on high 1 to 1-1/2 minutes as above. Stir in remaining vanilla; spread evenly over peanut butter layer. Cover; refrigerate until firm. Cut into 1-in. squares. Store in tightly covered container in refrigerator. **Yield:** 1-1/2 pounds.

INDIVIDUAL CHOCOLATE ESPRESSO SOUFFLES

(Pictured above)

Souffles get their airy texture from egg whites that have been stiffly beaten. They're customarily baked in a straight-sided souffle dish. Since souffles begin to deflate soon after being removed from the oven, they must be served immediately.

 2 tablespoons plus 3/4 cup sugar, *divided*
 1/2 cup baking cocoa
 1/2 cup hot water
 3 tablespoons instant coffee granules
 2 tablespoons butter *or* **margarine**
 3 tablespoons all-purpose flour
 3/4 cup fat-free evaporated milk
 4 egg whites
Pinch salt
Confectioners' sugar

Spray eight 6-ounce custard cups with nonstick cooking spray; sprinkle evenly with 2 tablespoons sugar. In a medium bowl, combine cocoa, water and coffee granules; stir until smooth. Melt butter in a small saucepan over medium heat. Stir in flour; cook, stirring constantly, for 1 minute. Stir in evaporated milk and 1/2 cup sugar. Cook, whisking frequently, for 2-3 minutes or until mixture is slightly thickened. Remove from heat. Add to cocoa mixture; stir until smooth. In a small mixing bowl, beat egg whites and a pinch of salt until soft peaks form. Gradually beat in remaining sugar until stiff peaks form. Fold one-fourth of egg whites into chocolate mixture to lighten. Fold in remaining egg whites.

Pour mixture into prepared cups, filling 3/4 full. Place on baking sheet. Bake at 375° for 18-20 minutes or until toothpick inserted in center comes out moist but not wet. Sprinkle with confectioners' sugar. Serve immediately. **Yield:** 8 servings.

FLUFFY TAPIOCA CREAM

Just what is tapioca? It's a starchy substance that's extracted from the root of the cassava plant. It's processed into granules, pellets and flours that are used to thicken everything from soup to pie filling. This yummy pudding is the best use we know of!

 3 tablespoons quick-cooking tapioca
 1/8 teaspoon salt
 5 tablespoons sugar, *divided*
 2 cups milk
 1 egg, *separated*
 3/4 teaspoon vanilla extract

Mix tapioca, salt, 3 tablespoons sugar, milk and egg yolk in a saucepan. Let stand 5 minutes. Meanwhile, beat egg white until foamy; gradually beat in remaining sugar and continue beating until mixture forms soft rounded peaks; set aside. Cook tapioca mixture over medium heat, stirring constantly until mixture comes to a full boil, 6-8 minutes. (Pudding will thicken as it cools.) Gradually add tapioca mixture to egg white mixture, stirring quickly just until blended. Stir in vanilla. Cool 20 minutes; stir. Serve warm or chilled. **Yield:** 4 servings.

CHOCO-ORANGE FLUFF

Cool and refreshing, this velvety chocolate pudding is accented with a hint of orange flavor. It's a low-fat favorite family and friends are sure to enjoy.

 1 envelope unflavored gelatin
 1/3 cup sugar
 1/4 cup baking cocoa
2-1/2 cups fat-free milk, *divided*
 1 teaspoon vanilla extract
 1/8 to 1/4 teaspoon orange extract
 1 envelope whipped topping mix
Fresh orange wedges, optional

In a medium saucepan, combine gelatin, sugar and cocoa. Stir in 2 cups milk; let stand 2 minutes. Cook over medium heat, stirring constantly, until gelatin is completely dissolved, about 5 minutes. Pour mixture into a medium bowl; stir in vanilla and orange extract. Refrigerate, stirring occasionally, until mixture mounds slightly when dropped from spoon.

Blend whipped topping mix and remaining milk in a small mixing bowl. Beat on high about 4 minutes or until topping thickens. Measure 1-1/2 cups; refrigerate remaining topping. Add 1-1/2 cups whipped topping to cocoa mixture; beat with wire whisk until blended. Spoon into dessert dishes. Refrigerate 3-4 hours or until set. Garnish with reserved whipped topping and orange wedges. **Yield:** 8 servings.

PEANUT BUTTER APPLE CRISP

Turn a simple meal into a special occasion by serving this appealing apple dish for dessert. The lovely streusel topping adds spicy cinnamon flavor and delightful texture.

    4 cups sliced peeled apples
    3/4 cup packed brown sugar
    1/2 cup all-purpose flour
    1/2 cup quick-cooking oats
    1/2 teaspoon ground cinnamon
    1/2 teaspoon ground nutmeg
    1/3 cup butter *or* margarine, softened
    1 cup peanut butter chips
Sweetened whipped cream, optional

Place apple slices in a greased 8- or 9-in. square baking dish. Combine brown sugar, flour, oats, cinnamon and nutmeg; cut in butter until crumbly. Stir in chips; sprinkle mixture over apples. Bake at 375° for 25-30 minutes or until topping is golden brown and apples are tender. Serve warm with whipped cream if desired. **Yield:** 6 servings.

TOASTED S'MORE SQUARES

(Pictured at right)

You don't have to go camping to enjoy the great taste of s'mores. You can whip up a batch of these tempting bars in your kitchen anytime, and you don't have to put up with mosquitoes!

    9 honey graham crackers, broken in half to
      make 18 squares, *divided*
    1 package (10 ounces) marshmallows,
      cut in half, *divided*
    1 cup (6 ounces) semisweet chocolate morsels

Arrange 9 graham cracker squares in a single layer on bottom of 9-in. square baking pan. Top with 36 marshmallow halves; sprinkle evenly with chocolate morsels. Top with remaining graham crackers. Arrange four marshmallow halves, cut side down, on top of each graham cracker. Bake at 350° for 9-11 minutes or until marshmallows are puffed and golden brown. Let stand 5 minutes. Cut into squares with a greased knife. Serve immediately. **Yield:** 9 squares.

RICE AMBROSIA

When you're stuck for ideas on how to use leftover rice, turn to this unique recipe. Full of old-fashioned flavor, this fruity pudding is ready in no time.

    2 cups cooked rice, chilled
    1 can (20 ounces) pineapple chunks, drained
    1/2 cup chopped maraschino cherries
    1/4 cup slivered almonds, toasted
    1 cup marshmallow creme
    1 cup whipping cream, *divided*

In a bowl, combine rice, pineapple, cherries and almonds. Combine marshmallow creme and 2 tablespoons whipping cream; mix until well blended. Whip remaining cream until stiff; fold into marshmallow mixture. Fold marshmallow mixture into rice mixture. Chill. **Yield:** 8 servings.

STRAWBERRY PEACH TRIFLE

(Pictured at left)

If you're looking to serve a lighter dessert, you'll appreciate this tasty trifle recipe. You can easily substitute raspberries for the strawberries—or sprinkle in some blueberries, too, if you have them on hand. You'll want to make it in a clear glass bowl or trifle dish to show off its fabulous colors.

 3 cups cold fat-free milk
 2 packages (1 ounce *each*) instant
  sugar-free white chocolate pudding mix
 1 prepared angel food cake (14 ounces),
  cut into 1-inch cubes
 3 cups sliced fresh strawberries
 2 cups fresh *or* frozen sliced unsweetened
  peaches
 1 carton (8 ounces) reduced-fat frozen
  whipped topping, thawed
Additional sliced fresh strawberries

In a mixing bowl, combine milk and pudding mixes. Beat on low speed for 2 minutes. Place a third of the cake cubes in a trifle bowl or 3-1/2-qt. glass serving bowl. Top with a third of the pudding, 1 cup of strawberries, 1 cup of peaches and a third of the whipped topping. Layer a third of the cake, a third of the pudding, 1 cup strawberries and a third of the whipped topping. Top with the remaining cake, pudding, strawberries, peaches and whipped topping. Garnish with additional sliced strawberries. **Yield:** 14 servings.

CHOCOLATE HONEY RAISIN CHEWS

These chewy candies are popular with home cooks because they are so easy to make. There's no cooking…just mix together and chill. The recipe contains sweet raisins and crunchy nuts blended with creamy peanut butter and a touch of honey.

   1 cup peanut butter
  1/2 cup confectioners' sugar
  1/2 cup baking cocoa
  1/2 cup honey
   1 teaspoon vanilla extract
   1 cup raisins
1-1/3 cups chopped nuts *or* shredded coconut
   or crushed cereal

In a bowl, combine peanut butter, sugar, cocoa, honey and vanilla; mix well. Stir in raisins. Form mixture into 1-1/4-in. balls. Roll in nuts, coconut or cereal until covered. Chill 2-3 hours. Store, covered, in the refrigerator. **Yield:** 3 dozen.

Luscious Banana Brittle Crepe Filling

Centuries ago, crepes were created in Brittany, the northwest region of France. Similar to pancakes, crepes started out as a type of bread. Eventually they were filled with savory or sweet fillings. After a surge in popularity in the 1970s, crepes have remained a menu item across the country.

> 3 ripe bananas, sliced
> 1 cup miniature marshmallows
> 1 cup crushed peanut brittle, *divided*
> 1 cup whipping cream, whipped, *divided*
> Basic Dessert Crepes (page 255)

In a large bowl, combine bananas, marshmallows, half of the peanut brittle and half of the whipped cream. Spoon mixture down the center of prepared crepes; roll up. Place 2 filled crepes, seam side down, on each serving plate. Top with remaining whipped cream and peanut brittle. **Yield:** 4 servings.

Custard Rice Pudding

Rice pudding is a wonderful, old-fashioned dessert. Simple ingredients that most cooks always have on hand create a creamy, warm concoction that fits the bill during comfort-food cravings.

> 1/2 cup uncooked long-grain rice
> 3 cups milk
> 1/4 teaspoon salt
> 4 eggs
> 3/4 cup sugar
> 2 teaspoons vanilla extract
> 1/2 teaspoon ground nutmeg

In a 4-qt. saucepan over medium heat, bring rice, milk and salt to a boil. Reduce heat to low. Cover; simmer 30 minutes or until rice is tender, stirring occasionally. Meanwhile, in a medium bowl, beat together eggs, sugar and vanilla. With wooden spoon, gradually stir beaten egg mixture into rice. Heat just to boiling, stirring constantly. Serve warm or cold. Spoon into dessert dishes; sprinkle with nutmeg. **Yield:** 3-1/2 cups.

Peach Cobbler

The name "cobbler" comes from the expression "cobble-up," meaning to put together fast. This tempting cobbler is a quick version of a deep-dish pie. The shortcake-like dough is spooned over the peaches, so you save the time and inconvenience of rolling out a pie crust, yet preserve the wonderful flavor.

> 4 cups thinly sliced, peeled fresh peaches
> 6 tablespoons sugar, *divided*
> 1 tablespoon cornstarch
> 1 cup all-purpose flour
> 1-1/2 teaspoons baking powder
> 1/2 teaspoon salt
> 1/4 cup butter *or* margarine
> 1/3 cup milk
> 1 egg, beaten

In an 11-in. x 7-in. x 2-in. baking dish, combine peaches, 4 tablespoons sugar and cornstarch; set aside. In a medium bowl, combine the flour, baking powder, salt and remaining sugar. With pastry blender or 2 knives, cut in butter until mixture resembles coarse crumbs. Stir in milk and egg to form a soft dough. Drop dough in 6 equal portions on top of peaches. Bake at 350° for 40 minutes or until topping is golden. Serve warm or cold. **Yield:** 6 servings.

Mocha Bread Pudding

Mocha generally refers to the popular flavor combination of coffee and chocolate. In this recipe, bread cubes are saturated with a sweet custard mixture that has been flavored with cocoa and instant coffee granules. Because it uses reduced-fat and fat-free ingredients, this light dessert will even please the waist-watchers in your clan.

> 1/4 cup sugar
> 2 tablespoons baking cocoa
> 2 teaspoons instant coffee granules
> 3-1/2 cups cubed French bread
> 1-1/2 cups (12 ounces) evaporated fat-free milk
> 2 eggs
> 1 teaspoon vanilla extract
> Confectioners' sugar, optional
> Reduced-fat frozen whipped topping, thawed
> Fresh raspberries, optional

In a small bowl, combine sugar, cocoa and coffee granules. Place bread cubes in a greased 8-in. square baking dish. In a medium bowl, beat evaporated milk, eggs and vanilla until well blended; stir in sugar mixture. Pour over bread, pressing bread into mixture. Place the square dish in a 13-in. x 9-in. x 2-in. baking dish; fill the larger dish with warm water to 1-in. depth. Bake at 350° for 30-35 minutes or until set. Sprinkle lightly with confectioners' sugar if desired. Top each serving with whipped topping. Garnish with raspberries if desired. Serve warm. **Yield:** 4-6 servings.

CHOCOLATE ECLAIRS

(*Pictured above*)

With creamy filling and fudgy frosting, these eclairs are extra special. People are thrilled when these finger-licking-good treats appear on the dessert table.

- 1 cup water
- 1/2 cup butter *or* margarine
- 1 cup all-purpose flour
- 1/4 teaspoon salt
- 4 eggs

FILLING:
- 1 package (5.1 ounces) instant vanilla pudding mix
- 2-1/2 cups cold milk
- 1 cup whipping cream
- 1/4 cup confectioners' sugar
- 1 teaspoon vanilla extract

FROSTING:
- 2 squares (1 ounce *each*) semisweet chocolate
- 2 tablespoons butter *or* margarine
- 1-1/4 cups confectioners' sugar
- 2 to 3 tablespoons hot water

In a saucepan, bring water and butter to a boil, stirring constantly until butter melts. Reduce heat to low; add the flour and salt. Stir vigorously with a wooden spoon until mixture leaves sides of pan and forms a smooth ball. Remove from the heat; add eggs, one at a time, beating well after each addition until batter becomes smooth. Using a tablespoon or a pastry tube with a No. 10 or larger tip, form dough into 4-in. x 1-1/2-in. strips on a greased baking sheet. Bake at 400° for 35-40 minutes or until puffed and golden. Immediately cut a slit in each to allow steam to escape. Cool on a wire rack. In a mixing bowl, beat pudding mix and milk according to package directions. In another mixing bowl, whip the cream until soft peaks form. Beat in sugar and vanilla; fold into pudding. Split eclairs; remove soft dough from inside. Fill eclairs (chill any remaining filling for another use). For frosting, melt chocolate and butter in a saucepan over low heat. Stir in sugar and enough hot water to achieve a smooth consistency. Cool slightly. Frost eclairs. Store in the refrigerator. **Yield:** 9 servings.

APPLE TURNOVERS WITH CUSTARD

Today, baking is easier than ever. Cooks can assemble turnovers from pie crust mixes, refrigerated dough, frozen pastry and canned pie fillings. But by rolling out pastry and filling a crust with fresh fruit, we can feel a kinship with Colonial women who did it all from scratch more than 200 years ago.

CUSTARD:
- 1/3 cup sugar
- 2 tablespoons cornstarch
- 2 cups milk *or* half-and-half cream
- 3 egg yolks, lightly beaten
- 1 tablespoon vanilla extract

TURNOVERS:
- 4 medium baking apples, peeled and cut into 1/4-inch slices
- 1 tablespoon lemon juice
- 2 tablespoons butter *or* margarine, diced
- 1/3 cup sugar
- 3/4 teaspoon ground cinnamon
- 1 tablespoon cornstarch

Pastry for double-crust pie
Milk

Combine sugar and cornstarch in a saucepan. Stir in milk until smooth. Cook and stir over medium-high heat until thickened and bubbly. Reduce heat; cook and stir for 2 minutes. Remove from heat; stir 1 cup into yolks. Return all to pan. Bring to a gentle boil; cook and stir for 2 minutes. Remove from heat; stir in vanilla. Cool slightly. Cover surface of custard with waxed paper; chill. Place apples in a bowl; sprinkle with lemon juice. Add butter. Combine sugar, cinnamon and cornstarch; mix with apples and set aside. Divide pastry into eight portions; roll each into a 5-in. square. Spoon filling off-center on each. Brush edges with milk. Fold over to form a triangle; seal. Crimp with tines of fork. Make steam vents in top. Place on greased baking sheets. Chill 15 minutes. Brush with milk. Bake at 400° for 35 minutes. Serve warm with custard. **Yield:** 8 servings.

WATERMELON BOMBE

You might not think of watermelon as a dessert. This one is! Sherbet is molded to look like actual watermelon slices—complete with "seeds"—when cut. It is fun to eat and refreshing, too.

About 1 pint lime sherbet
About 1 pint pineapple sherbet
About 1-1/2 pints raspberry sherbet
  1/4 cup miniature semisweet chocolate chips

Line a 1-1/2-qt. metal mixing bowl with plastic wrap. Press slightly softened lime sherbet against the bottom and sides of bowl. Freeze, uncovered, until firm. Spread pineapple sherbet evenly over lime sherbet layer. Freeze, uncovered, until firm. (Lime and pineapple sherbet layers should be thin.) Pack raspberry sherbet in center of sherbet-lined bowl. Smooth the top to resemble a cut watermelon. Cover and freeze until firm, about 8 hours. Just before serving, uncover bowl of molded sherbet. Place a serving plate on the bowl and invert. Remove bowl and peel off plastic wrap. Cut the bombe into wedges; press a few chocolate morsels into the raspberry section of each wedge to resemble watermelon seeds. **Yield:** 8 servings.

ORANGE CHARLOTTE

(Pictured at right)

On sunny summer days, give your meal a fresh-tasting finish with this light and fluffy citrus dessert.

  3 envelopes unflavored gelatin
3/4 cup cold water

  3/4 cup boiling water
1-1/2 cups orange juice
  2 tablespoons lemon juice
1-1/2 teaspoons grated orange peel
1-1/2 cups sugar, *divided*
2-1/2 cups whipping cream
  1/2 cup mandarin oranges
  3 maraschino cherries

In a large bowl, combine gelatin and cold water; let stand for 10 minutes. Add boiling water; stir until gelatin dissolves. Add juices, orange peel and 3/4 cup sugar. Set bowl in ice water until mixture is syrupy, stirring occasionally. Meanwhile, whip cream until soft peaks form. Gradually add remaining sugar and beat until stiff peaks form. When gelatin mixture begins to thicken, fold in whipped cream. Lightly coat a 9-in. springform pan with nonstick cooking spray. Pour mixture into pan; chill overnight. Just before serving, run a knife around the edge of pan to loosen. Remove sides of pan. Garnish with oranges and cherries. **Yield:** 10-12 servings.

Substitutions & Equivalents

Equivalent Measures

3 teaspoons	= 1 tablespoon		16 tablespoons	= 1 cup	
4 tablespoons	= 1/4 cup		2 cups	= 1 pint	
5-1/3 tablespoons	= 1/3 cup		4 cups	= 1 quart	
8 tablespoons	= 1/2 cup		4 quarts	= 1 gallon	

Food Equivalents

Grains

Macaroni	1 cup (3-1/2 ounces) uncooked	= 2-1/2 cups cooked
Noodles, Medium	3 cups (4 ounces) uncooked	= 4 cups cooked
Popcorn	1/3 to 1/2 cup unpopped	= 8 cups popped
Rice, Long Grain	1 cup uncooked	= 3 cups cooked
Rice, Quick-Cooking	1 cup uncooked	= 2 cups cooked
Spaghetti	8 ounces uncooked	= 4 cups cooked

Crumbs

Bread	1 slice	= 3/4 cup soft crumbs, 1/4 cup fine dry crumbs
Graham Crackers	7 squares	= 1/2 cup finely crushed
Buttery Round Crackers	12 crackers	= 1/2 cup finely crushed
Saltine Crackers	14 crackers	= 1/2 cup finely crushed

Fruits

Bananas	1 medium	= 1/3 cup mashed
Lemons	1 medium	= 3 tablespoons juice, 2 teaspoons grated peel
Limes	1 medium	= 2 tablespoons juice, 1-1/2 teaspoons grated peel
Oranges	1 medium	= 1/4 to 1/3 cup juice, 4 teaspoons grated peel

Vegetables

Cabbage	1 head	= 5 cups shredded	Green Pepper	1 large	= 1 cup chopped
Carrots	1 pound	= 3 cups shredded	Mushrooms	1/2 pound	= 3 cups sliced
Celery	1 rib	= 1/2 cup chopped	Onions	1 medium	= 1/2 cup chopped
Corn	1 ear fresh	= 2/3 cup kernels	Potatoes	3 medium	= 2 cups cubed

Nuts

Almonds	1 pound	= 3 cups chopped	Pecan Halves	1 pound	= 4-1/2 cups chopped
Ground Nuts	3-3/4 ounces	= 1 cup	Walnuts	1 pound	= 3-3/4 cups chopped

Easy Substitutions

When you need...		Use...
Baking Powder	1 teaspoon	1/2 teaspoon cream of tartar + 1/4 teaspoon baking soda
Buttermilk	1 cup	1 tablespoon lemon juice *or* vinegar + enough milk to measure 1 cup (let stand 5 minutes before using)
Cornstarch	1 tablespoon	2 tablespoons all-purpose flour
Honey	1 cup	1-1/4 cups sugar + 1/4 cup water
Half-and-Half Cream	1 cup	1 tablespoon melted butter + enough whole milk to measure 1 cup
Onion	1 small, chopped (1/3 cup)	1 teaspoon onion powder *or* 1 tablespoon dried minced onion
Tomato Juice	1 cup	1/2 cup tomato sauce + 1/2 cup water
Tomato Sauce	2 cups	3/4 cup tomato paste + 1 cup water
Unsweetened Chocolate	1 square (1 ounce)	3 tablespoons baking cocoa + 1 tablespoon shortening *or* oil
Whole Milk	1 cup	1/2 cup evaporated milk + 1/2 cup water

Cooking Terms

HERE'S a quick reference for some of the cooking terms used in *Taste of Home* Cooking School recipes:

Baste—To moisten food with melted butter, pan drippings, marinades or other liquid to add more flavor and juiciness.

Beat—A rapid movement to combine ingredients using a fork, spoon, wire whisk or electric mixer.

Blend—To combine ingredients until *just* mixed.

Boil—To heat liquids until bubbles form that cannot be "stirred down". In the case of water, the temperature will reach 212°.

Bone—To remove all meat from the bone before cooking.

Cream—To beat ingredients together to a smooth consistency, usually in the case of butter and sugar for baking.

Dash—A small amount of seasoning, less than 1/8 teaspoon. If using a shaker, a dash would comprise a quick flip of the container.

Dredge—To coat foods with flour or other dry ingredients. Most often done with pot roasts and stew meat before browning.

Fold—To incorporate several ingredients by careful and gentle turning with a spatula. Used generally with beaten egg whites or whipped cream when mixing into the rest of the ingredients to keep the batter light.

Julienne—To cut foods into long thin strips much like matchsticks. Used most often for salads and stir-fry dishes.

Mince—To cut into very fine pieces. Used often for garlic or fresh herbs.

Parboil—To cook partially, usually used in the case of chicken, sausages and vegetables.

Partially set—Describes the consistency of gelatin after it has been chilled for a small amount of time. Mixture should resemble the consistency of egg whites.

Puree—To process foods to a smooth mixture. Can be prepared in an electric blender, food processor, food mill or sieve.

Saute—To fry quickly in a small amount of fat, stirring almost constantly. Most often done with onions, mushrooms and other chopped vegetables.

Score—To cut slits partway through the outer surface of foods. Often used with ham or flank steak.

Stir-Fry—To cook meats and/or vegetables with a constant stirring motion in a small amount of oil in a wok or skillet over high heat.

Guide to Cooking with Popular Herbs

HERB	APPETIZERS SALADS	BREADS/EGGS SAUCES/CHEESE	VEGETABLES PASTA	MEAT POULTRY	FISH SHELLFISH
BASIL	Green, Potato & Tomato Salads, Salad Dressings, Stewed Fruit	Breads, Fondue & Egg Dishes, Dips, Marinades, Sauces	Mushrooms, Tomatoes, Squash, Pasta, Bland Vegetables	Broiled, Roast Meat & Poultry Pies, Stews, Stuffing	Baked, Broiled & Poached Fish, Shellfish
BAY LEAF	Seafood Cocktail, Seafood Salad, Tomato Aspic, Stewed Fruit	Egg Dishes, Gravies, Marinades, Sauces	Dried Bean Dishes, Beets, Carrots, Onions, Potatoes, Rice, Squash	Corned Beef, Tongue Meat & Poultry Stews	Poached Fish, Shellfish, Fish Stews
CHIVES	Mixed Vegetable, Green, Potato & Tomato Salads, Salad Dressings	Egg & Cheese Dishes, Cream Cheese, Cottage Cheese, Gravies, Sauces	Hot Vegetables, Potatoes	Broiled Poultry, Poultry & Meat Pies, Stews, Casseroles	Baked Fish, Fish Casseroles, Fish Stews, Shellfish
DILL	Seafood Cocktail, Green, Potato & Tomato Salads, Salad Dressings	Breads, Egg & Cheese Dishes, Cream Cheese, Fish & Meat Sauces	Beans, Beets, Cabbage, Carrots, Cauliflower, Peas, Squash, Tomatoes	Beef, Veal Roasts, Lamb, Steaks, Chops, Stews, Roast & Creamed Poultry	Baked, Broiled, Poached & Stuffed Fish, Shellfish
GARLIC	All Salads, Salad Dressings	Fondue, Poultry Sauces, Fish & Meat Marinades	Beans, Eggplant, Potatoes, Rice, Tomatoes	Roast Meats, Meat & Poultry Pies, Hamburgers, Casseroles, Stews	Broiled Fish, Shellfish, Fish Stews, Casseroles
MARJORAM	Seafood Cocktail, Green, Poultry & Seafood Salads	Breads, Cheese Spreads, Egg & Cheese Dishes, Gravies, Sauces	Carrots, Eggplant, Peas, Onions, Potatoes, Dried Bean Dishes, Spinach	Roast Meats & Poultry, Meat & Poultry Pies, Stews & Casseroles	Baked, Broiled & Stuffed Fish, Shellfish
MUSTARD	Fresh Green Salads, Prepared Meat, Macaroni & Potato Salads, Salad Dressings	Biscuits, Egg & Cheese Dishes, Sauces	Baked Beans, Cabbage, Eggplant, Squash, Dried Beans, Mushrooms, Pasta	Chops, Steaks, Ham, Pork, Poultry, Cold Meats	Shellfish
OREGANO	Green, Poultry & Seafood Salads	Breads, Egg & Cheese Dishes, Meat, Poultry & Vegetable Sauces	Artichokes, Cabbage, Eggplant, Squash, Dried Beans, Mushrooms, Pasta	Broiled, Roast Meats, Meat & Poultry Pies, Stews, Casseroles	Baked, Broiled & Poached Fish, Shellfish
PARSLEY	Green, Potato, Seafood & Vegetable Salads	Biscuits, Breads, Egg & Cheese Dishes, Gravies, Sauces	Asparagus, Beets, Eggplant, Squash, Dried Beans, Mushrooms, Pasta	Meat Loaf, Meat & Poultry Pies, Stews & Casseroles, Stuffing	Fish Stews, Stuffed Fish
ROSEMARY	Fruit Cocktail, Fruit & Green Salads	Biscuits, Egg Dishes, Herb Butter, Cream Cheese, Marinades, Sauces	Beans, Broccoli, Peas, Cauliflower, Mushrooms, Baked Potatoes, Parsnips	Roast Meat, Poultry & Meat Pies, Stews & Casseroles, Stuffing	Stuffed Fish, Shellfish
SAGE		Breads, Fondue, Egg & Cheese Dishes, Spreads, Gravies, Sauces	Beans, Beets, Onions, Peas, Spinach, Squash, Tomatoes	Roast Meat, Poultry, Meat Loaf, Stews, Stuffing	Baked, Poached & Stuffed Fish
TARRAGON	Seafood Cocktail, Avocado Salads, Salad Dressings	Cheese Spreads, Marinades, Sauces, Egg Dishes	Asparagus, Beans, Beets, Carrots, Mushrooms, Peas, Squash, Spinach	Steaks, Poultry, Roast Meats, Casseroles & Stews	Baked, Broiled & Poached Fish, Shellfish
THYME	Seafood Cocktail, Green, Poultry, Seafood & Vegetable Salads	Biscuits, Breads, Egg & Cheese Dishes, Sauces, Spreads	Beets, Carrots, Mushrooms, Onions, Peas, Eggplant, Spinach, Potatoes	Roast Meat, Poultry & Meat Loaf, Meat & Poultry Pies, Stews & Casseroles	Baked, Broiled & Stuffed Fish, Shellfish, Fish Stews

General Recipe Index

This handy index lists every recipe by food category, major ingredient and/or cooking method, so you can easily locate recipes to suit your needs .

Alphabetical Index

Refer to this index for a complete alphabetical listing of all the recipes in this book.